INTO THE I

READINGS AND PRAYERS FOR DIFFERENT OCCASIONS

Muriel McDonald

AT THE BEGINNING OF A NEW YEAR

Therefore, since we are surrounded by so great a cloud of witnesses, let us also lay aside every weight, and sin which clings so closely, and let us run with perseverance the race that is set before us, looking to Jesus the pioneer and perfecter of our faith, who for the joy that was set before him endured the cross, despising the shame, and is seated at the right hand of the throne of God.

Hebrews 12: 1, 2

For I am sure that neither death, nor life, nor angels, nor principalities, nor things present, nor things to come, nor powers, nor height, nor depth, nor anything else in all creation, will be able to separate us from the love of God in Christ Jesus our Lord.

Romans 8: 38, 39

PRAYERS

Only to thee dear Lord, can I confess the fears that shake my heart, the nameless apprehension and distress with which I start the course of a New Year. Give me that strength, O Lord, which comes I know sufficient for the day to meet its every need. And may it show my wavering steps the way to tread securely, leaning hard on thee the burden of my care, 'till thy deep peace stills my anxiety and I find courage there.

Source unknown

Father let me dedicate,
All this year to thee,
In whatever worldly state
Thou wilt have me be.
Not from sorrow, pain or care
Freedom dare I claim:
This alone shall be my prayer,
'Glorify thy name'.

If in mercy thou wilt spare
Joys that yet are mine;
If on life, serene and fair
Brighter rays may shine;
Let my glad heart, while it sings,
Thee in all proclaim,
And whate'er the future brings,
Glorify thy name.

Ancient & Modern Revised

FOR EACH NEW DAY

This is the day which the Lord has made; let us rejoice and be glad in it.

Psalm 118: 24

Dawn, a bird sings and splinters of light announce my resurrection from night's little death.
I am alive in a new day: reborn, breathing, hearing, seeing, thinking – alive by the grace of God, the giver of life, the Lord of life . . . .
To discover the source of life we must find the way, learn the truth.
So Thomas asked, 'How can we know the way?'
And Jesus said to him,
'I am the way, and the truth, and the life.'
Lord, as each day dawns, may I acknowledge that you are the giver of life,
you are the Alpha and Omega of all things.
You are the Lord of life.

Frank Topping

Look well to this day, for it is life,
The very life of life!
For yesterday is but a dream, and tomorrow is only a vision,
But today well-lived, makes every yesterday a dream of happiness
and every tomorrow a vision of hope;
Look well therefore to this day.

'Salutation to the Dawn'
from Martha's Prayer Book

PRAYERS

May the strength of God pilot us;
may the power of God preserve us;
may the wisdom of God instruct us;
may the hand of God protect us;
may the way of God direct us;
May the shield of God defend us;
may the host of God guard us against the snares of evil and the temptation of the world;
may Christ be with us, Christ before us, Christ in us, Christ over us; may thy salvation, O Lord, be always ours, this day and for evermore.

St. Patrick

We thank you, Lord, that you did not leave us without your blessing. You have put a new song on our lips and a new joy in our hearts. We praise you for a risen Saviour. We rejoice in a living Lord: and offer our lives today in thankful service to Jesus Christ our Lord.

Ian D. Bunting

All this day, O Lord, let me touch as many lives as possible for thee; and every life I touch, do thou by thy Spirit quicken, whether through the word I speak, the prayer I breathe, or the life I live. Amen.

Mary Sumner's personal prayer

THE WONDER OF CREATION

The Heavens are telling the glory of God;
and the firmament proclaims his handiwork.
Day to day pours forth speech, and night to night declares knowledge.
There is no speech, nor are there words; their voice is not heard;
yet their voice goes out through all the earth,
and their words to the end of the world.

Psalm 19: 1-4

The wonder of creation suggests another gateway to worship: the door of Beauty. Whatever kind of beauty stirs us to delight or to painful longing, we can use as a ladder to rise above ourselves. For this love of beauty is divinely implanted. The touch of beauty, when we feel it, is not to be merely a passing delight: it is the call of God, inviting us gently and sweetly to turn to Him. St. Augustine says: 'Thy whole creation praises Thee without ceasing . . . to the end that, using Thy creatures as stepping stones, and passing on to Him who made them so wonderfully, our soul might shake off its despondence and soar up to Thee. There is refreshment and true courage.' To the man or woman who 'means only God' the beauty of creation may become a transparent veil, half concealing and half revealing the presence of Love itself.

from 'The School of Prayer'
by Olive Wyon

PRAYERS

O God, of whose love comes sunshine and flowers, great spreading trees, sunset and dawn, and all the wondrous pageantry of the changing year, we praise thee that thou dost come to us through all the beauty of thy world. We thank thee for sudden swift glimpses of thy beauty: a sudden sight of flowers in city streets, raindrops shining in the sun: cobwebs gemmed with dew; stars reflected in a roadside puddle; shadows moving up a grassy slope; leafy trees in the lamplight; green moss on a stone wall; the sun on the bark of a fir tree. For these and all sudden showings of thy beauty we praise and adore thee.

Giles and Melville Harcourt

Lord,
teach me to rest in you.
Teach me to see the sky
and to think of nothing else
but the joy of it.
Teach me to look
at field and flower
and be soothed
by colours and seasons.
Teach me to close my eyes
and to rest
in the Love that has supported me
all my days.
Teach me, Lord,
to rest in you.

Frank Topping

THE BIRTH OF A CHILD

Thanks be to God for his inexpressible gift!

II Corinthians 9: 15

And suddenly there was with the angel a multitude of the heavenly host praising God and saying, 'Glory to God in the highest, and on earth peace among men with whom he is pleased!'

Luke 2: 13, 14

And they were bringing children to him, that he might touch them; and the disciples rebuked them. But when Jesus saw it he was indignant and said to them, 'Let the children come to me, do not hinder them; for to such belongs the kingdom of God. Truly, I say to you, whoever does not receive the kingdom of God like a child shall not enter it.' And he took them in his arms and blessed them, laying his hands upon them.

Mark 10: 13-16

PRAYERS

God our Father, maker of all that is living, we praise you for the wonder and joy of creation. We thank you from our hearts for the life of *this child*, for a safe delivery, and for the privilege of parenthood. Accept our thanks and praise through Jesus Christ our Lord.

ASB

God our Father, we pray to you for all who have the care of *this child*. Guide them with your Holy Spirit, that they may bring *him* up in the ways of truth and love. Through their care enable *him* to grow in grace and become daily more like your Son, our Saviour Jesus Christ.

ASB

AT TIMES OF DEPRESSION

Jesus wept.

John 11: 35

Fear not, for I have redeemed you; I have called you by name, you are mine. When you pass through the waters I will be with you; and through the rivers, they shall not overwhelm you; when you walk through fire you shall not be burned, and the flame shall not consume you. For I am the Lord your God, the Holy One of Israel, your Saviour.

Isaiah 43: 1-3

Cast your burden on the Lord, and he will sustain you.

Psalm 55: 22

PRAYERS

Lord, when this depression comes upon me I am weighed down and all joy leaves me. Help me to know that you are with me in the darkness and let me know that you love me. I have so little strength but I lift my troubled heart to you and ask for your peace. May I know that I rest in your hands as I wait for the return of light and the recovery of joy.

Hands who touched the leper,
touch my wounded heart;
Hands who healed the blind man,
heal my aching soul;
Hands who cured the lame,
mend my disjointed life;
Hands who embraced all life,
enfold me in your peace.
Lord,
merely touch and heal
cure and forgive.

Giles Harcourt

FOR THE GIFT OF CHILDREN

God is the creator of all things, and by the birth of children he gives to parents a share in the work and joy of creation.

ASB

We should say to each of them: 'Do you know what you are? You are a marvel. You are unique. In all of the world there is no other child exactly like you. In the millions of years that have passed, there has never been a child like you. And look at your body . . . what a wonder it is! Your legs, your arms, your cunning fingers, the way you move. You may become a Shakespeare, a Michelangelo, a Beethoven. You have a capacity for anything. Yes, you are a marvel.'

Pablo Casals

And a woman who held a babe against her bosom said, Speak to us of children.
And he said: Your children are not your children.
They are the sons and daughters of Life's longing for itself.
They come through you but not from you.
And though they are with you yet they belong not to you.
You may give them your love but not your thoughts,
For they have their own thoughts.
You may house their bodies but not their souls,
For their souls dwell in the house of tomorrow, which you cannot visit, not even in your dreams.
You may strive to be like them, but seek not to make them like you.
For life goes not backward nor tarries with yesterday.
You are the bows from which your children as living arrows are sent forth.
The Archer sees the mark upon the path of the infinite, and He bends you with His might that His arrows may go swift and far.
Let your bending in the Archer's hand be for gladness;
For even as He loves the arrow that flies, so He loves also the bow that is stable.

from 'The Prophet'
by Kahlil Gibran

PRAYERS

Heavenly Father, in your love you have called us to know you, led us to trust you, and bound our life with yours. Surround our children with your love; protect them from evil; fill them with your Holy Spirit; and receive them into the family of your Church; that they may walk with us in the way of Christ and grow in the knowledge of your love. Amen.

ASB

O God, our Father, we thank you for the gift of children and for the joy they bring. Look in your tender mercy on the children you have entrusted to us. In their weakness hold them in your strength. Help us to be sensitive to their deepest needs. Give us wisdom that they may grow up rooted in love, strong and courageous in life and steadfast in faith. May we, in our love, help and encourage them towards maturity and independence, through Jesus Christ our Lord.

THE JOY OF FAMILY LIFE

With a nurturing family immediately I can sense the aliveness, the genuineness, honesty and love. I feel the heart and soul present as well as the head.

I feel that if I lived in such a family, I would be listened to and would be interested in listening to others; I would be considered and would wish to consider others; I could openly show my affection as well as my pain and disapproval; I wouldn't be afraid to take risks because everyone in my family would realize that some mistakes are bound to come with my risk-taking – that my mistakes are a sign that I am growing. I would feel like a person in my own right – noticed, valued, loved and clearly asked to notice, value and love others.

from 'Peoplemaking'
by Virginia Satir

PRAYERS

Father of all, accept our thanks for the joys of family life.
Help us to live so that we may strengthen and enrich the life of the family.
Help us to build with you the kind of family which welcomes the stranger, the lonely and the needy.
Teach us through this small family to love the family of all mankind and to realize our part in it.
In the name of Christ we ask this.

Brother John Charles SSF

Heavenly Father, we bring to you in our prayers
all whom we love in our family circle,
knowing that your love for them
is so much greater than ours,
and that your will for them
is all that is for their good.
So have them in your keeping, O Lord,
and give them now and always
the fullness of your blessing;
for Jesus Christ's sake.

FOR THANKSGIVING

O shout to the Lord in triumph all the earth: serve the Lord with gladness and come before his face with songs of joy.
Know that the Lord he is God:
it is he who has made us and we are his
we are his people and the sheep of his pasture.
Come into his gates with thanksgiving and into his courts with praise:
give thanks to him and bless his holy name.
For the Lord is good, his loving mercy is for ever:
his faithfulness throughout all generations.
Glory be to the Father and to the Son and to the Holy Spirit;
as it was in the beginning is now and shall be for ever. Amen.

Jubilate (Psalm 100) ASB

Almighty God, Father of all mercies, we your unworthy servants give you most humble and hearty thanks for all your goodness and loving kindess to us and to all men. We bless you for our creation, preservation and all the blessings of this life; but above all for your immeasurable love in the redemption of the world by our Lord Jesus Christ, for the means of grace and for the hope of glory. And give us, we pray, such a sense of all your mercies that our hearts may be unfeignedly thankful, and that we show forth your praise, not only with our lips but in our lives, by giving up ourselves to your service, and by walking before you in holiness and righteousness all our days; through Jesus Christ our Lord, to whom, with you and the Holy Spirit, be all honour and glory, for ever and ever. Amen.

General Thanksgiving ASB

Now thank we all our God
With heart and hands and voices,
Who wondrous things hath done,
In whom his world rejoices;
Who from our mothers' arms
Hath blessed us on our way
With countless gifts of love,
And still is ours today.

O may this bounteous God
Through all our life be near us
With ever joyful hearts
And blessed peace to cheer us;
And keep us in his grace,
and guide us when perplexed,
And free us from all ills
In this world and the next.

All praise and thanks to God
The Father now be given,
The Son, and him who reigns
with them in highest heaven,
The one eternal God,
Whom earth and heaven adore,
For thus it was, is now,
And shall be evermore.

Ancient & Modern Revised

IN TIMES OF TROUBLE AND ANXIETY

Have no anxiety about anything, but in everything by prayer and supplication with thanksgiving let your requests be made known to God. And the peace of God, which passes all understanding, will keep your hearts and your minds in Christ Jesus.

Philippians 4: 6,7

Cast all your anxieties on him, for he cares about you.

I Peter 5: 7

One night a man had a dream. He dreamed he was walking along the beach with the Lord. Across the sky flashed scenes from his life. For each scene he noticed two sets of footprints in the sand; one belonging to him and the other to the Lord. When the last scene of his life flashed before him, he looked back at the footprints in the sand. He noticed that many times along the path of his life there was only one set of footprints. He also noticed that it happened at the very lowest and saddest times in his life.

This really bothered him and he questioned the Lord about it, 'Lord, you said that once I decided to follow you, you'd walk with me all the way. But I have noticed that during the most troublesome times in my life there is only one set of footprints. I don't understand why, when I needed you most, you would leave me.'

The Lord replied, 'My precious child, I love you and I would never leave you. During your times of trial and suffering, when you see only one set of footprints, it was then that I carried you.'

Source unknown

PRAYERS

Almighty God, you know us to be set in the midst of so many and great dangers, that, because of the frailty of our nature, we cannot always stand upright. Give us such strength and protection as may support us in all dangers and carry us through all temptations; through Jesus Christ our Lord.

ASB

Almighty and ever-loving God, the comfort of the sad, the strength of the suffering: let the prayers of all who cry out of any tribulation come unto you; and to every soul that is distressed grant mercy, refreshment and peace; for the sake of Jesus Christ our Lord. Amen.

Margaret Girdlestone

IN TIMES OF ILLNESS

The Lord is the everlasting God,
   the Creator of the ends of the earth.
He does not faint or grow weary,
   his understanding is unsearchable.
He gives power to the faint,
   and to him who has no might he increases strength

Isaiah 40: 28,29

For this reason I bow my knees before the Father, from whom every family in heaven and on earth is named, that according to the riches of his glory he may grant you to be strengthened with might through his Spirit in the inner man, and that Christ may dwell in your hearts through faith; that you, being rooted and grounded in love, may have power to comprehend with all the saints what is the breadth and length and height and depth, and to know the love of Christ which surpasses knowledge, that you may be filled with all the fulness of God.

Now to him who by the power at work within us is able to do far more abundantly than all that we ask or think, to him be glory in the church and in Christ Jesus to all generations, for ever and ever. Amen.

Ephesians 3: 14-21

PRAYERS

Heavenly Father, giver of life and health: comfort and restore those who are sick, that they may be strengthened in their weakness and have confidence in your unfailing love; through Jesus Christ our Lord.

Alternative Service Book

O my Saviour, lifted
From the earth for me,
Draw me, in thy mercy,
Nearer unto thee.

Lift my earth-bound longings,
Fix them, Lord, above;
Draw me with the magnet
Of thy mighty love.

Lord, thine arms are stretching
Ever far and wide,
To enfold thy children
To thy loving side.

And I come, O Jesus:
Dare I turn away?
No, thy love hath conquered,
And I come today;

Bringing all my burdens,
Sorrow, sin and care,
At thy feet I lay them,
And I leave them there.

Ancient & Modern Revised

WHEN FAITH IS LOW

Now Thomas, one of the twelve, called the Twin, was not with them when Jesus came. So the other disciples told him, 'We have seen the Lord.' But he said to them, 'Unless I see in his hands the print of the nails, and place my finger in the mark of the nails, and place my hands in his side, I will not believe.' Eight days later, his disciples were again in the house and Thomas was with them. The doors were shut, but Jesus came and stood among them, and said, 'Peace be with you.' Then he said to Thomas, 'Put your finger here, and see my hands, and put out your hand and place it in my side; do not be faithless but believing.' Thomas answered him, 'My Lord and my God!' Jesus said to him, 'Have you believed because you have seen me? Blessed are those who have not seen and yet believe.'

John 20: 24-29

Fear not, for I am with you, be not dismayed, for I am your God;
I will strengthen you, I will help you,
I will uphold you with my victorious right hand.

Isaiah 41: 10

He did not say, 'You shall not be tempest-tossed, you shall not be work-weary, you shall not be discomforted.' But he said, 'You shall not be overcome.' God wants us to heed these words so that we shall always be strong in trust, both in sorrow and in joy.

Julian of Norwich

PRAYERS

Lord Christ when you were here on earth you stretched forth your hand to those in need. You healed the sick, you fed the hungry, you lifted up the broken-hearted. You are the same yesterday, today and for ever. Make known to me now your grace and power; speak your word of peace to my restless heart and satisfy the hunger of my soul. Grant me living touch with you, for the glory of your name.

Lord, I believe, help thou mine unbelief.

Lord, prayer is dark and I cannot think at all. I know you can only be reached by love and not by the mind, but, Lord, my love seems dead and without feeling. I know nothing at all except that I want to love you and cannot. Give me courage to endure the darkness and faith to believe that you are with me in this emptiness.

Michael Hollings and Etta Gullick

WHEN FEELING AFRAID

The Lord is my light and my salvation; whom shall I fear?
The Lord is the stronghold of my life; of whom shall I be afraid?
Thou hast said, 'Seek ye my face.' My heart says to thee,
'Thy face, Lord, do I seek.' Hide not thy face from me.
Wait for the Lord; be strong, and let your heart take courage;
yea, wait for the Lord!

Psalm 27: 1, 8, 14

Be strong and of good courage; be not frightened, neither be dismayed; for the Lord your God is with you where-ever you go.

Joshua 1: 9

Finally, be strong in the Lord and in the strength of his might. Therefore take the whole armour of God, that you may be able to withstand in the evil day and having done all, to stand. Stand therefore having girded you loins with truth, and having put on the breastplate of righteousness, and having shod your feet with the equipment of the gospel of peace; besides all these taking the shield of faith, with which you can quench all the flaming darts of the evil one. And take the helmet of salvation, and sword of the Spirit, which is the word of God. Pray at all times in the Spirit, with all prayer and supplication.

Ephesians 6: 10, 13-18

PRAYERS

As Christians, we have no right to fear and yet we are afraid: of the neighbours, of the people we work with, and even of our own families. Frequently our faith is found behind the locked doors of our hearts. And yet, O Lord, you come to us with peace and the coming is enough to fill our hearts with joy. Burst the bars of fear that keep us silent and send us on your errands, your message not only in our hearts but on our lips. For your name's sake. Amen.

Ian D. Bunting

Calm my troubled heart; give me peace.
O Lord, calm the waves of this heart, calm its tempests!
Calm thyself, O my soul, so that the divine can act in thee!
Calm thyself, O my soul, so that God is able to repose in thee, so that his peace may cover thee!
Yes, Father in heaven, often have we found that the world cannot give us peace, but make us feel that thou art able to give peace; let us know the truth of thy promise: that the whole world may not be able to take away thy peace.

Sören Kierkegaard (1813-1855)

AT THE END OF EACH DAY

In peace I will both lie down and sleep;
for thou alone, O Lord, makest me dwell in safety.

Psalm 4: 8

The eternal God is your dwelling place, and underneath are the everlasting arms.

Deuteronomy 33: 27

And a great storm of wind arose, and the waves beat into the boat, so that the boat was already filling. But Jesus was in the stern, asleep on the cushion; and they woke him and said to him, 'Teacher, do you not care if we perish?' And he awoke and rebuked the wind, and said to the sea, 'Peace! Be still!' And the wind ceased, and there was great calm. He said to them, 'Why are you afraid? Have you no faith?' And they were filled with awe, and said to one another, 'Who then is this, that even wind and sea obey him?

Mark 4: 37-41

Thou does keep him in perfect peace, whose mind is stayed on thee, because he trusts in thee. Trust in the Lord for ever, for the Lord God is an everlasting rock.

Isaiah 26: 3,4

PRAYERS

Be present, O merciful God, and protect us through the silent hours of this night, so that we who are fatigued by the changes and chances of this fleeting world may repose upon thy eternal changelessness; through Jesus Christ our Lord. Amen.

Compline (Ambrosian)

Abide with us, O Lord, for it is toward evening and the day is far spent: abide with us, and with thy whole Church. Abide with us in the evening of the day, in the evening of life, in the evening of the world. Abide with us and with all thy faithful ones, O Lord, in time and eternity.

Lutheran Manual of Prayer

WHEN A LOVED ONE IS DYING

O God, be not far from me; O my God, make haste to help me!

Psalm 71: 12

Lo! I tell you a mystery. We shall not all sleep, but we shall all be changed, in a moment, in the twinkling of an eye, at the last trumpet. For the trumpet will sound, and the dead will be raised imperishable, and we shall be changed. For this perishable nature must put on the imperishable, and this mortal nature must put on immortality.

I Corinthians 15: 51-53

What is dying? I am standing on the sea-shore. A ship at my side spreads her white sails to the morning breeze and starts for the blue ocean. She is an object of beauty and I stand and watch her until at last she fades on the horizon. Then someone at my side says, 'She has gone.' Gone where? Gone from my sight – that is all. She is just as large in the mast, hull and spars as she was when she left my side. The diminished size and total loss of sight is in me and not in her, and just at the moment when someone by my side says, 'She has gone', others take up the glad shout, 'There she comes!'

Bishop Brent (1862-1929)

PRAYERS

Depart, O Christian soul, out of this world,
In the name of God the Father Almighty who created thee,
In the name of Jesus Christ who redeemed thee,
In the name of the Holy Ghost who sanctifieth thee.
May thy rest be this day in peace, and thy dwelling in the Paradise of God.

William Bright (1824-1901)

Father in heaven, you gave your Son Jesus Christ to suffering and to death on the cross, and raised him to life in glory. Grant us a patient faith in time of darkness, and strengthen our hearts with the knowledge of your love; through Jesus Christ our Lord.

ASB

THE END OF LIFE'S JOURNEY

Let not your hearts be troubled; believe in God, believe also in me. In my Father's house are many rooms; if it were not so, would I have told you that I go to prepare a place for you? And when I go and prepare a place for you, I will come again and will take you to myself, that where I am you may be also.

John 14: 1-3

The Lord is my shepherd, I shall not want; he makes me lie
down in green pastures.
He leads me beside still waters, he restores my soul.
He leads me in paths of righteousness for his name's sake.
Even though I walk through the valley of the shadow of death,
I fear no evil;
for thou are with me; thy rod and thy staff, they comfort me.
Thou preparest a table before me in the presence of my
enemies;
thou anointest my head with oil, my cup overflows.
Surely goodness and mercy shall follow me all the days of
my life;
and I shall dwell in the house of the Lord for ever.

Psalm 23

PRAYERS

Lord, I love you very much and really do want to be with you always, but I am afraid of dying. Give me the kind of faith in you that will not waver, the kind of hope which will help me to believe that you will be with me even to the end of the world, and the kind of love that will trust you completely whatever happens. Keep me in peace and guard me from fear, for the sake of your dear Son who knows human frailty so well.

Michael Hollings and Etta Gullick

Lord, you have loved me and have supported me all the days of my life, and I trust you. Now that the time of my death approaches, give me faith to trust you still and to know that you will continue to support me as you have always done. Death like life comes from you and like all your gifts must be good, so take away any fears I may have. When death comes to hush my last breath on earth, help me to remember that it will bring me to live more fully with you and this is the most wonderful thing that can happen to me, so into your hands I commend my spirit.

Michael Hollings and Etta Gullick

O think! to step on shore
And that shore Heaven:
To take hold of a hand
And that God's hand.
To breathe a new air
And find it celestial air.
To feel invigorated,
And to know it immortality.
O think! to pass from the storm and the tempest
To one unbroken calm.
To wake up
And find it glory.

Source unknown

AT A TIME OF BEREAVEMENT

The Lord is near to the broken-hearted and saves the crushed in spirit.

Psalm 34: 18

But we would not have you ignorant, brethren, concerning those who are asleep, that you may not grieve as others do who have no hope. For since we believe that Jesus died and rose again, even so, through Jesus, God will bring with him those who have fallen asleep. For this we declare to you by the word of the Lord, that we who are alive, who are left until the coming of the Lord, shall not precede those who have fallen asleep. For the Lord himself will descend from heaven with a cry of command, with the archangel's call and with the sound of the trumpet of God. And the dead in Christ will rise first; then we who are alive, who are left, shall be caught up together with them in the clouds to meet the Lord in the air; and so we shall always be with the Lord. Therefore comfort one another with these words.

I Thessalonians 4: 13-18

Surely he has borne our griefs and carried our sorrows.

Isaiah 53: 4

Faith is putting your hand out in the dark and finding it held.

Anon.

ON THE DEATH OF A CHILD

For the Lamb in the midst of the throne will be their shepherd, and he will guide them to springs of living water; and God will wipe away every tear from their eyes.

Revelation 7: 17

PRAYERS

O Father of all, we pray to you for those we love but see no longer. Grant them your peace; let light perpetual shine upon them; and in your loving wisdom and almighty power, work in them the good purpose of your perfect will; through Jesus Christ, our Lord.

Mothers' Union Service Book

We remember, Lord, the slenderness of the thread which separates life from death and the suddenness with which it can be broken.
Help us also to remember that on both sides of that division we are surrounded by your love.
Persuade our hearts that when our dear ones die neither we nor they are parted from you.
In you we may find peace, and in you be united with them in the body of Christ, who has burst the bonds of death and is alive for evermore, our Saviour and theirs for ever and ever.

R. H. L. Williams

Heavenly Father, our refuge and strength in every time of need, help and comfort us today in the loss of our beloved child. Lift us from the darkness of our grief into the light of your presence: may we find courage, hope and peace in your unfailing love.

IN PRAISE OF LIFE

Praise the Lord! Praise the Lord, O my soul! I will praise the Lord as long as I live; I will sing praises to my God while I have being.

Psalm 146: 1-2

The glory of life is to love, not to be loved,
To serve, not to be served,
To be a strong hand in the dark to another in the time of need,
To be a cup of strength to any soul in a crisis of weakness.
This is the glory of life.

Source unknown

The Glory of God is man fully alive.

St. Iranaeus

PRAYERS

Lord, Victor over death, sin, evil. By your power destroy in us all that makes for death. So touch us with your quickening power that we may be opened to your healing, be receptive of your gift of life, be so willing to die daily to sin, to be freed of fear, to be released from guilt, and to surrender all needless anxiety, that we may know, both now and forever, the joy of living in you and with you and by you and for you.

Brother John Charles SSF

Something in us is making music,
Something in us wants to dance.
Something in us wants to sing.

Sing a new song to the Lord.

Lord, it's you we should be praising,
Like a father, the best we can think of.
Lord, you're the best of anything we know.

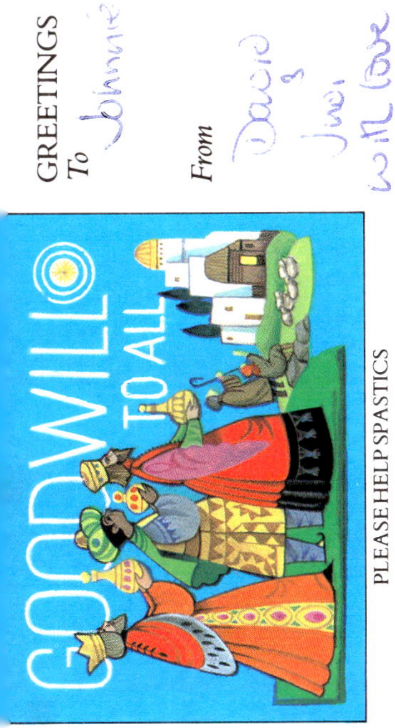

song to the Lord.

know, Lord, how things started.
a great voice, and a great light.
a great power, it's all a great mystery.

ning stars sang together
is of God shouted for joy.

eful for all the music of life,
oar, the song of a well-tuned engine
beauty of Mendelssohn
rhythm of jazz.

ning stars sing together,
is of God shout for joy!

these is the song inside us
s our own, coming from our hearts.
ause we are grateful, we praise because

song to the Lord.
are, Lord, with a new song to sing you.
very clean; we all have mixed motives,
very strong, and often fall
e with love, which is all we can boast of,
and a new song; Lord make us new.

Sing a new song to the Lord.

Simon H. Baynes

ACKNOWLEDGEMENTS

The Mothers' Union gratefully acknowledges copyright permission granted by writers and publishers. Every effort has been made to trace the sources of the readings and prayers used in this anthology, but where we have fallen short we beg forgiveness. Our thanks are due to:

The Church Pastoral Aid Society for Prayers by Margaret Girdlestone, Simon Baynes, Ian D. Bunting and R.H.L. Williams.

Wm. Collins & Co. Ltd. for The Jubilate (Psalm 100) from *The Psalms, A New Translation for Worship,* © English Text 1976, 1977 David L. Frost, John A. Emerton, Andrew A. Macintosh, all rights reserved. Also for two prayers from *Short Prayers for The Long Day.* Compilation © Giles & Melville Harcourt pub. Wm. Collins.

Darton, Longman & Todd Ltd. London, for Mother Julian quotation taken from *Enfolded in Love* edited by Robert Llewelyn, published and © 1980 by Darton Longman and Todd Ltd. and used by the permission of the publishers.

Eyre & Spottiswoode (Publishers) Ltd. for The General Thanksgiving as adapted from The Book of Common Prayer which is Crown Copyright and is used with permission.

William Heinemann Ltd. for extract from *The Prophet* by Kahlil Gibran.

The Lutheran Church for an evening prayer.

Lutterworth Press for quotations from *Lord of Life* by Frank Topping.

McCrimmon Publishing Co. Ltd. for quotations from *The Shade of His Hand* by Michael Hollings and Etta Gullick.

A.R. Mowbray & Co. Ltd. for prayers by Brother John Charles SSF.

SCM Press Ltd. for quotation from *The School of Prayer* by Olive Wyon 1943.

Souvenir Press Ltd. for quotation from *Peoplemaking* by Virginia Satir.

The Scripture quotations contained herein are from the Revised Standard Version Bible, copyright 1946, 1952, 1971 by the Division of Christian Education of the National Council of the Churches of Christ in the USA, and are used by permission.

The various Prayers and Collects from The Alternative Service Book 1980 are copyright © and are reproduced with permission of the Central Board of Finance of the Church of England.

Preface

This book is the result of the combination of two separate pieces of research by the authors, conducted with a total of 37 students, each of whom was interviewed during 2006 about their experiences of being at university. From these 37 individual stories, seven have been chosen for this book as illustrations of the experiences of mature-age female students in higher education. The book is written for educators and educational policy makers, students, prospective students, their families and their friends. As readers will discover, each of these women has a unique story to tell, yet despite the differences in their situations, common themes emerge. The challenges and triumphs that are part of the lives of so many mature-age women in higher education are represented within the stories of these seven. Above all, what emerges from these stories is a message about the transformative powers of education and the inherent value in facilitating, encouraging and supporting mature-age women to participate in education, discover their academic potential and achieve their goals.

Glossary

ABS:	Australian Bureau of Statistics
Enabling Programs:	Alternative entry programs into University.
HSC:	Higher School Certificate – Matriculation examination in New South Wales, Australia.
HECS:	Higher Education Contribution Scheme – Australian government loans scheme to fund university fees.
JET:	Job Education & Training – an Australian government job-seeking program for single parents.
OECD:	Organisation for Economic Co-operation and Development
SES:	Socio-economic status
STAT:	State Tertiary Admissions Test – an alternative university entry examination for Australian students
TAFE:	Technical and Further Education Colleges in Australia
UAI:	University Admission Index

Introduction

Going behind the scenes

This book tells the stories of seven women who decided to undertake higher education studies when they were all well into their 30s and 40s. All of them are embarking upon a 'second-chance' journey, a term often used in the literature in relation to mature learners (Cantwell, Archer, & Bourke, 2001; Giles, 1990; Rinne & Kivinen, 1996). Either they had never before contemplated university as an option, or having previously considered it when they were younger the time had not been right for them to continue down that path. It would even be true to say that, for these students, this is in fact more of a 'first-chance' journey, as never before in their lives had they the opportunity, let alone the means, to go to university.

None of these seven women has a parent who has been to university. Whether they had done well at school or not, most had received little encouragement to view themselves as capable of university studies or to consider a university education as important. Expectations of their parents and friends have not generally included the possibility that they would or could seek a university education. This book reveals how they made the decision to go, what made it possible for them to do so at this stage in their lives, what is helping and hindering their studies and how their lives are changing as a result.

The stories of the seven women are derived from two separate yet complementary qualitative research projects, examining the experiences of women and men returning to study as mature-age students (Stone, 2008; O'Shea, 2007). All seven women featured in this book, when interviewed, were enrolled in undergraduate degree programs at a large regional uni-

versity in Australia. All but one of them had entered university through an access course, known as an enabling program, run by that same university to encourage mature-age entry.

The research behind these stories used a narrative method to interview mature-age students, to analyse the data from the interviews and then to describe the student journeys, based upon each student's individual narrative about their experiences.

Using narrative inquiry

When individuals relate a story about some aspect of their lives, the events they describe are situated within and connected to other areas of their lives. Coffey and Atkinson (1996) make reference to 'chronicles of life'. Such chronicles are stories told by individuals, which describe and define how they managed to be where they are today. Certainly in the 'chronicles' of the women that follow, the reader is given an insight into the processes around their decision to attend university and their experiences as university students so far. Their decisions and experiences are intertwined with other developments in their lives.

One of the best ways to understand the actions of individuals is to be allowed to hear their personal stories as they themselves choose to narrate them. In the context of the research projects mentioned above, each of the women featured in this book was encouraged to describe her experience of coming to university and being at university. The rich accounts presented in the following chapters are based upon the ways in which each woman translated and interpreted this educational experience.

Pascall and Cox (1993) regard this type of small scale, detailed research as offering a way to explore and disclose individuals' processes of 'becoming' (Abrams, 1982). When events and experiences are presented in a narrative form, the reader tends to experience a sense of empathy with the narrator. In providing a structure in which to understand events, the narrator may refer to shared understandings, imagery and metaphors, all of which help the reader identify with the narrator. It is the narrator who decides what can and cannot be told; what is culturally acceptable and what is culturally taboo. The narrator is permitted to define and highlight the significance of certain life actions, ultimately negotiating 'human reality into wholes', serving to highlight 'human values' and 'bestow [ing] meaning on life' (Polkinghorne, 1988, p159).

The research behind the stories in this book focuses on 'first person accounts of experience' (Riessman, 1993, p17). Locating the 'stories' in these accounts enables the data to be considered and analysed creatively. The saturation of stories in everyday life means that this is a very familiar form of communication, utilised every day by all of us. However, narrative stories are not static forms. The story that someone tells today may differ from other versions, depending upon the ways in which events have unfolded, or even

how the person is feeling at the time of telling the story. Most of us tend not to regard such narratives necessarily as 'truthful' accounts (whatever truthful means) but we tend to regard them as reflections of values, meanings and experiences. Narrative accounts also have the potential to reveal experience in a collective sense, in that the narratives of a number of individuals may reflect on common life stages and turning points. In this sense, they are culturally located. In using a narrative inquiry method, it is ultimately the researchers who decide how to analyse and frame the stories that they have elicited from individuals. As the authors of this book, we have chosen to write the following seven chapters entirely in the words of the women interviewed, in order to enable the reader to hear the women's voices as they convey the rich detail of their lived experience as university students.

Through a semi-structured interview approach, the women were encouraged to reflect upon university in general, why they decided to attend at this point in their lives, their experience of being at university so far and how it had impacted upon them. One of the strengths of semi-structured interviewing is that it is the interviewee, rather than the interviewer, who ultimately determines the direction of the conversation. The interviewer adopts a less directive role, allowing subjects to tell their stories rather than simply respond to questions. While interviewers may have prepared some questions beforehand, they are willing to abandon these and instead allow the narrator to speak in depth about the issues that are most important to them at the time. This type of interview situation provides space for individuals to engage in lengthy monologues, which avoid the normal turn-taking conversational practices. Such an opportunity may encourage exploration of areas that in general conversation would remain unmentioned.

Background research

Access and equity in higher education

An exploration of previous research indicates that, globally, there was a flurry of activity in researching the mature-age experience through the late 1970s to mid-1990s, as widening of access began to become a priority for higher education institutions worldwide. This global movement to address inequality of access and participation in higher education gained pace through the late 1990s up to the present time (Skilbeck, 2006a), with an increase in international research focusing on students from socially and economically disadvantaged backgrounds. Coinciding with this has been an interest in mature learners in general, with research into adult education becoming more prevalent. Such literature provides valuable insights into gender and identity issues for mature-age students, including the different ways in which their lives can be transformed through education.

> Some people...may look to education, to universities, to help them in a struggle to rebuild and move beyond fragments of a life; a university may represent a space to understand self and others somewhat better and to revise a personal narrative as part of a process of rebuilding and constantly reshaping a life. (West, 1995, p150)

Mature-age students make up a significant proportion of the higher education population. Approximately 40% of the total domestic student population at all Australian universities is aged over 25, 27% is aged over 30 and 12% over 40 (Centre for the Study of Higher Education [CSHE], 2008). While most Australian universities define a mature-age student as someone who enters university over the age of 21 and not immediately following full-time secondary studies (Abbott-Chapman, Braithwaite, & Godfrey, 2004), most research with mature-age students has occurred with the over 25 age-group. A considerable proportion of mature-age students are entering university in their 30s, 40s and 50s, with even a small proportion (0.5%) aged in their 60s (CSHE, 2008). In terms of increasing participation of mature-age students, Australia is ahead of many other OECD countries, along with Finland, New Zealand, Sweden and the UK, with over 10% of 30 to 39 year olds enrolled in formal education, compared with the OECD country mean of 4.8: "the figures suggest that these countries offer more chances for adults to return to education" (Schuller, 2006, p. 9).

Mature-age students in Australia are also more likely to enter university via an alternative entry program, as many have come from backgrounds and situations which did not allow them the opportunity to complete high school or to achieve the qualifications necessary for university entrance (Cantwell, et al., 2001). Additionally, women are more likely than men to enter university later in life. In the over 35 age-group of university students, women outnumber men nationally by almost two to one (CSHE, 2004) and a greater number of women than men enrol in mature-age alternative entry programs (Cullity, 2006, p. 182).

Prior to the 1980s women were significantly under-represented in higher education on a worldwide level, including Australia. A 1975 report to the Australian Schools' Commission on "Girls, Schools and Society"(Bacchi, 1999) reported that, at every level, girls received less education than boys and that the subject choices of girls and boys at school perpetuated sex divisions in the labour market. The Australian government in 1990 formally identified women as an equity group in the higher education sector, introducing equity measures and targets to improve women's representation in non-traditional fields of study and postgraduate courses (Department of Education, Employment and Training [DEET], 1990). An analysis of equity groups (CSHE, 2004) for the period 1991-2002 reported that women had made progress in all areas of study, including at postgraduate levels.

Such equity measures aimed at women have been occurring against the backdrop of ongoing equity measures to improve participation in higher education of students, both male and female, of all ages, from lower socio-economic status (SES) backgrounds. There is considerable evidence

that, once enrolled, students from low SES backgrounds do just as well academically as do medium and high SES students across all age-groups (Archer, Cantwell, & Bourke, 1999; Cantwell, et al., 2001; CSHE, 2008). However, the problem of access remains, with low SES students remaining under-represented in university populations worldwide (Clancy & Goastellec, 2007). "People from low SES backgrounds participate below representative levels across most international higher education systems" (CSHE, 2008, p. 5).

One of the earliest and boldest attempts in Australia to increase low SES participation occurred in 1973, with the abolition of university tuition fees by the Whitlam Labor government. This led to an acceleration of enrolment in higher education across all age-groups with the most noticeable increase in the 30 and over age-group. This measure also had the effect of encouraging female participation, particularly amongst the mature-age cohort. The trend for women to enter higher education continued throughout the 1980s and by 1991, 55% of all new students were women, with the largest increase in female student participation occurring in the 25 and over age ranges (DEET, 1993). Free university education provided an opportunity for many women who, as lower income earners than men and/or financially dependent upon a male breadwinner, had not previously been in a financial position to undertake university studies.

The introduction of enabling programs as a particular type of alternative entry program for university began as another equity measure targeting the low SES equity group: "They emerged, as part of the move from the late 1970s onwards, to expand opportunities to wider constituencies of learners" (West, 1995, p. 136). Enabling programs were designed as entry courses to university, not in themselves higher education courses but ones that could lead to higher education entry (Chadwick, 2007). This also had the effect of increasing both mature-age and female participation, with a higher proportion of women than men enrolling in such programs (Ramsey, Tranter, Sumner, & Barrett, 1996). It is within the mature-age cohort entering university via alternative entry programs that the largest proportion of low SES students is found (CSHE, 2008). A mature-age student entering university via such a pathway is typically from the low SES group, did not complete high school and is the first in the family to come to university (Abbott-Chapman, et al., 2004; Cullity, 2006; Kavanagh & Stockdale, 2007).

Having succeeded in gaining entry to university, what then is the experience of such second-chance students? A search of the literature on the mature-age student experience over the past 20 to 30 years reveals that much of it focuses exclusively on the female experience from a feminist theoretical perspective. This is perhaps not surprising in the context of the increase in women's participation in higher education in general, particularly in the mature-age cohort, combined with the "second wave of feminist epistemology and methodology" (Fonow & Cook, 1991, p. 1) that developed over this period. Much of this research has utilised a postmodern feminist approach, which has developed from the interrelationship between *postmod-*

ernist and *feminist* theories. It is therefore worth devoting some space here to an explanation of these theoretical perspectives and the ways in which they interrelate.

Theoretical frameworks

Postmodernism

Postmodernist theory argues that reality is socially constructed, that it is "as much constructed in talking and writing as it is 'out there'" (Rice & Ezzy, 2000, p. 22). Postmodernism postulates that the meanings and understandings given to events and situations are culturally and temporally situated and therefore constantly liable to change, as a result of the political forces of oppression and power within the particular culture (Alvesson, 2002; Rice & Ezzy, 2000; Yeatman, 1994). The generation of knowledge is "an historically specific and contingent activity" (Yeatman, 1994, p. 20). Concepts such as truth and reality are represented and indeed determined by the particular political practices within a society. These practices are in turn reinforced by the "dominant discourses" (Alvesson & Skoldberg, 2000, p. 152), or the prevalent stories or narratives within a particular culture and time, which are themselves a representation of those same social and political practices. Therefore there is no fixed or pre-determined truth – "certainty must be regarded sceptically, if not rejected outright" (Gubrium & Holstein, 2003, p. 4) – but only the 'truth' that is representative of the dominant practices and discourses within a particular society. "The worlds we study are created, in part, through the texts that we write and perform about them" (Denzin, 1997, p. xiii).

An essential feature of postmodernism is the method of deconstruction of texts and narratives to reveal alternative meanings which have been suppressed or hidden by dominant discourses. "Postmodernism questions traditional assumptions and deconstructs them; that is, it shows the ambiguity and contextuality of meaning" (Gubrium & Holstein, 2003, p. 52). Through this process of deconstruction, other meanings, other stories, other explanations are revealed, with the potential to give voice and recognition to subjects and experiences previously subordinated to the point of invisibility. "Aspects that have been repressed to the limit of non-existence are elicited through deconstruction to be central; thus the marginal is transformed into the principal" (Alvesson & Skoldberg, 2000, p. 154).

Feminism

A number of writers (such as Alvesson & Skoldberg, 2000; Fonow & Cook, 1991; Olesen, 1994; Rice & Ezzy, 2000; Smith, 1987; Yeatman, 1994) credit *feminist* theories with having "politicised the research process" (Rice & Ezzy, 2000, p. 18) by actively challenging the dominant political practices

and power structures. By challenging conventional research methods that have been developed from the dominant male perspective, feminist theorists have advocated methods that allow women to talk about their own experiences from their own perspective (Harding, 1987; Oakley, 1981; 1992; Smith, 1987; 1996). Feminist approaches also demonstrate that texts can be studied from the female perspective, revealing very different stories and meanings (Swindells, 1989) and indeed that human behaviour can also be understood very differently (Gilligan, 1982). Feminist research acts to legitimise and prioritise the experience of the person being studied – in particular to legitimise women's knowledge and to prioritise "women as knowers" (Olesen, 1994, p. 160). "The only way of knowing a socially constructed world is knowing it from within" (Smith, 1987, p. 92).

Feminist research also highlights the political and ethical aspects of sociological research in general and draws attention to the process of reflexivity, where the researcher is intrinsically and significantly connected with the research process and outcomes (Rice & Ezzy, 2000). Fonow and Cook (1991) describe reflexivity as "the tendency of feminists to reflect upon, examine critically and explore analytically the nature of the research process" (p. 2). While reflecting upon the research process is not exclusive to feminist scholars – fieldwork and ethnographic studies may also be reflective in nature for example – Fonow and Cook (1991) make the point that:

> ...feminist epistemology carries this tradition of reflection one step further by using it to gain insight into the assumptions about gender relations underlying the conduct of the enquiry. (p. 2)

Post-Modern feminism

The interrelationship between postmodernism and feminism has become known as *postmodern feminism*, a deconstructive orientation in which minority or subjugated voices are privileged (Olesen, 2005; Yeatman, 1994). It seeks to question and challenge existing social and political practices, including the structures of power. "Science... is dismembered as a culture to reveal its practices, discourses and implications for control of women's lives" (Olesen, 2005, p. 247). It is where "a politics of representation comes together with a politics of difference" (Yeatman, 1994, p. 14). Gender relations and the social, cultural and political discourses on men and women are therefore inevitably sources of interest and enquiry for postmodern feminist research (Alvesson & Skoldberg, 2000). Such discourses are recognised as being culturally located and hence variable over context and time. Postmodern feminism would argue that:

> ...there can never be *a* [sic] feminist science, sociology, anthropology or epistemology, but only many stories that different women tell about the different knowledge they have. (Harding, 1987, p. 188)

In the words of Anna Yeatman (1994) "feminist theorising has introduced into postmodernism the politics of voice and representation" (p. 13). While postmodernist theory emphasises the meanings that are attached to events

through language and discourse (Alvesson, 2002), feminist theory makes visible the 'excluded other' (Yeatman, 1994).

In seeking to enquire into and 'make visible' women's experiences as mature-age students, the lens of postmodern feminism can be a helpful one, as the following discussion will reveal.

Gender constraints on women as students

Much of the research into the student experience indicates that males are more confident about their academic achievements and more likely to receive privileged time for their studies within their work, family and social situations. For females, time for study is not privileged in the same way, but is fitted in with their caring responsibilities of home, family and, in many cases, also paid work to supplement the family income. Feminist literature and research in this area highlight the gendered practices in the lives of the students and those around them, including the institution in which they are studying.

Research findings indicate that despite the greatly improved access to higher education for women that has occurred over the past 30 years, the problems and hurdles faced by mature-age female students have persisted over time. Christina Hughes (2002), in analysing the achievements of feminism since the 1960s, finds that "it is women's responsibilities in terms of the family that appear to be the most resistant to change" (p.33). Much research has demonstrated that care for others is overwhelmingly seen as women's work. Carol Gilligan's work (1987) on women's moral development led her to conclude that a sense of responsibility towards others heavily influences the decisions that women make. "Women not only define themselves in a context of human relationships but also judge themselves in terms of their ability to care" (Gilligan, 1987, p. 67). Gilligan maintains that this impedes a woman's sense of herself as an independent being, to the point where independent acts are perceived as acts of selfishness. Making the decision to go to university – an independent act in itself – requires therefore a considerable degree of resistance to these ways of thinking. It is perhaps not surprising that "often a return to school creates significant role strain and feelings of guilt, inadequacy and self-blame over difficulties in handling multiple roles" (Rice, 1989, p. 552).

Madeleine Leonard's (1994) research with 23 mature-age female university students in Ireland, for example, found that many family relationships were strained by the women's return to education, with the women experiencing lack of support or active hostility from partners. This multiplicity of roles and the sense of role conflict was highlighted by Rosalind Edwards (1993) in her research with 31 mature-age female students during 1988 and 1989, from a number of polytechnic colleges and universities in the UK. This research illustrates the multiple tasks which women undertake when combining study with the care of their families, the lack of support they

generally receive from male partners and the self-doubt that can ensue. Edwards found that the women's time was not their own; and that the demands they faced from others could not be accurately measured by linear notions of time. Hughes (2002) differentiates between "male time and female time" (p. 133), with 'male time' being linear, clock time and 'female time' as time given up to the demands and needs of others. She and other writers such as Davies (1990), Knights and Odih (1995) and McNay (2000) contend that society places a different value upon men's time and women's time, with men's time being seen as more valuable and productive.

Edwards' findings are supported by other research, such as that by Scott, Burns and Cooney (1993), Smith (1996), and Wolf-Wendel and Ward (2003), which in each case reflect upon "the gendered expectations of family obligations and the ongoing disparity with which women take on the 'second shift' through maintenance of children and home" (Wolf-Wendel & Ward, 2003, p. 113). Female students are also subject to gendered expectations and encounter similar difficulties in their academic studies as do female academics in their paid roles. A number of other feminist writers, such as Sandra Jackson (2000), contend that the term "academic" equates to "male" resulting in a situation where "women's voices in education are devalued and marginalised" (Jackson, 2000, p.281).

Yet, despite the difficulties for women in returning to study, research also reveals that going to university or college can lead to significant change in women's lives, through a sense of empowerment, independence and development of confidence in their own abilities and knowledge, as well as improved employment opportunities.

Education and identity

It has only been in very recent times that it has been acceptable for women to be educated at all. Terms such as 'scholar' and 'student' historically referred only to men. According to Jane Mills (1989) the only term that existed to describe a woman as a scholar, prior to the 20th century, was that of "bluestocking" (p. 30). From the early nineteenth century onwards, bluestocking was used derisively to describe "any woman who displayed signs of learning" which was itself perceived as "unnatural" (Mills, 1989, p.31).

The history of the term bluestocking is interesting in itself, in that it appears to date from the 18th century English 'salon', at a time when education for women was socially unacceptable (Bodek, 1976). The English salon, modelled after the French, became a place in which a woman could more acceptably "sharpen her wits and gather around herself other educated women and men" (Bodek, 1976, p. 185). Such gatherings were relatively informal and as blue stockings, in contrast to black, indicated less formality, they became known as bluestocking circles. 'To wear your blues' hence became a metaphor for intellectual discussion.

As the group developed, it became exclusively a women's group (Ferguson, 1985). In the context of the strong prejudice against educating women and hence against women of intellect, the word bluestocking therefore began to take on a derogatory connotation and women known as 'bluestockings' were generally regarded with suspicion. As such, the bluestocking circle, with its message to women to "be assertive, take the lead, wait for no man, write, create, be vocal, do not flinch from flouting custom" (Ferguson, 1985, p. 21) is now often regarded as an important predecessor of more recent feminist movements, with the term being reclaimed by later feminists as one meaning a woman of intellect, who challenges the social conventions of her time and fights for women's rights to education (Bodek, 1976; Ferguson, 1985; Ludwig, 2006).

Such issues continue to be of significance to women's educational experiences. Jackson (2002) for example, maintains that women continue to be denied full citizenship within higher educational classrooms, due to the "invisible pedagogies and mythical discourses" (p. 75) that operate to devalue women and women's contribution within higher education institutions:

> Within the public sphere of the university... being included intellectually and culturally can mean conforming to traditional male-defined and patriarchal definitions of culture and intellect. To succeed in higher educational institutions, women may have to take on men's way of knowing, unable to develop their own (Jackson, 2002, p. 68).

Other writers such as Letherby (1994) contend that "the dominant view in our society is that a woman's primary function is motherhood" and that "social attitudes encourage women to measure their own self-worth in terms of the capacity/desire to other" (p. 526). Figes (1994) discusses the lack of support and encouragement given to mothers who take on another role, such as paid worker or student even though "women are capable of more than one role at a time" (p. 76). She points out that, for fathers, it is expected that men will have significant roles in addition to fatherhood; hence they are not faced with these conflicts. However, "it is rare for the traditional roles to be completely reversed: only in 3% of families does the father take primary responsibility for children" (p. 94). The gendering of identities in which women are framed as *carers* and men as *breadwinners* (Lister, 2000; Orloff, 1996; Weeks, 2000) can significantly inhibit women with family and caring responsibilities from taking on the demanding additional role of student.

Implications for women as mature-age students

The impact of higher education on mature-age women appears to be profound, yet confusing, perhaps especially so for those who are first amongst their families and friends to enter university. The dominance of white middle class male culture within higher education institutions can also be particularly alienating. These students experience confusion and contradiction as they struggle to span the two different cultures of home

and university and to balance their domestic roles with their studies. The traditional role of 'woman as carer' mitigates against independent study and achievement.

However, for many women, university attendance comes to mean a lot more than simply gaining an education or further qualifications. While initial considerations usually include a desire to get a better job, the reasons for staying at university can change over time. The ultimate benefits of such a decision may well be unforeseen and unimagined at the start of the university journey. Quinn (2005), in her study of women as students, suggests that university provided her participants with an imagined space, a means to resist dominant discourses shaped by 'supermarkets, call centres and lonely train stations' (p.11). Women are able to re-imagine and legitimate self in relation to other members of the community; a truly transformative experience.

The following seven chapters each tell a story about a woman's journey into higher education, in her own words. Each tells of her reasons for coming to university, her expectations and the factors that contributed to her decision to undertake university study at this time in her life. How they managed the initial transition to university is also explored, such as reactions of others, coping with the early days and dealing with the anxiety associated with something so new and different.

Their stories also reveal the many sacrifices which all of them had to make, and the impact of these sacrifices on themselves and others around them. Gender issues are highlighted in the descriptions of the constant juggling involved as they find ways to combine their studies with the important relationships in their lives – partners, children and elderly parents – as well as with paid work. Also illustrated is the resilience and persistence of each of the women through difficult times, as well as their main sources of help and support. The transformative nature of their experiences as students, in terms of their own identity, vision for the future and potential impact upon generations still to come, is revealed through their stories.

The closing chapters summarise the common themes that emerge from the women's stories and bring these themes together in a coherent whole. Some practical ideas, based on these women's experiences, are offered to other women considering taking this path, or already beginning to tread it.

A number of recommendations are also offered to education providers and policy makers on ways to better support and encourage this important cohort of higher education consumers.

Throughout this book, the individual voices of these seven women – their experiences, challenges, difficulties and triumphs – can be clearly heard. Narrative theory informs us that the stories which individuals tell are, to a significant degree, products of the social and cultural times and places in which they are told (Elliott, 2005; Ewick & Silbey, 1995). It is therefore likely that the experiences of these seven women are reflective of the experiences of other mature-age students within a similar time and culture. Hence, their stories offer a powerful insight into the second-chance journey of the mature female learner in Australia at this particular time. In sharing

these stories, we, the authors, seek to engender a deeper understanding of the female mature-age student experience; one that is informed by student reality rather than institutional discourse.

As such, these stories can help to inform higher education policy and institutions on ways to better attract, teach and support women as mature-age students. In assisting them to maximise their individual student success, the broader societal goals of widening access and improving participation rates in higher education can also be furthered. In so doing, the educational outcomes for a higher proportion of the population may arguably be improved.

Katrina's Story

"When I came here it was very different from how I imagined it would be"

Katrina is 42, recently widowed with two children, aged 7 and 11. Before coming to university, she worked as an administrative assistant. Katrina did an enabling course to achieve university entry and is now in the second year of a Bachelor of Education degree, studying part-time.

I was told about the enabling program

I was always passionate about teaching, but I have no teaching qualifications. I thought, the only way to get a teaching qualification is to go to university. I didn't think I would be able to do this though, since I didn't finish school and didn't get the Higher School Certificate. But then I was told about the enabling program, and I was told this was a good way to get into university and get a qualification, so I did it.

I decided that now was the time to do it, as my husband was very sick and he wasn't able to function. I really needed to get things sorted out and needed to be in a position to be the breadwinner ...my husband passed away last year. He had been in hospital on average about three times a year. Each time he was in hospital for about three weeks, and they would get him better and get him stabilised, but the last time – he was in hospital and just didn't get any better.

I had started at university by then, and I think I was too scared to stop. I'm on a couple of scholarships and I didn't want to lose them.... I am basically dependent on them so couldn't afford to do without them. One of them is a learning scholarship, which I got from the university based on our income, and the other is one from the local council, and I really want to keep them. If I stop then they will both just be cancelled.

But, I must say that last semester was extremely hard. I had so much work and so many assignments to do, and I only just managed to get them all finished. I ended up only having a few days holiday after I got all the work done. I was so late with everything, and my children were still going to counselling and other things...

People tell me that I am amazing to have been able to keep on with my studies, and I know that I am in one sense, but in the other I can also see that my health declines from all that stress and not having the time or the ability to be able to have a quiet time and just reflect on things. It was only yesterday or the day before, I just got to that point where I said, maybe next year I could slow down a bit, maybe I could give myself just one subject next semester, and take things more slowly. I'm doing two subjects still, as I keep thinking I need to try to complete as soon as I can, because of my circumstances. I have some health issues as well, so it is really taking its toll on me.

The first six weeks were a nightmare

It probably wasn't the best time to take up studying, but it was needed, so I felt that I had to just get on with it. When I decided to do the enabling course my children weren't really very happy about it. My youngest child, he was then four, he was not very happy, and my daughter wasn't really happy about it either. In terms of the rest of the family, my brother thought I was mad. My husband was supportive though, as much as he could be, and he looked after the children more to give me time.

The first six weeks were a nightmare ... very overwhelming. I think my brain was a bit sleepy, and thinking hurts after so many years of not thinking much. I had worked for a long time as an admin assistant, and admin work is nothing like academic studies, so I found it all very frightening for the first six weeks and I was very close to just giving it all away... The place was just too big! But now I find it is fantastic; but when I started it was too big. I didn't know anyone; I didn't know who could help ...

When I got to the point that I wanted to give it up I spoke to someone in the Student Support office. I don't know why I didn't do that before, but I just didn't. They made an appointment for me with a Counsellor, and I had some counselling and that helped me to cope much better. It was really excellent, releasing all that fear and anxiety. I had one session on a Wednesday, when I was feeling absolutely sick, and on Friday I woke up and it was all gone.

It was one of my lecturers who pointed me in the right direction and told me to come to Student Support. I found that lecturer very, very supportive. She helped me to stay on. She made me agree to stay on at least for six weeks and when I hit that point when I said, “I can’t do this anymore”, then she got me to go along to student support.

I had pretty bad school experiences

I think it’s been even harder because there is no-one else in my family now who has been to university. My husband got his degree about 5 years ago, through external studies, but no one else has a degree, so there is no-one now in my family who knows what it’s like. When I was at school I was a good student – probably better than my brother. He was a real minimalist and he just did as much as was needed to get his School Certificate and didn’t care about anything else. He was still smart and I still find him very intelligent, but school had nothing to offer him. He just wasn’t interested. I didn’t like it either – I had pretty bad school experiences and that’s why I didn’t want to stay on and do the Higher School Certificate. I was still living in Denmark then, which is where I was born and grew up, and my brother is still there.

When we were growing up my mother worked in something to do with sales and my father worked in a management job. When I first came to university I wanted to know everything. When I’m involved in a course I have to know everything. But when I came here it was very different from how I imagined it would be. I don’t know everything... and I don’t have to...and I really enjoy just digging into one area and finding things out myself. I am so much busier than I used to be.

I had to make a lot of changes

Starting in the enabling course was a good way to start, in that it is easier than university, but it still very demanding. It’s a bit like kindergarten, all very friendly and helpful and looking after you. Once you start university studies, you might find lecturers like this, but you will also find lecturers who couldn’t care less. You are left on your own much more. If you find something difficult, well, you have to work it out yourself. You have to find your research material and so on, whereas in the enabling course they give you kind of a head-start and some ideas about how to start. But I must say it was an excellent preparation. I’d never written an academic essay before in my life and a few teachers said ‘well done’ and one teacher in particular was fantastic.

I had to make a lot of changes in my life once I started studying; less television, having long, long nights... Some nights I could be up to two or three in the morning. I found it very difficult last night, as my daughter was in tears. She didn’t know why she was crying, and I just had to put my essay

aside, even though I really needed the time to get it done. So, inside, I wanted to get things done, but she just wanted to be near me. In the end she was so exhausted she just fell asleep on the lounge. It is a big conflict for me, because we had a lecture and a presentation this morning and I didn't end up finishing my presentation until ten past ten in the morning at home, and I was supposed to be giving the presentation at ten in the class. I hopped in the car as soon as I was finished, and I rushed in and I opened the door. The lecturer said "What an honour", when I came in late. I felt terrible, and I said, "Look, I can tell you the big story about why I'm late, but let's just leave it at that....". So I did get the presentation done and I gave it ok in the class but I had no choice to give it much thought, I just put the points down, and in the end the lecturer was happy....

I think though that our biggest change was when my husband was first diagnosed and when he got so sick. After that, I think everything else maybe had an impact but I wasn't able to pin it down because there were other things that had a bigger impact.

I would like to be able to wave a magic wand

I just try and struggle to do things and I hope and hope that lecturers are understanding... and most of the time the lecturers are good. Not all of them though... I have had others who have been really difficult when I needed to change tutorial times or something like that. Often I have to miss tutorials because of other commitments, with the children and so on. Some lecturers are pretty easy and others are ... well, you've got to put this and that in writing, and they make it more difficult, which I find quite a strain. I find it quite demanding enough anyway, so when you are put under more and more pressure, well, it's hard.

I have no family here at all. My brother is still back in Denmark, and my parents are both dead now. My mother passed away 23 years ago and my father four years ago. My mother was only 60 when she died from complications of diabetes, and my father died at 78 of heart problems.... probably just old age really.

I do have one really good friend here at uni. She's on a different campus now though, but we see each other when we can and talk on the phone. She is very supportive in the way that I can spit the dummy, and I can whinge, and I can just sit there and say, "God this is all shit.... I don't know what I'm doing ...". In that way she's great. And I have another friend who takes my children every Sunday at the moment so I can get my assignments done. If I didn't have her I would definitely not be able to carry on.

Sometimes I think that I would like to be able to wave a magic wand.... It would be so much easier if there was more help from the government, or community services or something like that, that doesn't cost a fortune, or maybe even be free. I don't want to have to rely on my friend so much. Having my children every Sunday, well, that's more than enough for her to do.

One of the things that I used to find really helpful here at the campus was when we could have our essays and things proofread by the learning support person. That was so helpful, but that's been cancelled now, and because English is not my first language, I sometimes really struggle with getting the words just right. It would be great if that service could have continued, as now I just have to manage on my own and hope that it all sounds ok.

One thing that was really nice this year was when I robbed my children's bank accounts and we all went on a holiday up to the Gold Coast. Not really my style of holiday but it was for the children and it was really good for them. It was in January, and I made a very quick decision, and off we all went at the end of January, so the children actually started school a little bit later, but it was worth it.

In a way, my husband passing away was very much expected, although maybe not at that time. But we knew, and when he was diagnosed he was given 5 years to live and then there it is. I talked about it to my children to try to prepare them. A doctor recommended it. And even though we had talked about it so often, still, when it actually happened, my daughter reacted in such a way, as if she had no idea what was going to happen. Maybe in the years before, well, maybe they don't really want to listen to it and .... then they feel it anyway. You should talk to them, but still, again, when we started counselling ...we had one counselling session before we went on holidays... it was all unexpected... and my daughter was like ...why? So going on that holiday was one thing that helped at that time. We couldn't really afford it, but it was important to do.

When my husband was ill I had to get a few extensions on assignments and so on, and special consideration. I think I missed out a bit... looking at my results last semester. The lecturer was a really hard marker and I don't think my circumstances were really looked at enough. For example, in one subject I had to do three assignments. The first assignment my husband wasn't in hospital and I was ok within myself and I got a Distinction. But the middle assignment, I applied for special consideration because of the stresses, and I was given close to two months, and I just managed to cruise along, but not without a lot of pressure. For that second assignment I just got a Pass. And then for the last assignment, where my own health had picked up again, and he was in hospital and being looked after, I got a Distinction again. So it was the middle assignment where I didn't get the results, and I think if the lecturer had looked at the whole picture she would have easily given me 75 instead of 73...in the circumstances.

I have gained a lot of confidence

I'm a diabetic, which started when I was pregnant with my first child and at that stage it was the type that is confined to during the pregnancy, and once you give birth it's all better. But I had it again with my second pregnancy, and two years later I was diagnosed with diabetes, the type that isn't just in pregnancy, then I was on diet control and a year after that I was put on

insulin tablets. I must say studying doesn't really help diabetes because you just sit there and don't move, and I find when I have the time to exercise my diabetes is much better, but it's hard to get the time for that when you are studying....

But on the other hand I have gained a lot of confidence from doing my studies, and finding out I'm not dumb as I was told for many, many years at school.... maybe I wasn't told that precisely in so many words but yes, through comments... although my mother was very encouraging. I think I have just gained heaps of knowledge. Uni studies opens up an entire world of knowledge different to school, different to TAFE, just the amount of things you need to know and can know and it's all around you but you just don't think it's around you and worth knowing.

School and TAFE are more structured and you get presented with what you have to know in the lesson, whereas with uni you go into a lecture and the lecturer mentions this or that and then you do it by yourself. It's broader...also to me it's helped me to widen my interests. Just as one example, since starting in the enabling course my interest in Aboriginal culture has definitely been opened up. I think that this is one of the most fascinating cultures that have ever existed traditionally and so I've gone on in my uni studies to do more research into this.

Time-wise, it is very demanding

I think though that I have quite a restricted social life. I manage to keep two of my friends... but it's not that we see much of each other. For me, when assignments are due I really push myself to the edge, because I have hardly any time to switch off. No time to just sit in front of the TV sometimes and do nothing. I just keep going and going. Yesterday for example was just a normal day. After dinner I put my children to bed, and I had no time to just sit there to drink a coffee or do nothing, or maybe switch on the TV or listen to music. As soon as my children are in bed I'm in front of the computer or I'm reading uni books and articles. Time wise, it is very demanding.

When my husband passed away I really thought about leaving, just giving up uni. My children were like, yes, yes, take a break... they wanted me to stop. What kept me going were the scholarships. I think they were the main reasons... scholarships, and also I would think, well, having a break for a year would just push it even further away, my goal, and it's already a long way off because I'm only part-time anyway.

We try to support each other

Generally the lecturers are understanding, although of course there are some exceptions. I don't think there is anyone who has been really unhelpful though. The lecturer who was most helpful, I haven't had anything to do with her since the enabling course. She was my tutor in one of the subjects.

But most helpful are my friends, both of them because they both give me so much. One is extremely good for emotional support and the other is there with the children. We try to support each other.

If I want help or advice about my studies I usually go to other students, or to the learning support people in the library. I must say that I don't need them as much as I first thought. I definitely needed them when I was doing the enabling course. I almost lived in there... but not now. Sometimes I find it difficult when I start a new subject that I haven't touched before. This semester I started a new subject that I've never done before, and I found it very hard, extremely difficult, because I don't know the subject, and because I'm not from an English speaking background, and I need to get my head around it. So at the beginning I would go to the learning support people, and sometimes try to talk to the lecturer. I actually tried to do that this morning. I needed to do a 1500 word essay and I found it extremely difficult to put it into words. I'm very precise with my essays and actually go according to the criteria and try to write a very condensed and purely academic essay. But that one, 1500 words, I got to 1100 and I said, I can do no more... I can do no more; if I want to do more then it's really just "fluff". I said this to my lecturer and he said, "1100 words for a 1500 word assignment...?" And I said, "I know, that's why I'm here". And he said, "Oh well, don't worry about it, as long as the quality is there." So now I'm not sure...

One other problem for me here is that they changed the procedure for applying for student loans. With my husband having passed away and, it was a big expense as well, because it was ... how can I say.... I just didn't feel like cooking... Not that I don't... I just didn't feel like having all the responsibilities, with looking after the house, and household cooking, and I just needed basically my children around me. And this has cost me, apart from the holidays, the first three weeks probably cost five hundred dollars on going out, doing things differently, just not staying at home. I just couldn't, and I was really desperate for a loan, to help me out, and they've changed the procedure. It's all so, so difficult now. I've been asked to come back time and time again....

The last loan I think I applied for was probably a year ago or even longer, and there was the loans officer, and it was like, fill in one page, and showing her my health care card and telling her about income and payments, and just one page and she approved it, and this time I had to go back to Centrelink and pick up a statement and it just wasn't that one page ... I did get the loan in the end but it was all stress, and I felt like saying, please don't make it too complicated, I just can't handle ... I'm stressed enough. She couldn't help it, she was new, and if the other loans officer was still here, well, she knows you, and maybe it would have been easier.

What is most important to me

I think for other mature- age students coming to university, I would want to make him or her aware that they will find it very difficult until you adjust

to uni life and your brain starts kicking over again. You will find it very difficult, but remember it will pass, and there are people who can help and you can go to counselling, to student support and the learning centre. I think that universities need to keep on being really understanding about what mature-aged students are. We're not 19, we have family, we have responsibility, we have a house, we have a household, we have so many other things going on, work or whatever, children, and we are here, we are here to get our degree and, yes, our degree is very important to us, but we have other things as well, so many responsibilities, which affect our studies.

I just hope that I will finish my degree and I will be able to secure a job... maybe teaching.... maybe just in the education field somewhere. It may not have to be as a teacher particularly. I know that there is no guarantee, but hopefully I will be able to secure a job which will pay more and therefore economically I'll be able to support my children better than I would have been able to originally. That's really what is most important to me, and by being here and doing this degree, I can see that I have a chance to make this happen.

Barbara's Story

"It's definitely not just an educational experience; it's like a life learning experience too"

Barbara is a single parent with a young son aged 2. Just prior to starting university her marriage broke up and she relocated to a suburb closer to her parents. Before the arrival of her son, Barbara worked in a variety of roles and had completed some vocational qualifications in a technical college.

What planted the seed

I have a qualified trade but I left my job to move up to Sutton Cove with my husband. We were going to give it a good go, but everything fell apart 'cause I left work, and I was the one bringing in money. I was the responsible one. When we moved I fell pregnant and that's when it fell apart 'cause I wasn't the one keeping everything together.

I came back to this area on the pension and all of that lovely stuff. I decided I needed to work. When my marriage broke down it was a very, very tough time trying to work out what I was going to do in order to support my son, who is now two. My husband is not the best. He will not pay anything, so I realise that I have to provide everything. I didn't want to work six days a week 'cause then I wouldn't be able to spend time with Michael, and it's really hard to get baby-sitters at the weekends and with my trade they expect you to work Thursday nights and Saturdays or Sundays, and I just couldn't do that.

There is one girlfriend from Sutton Cove who really sort of encouraged me, 'cause it was her brother that was really looking into doing the course. I was asking him a few questions about it and that's what planted the seed. She's been the one who has been saying, "Why don't you look into it yourself?" and "Why don't you do this?" Sort of pushing me here...

It was good, as everyone has been very supportive, but my husband doesn't know yet. It will be curious to find out what he says when I actually tell him. He's the one that I am a bit nervous about, mainly 'cause he will probably use the five days in day-care against me, and all of that stuff. Yeah, he's just off on his own little tangent and so I don't have much contact with him. But he's the only one that I think will probably say, "But why are you doing this?" He's the only one I can think of that I might get a negative response from. Maybe that's why I haven't said anything to him, 'cause I don't want to hear that negative.

Uni was never really an option

I never considered uni 'cause I thought it would lock me in at too early an age, whereas I've had millions of jobs, and I was lucky to move from job to job at a young age. There was only one girlfriend that went to uni after school, and she went to be an accountant. We all thought she was a big nerd and all that stuff, so, yeah, I never. Way back then I wanted to be an air hostess and then I got into real estate and then I moved into hospitality. I was doing the functions and at that time my sister said, "You've got to have a trade, you've got to have a trade...get something behind you." So uni was never really an option. I just wanted to get out there and earn money and spend, and have my weekends to party.

I am doing the double degree of Bachelor of Arts, Bachelor of Teaching, and due to my prior studies through TAFE, that was enough study to get me into uni without doing the STAT test or an enabling program so I was lucky.

I just rushed into it headlong

I didn't think much about it as I thought I would probably scare myself off. I just rushed into it headlong. I've got to organise this, this and this, in order for me to get in. I didn't think about what I had to do at uni, 'cause otherwise I think I might not have done it. If I had really sat down and thought about it, "What am I getting myself into?", then there is the whole fear of the unknown and I might have lost courage. I had so many JET advisers tell me not to bother studying until Michael was seven 'cause I could stay at home until he was seven. But I was, like, "No, I want to do it now. If I don't do it now I'll never do it!" So I had to gauge my motivation and just not think about the big picture yet; just focus on getting in. Once I got in, I just focused on getting my computer, then just little steps, otherwise it would hit me.

When I arrived I was shocked by the expectations. I mean, I know that it's not like TAFE or like school where you get spoon-fed but... Okay, read chapter three by next week is fine if that is the only subject that you are doing, but I've got all these other things! It's just like, it was daunting to think, "Wow there is so much expected from me from day one". But it really comes down to time management. I have been doing a lot of those courses that Student Services have, and they have been really helpful; really putting it in laymen's terms so that you don't over-think things, 'cause that is my problem. I think too much about things and make a huge issue about something small. That's where I have to sort of step back and say, "Well, righto, if I just write a sentence on every single assignment I've started I can just go upwards from there". As long as I have started, and not let it become a major problem. So that is where I realised that you have got to be on top of things, and there are just so many young ones [young students] who haven't even thought of starting these assignments; and that's where I am ahead, 'cause I am thinking about how I've got to make time to do this, this and this, and still spend time with Michael. So it's making me feel a bit more motivated to sit at the computer and do my research a little earlier than probably I would have, but you have got to be motivated and just breathe deep....

A very steep learning curve

I dearly like to get the highest marks I can possibly get, 'cause I've always been very competitive. I'm always trying to do that extra bit to try and get that extra mark. But to start with, I did not put too much pressure on myself. I was just aiming for a pass until I got a bit of a grasp on what I was actually doing, and how to write the essays and all of that. When I felt a little bit more confident I aimed for the higher ones. I actually got a bit upset 'cause for my first assignments I got two D's, and I said to Mum, "Ohhh, I got two D's!". And then a girlfriend explained, that's a Distinction, and I went "Oh-hh! That's all right!" Yeah that took a bit of getting used to....

It is hard to work out exactly what the lecturers want and that's a very steep learning curve, and it's easy to get sidetracked. I'm finding that I have to put a little bit more work into that, and I have approached the tutor with a first draft three or four weeks before it is due and sort of said, "This is what I have so far. Am I on the right track?" I have approached them 'cause I didn't want to go off on my own tangent, so I didn't want to worry about it and let it all blow out of proportion. I deal with it when I could see, "Okay, I have done half of it", and I want to check that I am on the right track. I don't find that an issue with me, probably 'cause I realised that you can talk to your tute[tutorial] lecturers. You can talk to the lecturer and they are there to help you so I just I ask the silly questions!

I love the student mail too. I mean, I check it every single day religiously. That is just part of my day, and it is just so informative. Everything is on there. And using the library from home, that's just amazing... check on your

books from everywhere! I do the majority of my library stuff at home and look up journals and databases. It's just amazing and it's just so easy to use; really easy to use.

Some of the challenges

I find it still a challenge though, with home life with Michael. I'm finding that I'm relying on my parents a lot more than what I wanted to 'cause I'm needing an extra day to do assignments. And so I'm feeling a bit guilty with Michael 'cause I'm not spending the whole weekend with him like I wanted to. That's sort of eating away at me, thinking, "Okay, do I really want to spend so little time with him, and is the end result worth it?" 'Cause he's being a little bit naughty, and maybe it's just the terrible twos, but I just feel I want to be there a little bit more. So I'm at the stage now deciding whether or not I need to give up my work, which is only one day a week, but that's the extra money that I need. I'm enjoying being at uni, and I'm able to do it academically, it's just my time constraints that I'm finding quite hard.

I get up at six, well six-thirty usually, and then we have a bit of a play and have breakfast. I drop Michael off at eight and then I race down here. Depending on what time I finish at uni, I'll always pick him up between five and six pm and then we'll come home. He's usually had a pretty decent lunch at day-care, like seconds and thirds, so I know I don't have to do a major meal for him. So we'll just sit down and have something light, have another bit of a play, have a bath and he's in bed by seven. I'm pressuring him to go to bed on time and to stay in his bedroom, and that's adding extra pressure on me 'cause he senses that I'm getting a bit frazzled, so then he plays up. I've only got till ten-thirty some nights, but he's only been finally going to sleep at eight-thirty, so I've only got two hours to study. That's a little bit frustrating. I've tried to set the alarm for a little bit earlier so that I can get up before Michael, but as soon as he hears the alarm he's awake so that's what I'm finding just a little bit harder.

Mother guilt

I've got a lot of guilt with having Michael in day-care five days, and it's really hard, especially every morning when he bawls. That is really hard, but I've just got to think of the long-term picture. It's better than me working weekends and it's better than me working Thursday nights, so I've got to look at the positives that way. Sometimes I just think you have the mother guilt no matter what you do. Everyone has got guilt! Michael just loves day-care and I know he really does. He just so loves the children and he has got such a following! I can see that he just so enjoys it. He is just a social type. He needs that outlet, so even if I wasn't doing this I would probably be working anyway, and he'd be in day-care. He'd be there no matter what. I've got no choice. I do feel a bit guilty relying on my parents as much as I do, especially

with Michael sick and things like that, but you just get over it. I am doing this for our future, so this is what has to be done now. So there is no way around it, it's got to to be done!

I mean, there's only two of us, and we can eat baked beans for five nights and Michael couldn't care less. He thinks it's a party! I am also lucky that he is so young. He doesn't realize that we should be having different meals every single night. He couldn't care less as long as we are eating together and having a fun time, so that's why I am so lucky. I am so lucky...

That's the good thing about being a single mum. I don't have to go home and speak to my husband and try to spend time with him. I can just go home, have dinner time with Michael, put him to bed and then it's my time for the rest of the night. So really I have got it a little bit easier than a lot of other mums, 'cause I don't have that partner there.

What I have learnt

...about university

Mainly it's the time management; how to do things smarter, cutting out the non-necessary things and working out what is really important, and making time for me and family. Make the most of the time that you have got. I am a little bit more clever with my reading. I am only reading what I need to read and disregarding everything else. That's probably what I am doing differently, streamlining and making more use of my time. When I decide, I really don't feel like doing this, I won't push myself and I'll have a day off. There is no point spending a whole day to do something that could have only taken me a few hours to do once I am focused, so I give myself time out if I am not really feeling up to it. I won't do it rather than force myself to do it.

Over my holiday I ended up playing solitaire a lot 'cause every night I was still going into my study and pretending to study, so that Michael didn't get used to me watching TV, and I didn't want to get hooked on new shows and stuff like that. So through my holidays I was sitting down at my computer every night for at least an hour playing games, but Michael thought I was doing study, so I just wanted to keep that routine going 'cause it's too easy to lose it and then it's too hard to start all over again.

...about myself

I am not sure I want to be a teacher, much to Mum and Dad's dismay, but this has filled a void, and it's made me have a bit more confidence about myself again. I have gotten me back, 'cause I am using my brain. I can relate to people a little bit more, I'm more confident talking to people. Some of that might have been my confidence coming back after my marriage ended, so there might have been some of that there.

But I am getting back to the old Barbara, 'cause I have been through quite a bit, and so I am sort of feeling a little bit more confident with myself. I can do it, and I am just amazed that I am the most financially secure that I have been for a long time, and I am on the bloody pension! I mean, how can that happen? But I just feel so in control, and it's so good that I can feel that way after being so out of control for so many years.

There was still a lot of 'ifs and buts' at the end of last year, whereas now I sort of think that it is worth it, 'cause the end result will be so much worth it. Even if I don't become a teacher, even if I can't get a job as a teacher, I think that this has been such a learning experience that I have changed my thoughts. I have changed who I am, and I think I needed it, in order to do something entirely different that is not focused on me. It is focused on doing something. It is getting my mind thinking about things other than me.

I just got a feeling, it sounds really stupid, but... worthiness I think... I am worthy of being here and I can do it, and that just was great self empowerment to me. It really made me sort of think, well I am in a really great place right now and ... it was a culmination of everything working finally...I just think in total it was just such a steep learning curve but such a very enjoyable experience.

Anyway, I think I have learnt a lot and a lot of it has come from study, thinking about other things, so you are not going over and over it again, and then the thought might come in that things are really not too bad...

Highs and lows

Some of the highs have been passing! Definitely, that's been a bit of a boost. Some of the lows are not getting as high a mark as I had hoped for, 'cause I put so much work into it.

What I found really, really hard is that the timetable is unforgiving. I am the type of person I have to be at a lecture. When I hear somebody else say, "What is on that page?", sometimes just little things they say really click home to me, and I need to be in every single lecture. I couldn't miss it, and I need to be there rain, hail or shine, and that's what I have found really hard. Like, you couldn't go to a second lecture, like drop in on someone else's lecture and hear the same thing; that was your time slot. I sort of had to deal with that, as this is my timetable, and so I have to work out how I can get there

However, overall I found it to be a very big self-discovery, not just learning about subjects and things, but you are learning about yourself - what you are capable of, what you can actually do, that you can get through it, and that all the hard times are worth it 'cause you just feel proud of yourself for doing it really.

The future: I am in a better place now than what I was to start with

I don't think there has been a time in my life that would compare to this, and I will probably think that for the whole four years of uni. I think every year will be different. Your workload will be different 'cause you have some subjects that will click and some subjects that won't, and the ones that won't, you are just going to have to push everything else aside, just focus and get through.

I was in a supportive parenting program at Sutton Cove when I was up there as a 'mother-in-crisis' when Michael was one month old. That's when David [husband] first left. I didn't realise at the time, 'cause I was in my own little world, that I was watched quite heavily for signs of postnatal depression, and for, like, major things that might have happened. I could have gone either way. Recently, I called in there and the woman who ran the program said, "Wow, you are my happy ending!" Apparently, she has been speaking to quite a few mothers in a similar situation and saying how there was someone who was in this group and she is going really, really well at uni. It's actually really amazing to think that she uses me as an example for other people. Wow! Wow! It makes me feel good!

In the past, I never allowed myself to make plans 'cause so many things would happen, and so I just could never think, "Okay, next year, this is what I am going to do". I am now finding that I am planning my fourth year, what subjects I am doing, and that is really empowering that I can do that. I am even sort of thinking, "Now when I leave uni, these are some of the possibilities...", and that's something that I have never really been able to do before. So I think that anything will be a happy-ever-after from where I was to start with. I was way down there when I started, whereas now I am up here! I have got this far to go, but yeah, my little story will definitely be a happy-ever-after, 'cause I am different person now, and I feel like a different person. I feel like a better person, and I feel like I could be a better mum to Michael, and I feel like I am happy, and that is a really good feeling. But I am very proud of myself that I have come this far and I am doing it, and it is giving me back my sense of self-prowess, it's definitely not just an educational experience. It's like a life learning experience too.

I was quite messed up I must say. I came from a bad place, but I think the side-track of study made me get every other aspect of my life together. So I am going to wear one of those silly caps and capes. Yes, I am going to get there, and I am going to prove that it can be done, especially to show my ex-husband that I am worth something!

Mandy's Story

"I always wanted...something more..."

Mandy is 38 years old, married, with five children, ranging in age from 6 to 15. When Mandy left school she worked at a marketing company where she met her husband Mike. She continued working there until her children were born. While with the company, Mandy did a diploma at an Institute of Technology, as part of an employee staff development program. After having her children, Mandy returned to the paid workforce as a waitress, until deciding to do an enabling course to achieve university entry. She is now in the second year of a Bachelor of Civil Engineering degree, studying part-time. Mandy's husband is a manager in the same company where they first met.

I sort of had a yearning

My mother didn't encourage me to get my HSC. In fact, she told me I wasn't smart enough, so I joined the work force when I was sixteen. We lived out on a property, so I moved out of home at sixteen and lived in the city and worked at a marketing company. I met my husband there, doing training, and settled down. But I always wanted... something more. When I was in year 10, I wanted to stay on at school but I wasn't encouraged to do that. So it has always been a yearning. And then, when I was working for the company in their training section, before having my first child, I got this opportunity to do this Diploma of Adult Education, and I loved it. It was a real culture change, a real shock to the system, because I hadn't done my HSC, so I didn't have a clue what an essay was, and so I fuddled through that with a lot of help from Mike, because he had already done that Diploma a couple

of years before. So I got through, and got a pass, and ever since then I sort of had a yearning, looking for something, then falling pregnant and keeping on having babies.

As I got older I thought I was getting a bit wiser, but I was feeling quite mentally trapped. And then we moved around a bit for Mike's work, still with the same company, and I thought I was keen to study, so I was looking into doing some sort of preparatory type thing. The local TAFE where we were living at the time offered that, but somehow it just didn't happen. So, when we moved back here, it was still a part of me that wasn't satisfied, and I thought, I really should look into this. So I checked the website of the uni and saw that there was the enabling course. That was in the June. I was working part-time in a café, and it wasn't what I really wanted to be doing. I wasn't being mentally stretched and I didn't believe in answering to the 24 year olds who were working with me, who were quite threatened by my age. And so, anyway, I joined up for the enabling course.

None of my family has ever studied

I didn't really know what I wanted to do. I was tossing up what to do and was thinking about going on with Education, and doing a degree in that, but I just couldn't get excited about it – teaching I mean. I couldn't get excited about the subjects, and I have always been interested in building, drawing plans and things like that, and then I saw that the uni offered Civil Engineering, and I thought, 'What the hell!' I was actually more interested in getting into the construction management side, because that's where I think I would like to go, but being a mother of five children I knew that if I had to enter that building game, which is male dominated, then I needed some degree of respect. That's one thing I needed, and I thought, 'Civil Engineering!' and so I am plodding along and doing it.

The reactions were quite interesting. My parents were, like, "Can't you just focus on your family? Can't you just be happy with that? What are you doing this for? How are you going to find the time?" And one of my girlfriends was very negative. But generally speaking, everybody else was ok with it, and mostly they were very interested to know what I was studying, and how it was working. Some of them were interested in it for themselves, and asking me about it, thinking whether they might be able to do it too. Mike was very supportive and thought it was great, but there have been a few times, when trying to get an assignment done, I'd be having a temper tantrum, and he and the kids were having to eat cheese on toast for dinner six nights in a row, well then he didn't think it was too good.

My sister wasn't very supportive as well, but none of my family has ever studied and they don't understand what it's about and can't see the long term benefits. I'm the first in my family to do any study at all after school. When I did my diploma, when I was with the company, we had the big cap and gown thing at the end of it, and Mum and Dad refused to come to it. I don't understand why, but there was a lot of prejudice about studying and

getting qualifications. Even recently my sister was saying to me, "I don't know why you're studying civil engineering. Why don't you just go and work in real estate?" I said, "It's not what I want to do". They've got no idea. I got a high distinction for an assignment that I did. I was so thrilled and I was so proud, and I emailed it to my sister and asked her to give it to my Mum and Dad to read; they still haven't read it...but that's just the way it is.

My father was a builder, a carpenter by trade, working in a large corporate, commercial building. He was pensioned off rather early at 55, and retired to 'happy farm'... and Mum, well, I was a change of life baby, so that probably would account for a lot of things too. Mum was 40 when I was born and wasn't particularly happy about the fact that she was pregnant. Mum has never really worked outside the home. I've never known her to go to work, but I think that when she was younger she was mostly working in a cake shop, and other shop assistant jobs. I have no memory of her doing anything else. My brother was nineteen when I was born and my sister is nine years older than me – so we're on different planets. My brother passed away when I was nine and he was twenty-six, and I'm not overly close to my sister. We communicate in terms of what's going on with Mum and Dad, as she lives near them, but that's about all. My sister had always started TAFE courses and different things, but she never finished them. I remember my mother always berating her for starting things and not finishing them, and I used to think, if I start something I'm going to finish it.

I was worried at first

For me, coming from not having done anything for so long and not having had a particularly great experience with doing the diploma, I was worried at first about how it would be. But I felt that when I came here, I found everybody so welcoming and friendly, and the library staff so helpful, and it was like everybody was here for me and for us; whereas where I did the diploma, we were just treated like an interruption – that's how I felt. I was very anxious at first. I was very worried about my ability to be smart enough to do it, and I think that I was very nervous. But there was another part of me that was kind of quietly confident as well and thought, 'I can do this'. I did ancient history and linguistics in the enabling course, and when I saw that it was step by step, small essays to begin with, and that it was really an educational process in preparing you, I was able to embrace that, and I got quite enthusiastic and loved it.

It probably wasn't until I had started this degree that I truly became comfortable in the whole research side of things and confident in my arguments for essays. I certainly became more confident through the enabling course, but it wasn't until I'd done a few assignments and essays and things for the degree that I realised the true worth of the enabling course. I think it should be a must. In some ways there are some big differences between the enabling course and this degree, but in other ways there are similarities. This particular degree is a little bit different to lots of other degrees, in that

there's no exam and it's all assignments. The exam with the enabling course, I was really freaked out about, and that was one of the things that really swayed me to doing the subjects I am doing, simply because there were no exams. I really wanted to avoid the exams, even though I got good marks.

I found the lectures very hard at first. It was just the lecturer. Talk, talk, talk! No question and answer, and you couldn't generate conversation or discussion in the group, which was what I was used to in the enabling course, and I think that's a really beneficial learning tool. So I guess that's the difference between the enabling course and this particular degree.

It has been a really big adjustment

Things have had to change quite a bit at home since I started doing this. I had to let go of the housework. What a shame! Now we crunch around on rice bubbles and food ... and to begin with I didn't really mind, as I was quite caught up in the moment and enjoying the study and my brain was being challenged. But it's getting on top of me now, simply the fact that I can't find anything. Mike does the washing now and nothing gets put away, and because I've lost that control I'm finding it quite frustrating, the mess. I find it is really hard to focus on assignments and study when all this other stuff needs to be done. It is really distracting.

The kids have had to become more independent too. Most days I get home in time for them after school, but I was having to rely on babysitters in the morning to get the kids off to school. I've been commuting for an hour and a half each way to uni four days a week. The driving backwards and forwards has been really stressful, and the financial burden of the petrol and everything, and trying to go by train instead just wasn't logistically possible for me with the children.

It has been a really big adjustment curve for all of us. I think the children have coped best, but then I find that my stress levels rise, with due dates and assignments, and I can become very frustrated. And then sometimes when I was trying to do assignments I would have kids sick as well. I'd have it all planned for tutorials, assignments, classes etc, and then I would have the kids home sick and the plans would go out the door. But overall the kids have coped particularly well and Mike has been incredibly supportive, very much so. He has recognised particularly in recent times that I need him to help more. I had a big breakdown during the first semester, because the children were all sick, and we had lots of financial problems, and it looked as if our marriage was on the rocks. It was fabulous to know that the counselling facility was here ...and I would never had gone to see a counsellor before... but I found that incredibly beneficial to help me make objective decisions and talk through my plans. I was trying to hold on to this degree and it was the one thing that was mine, and I didn't want to let it go and didn't want to drop back, and then talking it through with people who were objective and removed from it, well...it helped. It's been stressful but everyone has adapted to it.

I no longer feel like I'm a dummy

It's possible that the problems between Mike and me would have happened anyway, but I think the studies have had a lot to do with it. I feel like, all of a sudden, I've got a brain. My opinion is worthy. I no longer feel like I'm on the back foot. He's a very bright man, and talented, and so I no longer feel like I'm a dummy. It's made me think a lot more, and I probably don't have as much respect for him as I once had, because I know I'm more confident and say what I think. So in that way it has highlighted the differences between us. I probably wasn't confident enough to express what I believed before. And I think that this has also affected my relationship with my children, perhaps more so with my fifteen year old. I noticed that within a few weeks of starting the enabling course, I'd be saying, "I've got to go and study". She was in year eight, and as soon as I started my study her attitude towards her homework changed. She studied more, went to the library... it was great. I can't say that's necessarily the case with the others, but it really has been very noticeable with her.

I have a couple of girlfriends who will look after my youngest if I need to come up to uni, and Mike's mother is quite helpful and supportive. There has been a lot of support and encouragement from her. And I think because I was having a bit of a difficult time with my marriage and sick kids – everybody – the lecturers were all very empathetic, and happy to work with me in terms of getting extensions. Here I find the librarians, the ladies in student support, the book shop, the cafeteria... everyone... are fabulous... and I think that if you didn't get that on your 'down' days, it would make it harder.

The situation with Mike just got me to the point where I couldn't concentrate on my work, because there were always financial issues as well ...financial difficulties. I haven't been able to just concentrate on my studies because of feeling pulled and dealing with all these other things. We've decided to sell our house, so I can focus on my studies and not worry about debt hanging over my head. The other big worry is my mother's ill health. She hasn't been a hundred percent. She was very ill four months ago, and about two months later she was back in hospital. I was in a lecture and no-one could get in touch with me, and she had a suspected heart attack. I was told, "You had better come down – it's not looking good" ... that was early in the semester. It didn't impact too much, but I was back and forwards to where she lives, about four hours away, which was taking out time. She's doing okay now though. They determined she had a heart murmur and stress, not a heart attack after all. And my father needs a hip replacement, which is another reason why I have had to drop back from full time to part time study. They are in their eighties – so now he is scheduled for surgery. I think whether I can go back to studying full time depends a lot on how Dad comes out of this surgery. I think it will be fine, but you never know. I may even have to defer depending on what happens of course, but it's something that

I'm not going to walk away from. To begin with I was, like, I have to get it done in three years, but now I realise I don't have to, and I have learnt not to put so much pressure on myself.

I have gained a lot of self confidence...empowerment...particularly having done the enabling course and getting some good marks. At one point, when I was at my lowest point, I was thinking I would defer or drop out, start again in a couple of years, and then I got these high marks so I thought, "I can do this". So I've gained self confidence and credibility amongst our friends. I know a lot of people in the building game, either engineers or 'tradies' [tradespeople] and over the years I've had such an interest in building and renovating and so on. I have always been interested in talking about what they're doing, and it's fascinating to see their change in attitude towards me now. They ask me to look at things, and all of a sudden there is common ground that a man can talk to me about ... my opinion counts. I was introduced to a man who was an engineer and when I said I was studying civil engineering, all of a sudden he was interested in me and wanted to talk to me.

It's something of mine

What I miss though is time with my children and time for me. I thought I could live without all that – but I realise I do need it. There have been lots of times when I've thought about quitting. Even in the enabling course, towards the end it was all getting a bit hard. I had sick kids, couldn't get to the lectures, and I wasn't real confident on the whole Blackboard [online interface] thing. I thought it was just too hard, and then when we came towards the exams I was worried I wouldn't be smart enough. I don't have a particularly good memory ...I don't think I do. I found it took an awful lot of preparation. And even now, in the last couple of weeks, again with the on-going financial burden, sick kids, and wondering about due dates for extensions, I'm really pushing it to get it all done. And then I find that I'm thinking of deferring, depending on how things go with Dad.

But I guess what has kept me here so far is the enjoyment I get from the research, from the writing, finishing each assignment... the fact that for the first time in 15 years I can just get in the car and drive up and get lost in books and research ...independence. And it's something of mine. I don't have to necessarily share it with Mike and the children. They don't have to be here. They don't have to have anything to do with it. Even though I would rate the difficulties as twelve out of ten, particularly too, when I sit in lectures with these nineteen and twenty year olds who live at home, and they still complain...

I chuck a lot of tantrums – I express it and that helps! Probably also talking it through with Mike is really helpful... his reassurance – "Keep at it, keep going, you're enjoying it", and utilising the counselling services here, that is enormously helpful, and just the support from my peers. When I didn't turn up for a while (I was trying to save money) peers would call and

ask if everything was well and hoping I could make it back. I wouldn't say that they are good friends of mine, as I am the oldest by far, with the next oldest only 24, but they are still very supportive. I made good friends in the enabling course, as they were all more my age, but now we mostly just keep in touch when we see each other around on campus, and with the odd text message. One of the girls I did the enabling course with, she is doing teaching and studying full time and working part time, and she was quite overwhelmed with the work load of the first semester, and it was nice to know that we were not all alone.

It hasn't been anywhere near as hard as I thought it would be

But without a doubt my immediate family is my biggest support, and my lecturers. Probably what's been the biggest problem is the negative attitude of my extended family. Nothing else. Except perhaps there are too many lectures where there's not much interaction. There are a lot of powerpoint presentations used, so I find those lectures pretty unnecessary as I could just look at the lecture on Blackboard. There were obviously times when they were beneficial, just being in the room and hearing a few questions that came out, and the answers, and being able to clarify, but overall, generally speaking, it has all been very positive.

If there's something I don't understand, well, as the first point of call, I always go to Blackboard and have a look at what the discussion board has been about. The discussion with students and the lecturers on line – I often find if I have a question someone else has too, and sure enough I find it on Blackboard. If I can't find it I send my lecturer an email and go from there, or I ask one of my peers the question. Most of the time I look on the internet and do my research and read books and books and books. But in terms of being able to maintain my focus, I do use the counselling service ... go and talk to the counsellor.

I think that it's important that mature-age students know that they can ask lots of questions, and not be afraid to use the services that are here. The librarians are a wealth of information. And it helps to just talk to people that might be sitting in the café, and there is also a mentoring program, with other students mentoring the new students. It's important to use all this. The only other thing I think is that the library needs to be open longer. My children are of an age where I can bring them along and they are happy to play on the computer, so it would help if I could use the library more after hours. I think there could also be some workshops that are geared towards a mature aged student. I must say I felt very old, and it would be good to have some of the essay writing courses and things like that geared to older students. I'm a little bit intolerant of a lot of the younger ones in the lectures. They are straight out of high school and they just want to talk all the time with their friends, and you just want to stand up and say "shut up".

But, you know, I was expecting uni to be really hard, and I was expecting it to be unfriendly and hard to navigate. I was worried that I was going to get lost, and I was really pleasantly surprised by the whole experience, because I didn't get lost at all. I was expecting a 3,000 word assignment in the first week. I wasn't expecting a gradual... "Let's hold your hand here, we're here to help you achieve exactly all your goals". I was expecting lots of smart people, and there are, but I was expecting to have to work really, really, hard, and it hasn't been anywhere near as hard as I thought it would be. It has been really enjoyable.

I'm far more confident now

The way I feel about myself has really changed, most definitely. I was writing a description of myself for something a while ago, and I was able to write that I regarded myself as an intelligent, attractive woman who is capable and confident and can hold an intelligent conversation; whereas maybe three years ago, I wouldn't have regarded myself that way. I feel like I'm better read, and I've got this desire to read... I want to read. I read papers, and I make far more analytical decisions now, and I really research and give a lot more thought to decisions, and I find my thought process is much faster and... yes, I think that other people see me differently now too. I also think that some people are a little bit threatened now, particularly this one girlfriend, and maybe my sister, and Mike's father is a builder as well and he was quite miffed that I got into civil engineering. He was, like, how could a ditz like you be doing that? No, sadly I don't think I have gained his respect or anything. I was brought up to be seen and not heard, but now, through the essay writing and researching, and because I've got this hunger for knowledge now, I find I'm a bit more opinionated.

I think my future is going to be much brighter than the past. I'm much more confident in terms of ... well, say, for selling our house. I'm not worried so much about material things anymore, and I don't have so much need to hang on to to all these material things and collections. And I'm far more confident. I have the ability to focus on goals that I haven't had before. First, I want to get this degree and then launch into my business, but now I'm happy to plod along and be a perpetual student. It's going to take longer to get the degree but I will probably enjoy the whole process a lot more. I have managed to get things in place. A bit of uni, a bit of exercise, more time with the kids... I've got some balance now, whereas before it was all uni and no family and no me. If I hadn't started at uni I'd still be unhappy, and being frustrated by a Neanderthal boss and...you know.

I think that for my children, they definitely will not be scared to study, because they are here in the uni environment; it is such a familiar place for them. I'm very keen for my husband to do a degree now. He needs to, because now at his age he is competing against people who have got a degree, and I think because he has seen it has been a relatively easy transition for

me, he's more open to thinking he might go back to uni. And a couple of friends and other mums, they are saying that it is an inspiration what I'm doing, with five kids and all.

Nerida's Story

"So I just thought, 'I'm not taking this anymore'..."

Nerida is 49, married with three adult children, aged 22, 23 and 26. Before coming to university, she worked as a customer service officer with a large national company. Nerida did an enabling course to achieve university entry and is now in the final year of a Graduate Diploma of Education, following completion of a Bachelor of Arts degree, studying full-time. Nerida's husband is a labourer.

The way it happened was this

Well, I'm 49 years old, and I certainly never expected that I'd ever get to uni – and never in a million years at this age! The way it happened was this. I had taken a package – a redundancy - and I'd spent six months at home and I was bored. I was arranging the information about uni for my second son. He was in the first year of the Higher School Certificate that had changed from how it used to be, and he got a really low UAI [entrance score for university]. The thing is, he really is quite brilliant and I knew that that wasn't right, so I was trying to arrange to get him into uni somehow, but he just wasn't interested. So, I thought, well bugger you! If you're not interested, I'll go to uni!

Because, someone said to me – at student services – well, what about yourself? And I said, I couldn't possibly go to uni, but they gave me information about how I could go to uni if I wanted to. So that's how it started.

That was in the middle of 2000, and then I did the research and I got all the information off everyone who would stand still and listen to me, and then I started in the enabling course in 2001.

I think that the reason I decided to do it, was simply that I was at the end of a career where I got nowhere. I knew I had a lot to give, but working for a large company and being a woman, meant I didn't have the necessary 'physical equipment' to make a manager. I had done all my manager training, I was a marketing officer, I worked in regional office, I worked in head office – anything that was going I was in it and I was still at base level, so I thought, I'm not doing this anymore.

The reason that I took the package out of my job was that the 'dork' in my training school, the one that we all helped get through training, was my manager when I left, and he was male! So I just thought, "I'm not taking this anymore".

I felt unfulfilled and looking for something

At that stage too we had one son go through uni – he was in his third year. I had another son who'd just done year twelve, I had another daughter going into year ten, and it was getting up to twenty years of my marriage, which is around the time that most marriages will stop! I felt unfulfilled and looking for something and I had to say, 'Well, do I leave and go and live in a cockroach-infested flat and take thirty years to recover, or do I make a go of what I've got?'

So I said, "Right!" and thought about it. We can't afford to live in our house here on what my husband has in his redundancy, so where can we survive until he's 65, and where I can work (because I'm ten years younger than my husband) for ten years, and then come back and live back here where the hospitals and medical are? We could go to the bush where there's lower real estate value, but what can we do in the bush? There's no jobs. The only jobs you can get in the bush are doctor, nurse, teacher. Right! I'll be a teacher!

I had wanted to be a teacher when I left high school, but my father had died between year ten and year eleven and Mum said 'I can't afford to buy your year eleven uniform. Do you mind getting a job?' So that was the end of that. Then I got married at twenty-one, and had a child at twenty-two – so I really felt I hadn't fulfilled what I really wanted to do. So, I came back and did the enabling course and got very good marks.

I want to soak up knowledge

I got into the Early Childhood [teaching degree] and went, "Oh my God! It's nappies! No, no, no!" So I jumped over in second semester to the Arts degree. I had done 50 units in the second semester and I had two days out in a school with an absolutely hideous teacher in a school, that was just so

horribly run, that I just said, there is no way I'm doing this; and I think through a combination of tiredness and the shock from the bad experience, I just said to my lecturers, "That's it!" And they said, "Don't go, don't go".

So I said, "Look, you're my age; you get out and work in that system". I said, "There is no morning tea, there's no lunch, there is no afternoon tea, there is no break; you don't get this and you don't get that; and coming from a work background where I got all those things...."

And then my sociology teacher said to me, "Look, you get high distinctions in sociology; why are you going teaching?" And a Masters' student had also said to us in the enabling course, that everyone starts in teaching. They think they are going to come here and be a teacher, but there are other things besides teaching. So I thought about it, and said to myself, I need to mature academically. What I want is an education, I want knowledge, I want to soak up knowledge. I want to learn classics; I want to learn to be able to deconstruct; I want to be able to argue politically; I want to be able to learn literature; I want an intellectual stimulus; and I thought, "Great!" I thoroughly enjoyed my journey by doing it that way.

I'm like a dog with a bone and never give up

By third year in I had to start to make some decisions. By this time, the brilliant son had decided, 'I'm going to do the enabling course Mum"; came back and did the enabling course and went through brilliantly of course, we knew he would, and he then said, the campus where I want to do my degree is in another state. So instead of him being through uni, and the first son being through uni and the daughter nearly through uni – allowing us to then break free and go to the bush – we had like a three year delay, and then we had a four year period of supporting two children at uni, plus accommodation and everything. We were pretty broke!

In second year I decided I'd do my honours, but in third year - I had to say, ok, this degree has cost me $33,000, through not working, so I thought, what can I do? The careers adviser said to me, "What are you doing honours for? Why don't you do a Masters, or a Diploma of Education?" And I went, "Perfect!" At that stage, all the way through my degree, I said, "Keep that distinction average. You might need that one day".

I'm like a dog with a bone and never give up. I applied to do the Diploma of Education. If I didn't get in I would have done the honours and been quite happy but still wouldn't have got a job. So this has been a long journey, but I'm getting to where I want to be and now I have applied for all of the rural areas [for teaching]. You know, I don't think a lot of people would have put up with it. They wouldn't have become as tenacious as I am – they would have just left. There were times when I was depressed and felt harassed, and felt incapable and was made to feel that I wasn't coming up to standard, and I could see why people would leave. What kept me going was my love of learning, my lecturers, our beautiful campus.

I think he secretly thinks I'm smarter than him

When I first decided to come to uni, people were a bit patronising – pat mum on the head, she'll be right. But, for my husband, I think it was a big slap to his pride and his ego and he has only in the last two years felt comfortable with the fact that I'm not going to get a degree in leaving!

We went to a marriage counsellor and we have gone through a process – we've been married 28 years now – and he had issues he had to deal with himself. I think he secretly thinks I'm smarter than him, which is so stupid. He's got beautiful interpersonal skills. He wouldn't be where he is if he wasn't the person he was – but it's his issue. But I think it was ego damaging for him to deal with.

But I will say this – he has supported me, one hundred and ten percent entirely – that was his way of dealing with it. He would say to other people, "I support my wife, she goes to uni – I'm the provider and I go to work and support all these uni students", and I went, "Fine!"

I've not had good memories of education

I was really worried about starting uni. I thought there'd be raving packs of young women who would pay me off and tease me – that was the biggest worry I had. What would the younger ones be like? I really thought uni would be like high school in year ten in the seventies. Of course, things have changed.

I've suffered with depression and anxiety all my life, but it wasn't diagnosed until the 1980s. When I went to kindergarten – even right up to sixth class - I sat alone, even in the rain and my best friend was the other outcast and she was the Polish immigrant child. Because I didn't get medication for depression and chronic anxiety until much later, I've not had good memories of education – and teachers did use sarcasm. They did ostracise people. It was a hard road.

But, in the bridging course I met a woman and she was lovely and - it was maths, God help us! I was doing this bridging course to do core mathematics and this woman was even more pathetic than me! She said, "I don't know anything about maths, but if I stand up and ask a question and you all think I'm dumb, I don't care. I'm going to ask as many questions as I need because I need to learn". I turned around and said, "My friend!" – and we are still friends.

Like trying to learn a foreign language

I did all the preparation courses here that I could do, six months before I started, and it was a great help. I had done all the bridging courses, learning support courses; and even though nothing can prepare you for an academic

essay - it was like trying to learn a foreign language - I got a credit in my first essay. I got help with that from [academic skills adviser]. So many students have had help from her on this campus. Just that direction I think is what it needs to kick-start people.

But one thing I will say; mature aged students do run at a disadvantage – all the way through – well, it's what the young ones have and they just accept it as normal – knowing how much effort to put in – knowing where to find things, the technology level, the ability to be able to pick out key words – what do you do with a key word? How do you use the internet? What do you mean, an email? All of this – they're all added challenges and it makes it really hard slog. It's like walking through mud.

I also had help from this lady I met in maths bridging class. And I knew some people then in Australian History. I don't know what would have happened if I hadn't met up with a couple of girls in that subject. I didn't want to do the geometry part, and the girls in Australian History said, "Why don't you come and do classical history?" And I think because the lecturers are around my age and because I'm from a corporate background and because I'm used to dealing with managers who were only men, and people in positions of power, I've never had that worry that I can't approach someone.

I'm a different person totally

It has been a big adjustment though; giving up gardening; giving up reading; giving up sewing; giving up relaxing; giving up going out with family visits; giving up socialising; giving up clothes (I buy from op shops); giving up spending money on anything; giving up having holidays. Lots of giving up! It's not just yourself – it's the normal giving up you have to do to get three children through uni as well. But I've learnt so much! I can't just <u>look</u> at a TV show anymore. I deconstruct everything! I can't just read a newspaper; I know what's behind the headlines, I know who is pushing the buttons. I can't just listen to politicians; I can see all the power play and all the crap and the nonsense that is going on in this world. I can see all the injustices. I'm a different person totally.

I also appreciate things very much. I really appreciate a Sunday afternoon with my husband. I appreciate being able to stay outside in the fresh air and sunshine; and I appreciate what my husband does for me, and I don't know if I used to do that.

My children also started to see me not just as a mother, but more of a person. I don't think my second son would have gone to uni if he hadn't seen me putting in the effort. And my daughter, well she would have just played, she was a social butterfly; she would have been fine, but would never have had anything. They say to me, "Mum, we don't know how you do it". My daughter calls me a freak – because when it comes to an essay, they struggle – and they will come to me and say, "I have gone as far as I can go. Can you

read it and tell me where I'm going wrong?" And I type it up – and they say, "That just sounds like a lecturer!" whereas in their year twelve, I couldn't help them at all.

Waves of inspiration

I think it has made my husband appreciate me. That is a mutual thing, and I think it has also allowed him to do a lot of things on his own, and that's a good way for him to reduce stress. I think we're much happier together, and I make it a rule that we go and have breakfast on Saturday and Sunday, and we realise now that is the only time we actually talk, away from everyone, and that's become a ritual – we have our coffee and our breakfast. He's also accepted the fact it's ok, because I am going to be there and I will provide for him while he goes out and does what he wants to do.

He supports me in lots of ways now - shopping, cleaning, washing the car, feeding me. He cooks tea every night. He has said to me, "Don't ever stop using your brain because you are not a person that can just sit at home."

With my children, we're more equal. We look at each other like adults, whereas before they looked down on me and were up above me with their father, and I was the object of ridicule; "Oh, silly old mum". Now I'm someone to come to for advice.

I even have more respect from the neighbours. "How are you going? Don't give in; it's only a couple more years to go". "I've got a couple of degrees on my wall", one old fellow keeps saying to me.

And then the children down the road, they call me up and ask for help and those kids - one of them is four - asks me if I'm a school teacher yet. "Are you finished your big school yet?" It's like waves of inspiration.

I'm the first one in my family to go to uni

But my family – my own siblings, fifteen years older and one either side of me - to the three older ones I'm a 'professional student'. I have said, "Please, I really don't like that term, don't speak of me like that." I find that offensive and they mean it disrespectfully.

The oldest sibling I don't see, but the youngest sibling, she went to TAFE and got 'student of the year', and her daughter at TAFE got 'student of the year' – she's probably a bit brighter than me. She said to me, "I think what you are doing is fantastic". She actually started [studying] about two years after I started. I think it made her put her thinking-cap on. I'm the first one in my family to go to uni. My niece went before me, but not any of my brothers and sisters.

Both my parents are dead now. Mum died last year. She was disappointed; she said, "I'm sorry I can't come to your party" – meaning my graduation, God love her, and I said, "Don't worry Mum, you know I'm going to get it" – and that was okay, and I knew Mum was proud of me, extremely.

My mother only went to third class for her education; couldn't do a crossword or couldn't write or read properly – so she was very proud. My mother was 81 when she died. She was always a stay-at-home mum; never worked until my father died. She didn't know how to pay bills; she was from that generation. She was a fighter. She struggled; she was the child of a divorced woman. Now that in those days was quite stigmatising. She used to say, "Whatever you do, be good at what you do". So she encouraged us to do the best at whatever we did.

My father was a boiler maker and he worked at a hospital. He did that as long as I knew. He had very little education. In winter he was sent up to the country to go rabbiting, because in those days they would get the rabbits. They sold the skin. It was the worst horrible thing to do. I think it affected him actually. So he had very little education and he was the eldest of thirteen. They didn't have education like we have now.

Even if you're feeling horrid there is always somewhere nice to go

Most of the help I've had here at uni has been from student support services; also from the woman in the shop, and the library woman, and talking to the girls in the café. I'm older, and so I just say, "I've had a bugger of a day", and I will talk to anyone, and I have always been like that.

The lecturers and tutors are better than good – they're approachable, you feel confident with them - you're not being fobbed off – they are really quite wonderful. I think just everyone who is here is generally really helpful. People who work here choose to work here – they will forego a pay rise to work here, and I think it's the ambiance of the place. Even if you are feeling horrid there is always somewhere nice to go.

What I would say to other mature age students

"Believe in yourself, acknowledge that not everyone is going to support you, acknowledge that you are going to change and not everyone is going to like it and be prepared for things that you don't think are ever going to happen". The amount of people who have left their husbands or gone through situations or have left uni because they haven't received support from family... I think, "Just don't give up". I think it's about time for Australian women to actually consider themselves to be of value, because we are valuable people, and we have a right. I've worked all my life and I'm not doing my degree to go home and do nothing. If you want to go home and do nothing, go and take up patchwork, but don't come to uni and take someone else's place for a education. And if you come and get an education, acknowledge when it's time to go and then take it with you. Don't use uni as a crutch.

It's a brand new start

I've got an interview with the Department of Education in September; I'm going to say, "I've been working five years towards this interview. Let's talk!"

If I get a position, which would be lovely, I'm prepared to go anywhere. It doesn't matter. I'm walking out. We've been working on this over the last five years. We know this is what we're doing. It's very exciting; it's my only window of opportunity. It's a brand new start.

I've got this ten year window of opportunity before my children start marrying and having children, and because my husband's ten years older than me, this is my time. I have said to all the kids, we can't give you money, we're not money rich, but we can give you a degree, but once you get your degree you've got to go out in the big wide world, and they're all doing it.

If I hadn't have come to uni I would have been like all those poor unfortunate women living on their own, wondering, "What happened to my life?" My marriage would have broken up. I left him three times, because I felt so under-valued. I was unhappy, but we have worked through it and now we're a great couple. Now I value myself, which is easy thing to say, but a very hard thing to do. If everything fell apart tomorrow I would be alright.

Fiona's Story

"I was really worried about meeting people, fitting in and everything..."

Fiona is 35 years old, single, with a son aged 7 and living with her parents. When Fiona left school she did a secretarial course at TAFE and then worked as a clerical assistant until her son was born. Fiona did an enabling course to achieve university entry and is now in the second year of a Bachelor of Social Science degree, studying full-time.

His starting school was the catalyst really

I decided to start the enabling course because my son started kindergarten and I thought, I could either go and get another boring office job, or I could do something that I actually want to do, and I love learning. So his starting school was the catalyst really. The relationship with his father had broken up a couple of years before, so I had spent that time trying to sort that out with him and my son, and then I thought, it's time to do something for myself.

I had seen a counsellor because of the breakup and stuff and I thought, wow, I really want to do this – to be a counsellor like she was. The lady that I saw was just fantastic and she said, "Go and do something." She really gave me that positive inspiration. I'm not sure if that's where I actually want to go now – but that was the whole reason I did the enabling course; it was to get into the Bachelor of Social Science. I thought that being on the other

side of the counselling chair put me in a better position if I was going to be on the other side, behind the desk, so I'd have a better insight into what people are going through, even though not all experiences are the same. But I thought it would have helped me to just to have a little bit of insight.

My family was very positive about it too. I moved in with Mum and Dad when the relationship split up, and so they were keen for me to do something, and they still are. They love helping out whenever they can. They take my son when I've got a heavy workload. They are very good.

The best thing in the world

I didn't really have many friends after the break-up. As a full-time mum I'd spent a lot of time at home. But there was one girl that I knew – she did the enabling program the year before I did. She really struggled. She doesn't have a very good grasp of language and expression and she didn't do very well, so she didn't go on with it. So I had heard about it from her, and then in the local paper they had the ad for the campus open day and I thought, this is really what I want to do. And it was so weird. I'm listening to what everyone is telling me, and then I saw this lady that I used to live next to when I was with my partner, and I hadn't seen her for, like, six years at least, and I saw her here on the campus on that open day. And she said, "You have to do the enabling course; it's the best thing in the world." She had her kids with her and she said, "It's flexible", and everyone there was really positive about uni.

My sister had done a teaching degree before and she was very positive as well. I was a bit worried though, as I hadn't studied, obviously, for a long time. Like, at work, you do in-house training or whatever the companies have, and that's one thing at least. You learn specific ways of doing things, like payroll, but I was little bit worried about studying again. But before the course had even started I was doing all the preparation and extra learning support classes. I did the essay writing, I did everything before it even started. I thought, I am not going into this blind. I'm going to get as much information as I can. So that definitely helped me to feel more confident about starting, and whenever anybody said, "I'm struggling", I would say, "Go and do this course". I was a big advocate.

You need a different headspace

Only my sister had been to uni, no-one else in my family. So it's still only me and my sister. My mother did nursing, back in the sixties before it was a uni degree. She was a shift worker and Dad was a cabinet maker. They are both retired now and they are never home. Mum does exercise and Dad plays bowls. He loves his bowls and the bowls nights and so on.

When I first started the enabling course I was really worried about meeting people, fitting in and everything. I was a bit shy and you kind of assume that everyone is younger, but we were all about the same age. And once you speak to someone and say, "I don't know how this works", and they would say, "I don't either", and then it's okay. I didn't have any problems with my son. He loved the fact that Mum was going to uni. He was really excited and he could see that it was positive as well. So I really didn't have any problems settling in, as doing all the courses before it started really helped.

When I moved from the enabling course to the undergraduate degree it was just the same really. Maybe the work load was a bit heavier, but that's obviously the way it is. The enabling course gave me a good grounding, and I think if I had of gone into uni straight from school I would never of got this far, because you need a different head-space, and I just don't think I would have been able to cope as well if I hadn't been able to get used to it through the enabling course. The other thing that's helped is just being a bit older – being a mum and going to work you get used to having dead-lines and having responsibilities, so having some life experience has made a difference.

I didn't ever think about going to uni before. The only reason I stayed on to year twelve at high school was because I didn't know what else to do. I wasn't a brilliant student or anything. I was pretty average. And then, in that Christmas holidays after year twelve had finished, my friends said, "There is a secretarial course starting tomorrow – do you want to go in?" I said, "Yes, okay." So that's what happened.

Since starting at uni I stay up later, reading. I wait until my son has gone to bed before I do any work because it's just too hard when he is around. He wants attention, needs to be fed and looked after and so on. So you don't see your friends as much, not at uni anyway. I do have social life but it's outside uni. So the change to routine has been the biggest change.

I'm close to Mum and Dad and they're supportive and help me whenever they can. I'm probably closer to my sister now, as she's been to uni too and we have that in common. I also have more friends now because of uni. Other girls that I did the enabling course with, I'm still with now, doing the same degree with two of them, and we help each other.

I also met Evan here at uni. We started going out and it kind of took my mind off my studies for a while. It had a big impact on my studies to begin with, as I just couldn't concentrate for a while and we were seeing each other all the time. But then we made a pact that we both had to try to concentrate on our studies first, and then we managed to fit in the two – studying as well as seeing each other. So we've been together for nearly a year now. It's had a really positive impact too because we can help each other with our studies, both being here together. He is a lovely man.

A sense of awareness I didn't have before

Since starting here I've definitely got more confidence and, I don't know how to say this really, but just being able to say "No", and to have an opinion

and be able to back it up. I'm more sure of my own opinions and I'm able to express myself more. That's it really. Just confidence. I like learning. I like to be engaged in something. And in Social Science I'm learning a lot about social issues and so on. It's kind of depressing at times, but there's so much to deal with, and I really want to stick with it. I've gained a sense of awareness that I didn't have before. I used to just be walking around with my head up my arse, but now it's like, "Oh I wish I could go back there, because everything's so confronting."

I know that if I had chosen to go to work instead of coming to uni when my son started school I would have more money. But I don't think that way, I think that's irrelevant. You can get caught up in the office politics and rubbish, and I can't stand that, so I don't think I'm missing out on anything by being here instead. Sometimes though it can be really difficult; just when I've got too many things on at once, and as well as being a single mum. Evan doesn't live with me, and although I live with my parents and they're there to help, I don't like to palm him [son] off. So just time-management really, can get quite difficult at times. I would like to be better at that, at managing my time. But in some ways I think I work better under pressure as well, so the pressure is positive sometimes. It gets the results.

I don't like to give up

I've never got to the point where I've thought of chucking it all in. I don't like to give up. Definitely not. When things get difficult I try to organize things better. I try to work things out. Sometimes if I had a better plan then things wouldn't get to that point of being so stressed, so I try not to get like that. But then sometimes it just happens, like last week we had an exam which was supposed to be done on-line – and that was the same day as when I had an assignment due. So I thought I would get that done, and then do the exam. But then it came on-line a few days earlier and it said it had to be in by then so that was really stressful. So I just burned the midnight oil and had no sleep. Evan helped then and Mum and Dad did too. I had to say to my son, "I've really got to get this done", and Mum and Dad took him to school and picked him up and stuff like that. He's their only grandchild and he's very much doted on.

If I need help with my studies and so on, first off I go to my friends. If we don't understand something we talk amongst ourselves. After that I would go to the lecturers. They're very approachable, and even though I haven't really used the Learning Centre courses, and I probably should have, I know they are there if I need them. Usually though I just nut it out by myself. The most helpful of all though are my friends here at uni. Last year we had lots of group work, and we were five in a group. Without them, it wouldn't have worked. If I'd been in another group I just don't think it would have been the same. But this semester there has been no emphasis on group work or co-operation, and, oh, it's been really hard, because that support base isn't

there, and even though we were doing the same subjects, we would be doing them differently and it was really hard to call on them and help each other. I think that group time really brings out the best in all of us.

But at the moment there's a lot of uncertainty about what's going to happen at this campus, as they are cutting courses and just offering them at the other campus. I came here to stay and I don't want to go up to the other campus. It would mean more time and more money, and it's not really feasible for me, with a young child, or even for any others, even those who have no children. Yes I think that is really negative. I think there is a risk that I might not be able to finish my degree here because of the cutting of courses. I'm not entirely sure, but I mean we've had some courses that aren't available this year, and some of the lecturers have left, and the fact that we don't know. That's the thing, we feel as if we are being kept in the dark, and there is all this rumour and suspicion.

I really got involved

Whenever I talk to any other mature-aged students I always tell them to come into Student Support, to do all the learning support courses and to ask the student mentors for help and information, and then to volunteer to be a mentor. I didn't need all that so much because I had the friends from the enabling course, and because we had already been here a year, so it wasn't such a big deal. But you can see how beneficial it would be for someone coming straight from school to meet people. I met a few people at the Mature Age club, that the Student Union runs, and also the Women's Collective. That was really good. I really got involved. It's important not to sit back and think, 'it's too much' and try to rely just on your own resources, because that is not enough.

I didn't find any lack of support here. I can't speak for other people, but the support is all there, it's all laid out. I was on the panel for the workshop that's run at the start of the year for new mature-age students coming in. We tried not to be negative, and said things like, "Oh yes, there is so much reading, but it's all good". People have to be prepared to go and access the help and support. That's the main thing. All these things need to be advertised too, to make people aware. I guess there is only so much you can do – you can't accost everyone in the café – and say 'are you having troubles'?

Mum and Dad always worked hard, and so they instilled in us hard work, and just get in there and do it. I hadn't done any other formal study since school, so I didn't really know what to expect when I started here. I guess I thought it would be more individualised. I didn't think that there would be so much cohesion, so that's why I was a bit apprehensive. I thought the lecturers would be more like school teachers, less approachable, but that's not the case. I didn't think it would be so relaxed, because it is relaxed. It's a very relaxed campus. We don't have those big lecture halls, so we're in classrooms and they actually talk to you. It's not like school at all. We're all even. The lecturers are easy to talk to and approachable, and I didn't think

they would be. I thought they would be more formal. Because it is a formal institution, I assumed it would be formal right down to the letter. Even at TAFE they kind of talk down to you, even though we were only doing typing and stuff. When I was at TAFE doing secretarial training, that was in 1985, they talked down to you, because we were kids really, only nineteen, but because now we're mature-age, and even the young people, they're not talked down to.

Coming to uni, I sort of bloomed

I'm a lot more confident and more outgoing. I'm the social secretary of the group! At school, I was always the quiet one. I wasn't popular, not part of the cool group. And then having a child, and being in that relationship, that didn't help my confidence either. But coming to uni I sort of bloomed. I'd organise nights out and everybody came, and we always had so much fun. That made me more confident to say to people, come and join us. Just the other day I organised everyone to have a study group. We had seven chapters and seven people and we all did a chapter each instead of trying to do it all by ourselves. Some people say I'm like my mother – she's a good organiser and confident socially, and now I'm getting to be that way too. It makes you feel good. When I started the enabling course I bought my books from a lady, and every time I see her now, she's like, "Oh, I can't get over how much you've changed. When I first saw you, you came in with this mousy look and asked for your books, and now when I see you you're everywhere, doing everything and it's great". So I'm much more outgoing. I've always been pretty organised at home, but coming here has really developed that outgoing side of me.

My future will be very different from before

I don't know yet what the future holds for me. I'm still kind of unsure where I want to go, what to do at the end; that kind of plays on my mind, because I haven't got a goal. I'm kind of up in the air about what I really want to do and I don't know. Someone said, "Go and see the careers counsellor", and I did at the beginning, but she couldn't help me because I couldn't help her. I couldn't say what I wanted to do.

Sometimes that's good, because if you don't have set ideas about what you want to be, or what you want to do, well, then you can go to any door that opens, but I like stability and I like to know what I'm doing. My first idea of wanting to be a counsellor, that's changed now. That's not what I want to do now. I want to have an interesting job, but I just don't know what.

I think that Evan's and my relationship is going pretty strong, and we would like to move out together. That would be great, but it's not feasible at the moment. But once I finish my degree I can get a job and move out and get a house together. I can see that my future will be different from before.

The work I did was very monotonous and I'm looking forward to being able to do something that I want to do, not something that I have to do; more rewarding and stimulating work, instead of just clerical stuff.

If I'd just gone back to clerical work, sure I would have had a bit more money, but then I wouldn't have had the time with my son. That relationship would be different. My aim was always to get off the pension, but not just to get off it and take whatever comes, but to aim higher. Financially I think my future will be better, than what it would have been, and better personally as well I think, because it has given me more confidence. I doubt whether I'm going to lose that. I know I won't lose it.

I'm also hoping that by my being here at uni will show my son that he doesn't have to take anything, and that he can aim higher. I worry about him. His Dad has a job where he works for his family's company and he doesn't actually get anywhere. He never has any money and stuff like that, so I want to be an example, a positive example for my son, and to show him that if you do the hard work and you will get somewhere.

So, generally, it has been a really positive experience for me, and I just love it and don't want to give it up. I'd really like to just keep studying. The campus is great, I love it. I can't think of one thing that is negative about it, except for the restructuring that I talked about before, but that's something that I can't control and you just have to deal with it. So it's all just positive.

Susie's Story

"I was so bored at home, you know, like I just couldn't cope..."

Susie came to university from an enabling course and is studying a Bachelor of Social Science. Prior to commencing her studies, Susie worked as a barmaid but after her degree she hopes to work with children in the Juvenile Justice system. Susie is 38, married with two young children, aged just 3 and 6.

It's something that I need to do for myself

I've always wanted to work for the police force. I want to be a profiler and so I came in and saw the university careers advisor, this was before the enabling course finished last year. I explained to her what I wanted to do and she advised me the best way to do that was to come to uni, go through the Bachelor of Social Science, do Psychology and then go into Juvenile Justice work so that I can profile juveniles instead of criminals. Because if I joined the police force at 38, I would be 65 before they even thought of me as someone high enough to be a profiler; you would have to start at the bottom. I've always wanted, you know, to help stop... I don't know how to say it really... but help stop things that maybe kids shouldn't do from a young age, instead of letting it progress up until they are over 18. There is nothing you can do

for them. Not that there is nothing you can do for them, but by then they are in jail anyway, so yeah, just to help kids understand there is more out there in life then blowing up the school or killing your classmates or stuff like that.

My husband said to me: "I don't want you working in a pub no more". There was a few fights and I was sort of one that would jump in and stop a fight and my husband says: "No, you are not doing that no more. I want you to do something else". I said: "I'm not qualified to do anything else" and he said: "Why don't you get qualified?" The lady in his band went through the enabling course, went to uni and is now a history teacher in high school, so he found out information from her. I went to my son's school and they gave me the information for the enabling course; that's how I found out about it. So my husband really pushed me, he said: "You go out and work and in five years time make a lot of money so that I can retire!" This [degree] also gives me something to do for the next six years. I was so bored at home, you know, like I just couldn't cope. It was just like, I've got to do something. Yeah, I can't cope staying at home, and he'd [husband] come home and I just smoked all the time and he said: "You need to do something" and I'm going: "That's what I've been telling you." I have always been interested in crime, always interested in crime, true crime not fake crime like CSI [television program - Crime Scene Investigations] and that but real CSI. Firstly, I was going to be a teacher but as soon as I got here I changed my mind 'cause I know what I wanted to do, I knew in myself what I want to do. He was a bit cranky when he found out I'd changed from Teaching into Social Science but I said to him: "I can go back and do a Dip Ed in Teaching and become a teacher". He goes "Is this something that you really want to do?" And I went: "Yeah" and he goes: "Well do it!" So he was cool with it and he's all smarty now so, yeah, he was pretty cool about it.

I haven't studied for over twenty years okay, and it is a real smack in your face when you come here, but yeah, I enjoy it and I love doing homework and things. I waited later in life to have my children so I always make sure that they come first, 'cause for the last thirty years I came first, so I make sure that they are first and make sure that my housework is done as fast as I can do it. Then I spend time on my study. Sometimes I am up until two in the morning studying but it's something that I need to do for myself, type of thing. On the weekends I spend time with the children and then Alan [husband] will take them and then I spend time studying.

I don't really care what they think to be honest with you

I've done it for me, and that's me, type of thing. My husband won't go to uni and I am trying to get him here, but with the mortgage he just won't come yet. But I said to him: "If you want to, when I am finished you go because I will be able to financially support the family and you can do what you want to do". I don't think someone in your family has to be a university student for you to go. Yeah, if you want to do it, do it.

My nieces are awesome about it, my older sister's two girls. They are both 29 and 27 and pretty cool. They're going: "Ahh, cool Aunty Susie". Yeah, most of them it was positive, just like two of them are real negative type feelings and that, but I just don't worry about them. Like my sister-in-law who belted the crap out of me one night from behind 'cause she thought it was a waste of time. She is a big toughie who has just got out of jail and she was very, very jealous of the fact that I was going to uni and she's just a fruit loop. Yeah, so she did not like it and going: "Why are you doing that? You're too old to be doing it, too stupid to be doing it". But I just let it pass, it's not a problem, she is not a very nice woman but my brother, it's his missus, I don't really talk to him anymore, but he was pretty cool about me doing it, and my sister, my older sister, she thinks it's great that I'm doing something. Yeah, but the rest of them, I don't really care what they think to be honest with you.

I started it, I'm going to finish it, don't care what anyone else says I'm going to finish this. Sometimes Alan and I have arguments about money 'cause he is the only one working, he is supporting the whole family and I only get $40 a week off the government so they don't give me anything really to help us. He does say sometimes, "Oh I wish you were working and you weren't going to uni", and that, but it's only like the heat of the moment. Just after, he thinks about it and he goes, "No I'm glad you're going to uni, forget what I said, just stay at uni", and I said, "Look, I'll quit uni and go back to work if you want to?" And he's: "No, no, no I don't mean it like that." So he says that he doesn't really mean it, type thing, it's just like frustration 'cause he's paying for everything at the moment. He's trying to, you know, just keep it all going but yeah, it's worth it all, but I think it's me, my determination to make it work.

It is very important to make friends here, yeah

It's like a culture shock because you are here with different people, with the very, very smart people okay that can just get it like that. I can get it but I can't write it. So it's just learning to write again and to get my thoughts down on paper the right way. So yeah, it's pretty hard, it's pretty scary too a little bit, but when you get to uni and you get friends, that makes it a bit better.

My husband is not doing it, so he can only advise me on some things whereas the people that are doing it with you are actually doing it with you and they know what you are going through. So it's like I help them and they help me, it's sort of like a two-way type of thing and it makes you feel a lot better. You can walk in and go,"How are you going?" and they go, "Well I'm having a shit day". But it's not going to be that bad, and then I can come in the next day and go, "I'm having a crap day – don't forget what you told me", and so, this type of thing, yeah, it is good and it is very important to make friends here, yeah.

There is a feeling of connectedness when you start knowing everyone, like the ladies in the library and the ladies in the bookshop, the lady in the little shop and the café and all that. Even the places around campus you get to know all the people, like, you get here and you have a coffee and you, like, de-stress from home and it's just, like, a nice relaxing place, and so I think you do become a part of it and it becomes a part of you, yeah.

My kids think it's cool that mummy is back at school

I always make sure the house and the kids are looked after, then do uni. I always make sure they're first. They've got to come first. During the weekends, they'll be playing and I'll be typing and stuff, and, "Mummy I'm hungry!" Fine, I'll make them some lunch and give them their lunch. I'll sit back down and type and they're pretty cool with that or they'll come and help me, you know, let them see what I'm doing, play a game or something, and they just toddle off by themselves and play. But they still come first. Uni just waits until everyone's in bed. I like it like that because it's quiet, then I can figure out what I want to do, sit down and do it. No "Mum, Mum, Mum!" It makes it a lot easier to concentrate without losing your concentration all the time.

I've had to sacrifice on some of the housework and I don't mind. My husband's been helping out which is great. I've had to sacrifice some of my motherly duties, which I don't mind at all. That's about it really. I am always one that likes a tidy house and my husband is too but, yeah, it's just a shambles, and really I don't care anymore 'cause there are four of us living there, one of us tidying up. Then I just let it get really bad one day and everybody's saying, "I can't find this and I can't find that", and I said, "Ah gee, maybe you need to tidy up after yourself, you might be able to find things!" It is just time, I think time with the housework that still has to be done 'cause if it doesn't get done, "Oh, you haven't cleaned the house today" and I think, "Oh well I am trying to study!" But now my husband knows. I think he realises that, yeah, that pressure is there now, he is starting to help me, so it'll subside a little, like, get a bit better. I am over the house. Like, if it is clean, it is clean, and if it is not, bad luck. I always make sure that the vacuum cleaning is done and if there is a pile of washing I don't stress no more, I just think, chuck it in the dryer and heat it up, shake it out and it is ironed!

Child-minding and the financial situation, they are two obstacles, like picking up my son from school and things like that, but I have got my Mum and Dad living with us, so I've always got someone there to pick up. But some mornings, if Mum and Dad are sick or whatever, like my Dad can't take him, I need to stay home and take him to school, so I miss the lecture. I always tell the lecturer and he's pretty cool with it. But that's the only little obstacle that I have to overcome, and the finances of it. Like, my husband got his inheritance last year after his father's death and he said, "Well, while we've got the money, go and do it!" So I thought fine, he didn't want me working in the pubs and so here I am.

The highs and the lows

The highs are getting the assignments in and the lows are trying to get them done on time! So yeah, the highs are actually when you hand them across the table to the lecturer and say, "There you go!" That is a high because you know that you've done it and the lows are, yeah, just trying to get it done with the family and all the research that needs to be done; just trying to fit it in with everything. My son got a little bit sick, he had an accident and hurt himself and ended up in hospital. So a little bit of time there where I couldn't do anything, and then my little girl got sick. So I was a bit pushed for time but, yeah, I got them in. One of them was one day late but that was a high because it was only one day instead of more. But the highs, yeah, getting the assignments in, it's one of the best highs I reckon. Don't care what the mark is but there you go. Oh, it's a great feeling when you hand them over. That is the ultimate high I reckon, just handing them across the table! Getting your mark back is pretty cool, but if you get really good marks it's really good, but if you get an average mark it's still good because you passed!

When I brought my assignments home, my husband was stoked with the twenty-two out of thirty. I also got the certificate from the enabling course sent to me because I couldn't make the ceremony, and he's been going around putting it up on the wall, he's so proud of me. It's so funny; it's so good to see. But he wants me to succeed and go to work so that he can stay at home with the kids. He wants to have that time with his kids. I can relate to that as I've had enough of them! I have never been one to stay at home and do nothing. You know, always independent, always had my own thing and earned my own money. Now I don't have anything, so it can be hard to keep coming here and not go to work, but my husband said, "Stick it out!" So I am going to stick it out 'cause it is really important that I pass for him too.

I am more open-minded to a lot of things

I think I got a bit more of a need to learn, especially, like, I didn't learn very much at school when I went to school, and now I've got a chance to learn I want to improve myself. I am a lot smarter now. I can come out with one-liners like you wouldn't believe now! It's made me more aware of my own rights and, like, being a female, and it gives you ideas to think about. I am doing male suicide at the moment and the effects that, like, us and society have on a male, and the statistics for male suicide are just incredible. Until you start researching something, you know, and then you get to these statistics, and you think, "My God!" You know what is going on. There's got to be something better for them out there than that, and what is it, and hopefully change it. Yeah, change the world!

I am more open-minded to a lot of things, yeah. I was always open-minded but now I am even more open-minded. You look through a narrow scope and uni has sort of broadened it; where you have still got a narrow scope but you are looking around that scope as well now, for other things. So, yeah, I think I have changed. I am more eager maybe to get information and more eager to learn. Some of the remarks that I have been spitting back at my husband when he's been saying things have just stopped him dead in his tracks, you know. I had a question for him the other night. I asked him, and he looked at me and I said, "You don't know do you?" And he said, "No, I think you'd better keep reading the book!" It's positive 'cause it's making him change his views and making him look at different ways. It's really weird seeing it, 'cause I come out with these things that he knows about, and I've never known about, and he's just like "Uhhhh", but yeah, so it is real positive, yeah.

Once upon a time, Susie was just a little barmaid, at home doing the homely thing and trying to work and look after the kids. And now, Susie sort of more stands up for herself and tells her husband that, "No, this isn't the thing no more 'cause I have rights in this world!" So my once upon a time is changing that, so he stays at home and I can go and work. Be like he was with me, just to show that women's life isn't easy you know. So once upon a time yeah, then I came to uni and everything changed ... I got wise and I started learning a lot of things but it was for the better.

When I get my degree I don't want to quit, I still want to keep doing courses so I can get the other courses in the area of human services so that I can go anywhere and not just Juvenile Justice, but see how it goes.

Simone's Story

"You only get one life to live and this is something that I wanted to do for a long time..."

Simone is 34 years old and is married with four children varying in age from 8 to 18. Simone is completing an enabling program in order to obtain entrance into a Bachelor of Education. Over the years, Simone has volunteered regularly at the local primary school where her children attend; this experience has led her to decide on a teaching career. She currently works part-time in a supermarket as a deli assistant.

I couldn't have left it any longer

I've just decided to go ahead with going to university this year. I started an enabling course hoping to go into a Bachelor of Education for next year. It's something I've wanted to do for a long time, but I started my family early and now it's my turn to go and do my part of my education. I completed year ten and then I had my first son the next year. I tried to go back to do year eleven when he was a little bit older but found it hard with a little baby and unreliable baby-sitters. If I had him in child-care it might have been different, so I dropped out of that and decided to just be a mum. I started being a mum for a long time, and now I've just thought this is something that I want to do, so go for it now.

I think I am a bit old to go back and do year eleven and twelve at school. I also think there is probably too much involved in it; that way you have to do lots of other subjects that I don't find relevant. I have a son at high school and I don't think I want to be there while my children are there so when I found out about the enabling course, I thought, "Oh I can do that. It sounds good!"

I couldn't have left it any longer. You only get one life to live and this is something that I wanted to do for a long time, and I kept putting it off and saying, "I'll do it one day; I'll do it one day", and one day never comes. So I am actually doing it, and I think to myself every day, this is so great! I never thought it was ever going to happen. I always wanted to be a teacher but I couldn't see how that was ever going to happen because I didn't finish year twelve and I started my kids young, so I sort of tied myself down, and then didn't have finances and things like that. But over the years, I have learnt how to work and how to buy a house and how to maintain things, and I can go and do other things. There is no "you can't do it"; you can do it if you want to do it. There is always a time in life. I see ladies here that are in their seventies and their sixties, they may never ever go to work after they get their degree, but they can at least say, "I have a degree".

I am ready for it now, I have the age, the maturity, the confidence

I actually started work at a supermarket last year and there are kids going through uni there, one who was only nineteen who was doing university to become a high school teacher. So I talked to her about it and she gave me a lot of information about what she had to do to get in. Then I met another lady who was twenty-seven and she had just finished the primary school Bachelor of Education, and so I hung around with her and asked lots of questions of what I needed to do. You see this is something that I have wanted to do since I was in year seven of high school. So yeah, I am ready for it now. I have the age, the maturity, and the confidence of being with little kids that I didn't have when I was eighteen, so I am doing it now.

I love working with kids and have been volunteering at the school for the last couple of years. The hours are getting longer and longer and longer that I am up there, and my husband was saying, "You never do this, you never do that, and you should go to work more often, you know all this volunteer work is clocking up." But it's just where I want to be, and I love being around the kids. The pay [teacher's] will be a lot better than what I am getting now and the hours will be a lot better than what I am doing now. I am working nights and cleaning, doing lots of physical stuff. I don't want to do physical labour anymore, I want to go out and have fun, play with the kids and see them play sports and interact with kids.

I think it was just me being very headstrong and wanting and wanting and wanting, and I sort of harped on my husband for a whole year and he's agreed to it. Initially, my husband didn't think I'd finish it, so I told him

we'll see how I go for this year with the enabling course, and if I finish it and I am happy with fitting the study in with work and family, he's quite happy to let me go ahead and do that.

But I've met single women here, single mums and they've got their kids and they are coming to uni. There is no partner, there is no help for them, and they are still coming. They are in the first year or second year or third year of teaching and I have thought, if everything else fails I can still do it. If he [husband] doesn't want to come with me, he can go on his separate path and I can go on my separate path. I am big enough and strong enough to fit in the uni, to fit in the work and to raise the kids, and he can just pack up and leave if he doesn't like it! That sounds terrible but that's what I have come to. If he doesn't want to support me for the next five years, if he wants to leave, leave, but I am not going to stop from doing it. This is what I want to do. We've been together for sixteen years and I've always followed him to do what he wants to do and I've never stopped and said, "Hang on I don't really want to do that!" I've gone his way, I wasn't happy but I'm happy doing this, and now it's his turn to realise that he can still have his way of things and I can have mine and we can work together. You know you don't have to do everything all the time in the same direction.

He has come to realise that I am a person, I do have a direction I want to go in. I don't want to spend the rest of my life doing something I don't want to do. I want to be happy, I want to work with kids and I have said to him, "Either I go on and do it this way or else I am just going to volunteer at the school and I won't earn an income". I'll just volunteer 'cause that's where I want to be, and they'll quite happily have me up there from 9.15 till 2.55 everyday if I wanted to. I'd rather be paid to be there for that time, so to get paid I have to do it this way.

I have one friend who thought I was being a bit selfish

Everyone is interested and asking how it is going so I just prattle on. I have a couple of mums from school, our kids all do sport together, so while they do sport we walk around the oval and we talk about it [uni]. One of them is a teacher's aide and the other one just volunteers a lot at school, so they are interested in how I am going and what I am doing.

Some are sceptical though. I have one friend who thought I was being a bit selfish, so that threw a spanner in the works when she said that. But I thought she was a bit too young and inexperienced to give me that sort of answer. She is only twenty-one and she lives with her grandparents. She doesn't have any children, she doesn't have a mortgage, and I thought, she doesn't know what I am living through as to whether or not I am being selfish. I quizzed my Mum and said, "Am I being selfish. Am I? Should I be waiting until I've paid off my house and then do this?" And she said, "No, if you don't do it now you won't ever come back to it". She was good that way.

My parents don't work, yeah. I don't know how to describe them. You try to be nice but my Dad has never really been interested in working and my Mum had the attitude of, "Well if he doesn't, I am not working." My Mum left school in year nine. She hated school. Her father said, "Well if you get a job you can leave". She did at one stage sell Avon [cosmetics] and she was very good at that but then she just stopped as something upset her. Now she just is a woman of leisure and Dad, he's a very intelligent man, it's a waste actually; all the knowledge that's in his head. I thought he might have come up with something by now if he didn't want to go to work that he could use it for. He was actually dux of the school, but I think he only went to year ten though. He never pursued anything else, but each to their own though. Gary's [husband] parents are both retired and they do a lot of travelling around in New South Wales and Queensland.

I actually haven't told his parents yet what I am doing. We think they will say, "Oh financially, we don't think that's a good idea". But it was our choice, so we have done that. My parents, well, they are pretty laid back, they are not real worried. They don't get involved much either, so it doesn't have any effect on them. I've got a younger brother, he is eight-and-a-half years younger than me, and he is just off doing his own thing. None of them are interested in getting involved, as far as going and doing it themselves. So I had no one, no one who could tell me what it was going to be like, apart from the people that I am meeting now. I can't just ring a cousin or a sister or a brother and say, "Oh I am having problems with this, how would you deal with it?"

The bank doesn't like me but the bank can get use to that!

I have sad days when different things are happening and I think I just want to pack up and get in the car and go and forget everything. And then I think "No!" I'll just wait till the end of this year and I'll do my exams. You can always defer for a year until I get my feet back on the ground. My husband hasn't been working this last year so it's been really tough financially, trying to fit in the study and knowing the bills are there, and I have to go and do extra hours at work to pay for the bills. I was feeling very angry and frustrated, and then last week he finally got a job! Last week was very emotional for me 'cause I thought, "Thank God!" I just hope he likes this job; I hope he sticks with it long enough to pay off or just to keep us financial each week. So that instead of doing thirty hours of work, I can do thirty hours of study and then go and do five or ten hours of work, instead of the other way round, you know.

I have had a lot of pressure on, trying to find time to study because I was either at work or had the kids pressurising me for time with them. I just wanted them to leave me alone and let me do what I needed to do. I had a workbook that needed to be finished and handed in; in the end I handed in work that I wasn't happy with. My results were pretty sad and I went home and I showed him [husband] and said, "This is because of the pressure of

having to do so many hours at work, and then coming home and having you, mainly, and the kids, demanding so much of my time. I had to let the study slip and I don't want to do that. It is not making me happy". They were complaining that I was angry and unhappy with them, and I said, "There is a simple solution, get a job and let me have some time to study and then I'll be happier".

We had the interest rates go up on the mortgage, and I had work that needed to be done on the car, and the car had to pass rego, and I had to renew my licence, and we had another insurance come up as well, and the rates. So it was just a matter of having to work as many hours as I could get, for weeks, and not do the study that I needed to. It was tough that they all happened at the same time. If they had happened one month and then another month, that would have been fine, but it all happened in the one month. So yeah, it wasn't happy days at our place, and the bank doesn't like me, but the bank can get used to that! I am spending all my time studying instead of shopping, so it doesn't really matter. I don't need the extra money anyway. As long as I've got enough to cover the bills, I am happy with that.

This week I am a lot happier because Gary is working 10.00pm till 6.00am, so I am studying from 8.30 at night when the kids go to bed until 12.30, and then I am going to bed and I am not being woken up during the night 'cause he is not there to wake me up! I am getting a good sleep and I am getting up happy in the morning, and he sleeps then during the day so that gives me extra time to study, and because he is working I don't have to go to work. I've had all week off work and I won't work again until tomorrow. I'm doing a five-hour shift tomorrow and I am happy with that. I know the bills are covered and I know that my study is getting done and the pressure is just a bit lighter.

I'll get a job as a teacher one day

I remember I was very nervous before that first lecture. I was up most of the night feeling sick in the stomach, and then I walked in on my own and thought, "Why am I doing this on my own?" You see the younger ones and they come in their groups and have friends here. I walked in knowing no one so that was a bit daunting. I didn't want to miss out hearing what was going on so I sat right down near the front and brought my tape recorder with me so that I could record it. Trying to take notes and trying to remember what they are saying and not get lost. I walked out of there and I think I went home and slept for about two hours afterwards, 'cause my brain was just exhausted from all the information going in, and I thought, "What am I going to be like next week?!" But it wasn't too bad. Yeah, your head is fairly full by the time you come out with all this information.

I think I was scared about doing essays as well, but I have handed in a few things now and come to the conclusion that it doesn't all have to be perfect. It doesn't all have to be a hundred percent right, and sometimes I think about things more than I should. It's not that hard just to back off a little

bit, so I am now learning to deal with that. Whereas before, when I read that first article, I read it seven times and then came to the lecture to talk to the teacher about it, who went through it with all of us. She was explaining bits and pieces about having to write answers to five questions relating to that story. It took days and I just found that very hard. I considered not handing it in!

That was around the time that my husband and I weren't on really good communicating levels and he thought that I was putting too much time in. I was really struggling with it and couldn't ask him for help. Eventually I did go and ask, and he was not happy with me that I had left it to the last minute to ask him for the help, but I stated to him later that I didn't feel comfortable enough with him to come earlier. I felt, you know, like he was sort of expecting me to fail, and I really didn't want to fail, but I didn't know how to ask him for the help either. He just listened to me read for an hour as I read this article out to him, and then he asked me the questions and what I thought. I told him what I thought and he said, "Well, you sound like you are on the right track." So I then went back and wrote down my answers and I didn't score too badly on it. I think you get the scores back and you think, "What was the big deal?" But it was a big deal at the time. It was really hard.

I have written pages and pages of stuff for just one essay, and it's just incredible the amount of time it takes. Then you have got to put it all together and then you've got to check, you know, that your spelling is alright and that your paragraphs are right and everything sounds like it's heading in some sort of direction. I think it will get easier though, the more you do. It has to get easier. Essays can't always be hard, can they?

My Mum, she was funny when I rang her to tell her what I got for my marks on the first five tasks for history. Her comment to me was: "Why didn't you do that well at school?" Then she laughed about it, but she said: "I knew you could do it. I've always known you could do it!" So she was very positive about it. But then, when I was at school, I didn't hand things in through fear of not getting good marks or because someone else would get better. But now I think I will succeed. I don't think I have to get a hundred percent anymore. I think, you know, a pass is good enough. You aim for higher but, yeah, you don't have to be perfect at everything all the time. So, yeah, I think I will succeed. I'll pass. I'll get a job as a teacher one day....

I have found out there is support and there are ways of doing things and people to ask, but just getting it in your head that if you have problems go and ask anyone. There's people there to ask, even if you think you know no-one you find someone, so just try, you've got to go and try! Every day's a new challenge, but they are all exciting challenges, and don't forget to ask if you need help.

You have really high days where you would just feel on top of the world and ... other days you are just hitting rock bottom

I am really missing spending time with the kids, and they are growing up and I am looking at them and I am thinking, "Where do I start? Where do I start to get back to knowing these kids again and doing things with these kids?" They have had so many days where Mum's at work, well, they are at school, and then when they come home I'm at work, or I am leaving to go to work. I have to learn to cope with that, and now I am trying to get back to, I want to be the Mum. I want to study and I want to be the Mum, and I only want to work a little. Sometimes I think I am being selfish, but other times I think, well, that is the way it is supposed to be.

I don't have a guilt feeling for studying. I am having it for working. I think it's good that I am studying, because the kids are seeing me study. My daughter will come and get her homework book and sit alongside me, and she is doing her homework with me doing my homework by me. Studying, it's good for the kids, and they are getting into better study habits with their homework.

But one of the obstacles I have to learn to cope with is the relationship between my daughter and myself. I had three boys; finally got the little girl that I wanted, and I am finding it hard, the fact that I don't have any time for her. She has now adopted the woman next door as her mother, and that, to me, is very hard to deal with. I think she is better off being there in the afternoons when I am working rather than being at home with her Dad and brothers. They are rough and they pick on her and things like that. Her father doesn't sort of understand her emotional side, where I can give her a cuddle and say, "Let's go and do something else". Then when I am there, and she says, "Can I go next door?", and I sort of don't want to let her go, but I know that I am being selfish. She goes to play with the little girl. She wants a little sister but I am not prepared to have another baby to give her another sister. I used to walk her to school every morning and now she doesn't want to. She wants to go and walk to school with next door. So I am feeling it; my little girl is becoming someone else's little girl, and I don't like that. All I ever wanted was a daughter, so, three sons, and then finally got the daughter, and she was the surprise. For me to get my little girl... but then why do I have to work in the afternoons? You know, why can't I have the afternoons?

So you have really high days where you would just feel on top of the world and coping with everything, and other days you are just hitting rock bottom. One of the teachers from school, she introduced me to her husband as "someone who is studying to be a teacher", so that meant a lot when she referred to me like that. I am not just the mother of kids that she has taught. I am going to be a teacher like her, so yeah, that was that was nice, the way she introduced me. It made me feel really good. It made me feel like I am going to actually be a teacher. I still have doubts every now and then, like, "What I am doing? Am I past it? Am I too old? Should I just go on and watch the

kids grow up and retire?" Instead, I am trying to find a career, so that when they get to high school I can not just work in a deli, but can go out and play with the kids and stay young at heart!

But I am determined to do it; I am not going to just have a half-hearted go at things. I want to do it properly and I am not going to drop out. This is what I want to do and I am not going to back down no matter what!

I am not as dumb as I thought I was

I think it was just a lot of soul searching, you know, to find out myself what I wanted and to make up my mind. I was letting everyone dictate where I should go and what I should do, and I didn't really want to do any of that. I wanted to do my own thing, which was coming here. I spent a lot of time on my own, just out on the back verandah. I would just go out there and pretend that I was reading or something, but just thinking about what my choices really are and how to deal with it. I pretty much shut myself away from everyone for a while, but then things just started to improve.

Over the years you just sort of dwindle as a person, and this year has just been a very big boost for my confidence. I can actually go and read a book and I can do an essay, which I had never done before. I was happy with the 70 I got for the first essay, and then the last one I got 83, and I was just "Wow! This is what it is all about!" Keep trying these new things, you know, and getting the rewards. So yeah, I am not as dumb as I thought I was.

I have more confidence in my own ability to do things, things that I thought were just very daunting and, "How do people do that?" You can do it. You are capable of doing things, and the more you try the better you get at them. I am loving it. I am loving looking at things that I used to look at and think, "I can't do that, I'll leave that for someone who is clever to do", and now I think, "I can do that. That's easy!" Even filling out forms, I used to always say to my husband, "Here you fill it out and I'll sign it". Now I just look at it and fill it out myself and don't have any worries about it. If people don't like what I have written, well they can come and see me about it! I am not going to crawl into a hole and go: "Ohhh don't look at me!" So I am happy with that side of it. I am not just putting up with passing the buck all the time and letting other people learn new skills. I am learning new skills and I am loving it. I don't let people pressure me into things. I make up my own mind, and if someone wants me to do something and I am not happy with doing it, I will just say "no". Whereas before, I would probably have tried to do what they wanted me to do, and you know, probably ended up in tears. But I am better than that; I can go on and do something different, so I am a lot more positive.

I think that when the next four years are over I am going to have learnt a lot about managing to strive for what I want, and encourage others to strive for what they want.

Transformations and Self-Discoveries

Themes that unite

Introduction

Each narrative in the preceding seven chapters charts a process of self-discovery. Their words indicate that the narrators are finding out who they really are and what they are capable of doing. Each narrative has been presented in a 'storied' (Gubrium & Holstein, 1998) fashion, where the individual and idiosyncratic nature of this student experience is foregrounded. This type of 'narrative knowledge' (Polkinghorne, 1995, p.11) does not look for overriding concepts or categories when analysing the data but rather explores the nuances of human experience in all its singularity.

Readers of storied descriptions can be touched in sensual and embodied ways as these stories offer the possibility of evoking a range of emotions specific to that particular experience. Such emotionality is arguably not possible when data is sliced or removed from its broader context to create what Polkinghorne (1995) terms as 'paradigmatic' categories or concepts. The inclusion of a diversity of stories also allows the reader to forge their own connections between and within a variety of cases rather than being presented with predetermined generalisations.

Brookfield (1995) suggests that all educational research should commence with the actual learners. It is essential to identify with students and for educational institutions to see themselves 'through student's eyes' or get 'inside student's heads' (p.92). The stories presented here for others to read, connect with and be touched by, reveal significant personal growth and internal transformations which, while articulated on a very personal level, also

have wider, more public implications. The women reflect upon these transformations in highly descriptive ways, such as by Fiona who describes how: *"Coming to uni I sort of bloomed....Much more outgoing..."* or Susie who is now *"...more open minded to a lot of things..."*

The women are all very familiar with defining themselves in relation to others, such as partners, parents and children – but are now beginning to define themselves differently, according to insights and understandings that are emerging during their educational encounters. Part of this is discovering their intelligence, as passionately articulated by Mandy:

> *I feel like I'm intelligent. I was writing a description of myself for something a while ago and I regarded myself as an intelligent, attractive woman that is capable and confident and can hold an intelligent conversation, whereas maybe three years ago I wouldn't have regarded myself that way...*

Katrina and Simone voice similar discoveries, both highlighting that they no longer consider themselves "as dumb", an identification they had previously held. In Katrina's case this categorisation was based upon prior education experiences: *"I'm not dumb as I was told for many, many years at school"*.

No doubt certain narratives and experiences will resonate more than others with particular readers. The narrators have adopted multiple standpoints, sometimes speaking as a mother, a wife, a daughter or a student. This positionality indicates the multiple choices available when one tells stories as well as the control an interviewee has in relation to what and how things are heard. Hence, it would be naive to assume that these stories provide a 'pristine' reflection of life as it is lived but rather these are subjective texts. However, it is precisely this that makes narrative such a meaningful form of expression, it is in the act of making sense and explaining events that lends narrative its evaluative and explanatory value. The stories contained in this book are evocative in the sense that they provide an understanding of "individuals' lives in social context" (Eliott, 2005, p.26).

Whilst each of the narratives is unique there are some common themes that emerge across the stories. This chapter explores these under the following broad categories, using the women's words to highlight each emerging theme:

- *The early days – decisions and transitions*
- *Losses and sacrifices – time and money*
- *Changes in relationships*
- *Persistence and determination*
- *A different view of themselves*
- *A different way of looking at the world*
- *What's ahead?*
- *The next generation*

The early days – decisions and transitions

Why did these students decide to come to university? And why at this point in time? Their stories indicate that there was some sort of catalyst for action, an event that had occurred which then led, directly or indirectly, to the decision to study. McGivney (2006) describes the path back into study for adult learners as being "often serendipitous" (p. 85). Her research highlights a number of factors that are influential in adults returning to formal study, such as "because others in their circle are doing it" and "because of the need to deal with an immediate situation in their life (life transitions, illness, redundancy, bereavement, divorce)" (p. 85). Such serendipitous factors also emerge from the stories in this book. For Fiona, it was her son beginning school;

> *My son started kindergarten and I thought I could either go and get another boring office job or I could do something that I actually want to do...*

For Susie, it was her husband's concern about fights in the pub where she was working;

> *My husband says, "No, you are not doing that no more. I want you to do something else. I said, "I'm not qualified to do anything else" and he said, "Why don't you get qualified?"*

while for Barbara it was the breakup of her marriage and the need to support her son;

> *When my marriage broke down it was a very very tough time trying to work out what I was going to do to support my son.*

For Mandy, Katrina and Simone, it represented the fulfilment of a long-term dream, Simone reflects how university was something she had "*wanted to do for a long time...*" whilst Katrina "*was always passionate about teaching*". Mandy describes her desire to study in terms of a "*yearning*":

> *I always wanted... to go and study... and I wasn't encouraged to do that... It has always been a yearning...*

...while for Nerida, it was something completely unexpected: "*I certainly never expected that I'd ever get to uni – and never in a million years at this age!*"

So why not before? Chapman, McGilp, Cartwright, De Souza, and Toomey (2006) identify a number of barriers that impede participation in education for adults, such as financial, geographic, personal and societal. Personal barriers include issues of identity and self-esteem, while societal barriers include lack of encouragement and support from others.

For these seven women, barriers they had faced included lack of encouragement from family, as voiced by Mandy.

> *My mother didn't encourage me to get my HSC, in fact she told me I wasn't smart enough, so I joined the workforce when I was sixteen...*

Growing up in families where neither parent had been to university, it just wasn't thought about. Fiona explains how "*I didn't ever think about going to university*' and "*Uni was never really an option*" for Barbara. Some, like Katrina, spoke of unhappy memories of school, which had inhibited consideration of further study, whilst Nerida had no choice but to leave school early:

> *My father had died between year ten and year eleven and Mum said I can't afford to buy your year eleven uniform, do you mind getting a job, so that was the end of that...*

So for each of these women, the decision to come to university was in itself a remarkable act and one that was influenced not only by particular circumstances but also by particular people.

"People who act as influencers, catalysts or change agents – are hugely important in leading others into learning" (McGivney, 2006, p. 87). This appears to hold true for these seven women. Sources of influence and inspiration included parents, friends, partners, teachers and work colleagues. Simone talks about two other women at work - *"one who was only nineteen who was doing university to become a high school teacher"* - who gave her information and encouraged her to pursue her long-term dream of being a teacher.

Barbara mentions a friend who had encouraged her:

> *She's been the one who has been saying, "Why don't you look into it yourself?" and "Why don't you do this?" Sort of pushing me here...*

For Fiona, it was a counsellor she spoke with after her marriage broke up, who told her to *"Go and do something"*... while for Susie it was her husband who *"really pushed"* her attendance. Perversely, in an indirect way, Nerida's son influenced her by his own lack of interest in going to university himself:

> *I was trying to arrange to get him* [son] *into uni and he wasn't interested and I thought 'well bugger you! If you're not interested, I'll go to uni'...*

Moving into higher education was also facilitated by undertaking preliminary studies at pre-university level. Mandy was inspired by a recent experience of other formal study to think about going on to university,

> *I loved it!* [TAFE Diploma] *It was a real culture change... and ever since then I sort of had a yearning, looking for something...*

Six of the women had done or were doing an enabling program. The importance of providing opportunities for adult learning at all levels has been demonstrated in other studies of mature-age students, such as that by Tett (2000) who found that the women she interviewed were all "able to give positive examples of learning which had taken place at a later point in their lives" (p.187). Similarly, McGivney's research (1999b) indicates that adult learning :

> ...often starts people with no qualifications or experience of post-school education on a continuing learning path by helping them to become confident and successful learners (McGivney, 1999b, p. vi)

So coming to university at this time was made possible by the presence of an enabling course. Once again, there was for some a serendipitous element to their finding out about this. For Fiona there was a chance encounter:

> *I saw this lady that I used to live next door to... on the campus on that Open Day and she said you have to do [the enabling program]. It's the best thing in the world...*

Susie's husband also heard about it by chance: *"the lady in his band went through [the enabling program]... so he found out the information from her..."*.

Once they had made the decision to return to study, each was faced with the difficult task of making the transition into university. For most it was an anxious time. Katrina describes how the *"first 6 weeks were a nightmare... very overwhelming... I was close to just giving it all away"*. Susie also explains how she was initially *"shocked by the expectations"* and Simone speaks of her trepidation:

> *I remember I was very nervous before that first lecture. I was up most of the night feeling sick in the stomach...*

There is much evidence to indicate that 'second chance' students place considerable pressure on themselves to achieve, feeling highly responsible for their own success or failure, adding further stress to an already stressful situation. Reay, Ball and David (2002) in their UK study researching the experiences of those students who withdrew or took leave from their studies, found that:

> ...it is the newly arrived working-class, minority and female cohorts who blame their own personal and educational inadequacies for their inability to make the transition to HE (pp. 14-15).

However, while the initial anxieties were intense at the time, the women's stories reveal that, in retrospect, these feelings were fairly short-term. Each quite quickly overcame the worst of their doubts and fears and began to make the adjustments in their lives necessary for the continuation of their studies. Their stories also reveal that there were longer-term changes and challenges ahead as they continued along their journey at university.

Losses and sacrifices – time and money

Each of the women are facing substantial challenges in the process of combining their lives as students with their existing responsibilities as parents, partners and employees. Meeting these challenges often requires considerable amounts of personal and financial sacrifice. Gendered expectations, held by the women themselves and others around them, play a significant role in determining both the quality and quantity of sacrifices that are made.

Previous research has identified a range of challenges that appear to be common to mature-age students as a group. Abbott-Chapman et al. (2004) for example, found in their research with mature-age students at the University of Tasmania, that it was the combined challenge of "family and employment pressures" along with "financial problems associated with giving up full-time employment" (p.114) that particularly impacted upon this older cohort. Similarly, McGivney's (1999b) research with older learners in the UK revealed that "practical problems such as costs and domestic commitments are the most commonly cited barriers to progression" (p. 70). The

stories of these seven women reveal similar challenges, including financial struggles, difficulties with organising and prioritising, dealing with changes in relationships with partners and children, balancing the needs of study with the needs of others and, in general, not enough hours in the day to do all that needs to be done.

Loss of time

Mature-age students who are juggling a range of other responsibilities are inevitably "time poor" (Reay, et al., 2002, p. 9). Fitting study in amongst work, child-care, domestic responsibilities and any possible social life requires a "complex negotiation of time" (Edwards, Hanson, & Raggatt, 1996, p. 213). As mentioned in Chapter One, a number of feminist writers contend that this is even more complex for women than it is for men, as a result of the "gender-laden and time-consumptive nature" (Morrison ,1996, p. 214) of a woman's role, in which time is collectively used for others and family "have a right to lay claim to" (p. 214).

Each of the women refer in some way to the challenge of finding enough time for everything and everyone, in particular their children, as well as finding time for their studies. Mandy indicates that the lack of time she now has for housework is a source of stress:

> *I had to let go of the housework... now we crunch around on rice bubbles and food... I'm finding it quite frustrating – the mess...*

and also describes her frustration at having to put assignments on hold...

> *I was trying to do assignments and I would have kids sick... have the kids home sick and the plans would go out the door...*

Similarly, Simone talks of the pressure of finding enough time, explaining how *"I was either at work or had the kids pressurising me for time with them. I just wanted them to leave me alone and let me do what I needed to do."* Fiona and Katrina also both describe the logistics of fitting study in around the care of young children, which sometimes means having less sleep themselves. Katrina explains how she is *"...having long, long nights, some nights it could be 2 or 3 am..."* whilst Fiona waits until her son is asleep as *"...it's just too hard when he's around... wants attention, needs to be fed and so on...."* For Barbara, trying to get up very early to study before her young son is awake also has its frustrations:

> *I've tried to set the alarm for a little bit earlier so that I can get up before Michael, but as soon as he hears the alarm he's awake, and that's what I'm finding just a little bit harder...*

Such examples highlight the multiplicity and demanding nature of their role within the family which impacts upon their experiences as students. Similar to other research findings, many of the women in this study describe a delicate "balancing act between wanting to study, meeting domestic responsibilities and needing to earn money" (Reay, et al., 2002, p. 10) and find that their approach to their studies is affected by "the weight of family responsibilities" (Scott, Burns and Cooney, 1996, p.240).

Katrina's story reveals the particularly difficult time that she had been through, with her husband's illness and subsequent death in the second year of her studies. His illness was a precipitating factor in her decision to study.

> *My husband was very sick and he wasn't able to function and I needed to get things sorted out and needed to be a bread winner...* (Katrina)

During her studies, Katrina not only cared for her husband, who had frequent hospital admissions but also managed to keep up with her studies and attend to the practical and emotional needs of her children.

These words of Katrina demonstrate how precarious and stressful this balancing act often feels for her.

> *I found it very difficult last night, she was in tears* [7 yr old daughter] *... and I put my time away to finish my essay, so inside I wanted to get things done... It's a big conflict because we had a lecture and a presentation this morning...* (Katrina)

Anxiety and guilt over taking time away from children is a common theme within each of the seven stories, with other examples being Simone: "*I am really missing spending time with the kids...*" and Barbara: "*I'm feeling a bit guilty with Michael 'cause I'm not spending the whole weekend with him like I wanted to...*"

Women with young children can also find it particularly difficult to work within traditional time management strategies as they try to fit 'more in' to their limited time, as articulated by Mandy:

> *I find it really hard to focus on assignments and study when all this other stuff needs to be done. Distracting!*

Morrison (1996) points out that the "linear time schedules" often encouraged as effective time management strategies for students "may be neither rational nor efficient for all humans, specifically those assigned caring and domestic roles" (p. 212). Her study of mature-age women undertaking part-time adult education courses revealed that the women learnt "to weave college and study times into a complex web, in which domestic-related/child-care time remains dominant" (Morrison, 1996, p. 223).

Certainly, what emerges from these stories is that each of the women find ways of managing time that are not based on traditional linear models of time planning. Often these appear to be chaotic, including staying up into the early hours to complete an assignment; missing a lecture to complete work, reading a text while feeding children or while waiting in the car to collect them from school, but it is strategies like these that enable the women to successfully fit study time into their fractured, interrupted days. For these women, considerable time is taken up in meeting the demands of others and there is no 'free time' for themselves.

> *Giving up gardening, giving up reading, giving up sewing, giving up relaxing, giving up going out with family visits, giving up socialising, giving up clothes, giving up spending money on anything, giving up having holidays. Lots of giving up!"* (Nerida)

"Giving up" any personal leisure time is a recurrent theme throughout the stories, something which has been found time and again in other research. Two decades of research into the mature-age female student experience

(Edwards, 1993; Leonard, 1994; Martin, 1988; Morrison, 1996; Reay, et al., 2002; West, Hore, Eaton & Kermond, 1986) has demonstrated that women's personal time for leisure and friends is sacrificed in order to facilitate the time required for university activities. At best, personal time is considerably reduced and at worst it becomes non-existent. Women with caring responsibilities tend to be at the more extreme end of the spectrum, putting family and domestic responsibilities first, study second and themselves last. With such limited time at their disposal, it is not surprising that many women end up with no personal or leisure time at all.

> The primacy of family life is unquestioned and the needs of the self are subordinated, even denied, until family responsibilities have diminished. (Britton and Baxter, 1999, p. 187).

Despite considerable social change, including a strong feminist challenge to traditional gender roles over at least the past 20 years, there appears to have been little impact upon gendered behaviours within the lives of the seven women telling their stories here. There is some evidence that adherence to more traditional gender roles is connected to lower educational, economic and employment status (Chapman, et al., 2006; McGivney, 2006; Tett, 2000). However, equally it could be argued that broader forces are at work here, in the form of government social policy (Thomson, 2000; Weeks, 2000) in which the Australian welfare state "has been constructed around families, with a silent but entrenched gendered division of labour" (Weeks, 2000 p. 55)

Australian welfare state legislation was initially framed on the traditional family unit of male breadwinner and female carer. Despite certain victories for women over the years such as the sex discrimination legislation of 1984 and the 1988 National Agenda for Women, this interpretation largely persists, in part due to a resurgence of conservative political agendas in Australia over the past 10-15 years, in which policies labelled as 'family friendly' have served to reinforce traditional gender roles. For example, Thomson (2000) argues that social policy continues to privilege the position of male workers and to maintain the perspective that child-care is the exclusive responsibility of women. She presents evidence that women are still more likely to be paid less than men, occupy casual jobs, bear the responsibility of juggling work and child-care, as well as carrying more of the domestic load in general. "The model of male breadwinner is no longer the norm" (Thomson, 2000, p. 84) yet it is a model that persists in social and welfare policy and continues to have a profound influence on gender roles, including in relation to family finances.

Loss of money

Financial stress is mentioned as a significant issue by almost all of the women. Simone explains how "*It's been really tough financially, trying to fit in the study and knowing that the bills are there*". In this case,finances were particularly tight as her husband was not in regular work either.

Katrina had needed to seek emergency financial assistance through Student Services, which had been a stressful exercise in itself: *"I was really desperate for a loan and they've changed the procedure. It's all so, so difficult now"*. Arguably, the increasing restrictions around access to welfare benefits witnessed over the past decade, including government assistance to students, has increased financial stress amongst the student population in general. This situation can only add to the difficulties for mature-age female students. For Susie, for example, this was at times an issue of contention between herself and her husband:

> *Sometimes Alan and I have arguments about money 'cause he is the only one working. He is supporting the whole family and I only get about $40 a week off the government, so they don't give me anything really to help us.*

The Centre for the Study of Higher Education [CSHE] (James, Bexley, Devlin & Marginson, 2007) reports that an estimated 12.8% of students in 2006 were "regularly [going] without food or other necessities because they could not afford them" (p. 2) and that around half of the students surveyed "had annual budgets that were in deficit [and] often worried about their finances" (p. 2).

This situation is not unique to Australia. Mature-age students in the UK similarly struggle financially if they are not in full-time employment themselves or being supported by a partner in full-time employment. Reay and colleagues (2002) in their study of working class mature-age students make the point that, despite the fact that "the UK policy rhetoric of commitment to widening access to higher education has identified mature students as playing a pivotal role" (p.5) the financial realities mean that mature students with a limited income also have limited opportunities to participate in higher education.

Changes in relationships

Another significant challenge that emerges from these stories is the impact that going to university has on the women's relationships with partners, children, families and friends. In turn, their relationships impact significantly on their studies, for better or for worse. Support, whether offered in practical terms or on an emotional level, emerges as an important part of their relationships. Indeed, the quality of the relationship is in some cases defined in terms of the perceived level of support that it offers.

A number of researchers make distinctions between various types of social support, which are commonly classified as practical support, informational support and emotional support (Darlington & Miller, 2000; Isaksson, Lexell, & Skar, 2007; Ringdal, Ringdal, Jordhoy, & Kaasa, 2007). Practical support is usually viewed as "instrumental aid, tangible" (Isaksson, et al., 2007, p. 23) often taking the form of task-focused assistance. Examples of such practical support relevant to this group of mature-age students might include assistance with tasks such as caring for children, transport, housework or household repairs, as well as financial assistance. Informational

support could include advice and information about university procedures, academic issues and availability of resources and services.

Emotional support is less easily defined, as the enacting of it may vary greatly depending upon the relationship and the situation. What constitutes emotional support is very much in the eye of the beholder. Perhaps an apt description is that by Ringdal and colleagues (2007) who describe emotional support as involving "verbal and non-verbal communication of caring and concern...believed to reduce distress by restoring self-esteem and permitting the expression of feelings" (p. 62).

There is general agreement amongst researchers about the significance of social support of all types, with evidence that, in the words of Isaksson et al. (2007, p.24) it is "positively related to life satisfaction". Research by Darlington and Miller (2000) reveals that, within families, "more adequate support is related to more intimacy and less conflict" (p. 72). It also demonstrates "the importance of receiving support that is appropriate and adequate for an individual's needs" (p. 66) and that it is the quality of support, rather than the quantity, which "is crucial in predicting family wellbeing and family functioning" (p. 74). Other research also demonstrates that social support "leads to motivation, which enables participation in occupation" (Isaksson et al., 2007, p. 28), a finding perhaps particularly relevant to this cohort in terms of their participation in higher education.

Not surprisingly then, the stories of these students indicate that their motivation for their studies and their sense of satisfaction within their relationships are influenced by the level and quality of support they feel they are receiving from others. Three of the married women – Mandy, Susie and Simone – do not appear to be receiving much support from their husbands in a day-to-day practical sense, although some felt that they were receiving a level of emotional support. Susie's husband for example, initially encouraged her to go to university and is reported as being largely supportive of her completing her studies, despite tension at times over finances. Ultimately though, her husband is supportive of her educational activities: "*He goes, 'No, I'm glad you're going to uni. Forget what I said. Just stay at uni'*".

Mandy says that her husband, Mike, has been "*incredibly supportive*", particularly since their marriage had been through a difficult time. However there is no indication that Mike provides much practical help, with Mandy relying largely on the children's growing independence and help from Mike's mother.

Interestingly, Reay et al.'s (2002) interviews with mature-age female students revealed "a subtext of women as 'uncared for carers'" (p. 17). Perhaps, for many women, lack of caring/support for themselves and their own pursuits is such an everyday experience, that they accept it unquestioningly. This may help to explain these apparent contradictions noticed by other researchers such as Wilson (1997) who describes "the woman who praises her family for their tremendous support but found the family difficulties... magnified because of her going to university" (p. 364); and Smith (1996) who concluded that partners were described as supportive as long as "there is no

change in the division of labour in the home... his time is not encroached upon either for his work or leisure [and]... the lives the children are not disrupted" (p. 67).

Simone's story indicates that her return to study into the enabling program was not initially welcomed by her husband, but rather than dismiss the idea she persisted and *"harped on my husband for a whole year and he's agreed to it"*. However, her continuation into a degree program appears to be conditional upon his approval and upon her ability to look after family and work part-time.

> *So I told him we'll see how I go for this year... and if I am happy with fitting in the study with work and family, he's quite happy to let me go ahead and do that.*

Nerida's story also reveals an initial level of resistance towards her studies from her husband, who perceived it as a threat to their relationship.

> *I think it was a big slap to his pride and ego... only in the last two years has he felt comfortable with the fact that I'm not going to get a degree in leaving!*

However, she now reports a very significant level of practical support from her husband. *"He supports me in lots of ways now – shopping, cleaning, washing the car, feeding me. He cooks tea every night."* In Nerida's words: *"that's his way of dealing with it"*.

A woman's decision to return to study can be a significant challenge to the traditional male/female roles in relationships. Certainly, some of the stories here reveal a change in the power dynamics in the relationship and indeed in the family as a whole. A number of the women describe a growth in confidence in their own knowledge and opinions, which has inevitably brought about a noticeable shift in their perceptions of themselves in relation to their partners.

> *I feel like, all of a sudden, I've got a brain... my opinion is worthy. I no longer feel like I'm on the back foot. He's a very bright man and talented – so I no longer feel like I'm a dummy... I probably don't have as much respect for him as I once had, because now I know I'm more confident and say what I think...* (Mandy)

> *I've always followed him to do what he wants and I've never stopped and said "Hang on I don't really want to do that." I've gone his way. I wasn't happy but I'm happy doing this, and now it's his turn to realise that he can still have his way of things and I can have mine...* (Simone)

Such quotes indicate that the traditional hierarchy within the family is being questioned, as the women begin to view their own opinions as worthwhile and to assert their independence. Shifts in relationships are also described in relation to their children, who are beginning to perceive their mothers as independent beings, rather than just someone at their beck and call.

> *They started to not see me just as a mother, but more of a person... we're more equal. Before they looked down on me and were up above me with their father and I was the object of ridicule – "oh silly old Mum"...* (Nerida)

The stories reveal the ways in which these women work continuously and conscientiously to develop measures and strategies to ensure that their children do not unduly miss out on their time and attention. The end result is that in most cases they perceive any effects of their studies on their relationships with their children, as positive on balance. While each noted having less time available for children, they indicate that the quality of time has improved.

There are also a number of observations about their children now being more independent and more actively engaged in learning, with some comments reflecting self-pride that, as more educated mothers, they can set an example for their children, as well as offer more practical help and encouragement over their children's school work. This has similarities with Reay et al.'s research (2002), which found that women undertaking enabling courses in the UK "saw themselves as role models for their children" (p. 11).

> *As soon as I started my study her attitude towards her homework changed. She studied more, went to the library...it was great...* (Mandy)

> *I don't think my second son would have gone to uni, had he not seen me putting in the effort. And my daughter, well she would have just played...she was a social butterfly. Now they will come to me and say "can you read it and tell me where I'm going wrong" – and I type it up and they say "that sounds just like a lecturer!"...* (Nerida)

> *I think it's good that I am studying, because the kids are seeing me study. My daughter will come and get her homework book and sit alongside me, and she is doing her homework, with me.* (Simone)

Women often have other close relationships in their lives for which they feel responsible, such as relationships with ageing parents. Amongst these seven women, both Mandy and Nerida refer to additional carer duties. In Mandy's case, the responsibilities she had for both her parents was impacting significantly on her studies:

> *She* [mother] *had a stroke in January this year, and about 2 months later she was back in hospital. I was in a lecture and no-one could get in touch with me and she had a suspected heart attack and I was told you had better come down, it's not looking good... I was back and forwards... which was taking up time... and my father – another reason why I had to drop back from full-time – he needs a hip replacement – they are both in their eighties – so now he is scheduled for surgery. I think a lot depends on how Dad comes out of this surgery... I may even have to defer depending on what happens...*

Nerida had to deal with the death of a parent after a long period of illness. Her story reveals that she was the main carer amongst her siblings, which seemed to exacerbate other problems in family relationships, adding to the strain.

> *It's awful to lose a parent but my mother was dying of diabetes, we knew she was dying... I think the way my siblings have treated me in the past 12 months has been unforgivable... there was so much scheming, swindling and trying to get rid of the executors of the will... really rotten, horrible stuff...*

Despite such difficulties, it is interesting to note that it is the positives rather than the negatives which are largely focused upon within the women's stories. For example, Mandy, who had been travelling up and down to another city, some four to five hours' drive each way, to visit her unwell

mother, comments *"it didn't impact too much"*, yet Mandy had changed to a part-time load largely because of her parents' ill health and was contemplating the possibility that she may need to defer altogether to care for them.

This minimising of the difficulties is consistent with an acceptance of the gendered expectation that women will carry the primary caring role in the family. In so doing, they are denied a sense of entitlement to personal time, including study time. Minimising the difficulties of university and the resulting impacts on caring roles possibly enables women to continue at university without too much self-censure and indeed, censure from others. For each of the women, family responsibilities are given priority and each makes sure that the competing responsibilities of study do not impact on family obligations. As long as academic activities are contained in this way then study can be seen as acceptable. Hence, there is every reason to be selective about what is revealed, to downplay difficulties and to manage a double load with cheerfulness and little complaint. Words such as "just" and "only" preface what, under other circumstances, would probably be regarded as significant losses or negative experiences. For example, Barbara views her single mother status through the positive lens of her university study, while Mandy minimises her financial difficulties (underlining indicates authors' emphasis):

> *I can sort of see that I am lucky I don't have to worry about anyone else I can be very selfish, yeah, which you have to be [to study].* (Barbara)
>
> *There were some financial losses, but they would be the only ones...* (Mandy)

'Satisficing' is a term used by Wolf-Wendel and Ward (2006) to refer to decisions that people make that, while not being optimal, are deemed to be 'good enough'. The act of 'satisficing' is apparent in these women's attitudes to study. The pressures of successfully juggling home, study and work translates into the act of 'satisficing' as certain things are sacrificed in order to meet the requirements of the course. 'Satisficing' is one of the ways in which the women manage and control university study in a life full of competing demands. Hence, both Simone and Fiona do not perceive themselves as being particularly disadvantaged, despite the challenges of managing their very limited time:

> *I'm still doing as much at home I only cut back a few hours in work but that's not a problem I usually work nights anyway... (Simone)*
>
> *Just time-management really, can get quite difficult at times. I would like to be better at that, at managing my time. But in some ways I think I work better under pressure as well, so the pressure is positive sometimes. It gets the results.* (Fiona)

This is also reflected in the way in which they perceive their future. There is a belief amongst all of them that their future will be substantially better as a result of coming to university. This focus on the future also provides the impetus for some to continue with their studies. Horstmanshof and Zimitat (2003) refer to the concept of possible or future selves in defining the reasons why students persist at university. These authors argue that fears and desires relating to the conceptualisations of these possible selves serve as powerful influences on persistence levels.

Conceptualisations of a 'hoped-for' self emerge as the possibilities afforded by university become more concrete. For example, Simone juxtaposes two alternative versions of her future, perceiving her options as either *'work in a deli'* or as a teacher, being able to *'go out and play with the kids and stay young at heart'*. This act of imagining these selves is undoubtedly one element contributing to Simone's persistence.

Persistence and determination

As their stories demonstrate, all seven women had multiple responsibilities, combining their studies with home, family and work demands, with money and time in short supply. Yet, they remain determined to continue at university, achieve their academic goals and experience that future self. Each of the student's stories indicates enormous determination. Fiona explains how she does not *"like to give up – definitely not"* Whereas Nerida describes how she is *"like a dog with a bone"*. In a similar vein, both Barbara and Susie explain their determination:

> *Yes, I am going to get there and I am going to prove that it can be done. (Barbara)*
>
> *I started it, I'm going to finish it. Don't care what anyone else says, I'm going to finish it. (Susie)*

Combined with this determination is a genuine enjoyment of their studies and *"love of learning"* as voiced by Nerida.

However, determination and love of learning can only go so far. There is considerable evidence from research, over many years, to suggest that support from others, both on and off campus, plays a major role in student persistence and retention. To name a few examples: students who withdraw before completion are less likely to have formed a significant relationship with someone on campus (Tinto, 1993); supportive relationships with others enable students to cope better with the study demands of higher education (Ostrow, Paul, Dark, & Berhman, 1986); those students who enjoy positive relationships with others are more likely to perform well academically and persist with their studies (Multon, Brown, & Lent, 1991); and first year students who experience low levels of support from others are more likely to encounter difficulties in adjusting to college life (Demakis & McAdams, 1994; Halamandaris & Power, 1999; Newland & Furnham, 1999).

Much of the more recent research into student retention, amongst all ages, continues to point to the significance of practical help and support, both on and off campus, in encouraging students to stay and progress (Abbott-Chapman, et al., 2004; Couvillion Landry, 2002; Krause, 2005; McInnes, James, & Hartley, 2000). For example, Skilbeck's (2006b) "superior conditions of learning" (p. 52) include the importance of learners feeling supported "by colleagues, family, employers etc" (p. 52). Also, Coffman and Gilligan's (2002) research found that "students who are satisfied with their supportive networks indicate higher levels of life satisfaction than students who are less satisfied with their supportive networks" (p. 152). In fact, ac-

cording to Skahill (2002/2003) "the most important criterion for staying in college is the student's social support network" (p. 39). Similarly, Rendon's (1998) work with mature-age and other non-traditional students in American colleges indicates the importance of "validation, when faculty, students, friends, parents and spouses made an effort to acknowledge these students and what they were trying to achieve" (p. 3).

So what keeps these seven students feeling supported and validated? What assistance, if any, are they receiving to enable them to develop and maintain the resilience required to succeed and progress with their studies? Their stories reveal a number of sources of assistance; fellow students, lecturers, university support services on campus, as well as family and friends off campus.

Supportive lecturers

Within the stories are references to help and support provided by lecturers.

> *The lecturers and tutors are better than good – they're approachable, you feel confident with them. You're not just being fobbed off. They are really quite wonderful...* (Nerida)

Having a supportive or "understanding" lecturer (Katrina), who is willing to give extensions for assignments at times of family difficulties, can make a crucial difference.

> *The lecturers are all very empathetic and happy to work with me in terms of getting extensions...* (Mandy)

The importance of supportive teaching staff in the success of adult learners has been identified in a number of other studies, dating back over many years (Lynch & O'Riordan, 1998; McGivney, 1999b; Rendon, 1998; Scott, Burns & Cooney, 1996). A more recent Australian research project (Chapman, et al., 2006) identified "good practice exemplars" (p. 157) amongst adult education programs in rural Victoria. The researchers found that the "dedication of the teachers and the care they extend to participants" (p. 158) was one important and noticeable element that contributed to the success of the programs and the participants. Adult learners were "treated with respect and given a voice, which increase[d] their sense of belonging and being a valued member of the group" (p. 158).

More recently still, the Australasian Survey of Student Engagement (AUSSE) that has been conducted for several years across nearly all Australian and New Zealand higher education institutions (ACER, 2008, 2009, 2010) demonstrates that student engagement with the institution is strongly linked "to perceptions of academic support" (ACER, 2008, p. ix).

University support services

Also named as helpful in these stories are university support services. Other research into adult learning environments stresses the vital role of institu-

tional support services in the success and progression of mature-age students. Skilbeck (2006b) identifies "a range of support services" as one of the key factors, which contribute towards "good practice" in adult learning (p. 63). Similarly, McGivney (1999b) outlines a number of factors that facilitate educational progression for adult learners, which include "support mechanisms that help people overcome any obstacle that might have prevented them from engaging in formal learning" (p. vii).

Mandy explains how the support extends beyond the teaching staff to "*...the librarians, the ladies in student support are fabulous, the book shop, the cafeteria...*"; a sentiment echoed by Nerida, "*...in the shop... the library woman.... I think just everyone who is here generally....*"

Specific professional support services such as personal counselling, learning support and student loans are also mentioned:

> *When I got to the point that I wanted to give it up I spoke to student support and – I don't know why I didn't do that before, but I just didn't – and I had some counselling and ... that was excellent, releasing fear and anxiety...* (Katrina)

The institutional support experienced by these students may well be a significant factor in their engagement with the university and hence their continuation with their studies.

Friendships

Fiona talks about the support, friendship and assistance she has received from fellow students and how: "*If we don't understand something we talk among ourselves*". Similarly Katrina explains:

> *If I want help or advice about my studies I usually go to other students, or to the learning support people in the library.*

These stories speak of new friendships at university. Fiona for instance has more friends than before, with the new friendships tending to be very significant and constituting an important part of her overall support network. She describes how the peer support networks can be aided, or inhibited, through different teaching approaches in class.

> *Last year we had lots of group work and five in a group, and without them it wouldn't have worked... but this semester there has been no emphasis on group work or cooperation... Oh it's been really hard, because that support base wasn't there and, like, even though we were doing the same subjects, we would be doing them differently and it was really hard to call on them.*

The importance of 'in-class' mechanisms for building social interaction has been demonstrated in previous studies such as that by Coffman and Gilligan (2002) in which they found that "in the classroom, faculty may further promote social interactions and support among students by designing assignments and class activities that encourage communication, interaction and cooperative learning among students" (p. 63).

Other informal activities on campus contribute to the development of friendships as well. "*Talking to the girls in the café*" was mentioned by Nerida as an important way of feeling supported, while Susie refers to:

> *"a feeling of connectedness when you start knowing everyone, like the ladies in the library and the ladies in the bookshop, the lady in the little shop and the café and all that."*

Quinn (2005) discusses the importance of engagement with a community of learners. Her research with second year female students at two higher educational institutions in the UK revealed that, for these women, connection with other students was of enormous importance to their sense of identity as university students; "a re-imagining of the self with and through others" (p.13) and that in having opportunities to meet together there develops what Quinn refers to as "an imagined learning community" (p. 5) – 'imagined' in the sense that, through connection with others, there is space "for dreaming new possibilities and sharing them with others" (p. 14). Quinn talks about the particular importance of these imaginings for women who are "staking claims to the learning community" (p. 12), from which they, as women, have been traditionally excluded.

As previously described, all seven students under discussion here came from family backgrounds where neither parent was university educated and all entered university through a different path than the usual route for school-leaver entry. In this sense they can be regarded as non-traditional (Abbott-Chapman, et al., 2004) and therefore traditionally outsiders in what was once regarded as "cloistered communities" (Quinn, 2005, p. 5) for the elite. Rendon (1998) talks about non-traditional students as being:

> ...students who do not consider themselves college material, ranging from students who didn't make good grades in high school to... single mothers and fathers coming back to college... students who have been told they will never amount to anything, students who have lived in poverty and who are the first in their family to attend college. (p. 2)

One or other of these descriptions would fit each of the women who have told their stories here. Similarly, Mann (2001) likens the experience of non-traditional students to that of being "a stranger in a foreign land" (p. 11). The forging of connections with others on campus can be seen as an important part of navigating "the new land of the academy" (Mann, 2001, p. 12) assisting in the development of their identity as university students.

Enabling program

These stories also reveal the value of the enabling program through which six of the women had entered or were entering university. This program had been particularly effective at welcoming them into the learning community, encouraging lasting friendships and providing them with a highly supportive environment in the very early stages of their studies. Such programs are designed to enable entry to undergraduate degree programs at university for "students who, for reasons such as poverty, gender discrimination and early school leaving, did not have the opportunity to enter university direc-

tly after high school" (Cantwell, et al., 2001, p. 221). Enabling programs are therefore designed to provide "both the subject-specific knowledge and the generic study skills that are required for effective studying in higher education" (Hayes & King, 1997, p. 8) as well as "support and encouragement from staff and other students" (Archer et al., 1999, p.50).

In order to assist students to learn and understand what is required for university study, more assistance and support in areas such as essay writing and study skills is provided within the enabling program curriculum than would be usual in undergraduate studies. With the recognition that the majority of students may be coming from backgrounds where there is little familiarity with higher education, there is also a greater emphasis on helping students to get to know each other, to encourage questions and discussion, to feel comfortable with the lecturer and to participate in class.

There is also evidence to indicate that those students who have completed an enabling program are more motivated and better prepared academically when entering undergraduate studies than those who have not, with "higher mastery goals and lower academic alienation... greater confidence in problem-solving, planning and self-appraisal" (Bourke, Cantwell & Archer, 1998, p. 1).

Certainly amongst this group of students the enabling program was credited with encouraging confidence as well as the development of supportive relationships.

> *Once you speak to someone and say, 'I don't know how this works', and they would say 'I don't either' and then it's ok.* (Fiona)

As well as building friendships, these programs provide students with important preparation for the rigours of academic study ahead and help to build confidence.

> *In the enabling course they give you a kind of head start... it was an excellent preparation. I'd never written an academic essay before in my life and...* [lecturer's name] *was fantastic...* (Katrina)

> *I certainly became more confident through the enabling course, but it wasn't until I had done a few assignments and essays and things for the degree that I realised the true worth of it.* (Mandy)

> *I think that if I had of gone into Uni straight from school I would never have got this far...* (Fiona)

McGivney's (1999b) work into informal and community based learning in the UK, indicates the value of educational opportunities that are open to all, free and locally based. She found that participation in this type of learning, particularly by those "who are educationally, economically and socially disadvantaged" (p. vi), leads to "progression... personal progression, social progression, economic progression and educational progression" (p. vi). Much like the experiences of the women in this book, McGivney (1999b) found that when this informal learning experience was positive, this provided the necessary motivation to continue into formal higher education studies.

A different view of themselves

The title of this book 'Transformations and self discovery' relates to the very tangible shifts that have occurred in these women's sense of identity. All the women speak eloquently of their university experience and the difference it has made to their perception of themselves; the use of words like *'confident'* and *'empowering'* suggesting that many of these women are undergoing dramatic transformations.

Barbara's story, for example, illustrates the ways in which university has emerged as something quite different from what was anticipated. Having entered university to explicitly fulfil vocational and financial ambitions, Barbara acknowledges attendance in more emotional and experiential terms. University emerges to fill a void in life, representing a move from conceptualising university as something for others, to an act for self, an 'intrinsic pleasure' (Blaxter & Tight, 1993, p15).

> *I just got a feeling, it sounds really stupid, but.. worthiness I think... I am worthy of being here and I can do it, and that just was great self empowerment to me. It really made me sort of think, well I am in a really great place right now and ... it was a culmination of everything working finally...I just think in total it was just such a steep learning curve but such a very enjoyable experience.* (Barbara)

While their domestic, family role remains an important part of their identity, these women are discovering that they can have another identity as well, independently from their identity as mothers, wives and partners. This is clearly articulated in a short "Once upon a time' narrative by Susie about her first year at university:

> *Once upon a time, Susie was just a little barmaid, at home doing the homely thing and trying to work and look after the kids. And now, Susie sort of more stands up for herself and tells her husband that: 'No, this isn't the thing no more 'cause I have rights in this world!'...So my once upon a time is changing that, so he stays at home and I can go and work. Be like he was with me, just to show that women's life isn't easy you know. So once upon a time yeah, then I came to uni and everything changed ... I got wise and I started learning a lot of things but it was for the better.*

University, then, can offer the possibility of having a separate or distinct identity; in the educational domain, women gain some control over their lives As earlier findings have demonstrated, university can be a catalyst for women to discover "an identity beyond that of wife and mother" (Scott, Burns & Cooney, 1998, p. 237).

This growth in personal identity and insight is evident in all of the women's stories, as expressed by Fiona:

> *just being able to say 'No', and to have an opinion and be able to back it up. I'm more sure of my own opinions and I'm able to express myself more.*

Also Nerida, who says:

> *I value myself, which is an easy thing to say but a hard thing to do. If everything fell apart tomorrow I would be alright...*

Quinn's (2005) research with women from low socio-economic backgrounds at university talks of "women carving spaces in order to resist and rebel" (p. 12). For the women in Quinn's research, university represented a place of resistance to the life from which they had come; a life typified by poorly paid and unsatisfying jobs and economic insecurity. For them, university was "a hard won freedom" and a means of "resistance to a destiny shaped only by supermarkets, call centres and lonely train stations" (p. 12). This resistance and rebellion is echoed in the words of Simone when she says:

> *If he doesn't want to come with me he can go on his separate path and I can go on my separate path. I am big enough and strong enough to fit in the uni, to fit in the work and to raise the kids, and he can just pack up and leave if he doesn't like it!*

The freedoms provided by study can, at least temporarily, liberate women from their usual occupation as carers.

> *The fact that the first time in 15 years I can just get in the car and drive up and get lost in books and research... independence. And it's something of mine. I don't have to share it with* [husband] *and the children, they don't have to be here, they don't have to have anything to do with it...* (Mandy)

Being a student therefore can be one way for women to gain freedom from their usual occupation and gain some legitimate time for themselves, albeit to engage in another form of occupation. Along with this comes the development of a greater sense of personal agency, independent achievement and future possibilities for even greater independence. As Nerida describes: *"This has been a long journey, but I'm getting to where I want to be..."* Similarly, Simone explains:

> *At the end of the day it's working towards where I want to be so it's definitely a positive ...there have been negatives lots of them, but overall, the end result is a positive.*

For these students, coming to be a student has not only translated to change in personal identity but also into a new status within the public domain. As Barbara explains, when she returned to the parenting centre she attended as a *"mother in crisis"*, she found out that she was being used as an exemplar for other mothers. Such recognition is bound to engender improvements in self-esteem and self worth. All seven women are discovering real possibilities of role change. Their role is changing from that of financially dependent carer or welfare recipient, with little personal freedom, to that of student, worker, breadwinner – and still carer – but with an increase in personal freedom and the prospect of more financial independence in the future.

Others are starting to see them differently as well, noticing changes in confidence.

> *When I started the enabling course I bought my books off a lady, and every time I see her now, she's like, 'oh I can't get over how much you've changed! When I first saw you, you came in with this mousy look and asked for your books, and now when I see you, you're everywhere, doing everything!' – and it's great!* (Fiona)

Indeed, the evidence suggests that for mature-age students engaging in education, there is not only an increase in knowledge, but also an increase in understanding (Beck, 2006; McGivney, 1999b, 2006; West, et al., 1986).

"Their interests widen and they often identify a desire for more information or new skills" (McGivney, 2006, p. 88). This leads to "more active citizenship" (McGivney, 1999b, p. vi) in terms of heightened interest and involvement in community, social and political interests and activities, as well as an increase in "intellectual interests, social liberalism, altruism, feminism and life satisfaction" (West, et al., 1986, p. 64). Change can also occur at the most fundamental level, even as an attempt to rebuild a life or just the opportunity to tell a 'better' story (Luttrell, 1997).

It is as if the process of coming to university has 'opened their eyes' to the world around them. Each indicates a growing awareness, a different and broader vision, in how they view life and society, which at times can be quite confronting.

> *I've gained a sense of awareness. I used to, like, go walking around with my head up my arse before, but now it's like, oh, I wish I could go back there, because everything is so confronting!* (Fiona)

> *I can't look at a TV show anymore... I deconstruct everything! I can't read a newspaper – I know what's behind the headlines. I know who is pushing the buttons. I can't listen to the politicians, I can see all the power play and all the crap and all the nonsense that's going on in the world... I can see all the injustices...* (Nerida).

There is also a sense of real exhilaration about the acquisition of so much knowledge and the impact that this is having upon them.

> *I think I have just gained heaps of knowledge... uni studies opens up an entire world of knowledge... just the amount of things you need to know and can know, and it's all around you...* (Katrina)

With the learning has also come a philosophical shift in priorities, with a decrease in focus on material and financial concerns.

> *I'm not worried so much about material things any more, and the need to hang onto all these material things and collections...* (Mandy)

Instead, there is more awareness of the importance of other less tangible aspects of life.

> *I really appreciate a Sunday afternoon with my husband. I appreciate being able to stay outside in the fresh air and sunshine.... and I don't know if I used to do that...* (Nerida)

Both current and future circumstances have changed for these women. They generally regard their futures in much broader strokes; there is better clarity about where they see themselves. This transformation is revealed in the sense of self-direction or 'control' that many describe in their narratives, one example being Barbara who talks about planning ahead and considering possibilities after she leaves university; something she could not do 'before'.

What's ahead?

With the attainment of higher education qualifications, all are looking ahead to a significantly different life from that of their parents and a better life than the one they had before.

> *A brand new start... I've got this ten-year window of opportunity before my children start marrying and having children. Because I got married and had a child straight away, because my husband's ten years older than me, this is my time...* (Nerida)

> *Financially I think my future will be better than what it would have been – and personally I think... because it has given me more confidence, and I doubt whether I am going to lose that... I won't lose it again....* (Fiona)

They are also looking forward to remediation of financial pressures through increased earning capacity and, as a result, a better quality of life.

> *Hopefully I'm able to secure a job which will pay more and therefore economically I'll be able to support my children better than I would have been able to originally. That's really what is most important to me, and by being here and doing this degree, I can see that I have a chance to make this happen.* (Katrina)

There is excitement about their dreams and plans for the future and the sense of a different life and a different self ahead.

> *I think my future is going to be much brighter than the past. I'm much more confident... far more confident... I have an ability to focus on goals I haven't had before. ...* (Mandy)

Running through the women's stories is a recurring theme of a vision of a more independent future, in contrast with the relative lack of prior opportunities for independence in their lives.

Some also express a desire to continue learning. This group of adult students had initially entered university as a means to an end, not necessarily expecting to actively enjoy the process, yet many had discovered that learning in itself has its own pleasures.

> *First I thought I want to get this degree and then launch into my business... but now I'm more than happy to plod along and be a perpetual student. It's going to take longer to get the degree but I will probably enjoy the process a lot more...*(Mandy)

> *I just love it and I don't want to go... I'd like to keep studying...* (Fiona)

The changes that these students envisage for the future are not limited purely to themselves. Achieving their university degree is seen as the start of a new cycle that may also have a profound influence on their children.

> *I'm hoping that it will show him that he... can aim for higher... I want to be a positive example...do the hard work and you will get somewhere...* (Fiona)

They are aware that their children will have some understanding of university and what it can offer, in a way that was not available to them when they were growing up.

> *I think that they will definitively not be scared to study, because they are here in the uni environment... such a familiar place...* (Mandy)

Hence not only individual transformation but transformation into the next generation is taking place, with the real possibility of "lasting change that has an impact, not only on the individual but also on communities in an ongoing basis" (Beck, 2006, p. 107).

> *I don't think my second son would have gone to uni if he hadn't seen me putting in the effort.* (Nerida)

The stories of these seven women, who have come to university as 'second-chance' students illustrate the transformative nature of their experiences in higher education. Adults participate in education for a number of reasons. These narratives indicate how such reasons can be associated with the management of change and crisis, both public and personal in nature. However, overcoming difficulties is truly 'empowering'; a sense of accomplishment can be derived from succeeding in activities previously regarded as too difficult or overwhelming. University attendance may present a 'risk of rupture' with existing relationships and identity (Brine & Waller,2004, p.111) but equally this is an 'emancipatory' experience (Merrill,1999). Being a student may not radically shift the gender and class inequalities experienced by female students but the decision to arrive and the resulting choices, changes and challenges should not be dismissed.

The following and final chapter will draw some conclusions about the experiences and insights of this particular group of students, which may assist others who are thinking about, or perhaps beginning, such a journey themselves. The implications for higher education institutions, in terms of providing opportunities and encouragement for women as mature-age students in general, to enter university and succeed with their studies, will also be explored.

And so the story concludes

Research into participation levels in higher education in Australia tells us that "mature age students from identified equity groups... suffer demonstrable educational disadvantage" (Abbott-Chapman, et al., 2004, p.7). We also know that "the success of mature-aged non-traditional entry appears independent of socio-economic background" (Cantwell, et al., 2001, p.233).

Despite more than a decade of equity measures, nationally and internationally, to improve the participation and academic success in higher education of students from lower socio-economic background across all age-groups, these students are still significantly under-represented worldwide (CSHE, 2008). In contrast, students from lower socio-economic status backgrounds are over-represented in enabling and other alternative entry programs, through which a majority of mature-age students enter university (Blaxter, et al., 1996; Cullity, 2006; Kavanagh & Stockdale, 2007). Supporting and encouraging mature learners to enter, participate and succeed in higher education is therefore of vital importance in furthering the equity agendas of universities.

As well as furthering broad long-term equity agendas however, there is another important reason to encourage mature-age university entry and academic success: that is, the benefits to the individual student, brought about by exposure to and involvement in the university learning community. From the stories of the seven women, featured throughout this book, have emerged findings of particular significance in increasing our understanding of the mature age female experience in higher education. Key findings emerging from the women's stories are discussed below.

The power to transform... for this generation and the next

The transformative power of engagement with higher education is well illustrated within the women's stories. Their stories reflect that, for each one of them, university has been, and is continuing to be, a truly transformative experience. Improvements in confidence, self-esteem, social skills, self-awareness and awareness of the world around them are considerable. Being at university as part of a learning community and expanding their knowledge has led these women to think very differently in a number of significant ways. They are developing a greater sense of personal independence and autonomy as they challenge the more restrictive aspects of their gendered role. They are looking forward to a different life, a better life, one with better work opportunities, a more comfortable and secure financial situation, achievement of career goals and, for some, further study. For all, there is a sense of dreams and ambitions being achieved.

The women are keenly aware of the positive influence that their studies are having upon their children and the likelihood that their children will consider university as an option for their own futures. They see themselves as role models for their children and as parents who will encourage and support their children into higher education, now that they know the value of it for themselves. A new cycle has begun, which will have potential ramifications for their children, their grandchildren and future generations to come.

The accessibility of an enabling program emerges as a major factor influencing the decision of nearly all these women to enter higher education. This supports previous research demonstrating that the provision of inexpensive, local access to education encourages adult learners, particularly those from lower SES backgrounds, to engage in further education and to want to continue learning (McGivney, 1999a, 1999b, 2006; McLaren, 1985; Reay, 2002; Skilbeck, 2006b). It also reinforces the premise that the expansion of free, locally-based programs which provide pathways into higher education will assist and encourage greater numbers of mature-age students, including those from lower SES backgrounds, to contemplate the possibility of going to university and to take the first steps towards this.

Influence of gender

Taking a feminist approach to the deconstruction of the women's stories reveals their gendered experiences. The role limitations for women as 'carers' (Lister, 2000; Orloff, 1996; Weeks, 2000) are evident throughout their stories and have shaped their experiences. The daily struggle of combining studies with the gendered role of 'carer' is revealed. They are carrying a double or even triple load of child-care, housework and paid work along with their studies. This is most clearly demonstrated in the ways in which they struggle

with the lack of time to manage the competing demands. The women's time for study is fragmented and fractured, melded in with other responsibilities such as caring for children and other various domestic duties.

Their stories reveal the interrupted nature of any study time and the virtual impossibility of having dedicated, privileged and uninterrupted time for study on a regular basis. These women consistently put family responsibilities first, yet still manage to succeed at their studies through artful juggling and often loss of sleep. Some have reduced their study load in order to manage to continue.

In terms of support from family and friends, the stories expose quite starkly how little help and practical support most are receiving at home from male partners. There are however indications that some are beginning to question or challenge the dominant view of male/female roles, with subsequent effects on relationships. This provides support for evidence which suggests that education encourages less conservatism and more open-mindedness to other possibilities, including different ways of conceptualising gender roles (Giles, 1990; West, et al., 1986).

Value of support

The importance of support from academic staff, university services and fellow students, is highlighted throughout all the stories of this group of women.

...from academic staff

Support and encouragement from academic staff is highly valued amongst this group. As mature-age students with many other conflicting responsibilities, they greatly appreciate any efforts made by lecturers to show understanding of their circumstances and a willingness to be flexible, to better accommodate their needs. This reflects other research into student experience in general (Krause, 2005; O'Shea, 2007; Rendon, 1998) which demonstrates that "student and staff interactions are one of the most important characteristics of high quality learning" (ACER, 2008, p. 8), particularly for non-traditional entry students.

...from university services

University support services have been of significant practical assistance, through financial support, disability provisions, learning support, and also emotional assistance via personal counselling. Easy and free access to such services is clearly of high importance in terms of supporting students to stay and succeed.

...from fellow students

The stories also reveal that friendships with fellow students play a significant role in persistence and resilience. Some have formed close friendships with other students and most refer to the sharing of academic and/or personal concerns with their peers on campus. This may take the form of talking over an essay topic, working together on a group project or catching up over a cup of coffee in the cafeteria. In whatever context, these interactions are important. Aspects of their stories reveal the helpful role that the institution can play in encouraging and supporting such interactions through ensuring that group work is part of the curriculum and organising time in class to talk and share work with each other. There is now considerable evidence to support the importance of student-to-student interaction for student engagement and academic success (ACER, 2008; Coffman & Gilligan, 2002; McGivney, 2006).

Financial struggles

Emerging from the stories is the very difficult financial situation that most are facing on a day-to-day basis. Inadequate financial support for these mature female learners is compounded by difficulties in the way such support is structured within a gendered, neo-liberal welfare state model (Lister, 2000; O'Connor, et al., 1999; Weeks, 2000). Under this model, the women with male partners receive little if any financial support for their studies and loss of income, while single parent benefits are reduced based on ages of children. Making ends meet is a daily challenge.

Advice to others

The women's stories contain a number of pieces of advice for other women who have begun, or may be contemplating, embarking upon a similar educational journey. These can be summarised by the following five points:

1. Ask for help, build friendships – and ask lots of questions

> *I think it's important that mature-age students know they can ask lots of questions and not be afraid to use the services that are here. (Mandy)*

All the women stress the value of asking questions, as well as seeking assistance from the services available at university campuses such as counselling, learning skills, career advice, student loans and so on. But apart from these designated university services, a number of the women also mention the value in getting to know, talking with and asking questions of a very wide

range of people at university – staff in the cafe, the bookshop, the library and, of course, lecturers and fellow students.

> *I have found out there is support and there are ways of doing things and people to ask, but just getting it into your head that if you have problems go and ask anyone.* (Simone)

Along with this goes the importance of building friendships with other students. As Susie found, *"it's pretty scary too a little bit, but when you get to uni and you get friends, that makes it a bit better"*.

2. Take time to adjust

In Katrina's words, it is important *"to be aware that they will find it very difficult until you adjust to uni life and your brain starts kicking over again"*.

3. Focus on what is most important

Managing their limited time by cutting out the less important aspects of their busy lives – such as reducing the amount of time spent on housework – is something that is mentioned by many of the women. As Barbara says, *"Make the most of the time you have got"*.

4. Believe in yourself

Having faith in oneself and maintaining confidence in one's ability to achieve the goal, despite setbacks, is another important factor that comes through from the women's stories. *"Don't just give up!"* is Nerida's message to others.

Part of building one's confidence is being prepared for what is ahead, which is the fifth piece of advice offered.

5. Be well-prepared

A number of the women had taken advantage of the preparation courses run by the university support services, particularly learning skills courses, and had found that these had given them a head start.

> *Before the course had even started I was doing all the extra preparation and extra learning support classes. I did the essay writing. I did everything before it even started. I thought, I am not going into this blind, I'm going to get as much information as I can. So that definitely helped me to feel more confident about starting...* (Fiona)

Where to from here? Implications for the future

While it would be a mistake to generalise the experiences of these seven women too widely, nevertheless many aspects of these narratives are con-

sistent with other research findings in the field of adult learning. It is also reasonable to assume that the stories of this group of women are, at least in part, reflective of the culture within which they are living their lives. Individual narratives tell us something of the wider community in which the individual is situated (Chase, 2003; Elliott, 2005). Hence, in coming to the end of this particular story about one group of mature-age women at university, it is possible to recognise some wider implications for education providers, policy makers and all who have a role to play in higher education, including students. It seems clear from the individual stories of these students, as well as other related research, that educational institutions have a vital role to play in developing greater awareness of "the relevance of lifelong learning to student personal and/or vocational well-being" (Cullity, 2006, p. 185). The narratives of this student cohort provide a valuable insight into the particular factors which have helped and hindered the progress of their 'second-chance journey' and into some possibilities for the future. To complete this story therefore, we offer some recommendations for action, based upon the experiences of the women whose voices have informed this research.

1. Pathways into higher education

Firstly, in order to attract more mature-age women into higher education, there is a need to expand the provision of appropriate, free and easily accessible enabling programs. Broadening the availability of such programs across the higher education sector is one important strategy to assist them to enter university, hence further widening access and participation. Enabling programs play a highly significant role in assisting mature learners to enter university. Equally importantly, they provide support for mature learners, academically and socially, in making a successful transition to higher education.

Currently, Australian institutions can apply for commonwealth grant scheme funding in order to provide enabling programs, with the funding agreement between the particular institution and the Australian government limiting the number of places which can be funded (Chadwick, 2007). An important step towards greater accessibility of higher education for mature-age students, women and men, would be to expand this funding to increase the number of free, open-entry places in enabling programs around the country. Adult education research tells us that mature learners are more likely to enter formal education when it is local and affordable; therefore offering a greater number of free enabling places at as many institutions as possible has the potential to significantly increase the number of mature-age students, particularly those from lower SES backgrounds, entering university. The "Participation and Equity" report (CSHE, 2008) identifies that rural and isolated areas in particular have low participation rates in higher education. It is therefore imperative that enabling programs are offered locally across rural areas and not only at city institutions.

2. Improved financial assistance

Another significant barrier to higher education access is a financial one. The financial implications of going to university can be an overwhelming deterrent, particularly for mature-age women with family responsibilities from lower SES backgrounds. Government assistance for students is clearly inadequate in general, as mentioned previously approximately 50% of students having difficulties managing financially and close to 13% often unable to buy enough food (James, et al., 2007). If higher education institutions are therefore serious about improving access and participation across all socio-economic groups, there needs to be considerable lobbying of governments to urge the provision of more adequate and appropriately targeted government financial support for students of all ages. Educational researchers have stressed that "it is imperative for Australia to both broaden access and increase participation in tertiary education" (Harris, 2008, p.1) and have urged "better financial support for students, and a shift in social attitudes to widening participation... to help disadvantaged communities to reimagine universities as "places for them" rather than places for the wealthy" (Bexley, 2008, p.3).

The dual imperatives of widening access and improving financial support have been recognised in the findings of the Bradley Review of Higher Education in Australia (DEEWR, 2008) with its recommendations to increase low SES participation and to significantly increase government financial support to disadvantaged students. Without adequate financial support targeted towards those least able to afford to go to university, and without sound measures to attract and retain students from all backgrounds, the goal of continuing to broaden higher education access and participation amongst those who are socially and economically disadvantaged will continue to be elusive.

3. Appropriate teaching styles

A third and equally important point is that the stories of these seven women indicate a need for teaching styles which take into account their particular situations and demonstrate an understanding of the gendered nature of the challenges which female mature learners face. Flexibility around issues of study time and assessment tasks, as well as classroom strategies which encourage interaction between students, teachers and other students, have all been demonstrated as being of key importance in encouraging and supporting such students to succeed with their academic endeavours. Teachers who encourage interaction with other students, who are more inclined to be flexible about assignment dates and who are willing to listen to the needs of individual students, including issues around child-care, family needs and lack of structured time, were the ones most highly valued and viewed as inspirational amongst this particular cohort of students. This type of support had

contributed significantly to the resilience and persistence of these students through difficult times. In Katrina's words: *"universities need to keep on being really understanding about what mature-age students are"*.

Feeling comfortable about approaching lecturers was something that these students also valued and this is emphasised by Shelton (2003), who argues that both individual academics and faculty need to take an active role in providing psychological support. Such support, Shelton suggests, should be based on qualities such as approachability; caring attitudes, respectfulness and 'genuine interest' toward students (p.64). First year students are generally expected to adapt and acculturise to the university environment in a timely and fluid fashion and some academics may not seem to fully appreciate or empathise with the very radical nature of this adjustment. Kantanis (2000) argues that the more traditionally focussed academics often foreground the imparting of knowledge rather than the teaching or supporting of students, adopting a 'sink or swim' philosophy in relation to these commencing cohorts.

Creating space and time for interactions with students may be difficult for many academics due to teaching demands. However, what is striking about the women's accounts is how minor incidents had a major impact on the quality of the student experience. In some cases, just small gestures could make a qualitative difference to learning experiences. For example, just knowing that you could 'see' a lecturer if this became necessary and being assured of an understanding response made a qualitative difference to the university experience. Undoubtedly, academics are faced with the dilemma of engaging in activities, which while beneficial to students and ultimately institutional budgets, may not necessarily be recognised as important or valuable, perhaps even regarded as eroding time needed for research. Many academic staff may genuinely wish to improve or positively negotiate student experiences but demands of the role combined with time constraints may preclude them from doing so.

In order to enhance the academic achievement of mature female learners, higher education institutions need to demonstrate a firm commitment to the effective teaching and learning of this cohort. It is important that strategies are developed to better equip academic staff to understand the particular learning needs of mature-age women at university, and the teaching styles which suit these needs. Teaching styles which demonstrate a level of individual flexibility and an understanding and respect for the many other demands that these students have upon their time – as well as for the innovative and sometimes unusual study habits they adopt in order to get their work done – are ones that these learners appreciate.

Equally important are classroom methods, which connect students meaningfully with their lecturers and with their peers. This combined with recognition and reward for those teaching staff who take the time to 'enable' these learners can maximise the potential for these students to fully engage with the learning community and succeed at their studies.

4. Adequate provision of university support services

The final recommendation relates to the provision of university support services. The courage of each of these women, often in the face of considerable adversity, is apparent to anyone who hears their stories. Their stories also highlight the importance of free, well-resourced, easily accessible support services on university campuses. These services are very important potentially for all students, but for mature-age female students they are absolutely vital.

Personal counselling provides such students with an opportunity to talk through the challenges and difficulties, as well as the confusion associated with changes in self and identity, helping them to overcome obstacles, understand the changes and to build a positive sense of their "new" self. Other services such as disability services, learning support and emergency financial assistance, emerge from these stories as making a significant and positive difference to these students, assisting them to continue at university through particularly difficult times. The ongoing provision of a range of well-resourced support and transition services is therefore another way in which institutions can demonstrate their commitment to engaging, supporting and encouraging students from all backgrounds and of all ages to stay and succeed at university.

Mature-age women are already entering higher education in significant numbers and as such constitute a highly important cohort. Yet, these mature learners remain largely unrecognised and unacknowledged for the different and important contribution that they make, not only to the classrooms and other learning and social activities of individual institutions, but also to the wider national and international higher education access agenda.

Our intention in bringing the narratives of these seven women to the page is to bring this valuable and courageous cohort of students into the spotlight. In making the recommendations above, we are advocating for a change in higher education for the future: a future in which the importance of attracting, supporting and retaining mature-age female students is better understood; a future in which the term "student" is widely recognised as one that applies equally across gender and age; most importantly, a future in which greater numbers of mature women have the opportunity to consider higher education as an option and to receive the institutional assistance and encouragement to enter, stay and succeed. In so doing, these students assist universities to move closer towards being places of equal access and opportunity, as well as of greater diversity. In the process, the women themselves are exposed to experiences which have the capacity to transform their lives, individually, socially and economically, as well as potentially those of future generations.

Reference List

Abbott-Chapman, J., Braithwaite, J., & Godfrey, J. (2004). Promoting Access, Increasing Opportunities for University Education: a study of mature-aged students from disadvantaged regions: University of Tasmania.

Abrams, P. (1982). Historical Sociology. Cornell University Press, Ithaca.

ACER (2008). Attracting, engaging and retaining: New conversations about learning. *Australasian Survey of Student Engagement,* Australasian Student Engagement Report. Melbourne.

ACER (2009). Engaging students for success: *Australasian Survey of Student Engagement,* Australasian Student Engagement Report. Melbourne.

ACER (2010). Doing more for learning: Enhancing engagement and outcomes. *Australasian Survey of Student Engagement,* Australasian Student Engagement Report. Melbourne.

Alvesson, M, & Skoldberg, K. (2000). *Reflexive Methodology*. London: Sage.

Alvesson, M. (2002). *Postmodernism and Social Research*. Buckingham: Open University Press.

Archer, J., Cantwell, R., & Bourke, S. (1999). Coping at University: an examination of achievement, motivation, self-regulation, confidence and method of entry. *Higher Education Research & Development, 18*(1), 31-54.

Bacchi. C. (1999). *Women, Policy and Politics: The Construction of Policy Problems*. London: Sage.

Beck, D. (2006). Together for a change: A partnership approach to individual and community learning. In J. Chapman, P. Cartwright & J. E. McGilp (Eds.), *Lifelong Learning, Participation and Equity*. Dordrecht, The Netherlands: Springer.

Bexley, E. (2008). Class-based assumptions hamper social inclusion. *Campus Review, 18*, 3.

Blaxter, L., Dodd, K., & Tight, M. (1996). Mature student markets: An insitutional case study. *Higher Education, 31*(2), 187-203.

Bodek, E.G. (1976). Salioneres and bluestockings: Educated obsolescence and germinating feminism. *Feminist Studies, 3* 185-199.

Bourke, S., Cantwell, R., & Archer, J. (1998). *Evaluation of an equity program for university entrance*. Paper presented at the HERDSA Annual Conference, Auckland, New Zealand.

Brine, J., & Waller, R. (2004). Working-class women on an Access course: risk, opportunity and (re)constructing identities. *Gender and Education, 16*(1), 97-113.

Britton, C., & Baxter, A. (1999). Becoming a mature student: Gendered narratives of the self. *Gender and Education, 11*(2), 179-193.

Brookfield, S. (1995). *Becoming a critically reflective teacher*. San Francisco: Jossey-Bass Publishers.

Cantwell, R., Archer, J., & Bourke, S. (2001). A comparison of the academic experiences and achievements of university students entering by traditional and non-traditional means. *Assessment & Evaluation in Higher Education, 26*(3), 221-234.

Chapman, J., McGilp, J. E., Cartwright, P., De Souza, M., & Toomey, R. (2006). Overcoming barriers that impede participation in lifelong learning. In J. Chapman, P. Cartwright & J. E. McGilp (Eds.), *Lifelong Learning, Participation and Equity* (pp. 151-174). Dordrecht, The Netherlands: Springer.

Chadwick, R. (2007). *Update on Enabling from DEST*. Paper presented at the Enabling Education 2007 - What works?, Newcastle, Australia.

Clancy, P, & Goastellec, G. (2007). Exploring Access and Equity in Higher Education: Policy and Performance in a Comparative Perspective. *Higher Education Quarterly, 61*(2), 136-154.

Coffey, A., & Atkinson, P. (1996). *Making Sense of Qualitative Data: Complementary Research Strategies*. Thousand Oaks, London, New Delhi: Sage Publications.

Coffman, D. L., & Gilligan, T. D. (2002). Social support, stress and selfefficacy: Effects on students' satisfaction. *Journal of College Student Retention, 4*(1), 53-66.

Couvillion Landry, C. (2002). Retention of women and people of colour: Unique challenges and institutional responses. *Journal of College Student Retention, 4*(1), 1-13.

CSHE. (2004). *Analysis of Equity Groups*. The University of Melbourne.

CSHE. (2008). *Participation and Equity*. The University of Melbourne.

Cullity, M. (2006). Challenges in understanding and assisting mature-age students who participate in alternative entry programs. *Australian Journal of Adult Learning, 46*(2), 175-201.

Darlington, Y., & Miller, R. J. (2000). Support received by families with dependent children: The importance of receiving adequate support. *Journal of Family Studies, 6*(1), 65-77.

Davies, K. (1990). *Women, Time and Weaving the Strands of Everyday Life*. Aldershot: Gower.

Demakis, G. J., & McAdams, D. P. (1994). Personality, social support and well-being among first-year college students. *College Student Journal, 28*, 235-242.

Denzin, N. (1997). *Interpretive Ethnography*. Thousand Oaks: Sage.

Department of Education, Employment and Training. (1990). *A Fair Chance for All*. Canberra. Australian Government Publishing Service.

Department of Education, Employment and Training. (1993). *National report on Australia's higher education sector*. Canberra. Australian Government Publishing Service.

Department of Education, Employment and Workplace Relations (2008). *Review of Australian Higher Education: Final Report*. Canberra: Australian Government.

Edwards, R. (1993). *Mature Women Students: Separating or Connecting Families*. London: Taylor and Francis.

Edwards, R., Hanson, A., & Raggatt, P. (1996). *Boundaries of adult learning*. London & New York: Routledge in assoc. with The Open University.

Elliott, J. (2005). *Using Narrative in Social Research*. London: Sage.

Ewick, P. & Silbey, S. (1995). Subversive Stories and Hegemonic Tales: Toward a Sociology of Narrative. *Law & Society Review, 29*(2), 197-226.

Ferguson, C. (1985). *First Feminists: British women writers 1578-1799*. Bloomington Indiana: Indiana University Press.

Figes, K. (1994). *Because of her Sex*. London: Macmillan.

Fonow, M., & Cook, J. A. (1991). *Beyond Methodology*. Bloomington: Indiana University Press.

Giles, J. (1990). Second Chance, Second Self? *Gender and Education, 2*(3), 357-361.

Gilligan, C. (1982). *In a Different Voice*. Cambridge MA: Harvard University Press.

Gilligan, C. (1987). Woman's place in man's life cycle. In S. Harding (Ed.), Feminism and Methodology (pp. 57-73). Bloomington & Indianapolis: Indiana University Press.

Gubrium, J.F., & Holstein, J.A. (2003). *Postmodern interviewing*. Thousand Oaks: Sage Publications.

Halamandaris, K. F., & Power, K. G. (1999). Individual differences, social support and coping with the examination stress: A study of the psychosocial and academic adjustment of first year home students. *Personality and Individual Differences* (26), 665-685.

Harding, S. (1987). *Feminism and Methodology*. Indianapolis: Indiana University Press.

Harris, K. L. (2008). Strategies for reform under spotlight. *Campus Review,18*, 1.

Hayes, K., & King, E. (1997). Mature students in higher education: 111 approaches to studying in access students. *Studies in Higher Education, 22*(1), 19-31.

Horstmanshof, L., & Zimitat, C. (2003, 9 - 11 July). *Do extracurricular roles impact on retention? A Social Exchange Theory perspective.* Paper presented at the 7th Pacific Rim First Year in Higher Education Conference. Enhancing the Transition to Higher Education: Strategies and Policies that Work, Brisbane.

Hughes, C. (2002). *Feminist Theory and Research*. London: Sage Publications.

Isaksson, G., Lexell, J., & Skar, L. (2007). Social support provides motivation and ability to participate in occupation. *OTJR, 27*(1), 23-30.

Jackson, S. (2000). Differently Academic? Constructions of 'academic' in higher education. *Higher Education Research & Development, 19*(3), 279-296.

James, R., Bexley, E., Devlin, M., & Marginson, S. (2007). *Australian university student finances 2006*. University of Melbourne: Centre for Study of Higher Education.

Kantanis T. (2000). The role of social transition in student's adjustment to the first year of university. *Monash Transition Program*. Retrieved 4 September, 2003, from http://www.adm.monash.edu.au/transition/research/kantanis3.html

Kavanagh, K., & Stockdale, R. (2007). Opportunity knocks: Opening the door to the university experience through the Open Foundation Program at the University of Newcastle. Paper presented at the *2007 Enabling Educators' Conference – What works?*

Kelly, S. (1987). *The Prize and the Price: The changing world of women who return to study*. Sydney: Methuen Haynes.

Knights, D, & Odih, P. (1995). "It's about time!" The significance of gendered time for financial services consumption. *Time and Society, 4*(2), 205-231.

Krause, K. L. (2005). Serious thoughts about dropping out in first year: Trends, patterns and implications for higher education. *Studies in Learning Evaluation Innovation and Development, 2*(3), 55-67.

Leonard, M. (1994). Transforming the Household: Mature Women Students and Access to Higher Education. In S. Davies, C. Lubelska & J. Quinn (Eds.), *Changing the Subject: Women in Higher Education* (pp. 163-177). London: Taylor & Francis.

Letherby, G. (1994). Mother or Not, Mother or What? Problems of Definition and Identity. *Women's Studies International Forum, 17*(5), 525-532.

Lister, R. (2000). Gender and the Analysis of Social Policy. In G. Lewis, S. Gewirtz & J. Clarke (Eds.), *Rethinking Social Policy* (pp. 22-35). London: Open University in association with Sage Publications.

Ludwig, K. (2006). Reinventing the feminine: Bluestocking women writers in 18th century London. Retrieved 21 February, 2011, from *http://www.katelynludwig.com/masters/index.html*

Luttrell, W. (1997). *School-smart and mother-wise: Working class women's identity and schooling.* London: Routledge.

Lynch, K., & O'Riordan, C. (1998). Inequality in higher education: A study of class barriers. *British Journal of Sociology in Education, 19*(4), 445-478.

Mann, S. J. (2001). Alternative perspectives on the student experience: Alienation and engagement. *Studies in Higher Education, 26*(1), 7-19.

Martin, J. (1988). *Second Chance. Women Returning to Study.* Ringwood Victoria: Penguin.

McGivney, V. (1999a). *Excluded men: Men who are missing from education and training.* Leicester: NIACE.

McGivney, V. (1999b). *Informal learning in the community.* Leicester: NIACE.

McGivney, V. (2006). Attracting new groups into learning: Lessons from research in England. In J. Chapman, P. Cartwright & J. E. McGilp (Eds.), *Lifelong learning, participation and equity* (pp. 79-91). Dordrecht, The Netherlands: Springer.

McInnes, C., James, R., & Hartley, R. (2000). *Trends in the first year experience in Australian universities.* Melbourne: Evaluations and investigations program Higher Education Division Centre for Study of Higher Education, Department of Education, Training & Youth Affairs.

McLaren, A. (1985). *Ambitions and Realisations: Women in Adult Education.* London: Peter Owen.

McNay, L. (2000). *Gender and Agency: Reconfiguring the Subject in Feminist and Social Theory.* Cambridge: Polity Press.

Merrill, B. (1999). *Gender, change and identity: Mature women students in universities.* Aldershot UK: Ashgate Publishing Ltd.

Mills, J. (1989). *Womanwords.* Harlow UK: Longman.

Morrison, M. (1996). Part-time: Who's time? Women's lives and adult learning. In R. Edwards, A. Hanson & P. Raggatt (Eds.), *Boundaries of Adult Learning* (pp. 211-231). London: Routledge.

Multon, K. D., Brown, S. D., & Lent, R. W. (1991). Relation of self-efficacy beliefs to academic outcomes: A meta-analytic investigation. *Journal of Counselling Psychology*(38), 30-38.

Newland, J., & Furnham, A. (1999). Perceived availability of social support. *Personality and Individual Differences, 27*(659-663).

O'Shea, S. (2007). Well I got here but what happens next? - Exploring the narratives of first year female students who are the first in the family to attend university. *Journal of the Australian and New Zealand Student Services Association, April*(29), 36-51.

Oakley, A. (1981). Interviewing women: a contradiction in terms. In H. Roberts (Ed.), *Doing Feminist Research*. London Routledge & Kegan Paul.

Oakley, A. (1992). *Social Support and Motherhood*. Oxford: Blackwell.

Olesen, V. (1994). Feminisms and Models of Qualitative Research. In N. Denzin & Y. Lincoln (Eds.), *Handbook of Qualitative Research* (pp. 158-174). London: Sage.

Orloff, A. (1996). Gendering the Analysis of the Welfare State. In B Sullivan & G Whitehouse (Eds.), *Gender, Politics and Citizenship in the 1990s* (pp. 81-97). Sydney: UNSW.

Ostrow, E., Paul, S., Dark, V., & Berhman, J. (1986). Adjustment of college women on campus: Effects of stressful life events, social support and personal competencies. In S. E. Hobfoll (Ed.), *Stress, social support and women* (pp. 29-45). Washington DC: Hemisphere.

Pascall, G., & Cox, R. (1993). *Women Returning to Higher Education*. London: The Society for Research into Higher Education and Open University Press.

Polkinghorne, D.E. (1988). *Narrative Knowing and the Human Sciences*. Albany: State University of New York Press.

Quinn, J. (2005). Belonging in a learning community: The re-imagined university and imagined social capital. *Studies in the Education of Adults, 37*(1), 4-17.

Ramsey, E, Tranter, D., Sumner, R., & Barrett, S. (1996). Outcomes of a University's Flexible Admissions Policies. In Training and Youth Affairs Department of Education (Ed.), *Evaluation and Investigations Program Higher Education Division*. Canberra: University of South Australia.

Reay, D. (2002). Class, authenticity and the transition to higher education for mature students *The Editorial Board of the Sociological Review 2002* (pp. 399-418). Oxford: Blackwell.

Reay, D., Ball, S., & David, M. (2002). 'It's taking me a long time but I'll get there in the end': Mature students on access courses and higher education choice. *British Educational Research Journal, 28*(1), 5-19.

Rendon, L. I. (1998). Helping non-traditional students be successful in college. *About Campus, March-April*, 2-3.

Rice, J. (1989). *Continuing education for women: Handbook of continuing education*. San Francisco: Jossey Bass.

Rice, P, & Ezzy, D. (2000). *Qualitative Research Methods*. South Melbourne: Oxford University Press.

Ringdal, G. I., Ringdal, K., Jordhoy, M. S., & Kaasa, S. (2007). Does social support from family and friends work as a buffer against reactions to stressful life events such as terminal cancer? *Palliative and Supportive Care, 5*, 61-69.

Riessman, C. (1993). *Narrative Analysis.* Newbury Park: Sage Publications Inc.

Rinne, R, & Kivinen, O. (1996). The second chance: The vital myth of equal opportunites in adult education. In R. Edwards, A. Hanson & P. Raggatt (Eds), *Boundaries of Adult Learning.* London & New York: Routledge in assoc. with The Open University.

Schuller, T. (2006). Education and Equity: Perspectives from the OECD. In J. Chapman, P. Cartwright & J.E. McGilp (Eds.), *Lifelong Learning, Participation and Equity.* Dordrecht, The Netherlands: Springer.

Scott, C, Burns, A., & Cooney, G. (1993). Single and Married Mothers as Students: obstacles to successful completion of studies. Paper presented at the *A Fair Chance for All in Access to Higher Education: Consolidation and Advancement into the 21st century: Australia's First National Conference on Equity and Access in Higher Education,* The University of Newcastle.

Scott, C., Burns, A., & Cooney, G. (1996). Reasons for discontinuing study: The case of mature age female students with children. *Higher Education, 31*(2), 233-253.

Scott, C., Burns, A., & Cooney, G. (1998). Motivation for return to study as a predictor of completion of degree amongst female mature students with children. *Higher Education*(35), 221-239.

Shelton, E. (2003). Faculty support and student retention. *Journal of Nursing Education, 42*(2), 68-76.

Skahill, M. P. (2002/2003). The role of social support network in college persistence among freshmen students. *Journal of College Student Retention, 4*(1), 39-52.

Skilbeck, M. (2006). Lifelong Learning for All: The Challenge to Adults and Communities. J. Chapman. P. Cartwright & J.E. McGilp (Eds.), *Lifelong Learning, Participation and Equity.* Dordrecht, The Netherlands: Springer.

Skilbeck, M. (2006b). Participation in learning: Why, what, where and how do people learn? In J. Chapman, P. Cartwright & J. E. McGilp (Eds.), *Lifelong Learning for All: The Challenge to Adults and Communities.* Dordrecht, The Netherlands: Springer.

Smith, D. (1987). Women's Perspective as a Radical Critique of Sociology. In S. Harding (Ed.), *Feminism and Methodology* (pp. 84-96). Indianapolis: Indiana University Press.

Smith, S. (1996). Uncovering Key Aspects of Experience: The Use of In-Depth Interviews in a Study of Women Returners to Education. In E.S. Lyon & J. Busfield (Eds.), *Methodological Imaginations.* UK: Macmillan Press.

Stone, C. (2007). Listening to individual voices and stories - the mature age student experience. *Australian Journal of Adult Education, 48*(2), 63-290.

Swindells, J. (1989). Liberating the Subject? Autobiography and 'Women's History'. In Personal Narratives Group (Ed.), *Interpreting Women's Lives* (pp. 24-38). Bloomington & Indianapolis: Indiana University Press.

Tett, L. (2000). 'I'm working class and proud of it':Gendered experiences of non- traditional participants in higher education. *Gender and Education,12*(2), 183-194.

Thomson, J. (2000). One size fits all?: Gender and the capitalist welfare state. In A.McMahon, J. Thomson & C. Williams (Eds.), *Understanding the Australian Welfare State* (pp. 82-100). Croydon, Vic: Tertiary Press.

Tinto, V. (1993). *Leaving college: Rethinking the causes and cures of student attrition* (2nd ed.). Chicago: University of Chicago Press.

Weeks, W. (2000). Women's Citizenship: Back into the family? In A. McMahon, J. Thomson & C. Williams (Eds.), *Understanding the Australian Welfare State* (pp. 55-81). Croydon, Vic: Tertiary Press.

West, L. (1995). Beyond fragments: Adults, motivation and higher education. *Studies in the Education of Adults, 27*(2), 133-156.

West, L., Hore, T., Eaton, E., & Kermond, B. (1986). *The impact of higher education on mature age students.* Higher Education Advisory and Research Unit, Monash University: Commonwealth Tertiary Education Commission.

Wilson, F. (1997). The construction of paradox? One case of mature students in higher education. *Higher Education Quarterly, 51*(4), 347-366.

Wolf-Wendel, L. E., & Ward, K. (2006). Academic life and motherhood: Variations by institutional type. *Higher Education, 52*, 487-521.

Wolf-Wendel, L., & Ward, K. (2003). Future Prospects for Women Faculty: Negotiating Work and Family. In B. Ropers-Huilman (Ed.), *Gendered Futures in Higher Education* (pp. 111-134). Albany: State University of New York Press.

Yeatman, A. (1994). *Postmodern Revisionings of the Political.* New York: Routledge.

CPSIA information can be obtained at www.ICGtesting.com
Printed in the USA
LVOW03s2138230315

431671LV00005B/163/P

9 781612 290300

Table of Contents

Dedicated to Anne Dunn, 1950-2012; sister, friend and mentor.

To the women who gave us their time and their stories, thank you for your honesty and your desire to encourage and assist others through your own experiences.

To our own families, thank you for your support, your interest and your patience.

First published in Champaign, Illinois in 2012
by Common Ground Publishing LLC
as part of The Learner series

Library of Congress Cataloging-in-Publication Data

Stone, Cathy.
Transformations and self discovery : stories of women returning to education / Cathy Stone and Sarah O' Shea.
p. cm. -- (Learner series)
Includes bibliographical references.
ISBN 978-1-61229-030-0 (pbk : alk. paper) -- ISBN 978-1-61229-031-7 (pdf)
1. Women college students--Australia--Case studies. 2. Adult college students--Australia--Case studies. I. O'Shea, Sarah. II. Title.

LC1571.A8S76 2012
378.19822--dc23

2011050679

TRANSFORMATIONS AND SELF DISCOVERY

STORIES OF WOMEN RETURNING TO EDUCATION

CATHY STONE AND SARAH O'SHEA

Common Ground

TRANSFORMATIONS AND SELF DISCOVERY

STORIES OF WOMEN RETURNING TO EDUCATION

CATHY STONE AND SARAH O'SHEA

comme les stigmates sur le corps du Christ.

Combien y en avait-il comme elle ? Des milliers ? Des millions ? Et leurs rejetons ingrats pullulaient, se reproduisaient de façon exponentielle. Il fallait nourrir toutes ces bouches, chaque jour, trois fois par jour. À la cantine, au restaurant, dans les foyers, les hôpitaux, les maisons de retraite. Des tonnes et des tonnes de viande, de pâtes, de fruits, de légumes qu'ils engloutissaient ou gaspillaient parce que personne ne se soucie de tous ces déchets qui s'amoncellent.

Il jouait avec la lame du couteau à cran d'arrêt. Clac ! Le bruit sec ponctuait chacune de ses respirations. Le mécanisme fonctionnait à la perfection. Clac ! Le mari venait de pénétrer dans la maison, sans un regard pour la malheureuse créature qui s'était donné la peine de l'attendre, comme chaque soir. Clac ! Encore quelques heures de patience et il pourrait enfin régler les comptes, réguler le flux infernal des naissances de cette race dépravée. Clac ! Il anticipait le moment où il leur donnerait le choix. Clac ! L'incompréhension dans leurs yeux. Clac ! L'impossibilité de raisonner. Clac ! La terreur. Clac ! La mort.

Chapitre 1

Avril 2015

La propriété des Salvant-Perret s'étendait sur plus de huit cents hectares avec ses vergers, ses champs fertiles et ses pâturages verdoyants où paissaient de robustes vaches normandes, prisées pour la richesse de leur lait. La famille, seulement composée de trois membres, s'y était installée une vingtaine d'années plus tôt. Des nouveaux riches que l'on avait regardés de travers au début.

Vincent Salvant-Perret exerçait le métier fort lucratif de marchand de biens. Sa femme, la discrète Hélène, avait enseigné le français dans le lycée de la commune jusqu'à son départ à la retraite. Quant à leur fils unique, Louis, après une scolarité chaotique, il avait fini par intégrer les forces de police, où il s'épanouissait, contre toute attente.

À défaut d'être aimés, les Salvant-Perret étaient respectés parce qu'ils employaient une dizaine d'autochtones à plein temps dans leurs champs et leurs fermes. Ils recrutaient des saisonniers parmi les villageois lorsque la période des récoltes pointait son nez. En homme d'affaires aguerri, Vincent avait vite compris qu'il lui fallait engager un régisseur du coin pour fédérer tout son personnel. Auguste Bénichou était cet homme. Un gaillard du Calvados avare en paroles mais à l'esprit et au regard aiguisés. Rien de ce qui se passait au domaine ne lui échappait.

Si Louis avait écouté ses parents, il aurait eu droit au repas dominical chaque semaine dans leur propriété. C'était sans compter sur son ex-femme, qui avait rapidement mis le holà à cette tradition familiale qui les condamnait à sacrifier tous leurs *week-ends* au nom d'une belle-famille dont elle ne partageait aucune valeur.

Depuis leur divorce, Louis avait repris le rythme des dimanches chez ses parents. Il avait besoin de cette routine pour se donner l'impression que l'ordre régnait dans sa vie de flic désormais célibataire. Il ne voyait sa fille qu'un dimanche sur deux et encore, lorsqu'il n'était pas accaparé par son boulot. D'où des rapports plus que tendus avec France-Alix, dont le caractère n'était déjà pas facile du haut de ses quinze ans. Quant aux vacances, qu'il aurait dû passer avec elle à raison d'une période égale à celle de son ex, il n'avait jamais réussi à se libérer plus de trois jours d'affilée en été. À Noël, c'était pire. On aurait dit que tous les malfaiteurs se donnaient le mot pour faire leurs sales coups à ce moment-là.

Anne en avait eu assez de ne pas pouvoir compter sur lui. C'était déjà le cas lorsqu'ils étaient mariés. Mais à présent que les liens étaient rompus, elle ne s'embarrassait plus d'une patience dont elle avait toujours été dépourvue : puisqu'il manquait à tous ses devoirs de père, il ne voyait plus sa fille. Problème réglé.

En ce dimanche d'avril, les fleurs des cerisiers étaient déjà passées. De petites billes vertes s'étaient formées au milieu du feuillage. Bientôt, les enfants des agriculteurs et des familles du coin viendraient s'empiffrer et se tordraient de coliques.

Vincent Salvant-Perret aimait se promener dans la cerisaie après un bon repas de famille. Louis l'accompagnait volontiers depuis quelques mois, ce qui n'avait pas été le cas ces dernières années. Il devenait plus attaché à la terre avec l'âge. Avec les épreuves de la vie aussi, sans doute.

— France-Alix a téléphoné à ta mère mercredi dernier. Elle a besoin d'un nouvel ordinateur.

— Quoi ? Mais je lui en ai acheté un à Noël dernier, qu'est-ce qu'elle en a fait ?

— Elle dit que c'est le fils du nouveau petit ami d'Anne qui s'en sert.

— Anne a un nouveau mec ?

— Ça fait six mois, Louis. Depuis combien de temps n'as-tu pas discuté avec ta fille ?

Celui-ci haussa les épaules en soupirant. Le temps passait trop vite, ou pas assez, tout dépendait du point de vue.

— Je ne sais pas, des siècles sans doute. De toute façon, Alix me traite comme un étranger les rares fois où elle vient à la maison. Elle arrive, elle jette ses affaires sur un fauteuil, s'enferme dans sa chambre pour fumer cigarette sur cigarette, et je ne la vois qu'au moment de manger. Quand elle daigne m'honorer de sa présence.

— Tu devrais faire attention avec cette enfant, essayer d'avoir une vraie discussion avec elle. Vous étiez si proches quand elle était petite ! Qu'est-ce qui s'est passé ? Qu'est-ce qui a changé ?

— Qu'est-ce qui a changé ? Tu me demandes ce qui a changé ? Papa, ouvre un peu les yeux : c'est la situation qui a changé, pas moi ! Tu sais bien que je n'ai jamais été très expansif comme garçon. Et avoir des enfants, ça me faisait flipper. Anne a insisté, j'ai cédé. Mais je l'avais prévenue que mon boulot passait avant le reste. Elle le savait, je ne l'ai pas prise en traître, je ne lui ai pas menti, je ne lui ai jamais caché qui j'étais.

— Mais ta fille n'y est pour rien, Louis. Elle n'a rien demandé à personne et elle est malheureuse.

— C'est très regrettable. Crois-moi, j'ai bien conscience de mes lacunes en tant que père, mais que veux-tu que j'y fasse ? C'est Anne qui en a la garde et Alix me déteste.

— Ne dis pas ça, ce n'est pas la vérité, temporisa Vincent. Tu es son père, elle t'aime. Je pense simplement qu'elle ne sait pas comment te le montrer parce que la situation a dégénéré. Et elle est à un âge où une jeune fille change. Qu'est-ce que tu comptes faire ?

Louis s'arrêta au beau milieu du rang de cerisiers. L'herbe venait d'être tondue, ça sentait bon, et le soleil apparaissait par intermittence entre deux nuages. Il fixa son père, les sourcils froncés.

— Tu ne m'as pas fait la morale depuis l'âge de douze ans, papa. À quoi tu joues exactement ? Alix n'a pas téléphoné simplement pour demander un nouvel ordinateur, n'est-ce pas ? Je n'y crois pas une seconde, ça ne tient pas la route. Alors, crache le morceau : qu'est-ce qui se passe au juste ?

Louis avait raison. Son père passait d'un pied sur l'autre, une main sur sa hanche, l'autre pinçant sa lèvre inférieure entre deux doigts, geste significatif chez lui lorsqu'il était dans l'embarras.

— Elle a demandé à venir vivre avec nous au

domaine.

— Anne est d'accord ? s'étonna Louis.

— Elle ne le sait pas. France-Alix nous a d'abord posé la question pour savoir si on accepterait avant d'en parler à sa mère. Mais la vérité, c'est qu'elle n'ose pas le lui dire. Alors, on avait pensé...

— Que je pourrais demander à Anne de laisser sa fille unique aux bons soins de son ex-belle-famille, en espérant qu'elle ne m'étrangle pas de ses propres mains, termina Louis avec un rire sans joie.

— Écoute, je sais que ce n'est pas facile. Mais pense au bon côté des choses. D'une part, France-Alix te sera reconnaissante de faire cette démarche pour elle. Et d'autre part, avec nous, elle ne manquera de rien. Tu crois que c'est une vie de partager son existence avec une nouvelle famille tous les six mois ? Anne en est à son troisième essai de concubinage depuis votre divorce et France-Alix est au milieu, la pauvre enfant !

— Pourquoi tu ne m'as pas dit tout de suite qu'elle voulait vivre avec vous ?

— Je ne savais pas quelle serait ta réaction. Et France-Alix craignait aussi que tu ne sois pas d'accord.

— C'est ridicule ! Pourquoi m'opposerais-je à ce qu'elle vive avec vous ?

— Je pense qu'elle craignait que tu lui en veuilles de préférer vivre avec nous plutôt qu'avec toi.

Louis se mit à rire franchement, cette fois. D'où venait cette soudaine culpabilité ? Sa fille lui adressait à peine la parole et elle s'inquiétait de froisser sa sensibilité ? C'était à n'y rien comprendre. En même temps, l'adolescence n'était déjà pas simple chez les garçons, il se rendait compte que c'était pire chez les filles. Non seulement Alix avait un comportement arrogant envers ses deux parents, mais au lycée, elle répondait aux professeurs, trichait aux évaluations parce qu'elle n'étudiait pas, séchait les cours et imitait la signature de sa mère afin de cacher ses forfaits. Anne ne la maîtrisait plus, son père encore moins.

— Je parlerai à Anne, finit-il par céder. Mais j'aurais préféré qu'Alix en discute avec moi d'abord. Je sais bien que je suis loin d'être parfait comme père, mais je ne l'ai jamais maltraitée.

— Personne n'a jamais prétendu le contraire non plus, admit son père. Et cesse de te rabaisser tout le temps, tu me fatigues !

Ils marchèrent en silence pendant quelques minutes, chacun absorbé par ses propres pensées. Une horde hurlante d'étourneaux passa en une masse désordonnée au-dessus de leur tête et les volatiles allèrent se poser sur les fils électriques dans le champ voisin. Bientôt, dès que les cerises seraient mûres, ils s'abattraient par centaines et pilleraient les arbres fruitiers.

Alors qu'ils atteignaient le bout du rang, le portable de Louis vibra dans la poche intérieure de son blouson de toile. Il l'en extirpa pour répondre à Antoine Amary, son supérieur. Fini le *week-end :* toute une famille venait d'être retrouvée assassinée à son domicile. C'était pas beau à voir, selon Amary. Seul le plus jeune des quatre enfants avait été épargné.

Louis partit sur-le-champ.

Chapitre 2

Les rubalises avaient été déployées autour du pavillon HLM afin d'empêcher les nombreux curieux et la presse de pénétrer sur le lieu du carnage. La police technique et scientifique avait déjà investi les lieux. Ses hommes, vêtus de combinaisons Tyvek, gantés de latex, chaussés de toile bleue, coiffés de charlottes faisaient un travail de prélèvement minutieux dans chaque recoin de la maison.

Louis montra sa carte à l'agent en faction, qui le laissa passer en soulevant la bande jaune, un léger sourire aux lèvres malgré la tension palpable. Ismaël Al Bakir, son binôme, vint à sa rencontre. Plus loin, il pouvait apercevoir Maud Cortès, leur « apprentie lieutenant », pliée en deux, appuyée contre une voiture de police. Ismaël suivit le regard de Louis :

– Je lui avais dit de ne pas entrer. Elle a vomi partout, juste sur le pas de la porte. Les PTS[1] vont pas apprécier.

Louis fit une grimace de dégoût bien qu'il eût pitié de cette malheureuse Maud, dont c'était la première scène de crime.

---

[1] Police Technique et Scientifique

— Qu'est-ce qu'on a ? demanda-t-il tout en enfilant les gants et les surchaussures que lui tendait Ismaël.

— Une famille de six, dont cinq zigouillés. Le père, la mère, deux ados de quatorze et quinze ans et une gamine de onze ans. Seul le petit dernier y a échappé, mais il est dans un sale état. Il est couvert de sang et va savoir de quel sang il s'agit dans ce merdier ! Si ça se trouve, il en a de chacun des membres de sa famille, le pauvre gosse. Il est dans l'ambulance pour l'instant, on a appelé les services sociaux, ils nous envoient quelqu'un pour le prendre en charge.

— Qui les a trouvés ?

— Un voisin qui passe par là tous les matins quand il va chercher son pain. On l'emmène au poste pour prendre sa déposition. Il a entendu le petit qui se cognait la tête contre la baie vitrée du salon, les mains et le visage en sang. Il n'a même pas essayé d'entrer tellement il a flippé, il a appelé directement la police.

— Des signes d'effraction ?

— On ne sait pas encore. En tout cas, rien de visible au premier coup d'œil : pas de vitre cassée ni de serrure forcée.

— Comment s'appellent les gens qui vivaient ici ?

— Lemonnier. C'est ce qui est écrit sur la boîte à lettres et sur les enveloppes qu'on a trouvées. Fabrice et Coralie. Pour les enfants, on ne sait pas encore.

Maud était blanche comme un linge, elle avait les yeux rougis d'avoir pleuré.

— Comment ça va, Cortès ? s'inquiéta Louis avec sollicitude.

— Mieux, merci. Je suis tellement désolée, je

pensais que je tiendrais le choc, mais mon Dieu ! Ce sont des gosses qu'on a égorgés là-dedans ! C'est monstrueux !

Maud ne retourna pas à l'intérieur. Louis la pria de rester auprès de l'enfant survivant jusqu'à ce qu'un éducateur spécialisé ou n'importe quelle instance adéquate arrive. Ismaël et lui enjambèrent la flaque de vomi de la jeune recrue avant de pénétrer dans l'antre de l'horreur.

L'odeur prit Louis à la gorge. Une odeur de fer et d'excréments qui vous soulevait l'estomac. Le lieutenant avait toujours un flacon de menthol dans sa poche, il en imbiba un mouchoir en papier qu'il appliqua sous son nez. Il répéta l'opération à destination de son coéquipier. Ainsi protégés contre cette puanteur morbide, ils déambulèrent dans le salon, où les corps étaient allongés dans leur dernière posture, baignant dans une mare de sang pas encore coagulé.

Les trois enfants avaient eu la gorge tranchée, la mère avait été éviscérée, et le cadavre du père pendait à une corde que l'on avait accrochée à la rambarde de la mezzanine. Son visage était cyanosé, sa langue sortait de sa bouche entrouverte en un masque d'épouvante. Les entrailles de la femme s'échappaient de son ventre, retombaient sur le parquet flottant. Louis se demanda si les enfants avaient assisté à l'exécution de leur mère ou s'ils avaient été tués avant, échappant à ce funeste spectacle.

Le tableau était insoutenable, même pour deux flics ayant quinze ans d'expérience. La mort faisait certes partie de leur quotidien, mais ce qu'ils avaient sous les yeux dépassait les limites du supportable.

Il y eut tout à coup des éclats de voix derrière eux tandis qu'ils observaient les cadavres en évitant de contaminer la scène. Louis se dirigea vers la porte d'entrée, où une petite brune à l'air furibond brandissait sa carte sous le nez d'un agent en uniforme :

– Je vous dis que je suis le médecin légiste, boudu ! Vous êtes bouché ou quoi ?

Âgée d'une petite quarantaine d'années, un visage poupin au maquillage impeccable, les cheveux courts, une tenue bariolée sous sa blouse, la nouvelle venue portait le nom prédestiné de Françoise Bonnemort. Quand elle parlait, on avait l'impression d'entendre les cigales et de griller au soleil sous un vent d'autan à décorner les bœufs. Son accent du Sud vous soufflait à l'oreille toute l'âme du canal du Midi.

– Demettre a enfin consenti à prendre sa retraite ? la questionna Louis sur le ton de la plaisanterie. Vous êtes la relève ?

Il fit un signe du menton à l'agent, qui la laissa passer.

– Daniel m'a formée, confirma-t-elle. Il m'a aussi mise en garde contre votre après-rasage et il avait raison : vous devez vider une bouteille chaque matin ! Cela dit, étant donné les circonstances, votre flacon de Cacharel est plutôt bienvenu.

Le moins que l'on puisse dire, c'est qu'elle avait de l'aplomb et un sacré tempérament. Ismaël souriait en coin pendant que Louis tentait de déceler l'odeur de son après-rasage en se frottant discrètement la joue. Il avait beau renifler sa main, c'était la puanteur des corps et les effluves de menthol sous ses narines qu'il sentait. Comment avait-elle pu reconnaître la marque de son parfum ?

Il finit par hausser les épaules, ne relevant même pas la provocation sous-jacente. Ce n'était pas dans ses habitudes de chercher le conflit. C'était un pacifique dans l'âme, même si cela lui avait coûté bien des déconvenues. Trop gentil signifiant souvent trop con.

Il préféra s'éloigner des cadavres que Bonnemort examinait l'un après l'autre.

Il n'y avait pas prêté attention en entrant, le regard focalisé sur le tableau de la tuerie, mais cette maison était dans un désordre sans nom. La propreté ne semblait pas non plus une priorité. Les meubles étaient couverts de toute sorte de choses hétéroclites allant d'une brosse à cheveux dont on ne voyait même plus les picots, en passant par un slip d'homme où une trace non équivoque laissait supposer une hygiène plus que déplorable. La poussière n'avait pas dû être faite depuis la construction de la maison.

Et c'était pareil dans toutes les pièces. Trois chambres où les vêtements jonchaient le sol ou débordaient des placards grands ouverts. Pas de bureau dans les chambres des enfants, qui devaient pourtant bien être scolarisés. Louis se demanda où ils faisaient leurs devoirs. Les faisaient-ils, d'ailleurs, dans de telles conditions ? Les lits étaient recouverts de cahiers, de papiers de bonbons froissés, de boîtiers de jeux vidéo. L'on ne distinguait pas le motif des housses de couette tellement elles étaient encombrées. Penser que les enfants dormaient sous ce ramassis d'objets chaque nuit le dépassait.

Louis déambulait souvent seul ainsi sur les lieux où il était appelé à enquêter. Cela lui permettait de se faire une idée de l'atmosphère, de mettre un décor autour des défunts. De cette façon, ils perdaient leur anonymat, ils prenaient une forme au milieu d'une sorte d'*aura* qu'il s'efforçait de ressentir.

Ismaël, plus enclin aux échanges, se chargeait en général d'interroger les témoins ou d'attendre les premières constatations du légiste. Ensuite, ils mettaient en commun les informations qu'ils avaient récoltées.

Après avoir fait le tour des chambres, Louis jeta un coup d'œil à la salle de bains. Là encore, la crasse dominait. Comment pouvait-on espérer se laver dans un endroit aussi répugnant ? L'émail du lavabo était vert à l'endroit où le jet d'eau du robinet coulait. Une épaisse pellicule marron recouvrait chaque paroi autrefois blanche. Quant au bac de douche, il était noirci par la moisissure qui courait sur les murs et au plafond. Les serviettes de bain, posées n'importe où, en tas informes, dégageaient une odeur de fraîchin absolument insoutenable en plus de celle de renfermé. Les tubes de dentifrice n'étaient pas rebouchés, des cheveux et des poils envahissaient chaque centimètre carré des surfaces. Le miroir, au-dessus du lavabo, ne reflétait plus que de vagues contours de la silhouette qui se trouvait face à lui, pauvre objet fatigué d'avoir à renvoyer l'image d'une laideur affligeante.

Un tel laisser-aller pouvait être le signe d'une addiction quelconque de l'un des parents, voire des deux : drogue ou alcool. L'on trouvait ce genre d'intérieur chez des hommes seuls parfois, ou des personnes n'ayant pas toutes leurs facultés mentales ; pas dans une maison où vivaient quatre enfants.

Louis retourna dans la chambre parentale, où il

n'avait fait qu'un tour d'horizon sommaire. Maintenant, il savait ce qu'il devait chercher pour étayer ses suppositions. Se penchant, un genou à terre, il trouva sous le lit une collection de bouteilles de mauvais porto, vides. Dans la penderie, deux autres, pleines celles-ci. Il devait y en avoir d'autres ailleurs. Il continua de fouiner et, dans les toilettes, il dénicha une bouteille du même alcool, cachée dans la bouche d'aération dont les vis ne retenaient plus la grille que par miracle. Il faisait attention à ne toucher à rien, examinait ce qu'il voyait, se servait autant de ses yeux que de son nez. Et ce n'étaient pas les odeurs qui manquaient, ici ! Mais ce n'était rien en comparaison des exhalaisons putrides qui se dégageaient des corps au salon, où il se rendit de nouveau après avoir fait le tour du garage.

Les scientifiques, qui avaient passé l'endroit au peigne fin, étaient à présent sur le départ. Une armée de fourmis blanches prit la direction des véhicules, où elles déposèrent matériel et tenue. Le flash de l'appareil photo bombardait les cadavres maintenant que la légiste avait fait ses premières analyses. Françoise Bonnemort, sa sacoche à la main, était en grande conversation avec Ismaël qui, visiblement, ne pouvait pas en placer une. La voix chantante de son interlocutrice faisait se retourner les têtes. Certains souriaient d'entendre cet accent plein de gaîté au milieu de ce cauchemar.

Lorsque Louis les rejoignit sur le pas de la porte, qui avait été nettoyé, elle se tut et disparut en lui faisant un signe de la tête.

— Elle est pas croyable, cette bonne femme ! fit Ismaël.

— D'origine italienne.

Ismaël leva un sourcil, sceptique.

— Comment tu sais ça, toi ?

— Tu n'auras qu'à vérifier, mais j'ai du flair pour ce genre de trucs. Qu'est-ce qu'elle t'a dit ?

Ismaël lui fit un topo sur ce que Bonnemort avait conclu. L'heure des meurtres se situait vers deux heures du matin. Sans surprise, la cause de la mort des trois enfants était l'exsanguination. L'artère carotide avait été sectionnée à l'aide d'un couteau. La mère avait succombé à l'éviscération et il faudrait attendre l'autopsie pour définir si l'homme s'était pendu. Auquel cas, l'on était en droit de supposer qu'il avait peut-être tué toute sa famille avant de se donner la mort à son tour. Ce n'était malheureusement pas un scénario inédit.

En émettant cette hypothèse à voix haute, Louis vit une faille non négligeable.

— Si c'est le père qui a pété les plombs, pourquoi laisser un des enfants en vie ? En général, dans ce cas de figure, tout le monde y passe. Il faut peut-être envisager qu'on ait un tueur dans la nature.

— Ouais, mais quel genre de taré serait capable d'égorger des enfants ? Et surtout pourquoi ?

— Je ne sais pas, répondit Louis, pensif. L'arme a été retrouvée ?

— On a un couteau, oui. Va falloir attendre qu'il soit analysé par les gars du labo.

Le lieutenant sentait que ce massacre avait une raison d'être, une certaine logique dans son horreur. Son instinct lui disait qu'il leur faudrait creuser au-delà des apparences pour découvrir ce qui avait motivé ces homicides. Pour l'heure, les deux hommes n'avaient plus rien à faire à l'intérieur de la maison, où les experts avaient déjà fait leur travail. Ils contournèrent le jardinet, à la recherche d'empreintes éventuelles de pas au pied des fenêtres. Mais ils ne virent rien de suspect.

Ismaël se chargea d'envoyer des agents interroger les habitants des maisons voisines. Peut-être que l'un d'entre eux aurait vu ou entendu quelque chose. Quoique, à l'heure tardive où le malheur s'était produit, les gens n'étaient pas à la fenêtre à épier leurs voisins mais dans leur lit, en prévision d'une dure journée de labeur. Mais sait-on jamais ?

En attendant, Louis s'approcha de l'ambulance, dont les portes étaient restées ouvertes. L'on distinguait Maud et une jeune femme qu'il ne voyait que de dos, mais dont le jean moulant révélait des formes plus qu'harmonieuses. Il y avait bien longtemps qu'une paire de fesses lui avait procuré autant d'émoi. Et le reste du corps était à l'avenant. Des jambes musclées, fines et élancées, un buste svelte et une chevelure châtain clair, soyeuse et abondante, des anglaises cascadant sur des épaules délicates.

Lorsqu'il fut à quelques mètres, sa collègue descendit du véhicule. Elle avait meilleure mine.

— La spécialiste est arrivée, annonça-t-elle. Elle va accompagner le gamin à l'hôpital. Je lui ai demandé de récupérer ses vêtements pour les confier au labo. Il faudrait qu'on puisse aller chercher des affaires de rechange à l'intérieur.

— Allez-y, Cortès. Et bon courage pour trouver des fringues propres dans ce taudis ! Vous n'aurez qu'à les apporter à l'hôpital avant de nous rejoindre au central. Demandez à un agent de vous faire entrer par la porte de derrière, histoire d'éviter les remontées gastriques intempestives...

Louis adressa un clin d'œil amical à Maud, qui appréciait toujours la délicatesse du lieutenant. Ça ne faisait qu'un mois qu'elle travaillait avec le binôme Louis/Ismaël. Elle avait conscience de la chance qu'elle avait d'être tombée sur deux flics aussi intègres que bienveillants. Ce n'était déjà pas facile d'être une femme dans ce corps de métier, alors si elle pouvait éviter le bizutage en prime, c'était le paradis.

Une fois que Maud eut tourné les talons, Louis toqua à la porte de l'ambulance. L'envoyée des services sociaux, penchée au-dessus du garçon sur le brancard, tourna un visage incroyablement expressif dans sa direction, l'arc parfait de ses sourcils relevé dans une mimique interrogative.

— Chut, fit-elle, un index sur ses lèvres légèrement rosées. On a été obligés de le mettre sous sédatif, il a fini par s'endormir. Vous êtes le lieutenant Salvant-Perret ? Votre collègue m'a informée que vous alliez venir aux nouvelles. Je suis le docteur Agathe Delcourt, psychologue-victimologue-traumatologue-criminologue spécialisée.

Elle lui tendit une main qu'il serra sans réfléchir, subjugué qu'il était par la fraîcheur et l'entrain qui se dégageaient de cette jeune femme.

— Ça fait beaucoup de « -logue » ! Spécialisée en quoi ? demanda-t-il bêtement.

— Dans les pathologies de l'enfant, bien entendu ! Vous vous sentez bien ?

Oui, bonne question : est-ce qu'il se sentait bien ? Heureusement, son portable se mit à vibrer dans sa poche, lui évitant ainsi d'avoir l'air encore plus stupide. Il s'excusa gauchement auprès d'elle et regarda son écran. C'était un SMS de son père qui lui rappelait de joindre son ex au sujet de leur projet d'accueillir France-Alix à la propriété. Du coin de l'œil, Louis observait la psychologue plus en détail. Elle avait un côté décontracté, sportif et raffiné à la fois qui l'émoustillait. Il fallait qu'il se reprenne. De plus, cette histoire avec Anne ne l'enchantait pas du tout. Il répondit un OK laconique à son père avant de se concentrer sur la charmante Agathe, qui ne cachait pas son impatience en tapant du pied, les mains dans les poches de son adorable jean délavé.

— Savez-vous comment s'appelle le gamin ? questionna Louis d'une voix qu'il voulait assurée mais qui partit un peu trop dans les aigus.

— C'est vous le policier, le moucha-t-elle. Il est très choqué, il n'a pas été capable de parler pour l'instant. Je pense que ça va prendre pas mal de temps avant qu'il se remette. S'il s'en remet un jour. Votre collègue m'a décrit la scène à l'intérieur, je vous laisse imaginer l'impact d'un tel cauchemar sur un enfant de six ou sept ans.

— Il faut qu'on sache s'il a vu ce qui s'est passé. S'il a vu quelqu'un tuer sa famille. Est-ce qu'il est blessé ?

— J'ai bien cru que vous ne poseriez jamais la question ! lui reprocha-t-elle ouvertement. Le médecin urgentiste n'a relevé aucune lésion ni aucun hématome. Il n'a pas été frappé, apparemment. Le sang dont il est recouvert est donc celui des membres de sa famille. À vous de tirer vos propres conclusions quant à sa capacité à décrire un carnage pareil ou à en désigner le responsable.

— Je comprends bien que le traumatisme est sévère, dit Louis, qui ne voulait pas perdre la face.

Mais d'après vous, dans combien de temps pouvons-nous espérer l'interroger ?

— Vous ne l'interrogerez pas, monsieur Salvant-Perret, soyez-en assuré. Jusqu'à nouvel ordre, cet enfant est placé sous ma responsabilité uniquement, et je serai la seule personne à communiquer avec lui en dehors du personnel médical. Est-ce que c'est bien clair ?

Elle ne lui laissa pas l'opportunité de répondre, mais lui tendit une carte de visite :

— Voici les coordonnées de l'établissement où j'exerce. Dans un premier temps, l'enfant va rester en observation à l'hôpital général. Ensuite, il sera transféré dans mon service. Je vous dis donc à très bientôt, lieutenant. De mon côté, je sais où vous joindre.

Et elle fit un demi-tour sur elle-même pour remonter dans l'ambulance. Ses cheveux longs effleurèrent la joue de Louis, laissant dans leur sillage un doux parfum sucré et poivré à la fois. Le médecin urgentiste referma les portes du véhicule de secours, qui s'éloigna rapidement. Toutefois, le chauffeur s'abstint de mettre la sirène puisque les jours de l'enfant n'étaient pas en danger.

D'autres *vans* attendaient d'embarquer les corps du reste de la famille massacrée. Une petite foule de badauds stationnait devant le périmètre de sécurité. Plusieurs journalistes commentaient déjà l'événement devant les caméras. Louis s'aperçut qu'il y en avait de plus en plus, notamment des *reporters* de chaînes nationales. L'un d'eux l'interpella par son prénom, ce qui ne manqua pas de l'étonner. Il ne connaissait aucun journaliste, tâchait autant que possible de les éviter. Il ne voyait pas comment l'un d'entre eux aurait pu savoir comment il s'appelait.

Louis s'approcha de l'homme, essayant de mettre un nom sur ce visage un peu androgyne. Mais il avait beau fouiller dans sa mémoire, cet individu ne lui disait rien. Voyant qu'il avait capté l'attention du lieutenant, le journaliste força le passage, main tendue :

— Salut, je suis journaliste pour *Le Petit Parisien*. Toute une famille assassinée avec un seul survivant, c'est plutôt hors du commun. Qu'est-ce que vous avez ? C'est le père qui a tué tout le monde ? Où est-ce qu'ils ont emmené le petit ? Allons, Louis, donnez-moi quelque chose à me mettre sous la dent !

— Est-ce qu'on se connaît ? répliqua le lieutenant, que les manières pour le moins familières du journaliste irritaient.

— Oh ! Un autre que moi pourrait se vexer, mais ce serait de mauvais goût. Disons que nous nous sommes déjà croisés sur une autre affaire sur laquelle vous avez enquêté.

— Je n'ai aucun souvenir de vous et je n'ai aucune information à vous donner. Il y aura une conférence de presse si le procureur le décide, point final.

— Parfait ! se défendit l'homme en levant les mains en signe de reddition. C'était qui, la bombasse dans l'ambulance ?

Cette fois, le journaliste arborait un sourire carnassier qui agaça prodigieusement Louis. D'autant qu'il faisait référence à la troublante Agathe et qu'elle avait marqué son esprit au point que son visage apparaissait régulièrement devant ses yeux, comme une enseigne lumineuse clignotant dans la nuit. Le journaliste n'eut aucun mal à interpréter le changement d'expression sur le visage du lieutenant.

— Je vois, c'est chasse gardée. Son Altesse Salvant-Perret se réserve la belle doctoresse ? C'est ce que nous verrons...

À ce moment-là, l'homme prit son mobile en main et répondit à un appel sans quitter Louis des yeux, le provoquant :

— Ils se dirigent vers l'hôpital général ? Très bien, tu ne les lâches pas d'une semelle, j'arrive.

Il coupa la communication, son sourire de vautour cloué à ses lèvres. Son collègue, un homme encombré d'une caméra qui lui cachait à moitié le visage, filmait la sortie des corps enveloppés dans des housses mortuaires. Alors que Louis s'apprêtait à formuler une repartie bien sentie à l'intention de l'arrogant personnage, Ismaël lui tapota l'épaule.

— Laisse tomber ce *loser,* Louis. Les techniciens ont trouvé quelque chose, on est attendus à l'intérieur.

— Hé ! se rebiffa l'autre homme, j'ai entendu ce que t'as dit, Ben Laden !

Le sang d'Ismaël ne fit qu'un tour à cette appellation. Il attrapa le journaliste par le col et s'exprima à deux centimètres de son visage devenu livide :

— Pour ton information, Ben Laden était né à Riyad en Arabie Saoudite, je suis né à Lyon. Je suis sans doute plus français que toi. Si tu ne retires pas tout de suite ce que tu viens de dire, je te fais coffrer pour insulte à officier dans l'exercice de ses fonctions et pour propos racistes. Et puis peut-être bien pour attentat à la pudeur aussi, vu la couleur de ta misérable cravate.

Louis saisit son coéquipier par le bras, mais il ne put s'empêcher de rire à sa dernière menace. Car à bien y regarder, la cravate du journaliste était en effet fort laide. Ce dernier se dégagea de l'étau des doigts d'Ismaël en se rajustant, mais il n'émit aucune excuse.

— Ça va aller ? fit Louis sur le chemin de la maison encombré d'hommes et de femmes absorbés par le spectacle des allées et venues des policiers.

— Quel con ! Tu devrais pas traîner avec ce type-là, il a une sale tête.

— Je ne traîne pas avec lui. Je suis allé le voir parce qu'il connaissait mon nom, ça m'a juste étonné. Mais t'as raison, c'est un sale con.

Intérieurement, Louis espérait que la jolie Agathe n'aurait pas affaire à ce sale type. Imaginer qu'il puisse la draguer et qu'en plus, elle réponde à ses avances lui donnait des palpitations. Décidément, il n'arrivait pas à enlever cette femme de sa tête.

Dans le salon maculé de sang, de matière fécale et autres réjouissances, il ne restait plus qu'un cadavre que l'on était en train d'emballer.

— C'est par ici, leur indiqua un technicien.

L'homme les emmena dans une des chambres, où tout avait été minutieusement fouillé. Les matelas étaient retournés et, sur l'envers de l'un des deux, la lettre « L » était nettement tracée, au feutre noir indélébile.

— C'est un L ? questionna Ismaël.

— Ou cinquante en chiffre romain, proposa Louis.

— Ou la première lettre du prénom d'un amoureux, renchérit Ismaël.

— C'est peut-être un des gamins qui l'a tracé il y a longtemps, non ?

— Ça vient d'être fait. Approchez-vous, ça sent encore le marqueur à plein nez. Et on n'a trouvé aucun marqueur nulle part pour l'instant.

— Qui dort dans ce lit ? se demanda Louis à voix haute.

— L'un des deux plus grands, répondit le technicien, sûr de son fait. Il cachait des mouchoirs maculés de sperme sous l'oreiller. C'est pas le gamin de sept ans qui s'adonne à la masturbation, d'après moi. Et comme la fille partageait la chambre du plus jeune, la conclusion s'impose d'elle-même. On saura exactement qui dormait où après analyse des prélèvements.

— Ouais, autant dire dans trois mois, râla Ismaël.

Le technicien haussa les épaules en signe d'impuissance et abandonna les deux lieutenants dans la chambre, où trois autres experts opéraient encore, armés d'instruments dont Louis ignorait jusqu'au nom.

— On va pas attendre leurs foutus résultats, dit celui-ci en inspectant les montants du lit où la lettre avait été trouvée. Il chaussa ses lunettes et se pencha, les yeux plissés, observant les moindres stries, les moindres aspérités. Sur la surface du dessous, il remarqua un agglomérat d'une matière indéfinissable, concentré à hauteur du torse du dormeur.

— C'est quoi, ça, d'après toi ? fit Louis.

Ismaël s'approcha puis, du bout de l'ongle, fit sauter un petit bout de la substance.

— Ce sont des crottes de nez, ça, monsieur Salvant-Perret.

— Quoi ? Putain, mais c'est dégueulasse ! s'écria Louis avec un mouvement de recul. Ce gamin a des mouchoirs plein le dessous de son oreiller et il colle ses mickeys sous son lit ! Et comment tu sais que ce sont bien des crottes de nez, d'abord ?

— Ma sœur faisait la même chose quand elle était gamine. Ça rendait ma mère folle de rage.

— Je ne regarderai plus jamais ta sœur de la même façon, répliqua Louis, du dégoût dans la voix.

Néanmoins, il reprit l'examen des montants de bois. Des éraflures dans tous les sens, plus ou moins profondes. Quelques symboles ou dessins au stylo ou au feutre et enfin, gravé profondément vers l'intérieur de la barre, le prénom Enzo.

Du travail de bureau les attendait, à présent.

Automne 2000

Entrer dans une maison au milieu de la nuit ne posait pas de problème. Il s'était entraîné, il avait passé des mois à préparer cette première épuration. Le choix de cette famille en particulier n'était pas dû au hasard, mais il aurait pu opter pour des centaines, des milliers d'autres.

Le foyer voisin, par exemple. D'origine marocaine, père au chômage longue durée, mère sans emploi ne parlant pas un mot de français, et trois enfants dont deux adolescents qui, au lieu d'étudier au lycée où ils étaient inscrits, dealaient du hachich dans les halls d'entrée de la cité voisine. Marché lucratif, le hachich : les deux jeunes gens ne s'habillaient qu'avec des vêtements de qualité, portaient des chaussures de sport de grandes marques, des lunettes de soleil hors de prix. Ils possédaient bien sûr les derniers smartphones *à la mode, même leurs mini-enceintes Bose crachaient un son digne de celui d'une boîte de nuit.*

Mais il ne voulait pas que l'on pense que ce qu'il faisait avait quelque chose à voir avec un acte raciste. Même si ces gens profitaient d'un système à bout de souffle, ils n'étaient pas sa cible ; ils n'étaient pas l'objet de sa haine, de son écœurement, de sa phobie. Ils y contribuaient, comme tous les autres. Comme lui-même aussi, d'ailleurs. Mais si l'on venait à découvrir son œuvre, autant que l'on sache pourquoi c'était nécessaire.

Dans quelques années, le monde prendrait conscience de ses limites. Le réchauffement climatique engendrait d'énormes catastrophes. Cela n'irait pas en s'arrangeant. Et l'homme seul en était responsable. Cette race égoïste, arrogante, destructrice, pervertie, ordurière. Il se sentait investi d'une mission de la plus haute importance pour la planète. Une mission d'épuration. Une mission d'extermination.

Juste avant de monter se coucher, l'employé de la CAT sortait fumer une dernière cigarette dans le jardinet derrière la maisonnette. Il refermait ensuite la porte, mais laissait la clef dans la serrure. La faire tomber sur une simple feuille de papier qu'il glissait ensuite sous la porte était un jeu d'enfant. Les maisons de ce quartier dataient d'avant les années soixante-dix et, comme les locataires ne gagnaient pas suffisamment pour les rénover, les fermetures dont ils disposaient laissaient à désirer. Quant aux propriétaires, ce n'était plus leur problème depuis longtemps. Ils se contentaient de récolter les loyers.

L'homme entra comme s'il était chez lui. Il était déjà venu. Dix fois au moins, sans que les occupants s'en soient jamais aperçus. Pour s'entraîner. Pour être sûr. Pour ne pas avoir de mauvaise surprise le jour où il se sentirait prêt.

Ce jour était arrivé.

La cuisine dans laquelle il se trouvait exhalait des relents de friture et de graillon. La vaisselle n'avait pas été faite depuis des jours, des semaines peut-être. Il y avait des assiettes sales sur la table en formica, ainsi que des gamelles où la nourriture s'accrochait au fond en une pellicule sombre que seul un marteau-piqueur serait parvenu à décoller. Des bols de petit déjeuner trempaient dans une eau verdâtre stagnante où surnageaient des éléments solides indéfinissables. Répugnant !

Poussé par la curiosité, il ouvrit le réfrigérateur. La poignée, ainsi que tout l'espace autour de celle-ci, était couverte de traces de doigts sales. Les empreintes digitales de toute la famille se trouvaient là, ainsi qu'une collection sans doute impressionnante de germes et de microbes, un véritable élevage à ciel ouvert ! L'intérieur n'était pas plus ragoûtant. Les clayettes étaient maculées de toutes sortes de traînées alimentaires. Des cercles collants se superposaient, un citron moisi se désagrégea entre ses doigts gantés lorsqu'il voulut le saisir. Dans le compartiment à légumes, tout en bas, une salade suintait un liquide noir qui dégageait une odeur putride.

Il y avait tout de même du lait encore consommable, quelques yaourts, de la mauvaise épaule de porc sous vide et des œufs. Comment pouvait-on prétendre au nom de « parents » quand on était incapable d'élever correctement ses enfants ? Pourquoi mettre au monde trois bouches à nourrir quand on ne savait pas s'alimenter soi-même ?

La réponse était plus qu'évidente : pour toucher les allocations familiales, bien sûr ! Ces gens-là n'en avaient rien à faire du bien-être de leur progéniture. Seul comptait l'argent qu'ils leur rapportaient chaque mois pour se payer de quoi assouvir leurs misérables addictions.

On verrait bien jusqu'où allait leur indifférence tout à l'heure.

Il attrapa son masque souple dans la poche arrière de son pantalon et, se plantant devant le miroir crasseux du buffet, l'ajusta consciencieusement sur son visage. Une tête de chat noir aux yeux bleus perçants se refléta. Tout le monde aime les chats.

L'homme sourit. Le félin le regarda avec un désintérêt total.

C'est propre, un chat. C'est calme, discret et débrouillard, un chat. Ça n'a pas besoin de l'Homme pour se nourrir. Un chat trouve toujours un abri lorsque les éléments se déchaînent. Et surtout, ça ne lâche jamais sa proie quand il l'a entre ses griffes. Le chat prend son temps, il joue, feint l'indifférence, puis attaque de nouveau jusqu'à épuisement de sa victime. Ensuite vient la mise à mort.

Dès qu'il mettait ce masque, il avait l'impression qu'un poids énorme s'envolait tout à coup. Sa respiration était calme, régulière. Les battements de son cœur allaient au rythme d'un métronome en position adagio. Il se sentait léger, invulnérable, invincible. Un peu comme Batman lorsqu'il enfile son costume de super-héros. Oui, c'est ça, lui aussi était un super-héros. Il allait sauver non pas la veuve et l'orphelin, mais la planète ! Existait-il tâche plus noble ?

À pas de loup, il quitta la cuisine, direction les chambres, son couteau dans la main droite. Ses gants de cuir souple étaient comme une seconde peau, ses chaussures de sport ne faisaient aucun bruit. Tel le félin en chasse, il monta jusqu'à l'étage sans avoir besoin de s'éclairer en aucune façon. Il était déjà venu si souvent qu'il connaissait les lieux parfaitement.

D'abord, il alla dans la chambre de Victor, le plus jeune de la fratrie. Les deux sœurs partageaient la même pièce, juste à côté.

Combien de fois était-il venu se pencher au-dessus du garçon endormi ? Les narines dilatées, il respira le tendre cou du dormeur, remonta le long de sa joue imberbe et enfin s'attarda sur les cheveux en bataille, un peu trop longs pour un garçon. Il sentait encore l'enfant, mais son manque d'hygiène régulière donnait une âcreté particulière à l'odeur de transpiration qui se dégageait de son cuir chevelu. C'était comme sniffer un rail de cocaïne. Cela lui montait au cerveau. Il ferma les yeux en relevant la tête, enivré, exalté.

Sa main droite serrait compulsivement le couteau à cran d'arrêt dont la lame attendait, sagement insérée dans le manche en corne de rhinocéros. Faire claquer la lame en appuyant sur le bouton d'éjection le démangeait. Tout son corps était parcouru de frissons, il avait la chair de poule en imaginant le couteau s'enfoncer dans les chairs. Peut-être pas dans celles du garçon allongé là, mais le sang coulerait à flots cette nuit, ils n'y échapperaient pas.

Tout à coup, après avoir longuement observé la cage thoracique de l'enfant s'abaisser et se soulever au rythme lent de sa respiration, l'homme plaqua sa grosse main sur la bouche de sa victime. Le garçon s'agita doucement d'abord, encore dans les limbes du sommeil. Puis frénétiquement lorsqu'il vit l'énorme tête de chat penchée au-dessus de lui.

Il voulait hurler, mais c'était impossible. D'autant qu'à présent, il sentait la morsure glacée d'une lame sur son cou. Une piqûre qui le transperça d'une douleur telle que deux grosses larmes brûlantes et silencieuses roulèrent sur ses joues pour finir leur course sur le gant de l'homme, qui les absorba. Du sang chaud coula le long de son torse secoué de sanglots terrifiés, son pyjama se colora de rouge. Ses petites mains avaient agrippé les bras de l'agresseur en vain ; sa force d'enfant ne faisait pas le poids contre ce monstre.

– Chut..., lui murmura alors l'homme-chat. Ne fais pas un bruit ou je t'égorge tout de suite dans ton lit et tu ne reverras même pas ton papa et ta maman. Avoue que ce ne serait pas drôle ni pour toi ni pour moi.

Cette voix. Si calme. Si posée alors que la pointe du couteau restait plantée dans le cou de l'enfant. Il y avait une douceur insupportable dans cette voix.

Instinctivement, le garçon sut que les portes de l'enfer dont on parlait au cours de pastorale venaient de s'ouvrir.

Chapitre 3

Avril 2015

Louis Salvant-Perret ne rejoignit son domicile que tard dans la soirée de dimanche. Avec Ismaël, Maud et le capitaine Hébrard, ils avaient fait un *débriefing* au central et s'étaient acquittés des tâches administratives relatives à cette nouvelle affaire.

Ils avaient à présent les identités de chacun des membres de la famille Lemonnier ; ou du moins ce qu'il en restait. En l'occurrence, le plus jeune se prénommait Nathan. D'après le capitaine, Fabrice Lemonnier, pour une raison encore indéterminée, avait assassiné toute sa famille avant de se pendre. Rien ne laissait supposer que quelqu'un d'autre l'ait suspendu à cette corde et les lésions constatées corroboraient cette hypothèse. C'est ce que l'on servit aux médias.

Le fait que le père de famille ait épargné le plus jeune de ses enfants pouvait s'expliquer de plusieurs manières. La plus évidente étant bien sûr l'incapacité émotionnelle de tuer un garçon si jeune. Mais le gamin pouvait tout aussi bien s'être caché au moment de la tragédie.

La présence de la lettre « L » à l'envers du

matelas restait pour l'instant une énigme. En revanche, l'on avait retrouvé sur place le couteau de cuisine ayant servi à éviscérer la mère et peut-être également à égorger les enfants.

À ce stade de l'enquête, on n'avait pas grand-chose. Il faudrait attendre pour obtenir les résultats des autopsies, puis des relevés d'empreintes digitales. Quant aux analyses ADN, c'était encore plus long.

La vue du massacre avait fortement éprouvé la fragile constitution de Maud. Louis n'en menait pas large non plus. Ce n'était pas tous les jours que l'on tombait sur une scène aussi terrifiante. Et heureusement, sans ça, il aurait changé de métier depuis longtemps !

Après une longue douche, il s'accorda une bière, qu'il but à même la bouteille devant la télévision. La chaîne d'informations rendait compte régulièrement du multiple homicide perpétré par un père de famille sans doute victime d'un *burnout* sévère. Plus il entendait cette version, moins il y croyait. Ce n'était qu'une impression, il ne l'avait pas encore clairement formulée à ses collègues, mais il sentait que le coup de folie ne collait pas.

Il se rendit compte qu'il n'avait rien avalé depuis le repas de midi chez ses parents lorsque son ventre se mit à gronder bruyamment. Il faut dire que personne n'avait songé à manger après ce qu'ils venaient de vivre. L'odeur épouvantable qui empoisonnait l'atmosphère chez les Lemonnier était restée accrochée à leurs vêtements jusqu'au central.

À présent qu'il était douché, des affaires propres sur le dos, Louis revenait à la vie. Il se rendit à la cuisine et là, sur le plan de travail, il découvrit une boîte Tupperware avec un petit mot plié sur le couvercle, bien en évidence. Sa mère était passée dans l'après-midi et, se doutant bien qu'il n'aurait pas envie de faire la cuisine un dimanche soir après une intervention, elle lui avait apporté une généreuse part des lasagnes qu'ils avaient mangées le midi.

Depuis qu'il était divorcé, Hélène avait hérité du trousseau de clefs d'Anne. Quand ils étaient mariés, celle-ci n'aurait pas supporté d'imaginer que sa belle-mère pût débarquer comme ça, n'importe quand, chez elle. Et Louis ne l'aurait pas accepté non plus. Les temps avaient changé. Il fallait bien avouer que Louis s'était laissé aller. Il n'avait émis aucune objection à ce que sa mère récupère les clefs de chez lui, parce qu'il savait que cela signifiait davantage de facilité pour lui. Ça lui était égal si les gens parlaient dans son dos, s'ils pensaient qu'être chouchouté par sa maman à trente-huit ans, c'était pas bien reluisant.

La maison était bien trop grande pour un homme seul. Son père avait déniché ce petit bijou d'architecture dix ans plus tôt. Un couple en plein divorce qui souhaitait se débarrasser au plus vite de ses biens en commun. Il avait bradé la demeure. Par conséquent, celle-ci était la propriété de Vincent Salvant-Perret, et cela avait évité à Louis de se retrouver à la rue. S'ils l'avaient achetée avec Anne, la connaissant, elle aurait mené une bataille acharnée pour garder la maison.

Après avoir englouti le plat réchauffé aux micro-ondes, Louis se décida à appeler son ex-femme. Il fallait régler cette histoire à propos de leur fille rapidement. Ce n'est pas de gaîté de cœur qu'il attendit que les sonneries aboutissent. Il appréhendait toujours les échanges avec Anne, et ce depuis si longtemps qu'il se demandait s'ils avaient un jour réussi à communiquer sans se déchirer.

Il tomba sur le répondeur, hésita quelques secondes à laisser un message, se décida finalement.

— Anne, c'est moi, Louis. Il faudrait qu'on parle. À propos de France-Alix. Rappelle-moi, s'il te plaît. Salut.

En appuyant sur la touche de fin d'appel, il se rendit compte que son cœur pulsait de façon anarchique, comme s'il avait omis de respirer pendant qu'il parlait. Quel message pathétique ! Il avait ânonné plus qu'autre chose et se sentait vraiment stupide. Était-il un homme, oui ou non ? Son manque d'assurance dans ses relations personnelles le désespérait, même s'il essayait de garder la face la plupart du temps.

Il jeta un œil à sa montre : vingt-deux heures quinze. Peut-être un peu tard pour une discussion avec son ex.

Mais contre toute attente, son téléphone vibra quelques minutes plus tard et, lorsqu'il décrocha, ce fut une Anne en pleurs à laquelle il dut faire face. Il se sentit encore plus désemparé que si elle avait été en colère.

Elle ne parvint qu'à prononcer son prénom avant d'éclater en sanglots. Louis ne savait absolument pas quoi dire. Il choisit donc de garder le silence, resta en ligne et attendit une accalmie. Il crut percevoir des bruits de portes que l'on referme, un déplacement, puis des sons extérieurs. Elle avait dû sortir de la maison pour pouvoir parler plus librement.

— Qu'est-ce qui se passe, Anne ?

Des reniflements, une respiration entrecoupée de

hoquets.

— Calme-toi, ça va aller, la rassura-t-il presque machinalement. Tu veux que je te rappelle demain ?

— Non, non, ça va...

Il ne lui vint pas à l'esprit que c'était elle qui l'avait rappelé. Cela signifiait donc qu'elle éprouvait le besoin de lui parler.

— Tu sais comment je suis, je m'emporte en moins de deux. Je suis trop impulsive et je m'emballe. Quelle conne !

Et les pleurs recommencèrent de plus belle. Il n'y avait rien d'autre à faire qu'attendre la fin de cette nouvelle salve de sanglots. Bizarrement, Louis respirait plus librement que lorsqu'il avait affronté le répondeur. La détresse d'Anne lui donnait davantage confiance en lui. Il lui parla doucement, la réconforta. Au bout de quelques minutes, cela eut l'air de fonctionner. Elle se reprit. Il l'entendit se forcer à respirer calmement, à fond, plusieurs fois.

— Dis-moi ce qui t'arrive.

— J'ai fait une erreur. D'ailleurs, je passe mon temps à faire des putains d'erreurs !

— Ça ne peut pas être si grave, temporisa Louis.

— Oh si, ça l'est ! Mais qu'est-ce que tu voulais me demander au sujet d'Alix ? Si tu as encore une catastrophe à m'annoncer, vas-y, au point où j'en suis...

— Eh bien, en fait, que dirais-tu si Alix allait vivre chez mes parents pendant quelque temps ? Histoire de lui faire changer d'air et de fréquentations. Tu sais à quel point c'est devenu un problème de...

— OK.

Louis allait continuer lorsqu'il réalisa qu'elle venait de donner son accord. Il n'arrivait pas à croire que cela avait été si facile, si rapide ! Il y eut un silence.

— Ce sera bien mieux pour elle, reprit Anne. Et ça me permettra de faire un peu de ménage dans ma vie par la même occasion.

— Tu as besoin d'un pied-à-terre ? proposa Louis, toujours prêt à rendre service.

Son ex-femme émit un rire sans joie.

— Pourquoi es-tu si gentil avec moi après tout ce que j'ai pu te dire comme atrocités ?

Louis haussa les épaules alors même qu'elle ne pouvait pas voir ce geste de dépit. Il était comme ça, personne ne le changerait à son âge. Ils avaient un enfant en commun et à ce titre, si Anne se retrouvait à la rue, il était hors de question que leur fille ait à en souffrir.

— L'appartement à Boulogne est inoccupé, si tu as envie de te ressourcer. Et pour Alix, tu n'as qu'à me dire quand ça vous arrange et je viendrai la chercher, si tu ne veux pas avoir affaire à mes parents.

— Je crois que je vais accepter, dit Anne d'une petite voix, entre deux reniflements. Je te tiens au courant, Louis, d'accord ? Ça m'a fait du bien de parler à quelqu'un.

— Je n'ai rien fait.

— Au contraire, tu as fait énormément. Merci.

— À bientôt, alors.

Anne coupa la communication sans lui dire au revoir. Elle était bouleversée, Louis ne se formalisa pas. D'autant qu'il n'avait pas eu à batailler comme il l'avait craint.

Dès le lendemain matin, avant de partir au central, il informa sa mère que son ex avait accepté leur proposition sans faire d'histoires. Hélène contacterait le lycée où elle avait enseigné jusqu'à la fin de sa carrière afin d'y inscrire France-Alix. Elle était enchantée à l'idée de s'occuper de sa petite-fille, même si elle avait bien conscience qu'une adolescente à la maison allait bousculer leur quotidien. Quant à Louis, il se disait qu'au moins, il pourrait voir sa fille chaque dimanche, autrement que dans sa maison gigantesque et déserte où ils s'évitaient la plupart du temps.

Quand il arriva dans le bureau du commissaire Amary, Maud avait distribué cafés et croissants à chaque membre de leur petite équipe. Antoine Amary, un homme immense à la peau noire, venait de terminer la lecture des rapports de la veille sur le massacre de la famille Lemonnier. À l'instar du capitaine Hébrard – pour l'instant à moitié somnolent dans un fauteuil de bureau à roulettes –, il penchait pour l'hypothèse du suicide du père de famille qui aurait pété les plombs.

– Le rapport préliminaire des techniciens ne révèle aucune trace d'effraction. Donc *a priori*, personne n'est entré dans cette maison sans y être invité.

– Je peux y jeter un œil ? demanda Louis.

Le commissaire Amary tendit un bras d'une longueur remarquable et Louis se saisit du dossier qui l'intéressait pendant que les autres continuaient de discuter de l'affaire. Le café qu'il sirotait venait du Starbucks. Noir, serré, sans sucre. Maud mettait un point d'honneur à connaître les goûts de chacun d'entre eux. Elle ne se trompait jamais. Depuis que l'enseigne américaine avait ouvert ses portes à deux pas de leurs bureaux, la machine automatique à pièces avait été abandonnée. D'ailleurs, elle avait disparu la semaine précédente, remplacée par une bombonne d'eau minérale.

Louis prit le temps de lire chaque ligne du rapport. Pour le moment, il ne semblait pas y avoir d'autres empreintes que celles des membres de la famille et en effet, aucune issue n'avait été forcée. Rien ne laissait donc supposer qu'un individu se soit introduit chez les Lemonnier pour les massacrer. Aucun objet de valeur n'avait été dérobé. Les appareils électroménagers, vidéo ou électroniques ne manquaient pas à l'appel. Même l'argent liquide, les chéquiers et les cartes de crédit du couple avaient été retrouvés.

— Vous allez vous pencher sur la vie de tous les Lemonnier un par un, annonça Antoine Amary. Vous connaissez la musique, chacun sait ce qu'il a à faire. Maud, vous vous occupez de savoir où et quand le petit Nathan est transféré. Il est encore à l'hôpital ?

— Oui, Monsieur, répondit Maud, de la déférence dans la voix. Je n'ai pas pu le voir, mais hier, il était en chambre sécurisée. Il y avait un gardien de la paix devant sa porte.

— C'est moi qui ai donné l'ordre que le gamin soit sous protection jusqu'à ce qu'on soit sûrs qu'il n'est pas menacé. Par contre, dès qu'il sera en centre spécialisé, il sera impossible de garder un œil sur lui. Concentrez-vous sur le père de famille. Qu'est-ce qui peut justifier qu'il en soit arrivé à ces extrémités ? Je veux tout savoir : ses relations avec ses collègues de boulot, s'il avait une ou plusieurs maîtresses, s'il buvait ou se droguait, s'il avait des dettes de jeu. Qui il fréquentait. Son passé, même lointain, vous n'oubliez rien.

Ismaël était déjà debout, son gobelet blanc et vert

à la main, les lèvres brillantes à cause du beurre des croissants dont il s'était empiffré. Maud rassemblait les miettes qu'ils avaient fait tomber sur le lino, du bout du pied, qu'elle poussait en direction de la corbeille. Elle avait toujours ce genre de délicatesse. Elle pensait au travail des autres, qu'elle tâchait de faciliter autant que faire se peut.

Une fois dans leur bureau commun, le trio se mit au travail. Louis se pencha sur l'aspect professionnel de la vie de Fabrice Lemonnier pendant qu'Ismaël recherchait des renseignements sur son enfance, ses parents, les écoles qu'il avait fréquentées. Maud prévoyait de fouiller dans ses comptes. C'est dingue tout ce que l'on peut apprendre de quelqu'un en examinant ses dépenses ! Les poubelles sont aussi une source incroyable d'informations sur les habitudes des gens. Il n'était d'ailleurs pas exclu qu'ils aient à mettre le nez dans les ordures de la famille Lemonnier à un moment ou à un autre. La maison était sous scellés, tout ce qui se trouvait à l'intérieur n'en bougerait pas, y compris les containers d'ordures.

Louis aimait particulièrement les débuts d'enquêtes, lorsqu'ils ne disposaient que de très peu de renseignements, que tout restait à découvrir. C'était comme regarder chez les gens par le trou de la serrure avant d'ouvrir la porte en grand et de faire entrer la lumière.

Ismaël leur apprit que Fabrice Lemonnier, âgé de quarante-quatre ans, était né le 19 janvier 1971 à Lille. Son père exerçait le métier de charpentier. Quant à sa mère, elle avait fait des ménages pour diverses sociétés. Tous deux étaient décédés en 2001 dans un accident de voiture. Fabrice avait eu un jeune frère, mais ce dernier était également mort à l'âge de treize ans, d'une leucémie. À première vue, il n'avait donc plus de famille.

L'homme ne devait pas briller scolairement parlant, il avait été envoyé en préapprentissage dès la fin du collège. Il n'avait jamais mis les pieds dans un lycée, sauf peut-être pour en refaire le toit.

— Pas un sportif non plus, ajouta Ismaël. Aucune inscription nulle part, même pas à l'union sportive de son collège.

— En même temps, l'UNSS, c'était pas franchement réjouissant, fit remarquer Louis. Passer ses mercredis après-midi dans des gymnases pourris !

— Moi, j'étais en club, je faisais du foot. J'imagine que toi, tu suivais ton père sur le *green ?*

Et il éclata de rire.

Chambrer Louis à propos de son enfance de nanti était le grand jeu au central. Quand on travaillait avec des flics, il fallait s'attendre à ce que son passé ne reste pas derrière soi très longtemps. Tout le monde savait qu'il habitait un pavillon dans un quartier huppé de la capitale et qu'il avait la jouissance non seulement d'un appartement à Boulogne, mais aussi d'une villa à Deauville. Bien sûr, aucun de ces biens immobiliers ne lui appartenait en propre, mais il en hériterait forcément un jour. Il était surnommé le prince du central par tous ses collègues. Ce sobriquet lui avait collé à la peau dès le début de sa carrière. Les premières années, cela le mettait très mal à l'aise, mais à la longue, il avait compris que c'était plutôt dans un esprit bon enfant. Alors il laissait dire.

Par ailleurs, lorsque le commandant Fontaine s'était séparé de sa deuxième femme, Louis lui avait généreusement proposé d'occuper l'appartement de Boulogne sans rien lui demander en retour. Il était aussi arrivé qu'il prête la villa normande à un collègue ou deux pour le *week-end*. En résumé, Louis avait la réputation d'être grand prince, d'où son surnom, et on l'appréciait pour ça.

Il ne faisait pas l'étalage de la fortune de ses parents. C'étaient les autres qui y faisaient référence, pas lui. Parce que pour être tout à fait honnête, il portait des vêtements basiques, rien sur lui n'indiquait qu'il venait d'une famille aisée, si ce n'est une sorte d'*aura* naturelle sur laquelle il n'avait aucun contrôle.

Bien sûr, il y avait toujours des jaloux, des mauvaises langues qui disaient dans son dos que c'était facile quand on n'avait pas de loyer ou de crédit à payer ni de location d'été. Il n'avait pas besoin de se priver pour passer ses vacances à la mer, tout lui tombait du ciel ! Ceux-là n'étaient que des envieux qui ne le connaissaient pas. Car en fait de vacances, s'il se permettait une semaine au mois d'août, il la passait le plus souvent chez lui, à Paris.

— Pour ta gouverne, je faisais du tennis, répondit Louis d'une voix parfaitement maîtrisée.

— J'ai vérifié ses antécédents, intervint alors Maud.

Louis et Ismaël se tournèrent vers elle, dans l'expectative, mais la jeune enquêtrice n'avait pas l'air décidée à continuer. C'était frustrant.

— Eh bien ? Développe ! l'encouragea Ismaël.

— Oh oui, pardon ! Je terminais de lire, voilà. En fait, à part des infractions au Code de la route, il n'y a rien de vraiment remarquable. Excès de vitesse, feu rouge grillé, véhicule en stationnement interdit. Il n'a plus que quatre points sur son permis et je ne vois aucune inscription à un stage de récupération de points.

Maud s'interrompit, mais Louis se rendit compte que quelque chose retenait son attention sur l'écran d'ordinateur. Elle mit quelques secondes avant de reprendre la parole.

— Dites-nous tout, Maud, qu'y a-t-il d'autre ?

— Un accident qui date d'il y a quinze jours. Lemonnier était en tort, il est rentré dans l'arrière de la voiture d'un certain Christian Blanchard, avec qui il s'est battu. J'ai le procès-verbal sous les yeux. Lemonnier a prétendu que l'autre automobiliste avait freiné sans aucune raison et n'a pas voulu reconnaître qu'il était en tort. Il a mis son poing dans la figure de Blanchard et le gars s'est retrouvé à l'hôpital. On lui a fait six points de suture à l'arcade gauche.

— Une plainte a été déposée ?

— Non, Blanchard n'a pas porté plainte.

— Bizarre, fit Ismaël. Le mec se fait défoncer la voiture et la tête par la même occasion et quoi ? Il tend l'autre joue ?

— Dans quel état était la voiture de Blanchard ?

— Apparemment, c'est juste le pare-chocs qui a pris. Les dégâts les plus importants étaient sur la voiture de Lemonnier. Je suppose que c'est ça qui l'a mis en colère. Non seulement il allait devoir payer pour les dommages causés sur la voiture de Blanchard, qui n'avait presque rien, mais en plus sur la sienne. L'officier qui a rédigé le PV précise que Lemonnier était très virulent, ils ont failli l'embarquer.

— Il serait peut-être intéressant de parler à ce

Christian Blanchard ? fit Louis à personne en particulier. Je serais curieux de savoir ce qui l'a retenu de porter plainte. Lemonnier l'a peut-être menacé. Notez-nous les coordonnées de ce monsieur, Maud, et convoquez-le au poste le plus rapidement possible.

— Je m'en occupe. Et ensuite, je remets le nez dans les comptes de Lemonnier.

La matinée passa à toute vitesse. À l'heure du déjeuner, Maud rentra chez elle tandis qu'Ismaël et Louis descendaient prendre un plat du jour au troquet d'en face.

— Pourquoi tu t'intéresses à ce Blanchard ? questionna Ismaël au moment des desserts. Tu crois que le gars serait venu décaniller toute la famille Lemonnier juste à cause d'un malheureux accident ?

— Et d'un coup de poing qui l'a conduit à l'hôpital, précisa Louis. Il y en a qui tuent pour moins que ça. Si tu ne veux pas de tes cigarettes russes, je les veux bien.

— Pourquoi je ne voudrais pas de mes cigarettes russes ?

— La dernière fois qu'on en a eu avec nos glaces, tu as dit que tu n'aimais pas ça.

— J'ai dit ça ?

Louis considéra Ismaël en fronçant les sourcils, cherchant à savoir s'il se moquait de lui.

— Par respect pour la religion de ta famille, je ne te demanderai pas si c'est du lard ou du cochon, finit-il par lâcher, un petit sourire aux lèvres.

Les deux hommes se mirent à rire. Ismaël, dont la famille était d'origine marocaine, était le seul Maghrébin de la connaissance de Louis qui mangeât du saucisson. De plus, comme il était marié à une

Basque, les charcuteries faisaient partie de la culture de sa femme.

— OK, tu peux prendre ces infâmes gâteaux. Mais pour ce qui est de notre affaire, tu ferais mieux de me dire le fond de ta pensée. Tu crois que quelqu'un est entré dans la maison des Lemonnier et les a tous tués ? Ça ne colle pas avec le suicide du père.

— On n'en sait encore rien. Quand on aura le rapport du légiste, on pourra avancer des hypothèses plus solides. Le problème, c'est qu'avec quatre corps à autopsier, ça va prendre un max de temps. D'ailleurs, qui se dévoue pour y assister ? On ne peut raisonnablement pas envoyer Cortès, elle va nous claquer entre les doigts.

— OK, je m'y colle, céda Ismaël. Mais tu ne crois pas que le père soit responsable de la tuerie et qu'il se soit pendu après ?

— Parce que tu y crois, toi ? Quel père de famille égorgerait ses propres enfants au couteau ? Dans la plupart des massacres commis par l'un des membres d'une famille, le coupable utilise un pistolet ou un fusil, pas une arme blanche. Le couteau implique une proximité avec la victime incompatible avec ses liens familiaux, tu comprends ? Et puis aller ouvrir le ventre de la mère de ses enfants, franchement, quel genre de monstre ferait une chose pareille ? Et peut-être même sous les yeux de ses gosses ! Non, je n'y crois pas.

Ils dégustèrent leurs boules de glace en silence pendant quelques minutes. Dehors, il s'était mis à pleuvoir. Louis détestait la pluie, surtout en ville. À la campagne, c'était différent. Les gouttes qui tombaient sur les feuillages avaient un bruit doux et apaisant. L'eau faisait ressortir les odeurs de terre et d'humus. Tandis qu'ici, l'on n'entendait que les sons discordants des gouttières débordant, des tôles de voitures frappées par l'ondée. Les gens vous éborgnaient avec leurs parapluies, les voitures vous éclaboussaient en roulant dans les caniveaux saturés, les rues pavées étaient dangereusement glissantes, les citadins nerveux et agressifs.

— Ton raisonnement se tient, approuva Ismaël. Mais dans ce cas, ça voudrait dire que ton tueur présumé a convaincu le père Lemonnier de se pendre. Sacré pouvoir de persuasion, quand même !

— Il est facile de maquiller un meurtre en suicide, et tu le sais aussi bien que moi. Et puis tu sais, quand on menace tes enfants, je crois que tu serais prêt à faire n'importe quoi pour leur sauver la vie. Tu verras quand vous aurez des gosses avec Jade.

— Ben en fait, maintenant que tu en parles... Je voulais attendre un peu pour l'annoncer, mais Jade est enceinte.

Le sourire radieux d'Ismaël fut contagieux. La joie de cette nouvelle se transmit à Louis, qui le félicita avec effusion. Le futur père pria néanmoins son coéquipier de garder ça pour lui. Jade n'avait pas donné son feu vert, c'était trop tôt, elle préférait attendre le cap des trois mois et ils feraient ensuite une fête chez eux avec les collègues.

Louis se sentit honoré d'être le seul dans la confidence. Quand ils sortirent dans la rue, sous une averse soutenue et sans parapluie, cette météo déplorable fut moins dure à supporter, du coup.

Chapitre 4

Dans son petit bureau du service psycho traumatologie infantile, Agathe Delcourt étudiait le dossier médical du jeune Nathan Lemonnier. Arrivé la veille en ambulance, l'enfant avait été placé en chambre sécurisée, avec caméra de surveillance et personnel soignant ayant une vue permanente sur le patient. Tout un côté était fait de vitres en plexiglas, comme dans certains services de réanimation des hôpitaux.

L'institut Saint-Jean était un des rares établissements du pays à posséder un service spécialisé dans les traumatismes sévères liés à des événements violents chez l'enfant. Il n'était pourvu que d'une dizaine de chambres, dont seulement trois étaient occupées pour l'heure. Le personnel était trié sur le volet. Marie-Thérèse Bosquet, directrice de l'institut, tenait à la réputation irréprochable des lieux, acquise grâce à son père, qui occupait la direction avant elle.

Les murs des locaux appartenaient au diocèse du Calvados. Une des parties de l'institut était d'ailleurs encore habitée par la congrégation des sœurs de Saint-Jean. Le bâtiment possédait sa propre chapelle, où une messe était célébrée chaque soir à dix-neuf heures par le curé de la paroisse, le père Pondillac.

Ainsi installés non loin des côtes de la Manche, le personnel et les pensionnaires bénéficiaient de l'air marin, mais aussi du climat pluvieux propre à la Normandie. De sa fenêtre, Agathe avait une vue imprenable sur le magnifique parc, sur le jardin potager entretenu par les sœurs et, au-delà, sur les pâturages verdoyants et vallonnés.

Depuis cinq ans qu'elle exerçait à l'institut Saint-Jean, c'était la première fois qu'elle se retrouvait confrontée à un cas aussi extrême que celui du petit Nathan Lemonnier.

La plupart des enfants dont elle s'occupait étaient victimes d'inceste à caractère violent ou d'actes de barbarie de la part de leurs parents. Une fois, elle avait eu affaire à un garçonnet à qui les parents administraient des doses hallucinantes d'héroïne afin d'avoir la paix lorsqu'ils organisaient des parties de défonce qui tournaient à l'orgie. Une monstruosité. Mais grâce à ses efforts soutenus et avec l'aide du personnel accompagnant, l'enfant avait pu être sauvé. Il avait été confié à une famille d'accueil qu'Agathe avait choisie personnellement. Il coulait à présent des jours heureux loin de ses parents biologiques qui, eux, étaient emprisonnés pour de nombreuses années.

Si Agathe avait été sélectionnée pour le poste de pédopsychologue spécialisée à l'institut Saint-Jean, c'était d'abord pour ses brillants résultats à la faculté, où elle avait terminé major de sa promotion. Elle avait ensuite suivi une spécialisation dans un hôpital réputé avant de postuler auprès de madame Bosquet.

Cette dernière avait été charmée par la vivacité

d'esprit de sa future recrue, mais aussi par ses idées novatrices en matière de psychologie enfantine. Sa douceur et sa beauté ne faisaient qu'ajouter à ses qualités professionnelles. À trente-deux ans, Agathe Delcourt faisait se retourner les hommes sur son passage, bien qu'elle feignît de l'ignorer.

L'on ne lui connaissait aucun petit ami. Sur sa fiche de candidature, il était spécifié : « célibataire sans enfant ». Très réservée, elle ne laissait rien filtrer de sa vie privée sur son lieu de travail, et elle maintenait une telle distance envers ses collègues que nul n'aurait osé s'aventurer à lui poser des questions d'ordre personnel.

Elle s'investissait totalement avec les enfants dont elle avait la charge, passait le plus clair de son temps à l'institut, ne comptant pas ses heures. Il était évident pour tout le monde que la jeune psychologue aimait profondément son métier et surtout les enfants.

Après avoir parcouru son dossier avec attention, Agathe décida de se rendre dans la chambre de Nathan Lemonnier. Exténué, le garçon n'avait pas quitté le lit de la journée. Quand elle entra, il avait le visage tourné vers la fenêtre aux stores à demi baissés, le regard fixé sur un point indéterminé. La lumière était diffuse. Comme le temps était très nuageux, une atmosphère un peu mélancolique flottait dans la pièce.

Nathan n'avait pas émis le moindre son depuis la tragédie. Agathe avait refermé la porte vitrée derrière elle, sans faire de bruit. Elle s'approcha à pas lents mais réguliers en direction du lit. De profil, les traits de l'enfant étaient très fins. Un nez minuscule, un ovale parfait, un petit menton rond, de longs cils noirs et une chevelure qui lui tombait dans les yeux ; deux billes aussi sombres que l'enfer dans lequel il venait de tomber.

Agathe savait que les mots manquaient aux jeunes victimes. Que la souffrance, le souvenir abominablement vivace de ce qu'elles avaient vécu ne pouvait s'extérioriser par le discours comme chez les adultes. Il faudrait aller creuser tout autour du mal par le biais de dessins, de jeux, d'histoires que la thérapeute choisirait de lire à l'enfant.

Pour l'instant, la jeune femme se contenta de venir près de Nathan, quoique à une distance calculée pour qu'il ne se sente pas agressé, sans parler d'abord. Elle l'observait avec toute la bienveillance dont elle était capable. Elle était convaincue que tout être vivant dégage des ondes, positives ou négatives, qui se transmettent sous forme d'énergie dans l'air que l'on respire, influant sur notre perception de l'autre.

Nathan savait qu'elle était là, même s'il n'avait pas bougé d'un millimètre. Quelque chose dans la pièce s'était modifié qu'Agathe ressentait jusqu'au plus profond d'elle-même.

Elle fit le tour du lit, sans quitter l'enfant des yeux et enfin, elle lui parla d'une voix pleine de douceur, destinée à affirmer sa présence avec lui :

— Je m'appelle Agathe. On va passer un peu de temps ensemble, toi et moi. Pas trop longtemps, j'espère, sinon on risque de se lasser l'un de l'autre.

Même si le garçon ne la regardait pas, elle sourit. Et ce sourire se retrouva dans sa voix lorsqu'elle continua :

— Tu ne seras pas obligé de parler si tu n'en as pas envie. Et ce qu'il y a de bien, c'est qu'ici, tu ne seras pas obligé d'aller à l'école non plus. À moins que tu n'en émettes expressément le souhait, bien sûr... Mais tu sais, je me suis occupée de beaucoup d'autres enfants de ton âge et aucun d'entre eux ne s'est jamais plaint de ne pas pouvoir aller à l'école.

Tout en parlant, Agathe s'était positionnée près du visage de Nathan, de façon qu'il l'ait dans son champ de vision. Ainsi, même s'il ne voyait pas ses traits, il pouvait distinguer sa silhouette et, plus important encore, il percevait parfaitement le timbre de sa voix. Or, pendant plusieurs jours, voire plusieurs semaines ou mois, Agathe sentait que le son de sa propre voix serait tout ce qu'elle entendrait face à ce garçon perdu.

Ce qui l'inquiétait le plus, c'était qu'il n'avait pas versé la moindre larme. Plusieurs explications pouvaient être avancées mais, à ce stade, aucune conclusion n'était envisageable.

Elle s'était renseignée auprès des services de police : Nathan se retrouvait seul au monde après le massacre de ses parents et de ses frères et sœurs. Pas de grands-parents ni d'un côté ni de l'autre, pas l'ombre d'un oncle ou d'une tante nulle part. Personne qui pût s'inquiéter de lui ou donner des indications quant à son tempérament, ses habitudes, ses goûts. Il faudrait qu'elle mène sa propre enquête auprès des enseignants de l'école qu'il fréquentait, éventuellement des commerçants du quartier que la famille avait habité.

Parfois, elle se faisait l'effet d'un détective privé lorsqu'elle partait en expédition, à la chasse aux informations sur ses petits patients. Tous les psychologues ne faisaient pas ce genre de démarches, mais elle était comme ça, Agathe. Afin d'optimiser ses méthodes, elle n'hésitait pas à sortir des sentiers battus.

En règle générale, il y avait toujours un ou plusieurs membres de la famille susceptibles de l'éclairer quant à ses petits pensionnaires. Nathan était un cas exceptionnel à tous les niveaux. Plus elle observait son visage figé, plus elle était persuadée qu'il lui donnerait du fil à retordre. Un enfant de sept ans qui ne pleurait pas, cela n'augurait rien de bon. Mais elle était prête.

Lors de cette première rencontre, elle resta une bonne demi-heure dans la chambre de Nathan. Elle s'installa sur la chaise à son chevet et lui expliqua patiemment comment se dérouleraient désormais ses journées à l'institut Saint-Jean. Elle ne lui parla pas comme à un enfant, mais bel et bien comme à un jeune adulte qui comprend parfaitement ce qu'on lui dit. Car malgré son mutisme, elle sentait qu'il l'écoutait, qu'il ne perdait rien de ses paroles au débit régulier.

Les activités qui lui seraient proposées, les heures de repas, de promenade, de jeux, de temps libre, de thérapie, de coucher ; Agathe lui exposa son futur emploi du temps sans le quitter du regard une seule seconde.

Cela n'avait l'air de rien, mais lorsqu'elle rejoignit son bureau, elle était vidée. Sa concentration avait été telle qu'elle avait l'impression d'avoir passé un oral d'examen. Elle avait fait attention à chaque mot qu'elle avait utilisé, à chaque tournure de phrase, au ton de sa voix, à l'expression de son visage. Car tout avait de l'importance lors d'un premier contact. Elle ne laissait rien au hasard. Surtout pas avec un enfant ayant vécu un tel choc émotionnel.

Dans le dossier qu'elle avait créé dans son ordinateur, elle nota ses constatations préliminaires. Le caractère exceptionnel de la situation de cet enfant la touchait particulièrement. Il était difficile de mettre ses émotions de côté. C'était la première fois qu'elle avait affaire à un cas aussi délicat.

Son téléphone vibra sur son bureau. Elle s'interrompit dans son compte-rendu, posa les yeux sur l'écran. Numéro inconnu. Elle ressentit un léger malaise, mais prit quand même la communication.

Personne ne répondit à ses « Allô » répétés. On n'entendait absolument rien. Aucun bruit de fond, aucune respiration. Puis la personne raccrocha et l'écran d'accueil, avec ses icônes familières, réapparut.

Depuis quelque temps, elle recevait régulièrement ce genre d'appel avec personne au bout. Elle n'aimait déjà pas le téléphone, alors ces intrusions silencieuses dans sa vie commençaient à lui taper sur le système. Cela se produisait environ une fois tous les deux jours. Fallait-il signaler le désagrément à son opérateur ? Ou à la police, peut-être ? Elle se promit d'y réfléchir plus sérieusement si cela se reproduisait.

Pour l'heure, elle tâcha d'oublier l'incident et se replongea dans l'analyse de sa première entrevue. Les jours prochains allaient être décisifs. Elle devait programmer une méthodologie précise, mais suffisamment souple pour lui laisser une marge de manœuvre. On ne pouvait jamais vraiment savoir à quoi s'attendre avec les enfants. Ils étaient imprévisibles. C'est sans doute pour cette raison qu'elle les aimait tant.

On frappa à sa porte. Fanny, l'une des aides-soignantes, passa la tête dans l'entrebâillement, sourire timide aux lèvres, la crainte de déranger se lisant dans son regard.

— Mademoiselle Delcourt, le petit Nathan aurait bien besoin de vêtements de rechange. Qui devons-nous contacter ?

— Oui, vous avez raison. Je m'en occupe, ne vous inquiétez pas.

Dès qu'elle eut formulé sa requête, Fanny eut l'air soulagé. Elle avait toujours peur de mal faire, n'était pas sûre d'elle alors qu'en réalité, tous s'accordaient à dire qu'elle faisait un excellent travail. Comme Fanny semblait attendre, Agathe s'inquiéta :

— Il y a eu un problème ?

— C'est-à-dire qu'il s'est endormi et qu'il a encore fait pipi. C'est arrivé cette nuit aussi. On lui a mis une couche.

Agathe se demanda si l'énurésie était un phénomène récurrent chez Nathan ou s'il s'agissait d'une réaction traumatique.

— A-t-il parlé ou crié pendant son sommeil ? questionna la psychologue.

— Il était très agité, mais il n'a pas crié ni pleuré.

Agathe prit quelques notes supplémentaires à ce sujet, puis demanda s'il y avait autre chose dont Fanny aurait voulu l'informer. Comme ce n'était pas le cas, l'aide-soignante se retira sans faire le moindre bruit en refermant la porte alors que la thérapeute décrochait le téléphone sur son bureau. Elle composa le numéro du commissariat qui était sur l'affaire Lemonnier.

Au standard, après s'être présentée, elle demanda à parler au responsable de l'enquête. Elle fut mise directement en relation avec le commissaire Amary.

Après les politesses d'usage, Agathe entra dans le vif du sujet. Elle avait besoin que quelqu'un lui apporte davantage de vêtements pour Nathan et elle désirait savoir s'il y avait des traces d'urine dans le lit du petit garçon.

— Peut-être pourrais-je avoir un double du rapport des experts dès que vous l'aurez ?

— Je crains que ça ne soit pas possible, mademoiselle Delcourt, je regrette. Mais je vais demander que l'on vous donne le renseignement que vous souhaitez dans les plus brefs délais. Il faut encore attendre, ce genre de chose prend du temps, vous le comprenez, n'est-ce pas ? Ce n'est pas la première fois que vous travaillez avec la police, j'imagine.

— Certes, concéda Agathe. J'attendrai. En revanche, pourriez-vous m'envoyer les vêtements dans la journée, s'il vous plaît ? Je ne veux pas vous ennuyer avec des considérations aussi triviales, mais étant donné ce qu'il a vécu, cet enfant aurait bien besoin d'avoir avec lui des choses qui lui sont familières. Des vêtements d'une part, mais si vous pouviez aussi lui apporter quelques jouets provenant de sa chambre, un ours en peluche ou un doudou quelconque, je ne sais pas ?

— Bien sûr, je vous envoie un de mes lieutenants aujourd'hui même, lui assura le commissaire Amary. Et je vais aussi vous donner le numéro de ma ligne directe, ça vous évitera de passer par le standard. Vous avez de quoi noter ?

Agathe fut sensible à cette attention. Déjà, lors de sa première intervention, le jour du drame, les deux officiers de police auxquels elle avait eu affaire lui avaient fait une excellente impression. La jeune femme, Maud Cortès, avait été d'une gentillesse et d'une douceur inattendues dans un corps de métier où une certaine dureté de caractère était de mise. Quant au grand ténébreux qui l'avait badée et dont elle avait oublié le nom, elle l'avait trouvé bien différent des officiers auxquels elle s'était déjà frottée. La bienveillance de leur commissaire avait peut-être déteint sur toute l'équipe ?

— L'un de vos hommes a déjà ma carte si vous avez besoin de me joindre, termina Agathe après avoir inscrit le numéro du commissaire. Merci pour tout.

Chapitre 5

Lorsque le commissaire Amary fit part à son équipe des requêtes de la psychologue, Louis Salvant-Perret se proposa aussitôt pour se rendre à l'institut Saint-Jean. Maud l'accompagnerait.

Le sourire en coin d'Ismaël trahissait ses pensées. La jolie pédopsy avait tapé dans l'œil du lieutenant, son empressement à la revoir était plus que révélateur. Cependant, il ne fit aucune remarque et Maud ne sembla pas soupçonner quoi que ce soit. Elle était enchantée de quitter la capitale pour l'air plus pur de la Normandie.

Avant de se rendre à l'institut, ils se munirent d'un grand sac de sport que Louis gardait dans son coffre de voiture et firent une halte au domicile des Lemonnier. Ils brisèrent les scellés provisoires, il leur suffirait de les confectionner de nouveau après leur passage.

— Maud, ça ne vous ennuie pas de vous occuper des habits et des jouets du gamin ? Il me semble que vous serez meilleur juge en la matière. De mon côté, je vais vérifier s'il y a des traces d'urine sur son matelas.

— Bien sûr, pas de problème, dit-elle en se saisissant du sac que le lieutenant lui tendait. C'est quand même drôlement sinistre de pénétrer comme ça dans une maison où de telles horreurs ont été perpétrées.

— Vous vous y ferez, la rassura Louis tandis qu'ils entraient dans la chambre de Nathan et de sa sœur.

— Que le ciel vous entende ! Je voulais faire médecine au départ. Le problème, c'est que j'ai les boyaux qui se retournent dès que je vois du sang.

— Oui, j'ai cru remarquer, ironisa Louis.

Maud eut un rire cristallin qui se répercuta dans la pièce sens dessus dessous. L'on ne pouvait pas poser un pied sans marcher sur un vêtement, un stylo, un livre de classe ou une cannette de soda vide.

Pendant plusieurs minutes, ils travaillèrent chacun de leur côté, silencieusement. Louis ne remarqua aucune auréole suspecte sur le matelas de l'enfant. *A priori*, faire pipi au lit n'était pas dans ses habitudes. L'analyse des prélèvements effectués par les techniciens confirmerait ses constatations.

— Vous croyez que je prends la trousse de crayons de couleur et le cahier de coloriage ? questionna soudain Maud.

— D'après moi, c'est inutile, ils doivent avoir tout ce qu'il faut là-bas. La psy a demandé des objets personnels. Vous n'avez pas trouvé une peluche ?

— J'ai ça, fit-elle en tendant un misérable morceau de serviette éponge crasseux. On dirait un doudou. Ma fille a traîné un vieux torchon à vaisselle pendant des années avant de s'en séparer à l'âge de dix ans. Et vu l'odeur que dégage celui-là, ma main au feu que ça appartient au gamin. De toute façon, on verra bien. Je l'embarque et tant mieux si c'est bien son doudou. Il y a aussi une figurine Transformers, je la mets dans le sac.

Maud prit quand même la précaution d'enfermer le tissu douteux dans un sachet plastique afin de ne pas salir les vêtements passablement propres qu'elle venait de plier. Puis elle referma le sac à l'aide du *zip,* qui émit un bruit sec dans le silence de cette chambre où l'on avait l'impression d'entendre hurler les âmes des enfants.

En *gentleman,* Louis prit le sac de sport des mains de Maud. Décidément, cet homme avait du savoir-vivre, ce qui n'était pas pour déplaire à la jeune enquêtrice.

Une fois remontés en voiture, alors que Louis avait pris le volant, celle-ci extirpa un cabas que son collègue n'avait pas remarqué et en sortit un ouvrage de tricot, avec pelote de laine et aiguilles. Il ouvrit de grands yeux en voyant qu'elle se mettait tranquillement à tricoter.

— Ça vous ennuie ? lui demanda-t-elle, notant l'air stupéfait qu'il affichait.

— Eh bien, c'est-à-dire que... je ne sais pas. C'est très inhabituel dans une voiture de flic.

— On en a pour presque trois heures de route et j'ai promis à Anaïs de lui terminer cette veste avant l'automne. En plus, la voiture est banalisée, qui va savoir qu'on est des flics en nous croisant sur l'autoroute ?

Louis n'en revenait pas de l'incongruité de la chose. Il finit par éclater de rire en secouant la tête. Maud ne cessait jamais de le surprendre, mais finalement, qu'elle fît du tricot pendant qu'il conduisait n'avait aucune importance. Alors, il haussa les épaules et elle le remercia d'un de ses sourires remplis de bonté dont elle seule avait le secret.

Il avait un peu l'impression de conduire sa grand-mère, mais l'un dans l'autre, Maud resta concentrée sur son ouvrage et il n'eut pas à faire la conversation, ce qui lui convenait plutôt bien. Il mit la radio en marche ; une station musicale qui n'abrutissait pas trop ses auditeurs avec les publicités. Maud fredonnait les airs qu'elle connaissait, Louis tapotait le rythme sur son volant.

Au bout d'une demi-heure de trajet, le système *Bluetooth* de son véhicule détecta un appel sur son portable. C'était Anne. Elle ne lui laissa pas le temps de parler :

— Louis, bonjour. Dis-moi, ça tient toujours pour l'appartement ? Non, parce que sinon, j'avais pensé qu'on pourrait se donner rendez-vous à Boulogne ce soir. Disons à vingt heures trente. Tu me donnes les clefs de l'appart et tu repars avec Alix. J'ai pas trop d'autres possibilités et depuis que je lui ai dit que c'était OK pour qu'elle vive un moment chez ses grands-parents, elle ne tient plus en place. Elle ne veut plus mettre les pieds au lycée.

Louis jeta un regard furtif en direction de Maud. Imperturbable, celle-ci gardait les yeux sur ses mailles, trop polie pour paraître s'intéresser le moins du monde à la conversation, qu'elle entendait pourtant parfaitement.

— Alors, on fait comme ça ? C'est bon pour toi ?

— Je vais m'arranger…

— Super ! À ce soir, alors.

Il n'avait pas pu aligner une phrase complète qu'elle avait déjà coupé la communication. Louis regarda sa montre. L'après-midi était déjà bien entamé et, le temps de rencontrer la psychologue, de faire le trajet retour et de rendre compte au commissaire Amary, il avait plutôt intérêt à ne pas traîner. En plus, s'il ne contactait pas ses parents tout de suite, il serait contraint de garder sa fille pour la nuit et il était bien certain que celle-ci lui en voudrait de ne pas avoir pris ses dispositions de façon qu'elle dorme le soir même chez ses grands-parents. En cela, elle était aussi impatiente que sa mère !

Or, il était en route pour le Calvados. La propriété des Salvant-Perret se trouvait à quelques kilomètres de l'institut, il était hors de question qu'il refasse le trajet une fois sa fille récupérée à Paris.

— Excusez-moi, Maud, mais j'ai une affaire personnelle et plutôt urgente à régler. Je vais être obligé de téléphoner à mes parents, désolé de vous infliger ça.

Maud haussa les sourcils en signe d'étonnement.

— Mais c'est tout naturel, vous n'avez pas à vous excuser. La famille avant tout. Vous pouvez vous arrêter sur une aire de repos si vous voulez être tranquille.

— Bonne idée, fit Louis, merci. Ça ne prendra que quelques minutes.

Louis tint parole. La conversation avec sa mère fut brève. Cette dernière se demanda pourquoi il ne pouvait pas conduire France-Alix lui-même chez eux, mais lorsqu'il lui expliqua la situation, elle n'insista pas. Elle fut simplement déçue de le savoir à deux pas de chez eux sans qu'il pût leur rendre visite.

L'affaire serait finalement réglée dans la soirée, cela lui enlevait une belle épine du pied. Maud, de retour dans le véhicule, ne posa aucune question. Le reste du trajet se fit au son de la radio et du cliquetis des aiguilles à tricoter, qu'elle maniait de façon experte.

Quand ils atteignirent l'institut Saint-Jean, ils furent agréablement surpris par le cadre pittoresque du lieu. Le vaste bâtiment était majestueux, mais cela ne ressemblait en rien à une maison de repos, il fallait bien l'avouer.

Passées les grandes grilles du portail, Louis se gara devant ce qui lui parut être une église. Il adressait un regard perplexe à Maud lorsqu'une religieuse surgit au détour de la bâtisse, se dirigeant vers eux, un sourire bienveillant sur les lèvres, son voile sombre flottant dans son sillage.

— Qu'est-ce que c'est que ça ? maugréa Louis. On s'est trompés d'endroit ou quoi ?

Les deux policiers sortirent de voiture, aussitôt fouettés par le vent qui soufflait fort à cause de la proximité du bord de mer. Maud poussa un petit cri d'excitation en riant quand ses cheveux furent secoués en tous sens.

— Ces messieurs dame viennent sans doute au centre de repos ? Vous êtes passés par la mauvaise entrée. Ici, vous vous trouvez à la congrégation des sœurs de Saint-Jean. Mais vous pouvez rejoindre l'institut par l'intérieur, il vous faut repartir par là, vous voyez ? Vous contournez la chapelle, vous prenez sur votre gauche, et puis après c'est indiqué, vous ne pouvez pas vous tromper.

— C'est très gentil, madame... ma sœur, je veux dire, bafouilla Louis, peu habitué aux ecclésiastiques.

— Je suis sœur Constance. Excusez-moi, je suis peut-être curieuse, mais vous êtes de la police ?

Louis n'y avait pas prêté attention lorsque la religieuse se dirigeait vers eux, mais maintenant qu'elle se tenait à deux pas de lui, il se rendit compte qu'elle ne devait pas être âgée de plus de vingt-cinq ans. Bizarre de consacrer sa jeunesse à Dieu et de vivre cloîtrée à l'ère des *smartphones* et du mariage pour tous ! Louis ignorait d'où lui était venue cette pensée, mais il imaginait tellement mal sa propre fille épouser de telles conditions de vie ! Il se demanda si sœur Constance et ses comparses avaient accès aux réseaux sociaux, ou bien si cela était proscrit. Elles devaient avoir Internet, quand même ?

— ... en tout cas c'est très gentil de nous avoir indiqué le bon chemin, terminait Maud alors que Louis, tout à ses pensées, n'avait rien suivi de la conversation. Lieutenant Salvant-Perret ? On y va ?

Sa collègue le regardait avec une sorte d'inquiétude, comme s'il avait l'air souffrant. Louis se ressaisit. Ils reprirent la voiture et se retrouvèrent quelques secondes plus tard devant un bâtiment beaucoup plus moderne où des panneaux indiquaient les différents services, ainsi que l'accueil, vers lequel ils se dirigèrent.

Cette fois, ce fut à une femme replète, affublée d'une chevelure rouge criard, qu'ils eurent affaire. Louis préférait la douceur et la sobriété de sœur Constance. D'un naturel plutôt conventionnel, il jugea cette couleur pour le moins tapageuse. Le problème, c'est que malgré ses efforts pour cacher ce qu'il pensait, l'expression de son visage le trahissait à coup sûr. Leur interlocutrice se rendit immédiatement compte qu'il désapprouvait son choix capillaire. Tout en répondant le plus courtoisement possible à Maud, qui demandait où se situait le service de la thérapeute, elle fusillait Louis du regard.

Les renseignements obtenus, les deux lieutenants prirent l'ascenseur, direction le deuxième étage : le service spécialisé grand trauma de l'enfant où Agathe Delcourt attendait leur arrivée.

La jeune femme se révéla encore plus belle que dans le souvenir pourtant vivace de Louis. Si son visage avait affiché une aversion non dissimulée envers la malheureuse créature de l'accueil cinq minutes plus tôt, la lueur pétillante dans ses yeux et le sourire un peu niais qui se dessinait inexorablement sur ses lèvres en disaient long sur son revirement de sentiments. À bâbord toute ! Hissez la grand-voile, un vent délicieusement chaud se lève !

Sa blouse blanche déboutonnée laissait voir un débardeur rose très échancré. Louis plongea dans ce céleste décolleté sans pouvoir se réfréner. Là encore, il sut que son regard avait été surpris. Tandis qu'il levait les yeux, il vit de l'amusement dans l'expression d'Agathe, ce qui lui fit piquer un fard. Il y avait tellement longtemps que cela ne lui était pas arrivé qu'il se sentit mortifié et se détourna, faisant mine d'examiner les lieux.

Quand la jeune femme s'approcha de lui, il avait recouvré ses couleurs naturelles, mais ne comprit pas pourquoi elle lui tendait la main.

— Vous me le donnez ? demanda-t-elle comme si elle s'adressait à un enfant rétif.

— Quoi donc ?

— Le sac.

— Oh ! Oui, excusez-moi, j'étais ailleurs.

Ça, pour sûr qu'il était ailleurs ! Le petit sourire qu'elle lui adressa marquait son indulgence, habituée à la maladresse des hommes face à elle.

Le sac de sport passa de sa fine main aux ongles courts à celle d'une aide-soignante à qui elle avait fait signe de venir récupérer les vêtements.

— Fanny va se charger de ranger les affaires de Nathan et vous pourrez récupérer votre sac avant de repartir, comme ça. Je suis navrée de vous avoir fait faire tout ce chemin, mais nous avions vraiment besoin d'affaires propres. Vous avez réussi à trouver son jouet préféré ? J'ai cru comprendre que la maison où il vivait était dans un état déplorable.

— Qui vous a dit ça ? s'enquit Louis avec un peu trop de véhémence.

Il savait que la psychologue n'avait pas mis les pieds dans la maison des Lemonnier et, en dehors des forces de police, personne n'était entré. Il ne voulait pas se l'avouer, mais en réalité, il redoutait que ce petit écrivaillon de journaliste n'ait contacté la belle thérapeute, lui dévoilant quelques détails de l'enquête, histoire d'obtenir ses faveurs.

— Mais c'est vous-même. Enfin, votre collègue qui discute avec mon aide-soignante. Quand nous étions dans l'ambulance, le jour du drame. Cela a l'air de poser un problème ?

— Non, non, pas du tout.

Elle lui fit signe de la suivre tandis qu'elle reprenait :

— En tant que psychologue, il m'est très utile de connaître l'environnement dans lequel évoluent mes patients. D'autant que lorsqu'il s'agit de jeunes enfants, ce qu'ils perçoivent de la réalité peut être déformé, idéalisé ou au contraire diabolisé.

— Je comprends, approuva Louis. Surtout que dans le cas qui nous occupe, il n'y a plus personne pour nous fournir ces renseignements.

— Vous n'avez trouvé aucune famille restante à ce garçon ?

Le ton d'Agathe Delcourt était plein de compassion, à la limite de la tristesse. C'était touchant de penser qu'après tout ce qu'elle avait dû voir de par son métier, elle ressentait encore ce genre d'émotions. Louis, de son côté, s'était blindé avec le temps. La misère des gens ne le bouleversait plus comme aux premières heures de sa carrière.

— Je crains qu'il ne soit seul au monde, déplora-t-il. Mais il vous a, vous, ajouta-t-il non sans arrière-pensée.

Elle le considéra, la tête légèrement penchée, s'étant arrêtée au beau milieu du couloir aseptisé le long duquel ils marchaient.

— Êtes-vous en train de flirter avec moi, lieutenant ?

Décontenancé, Louis eut un moment d'hésitation avant de répondre :

— Peut-être un petit peu, je dois le reconnaître. Mais c'est fini, je... c'est fini !

Il battit des bras tout en débitant sa tirade d'un ton qui fit rire Agathe, car à la vérité, son sérieux détonait avec les regards pleins de désir qu'il lui décochait. Néanmoins, il constata avec plaisir qu'il avait quand même réussi à la faire rire.

— Où en étions-nous ? reprit-elle tout en reprenant sa marche. Ah, oui ! Je voulais vous demander si vous aviez trouvé des traces d'urine sur le matelas de Nathan. J'avais fait part de cette requête au commissaire Amary. Savez-vous si quelqu'un s'est renseigné à ce sujet ?

— Je m'en suis personnellement chargé et je n'ai rien détecté.

— Dans ce cas, de deux choses l'une : soit il s'agit d'un symptôme lié au souvenir du traumatisme qu'il revit pendant ses cauchemars, soit c'est un comportement régressif dont les origines sont de toute façon les mêmes. Je pensais que c'était peut-être un phénomène récurrent. Ça arrive souvent chez les jeunes garçons. Mais vous venez de m'apprendre que non.

Ils étaient parvenus devant la chambre de Nathan. À travers la vitre, l'enfant offrait un triste spectacle. Allongé sur le lit, le haut du corps surélevé par de gros oreillers, il était d'une immobilité anormale, apathique et aphasique, selon les termes de la psychologue.

Derrière eux, Maud et l'aide-soignante discutaient à propos du morceau de chiffon – le doudou présumé – et de la figurine Transformers.

– Présentons-lui les deux, avança l'aide-soignante.

Elle lança un regard interrogatif à Agathe Delcourt, qui acquiesça discrètement d'un mouvement de tête. Louis fit un pas avec l'intention de suivre l'aide-soignante dans la chambre du garçon, mais la thérapeute le stoppa en le retenant par le bras :

– Je ne crois pas que ce soit une bonne idée, dit-elle avec douceur, mais de telle façon qu'il n'eut d'autre choix que de lui obéir. Je sais bien que vous n'attendez qu'une chose : c'est de l'interroger sur ce qui s'est passé. Mais il est bien trop tôt et vous le savez.

Le ton qu'elle employait semblait sous-entendre qu'elle le connaissait suffisamment pour savoir qu'il ne discuterait pas un argument aussi évident. Elle créait une sorte d'intimité qui fonctionnait à merveille avec Louis. Il n'opposa aucune résistance, proposa de se rendre jusque dans le bureau de la psychologue afin de s'entendre sur la marche à suivre. Maud, de son côté, alla glaner des informations auprès des infirmières.

— Pourquoi tenez-vous tant à entendre ce que l'enfant a vu ? demanda-t-elle une fois qu'ils furent installés devant une tasse de café qu'elle lui proposa. Les choses semblent pourtant claires : son père a tué tout le monde avant de se donner la mort à son tour. Malheureusement, j'ai déjà vu ça.

— Il y a déjà eu un cas comme celui de Nathan Lemonnier ? s'étonna Louis. Vous avez déjà eu affaire à un survivant ?

— Ce n'est pas ce que je voulais dire, non, s'embrouilla la jeune femme. Disons que ce genre de tragédie n'est pas un fait nouveau. Il y a des précédents.

Louis sentit le trouble chez la thérapeute. Il ignorait pourquoi, mais elle se rembrunit, le regard fuyant, les sourcils légèrement froncés. Elle coupa court à la conversation, revint sur sa question initiale :

— Qu'espérez-vous obtenir en venant ici, lieutenant Salvant-Perret ? Vous auriez pu envoyer un subalterne apporter ce sac de vêtements. Mais vous êtes venu en personne, sachant parfaitement qu'il était trop tôt pour interroger l'enfant.

— L'air est plus respirable en dehors de Paris, rétorqua Louis. Et la vue bien plus agréable.

Il dit cela sans la quitter des yeux. Elle comprit le message.

— Mais j'avais promis d'arrêter, se reprit-il aussitôt. Puis, après une fraction de seconde de réflexion :

— Un dîner, ça vous dit ?

La psychologue se rejeta contre le dossier de son fauteuil de bureau en ouvrant la bouche sur un « Oh ! » muet de stupéfaction, les yeux grands ouverts, un air à la fois outré et amusé sur le visage.

Un silence s'installa. Louis n'osait plus émettre le moindre son et Agathe Delcourt n'avait visiblement pas l'intention de répondre à ses avances. En même temps, qu'est-ce qui lui était passé par la tête ? Elle devait le prendre pour un mauvais dragueur impénitent alors que c'était tout le contraire. Il ne se reconnaissait pas.

— Oubliez ça, dit-il en se levant. Je ne suis pas moi-même, aujourd'hui. Un truc au déjeuner qui a dû mal passer...

Dieu, que cette dernière remarque était nulle ! Il aggravait son cas, mais c'était trop tard. Heureusement pour lui, Maud se présenta à ce moment-là dans l'encadrement de la porte restée ouverte. Il en profita pour prendre congé de la jeune femme, la salua maladroitement sans croiser son regard, et entraîna sa collègue loin de ce bureau.

Même durant les pires épisodes de son adolescence, il ne s'était jamais autant ridiculisé devant une représentante de la gent féminine !

Automne 2000

Assise par terre dans la salle de séjour, la famille formait une ronde bien étrange, chacun de ses membres attaché à l'autre par des foulards liés aux poignets. Les tissus bariolés appartenaient à la mère et c'est elle qui avait été chargée de ligoter son mari et ses enfants. L'homme au masque de chat l'avait ensuite fait asseoir avec les autres et avait noué le dernier foulard aux poignets de la femme et de son plus jeune enfant, fermant ainsi le cercle.

Personne ne bronchait et pour cause : leur persécuteur avait commencé par trancher la gorge de la plus grande des filles sans sommation, froidement, comme on se débarrasse d'une mouche agaçante.

Cela s'était passé très vite, alors qu'ils venaient de se rassembler dans cette même pièce. Victor avait été pris en otage le premier, la pointe du couteau de l'homme toujours plantée dans son cou, il offrait un spectacle désolant. Ses sphincters avaient lâché à cause de la terreur, une odeur forte d'excréments l'enveloppait.

Au début, il avait servi de porte-parole. L'homme-chat chuchotait ses ordres à l'oreille de l'enfant, qui répétait ensuite à voix haute, entre deux sanglots, de s'asseoir par terre, de ne surtout pas ouvrir la bouche sous peine de subir le même sort que l'adolescente sans vie. La vue de son corps gisant à deux pas de leur cercle était suffisante pour leur passer toute envie de se rebeller. L'odeur écœurante du sang se mélangeait à celle du pantalon de pyjama souillé de Victor. C'était à vous donner la nausée, mais leur tortionnaire ne semblait pas affecté le moins du monde.

À présent, il se tenait debout, immobile au milieu de leur ronde macabre. La seconde fille et son petit frère pleuraient et reniflaient sans discontinuer, la mère avalait ses larmes et la morve qui coulaient jusqu'à ses lèvres desséchées tandis que le père tremblait de tous ses membres en silence, les yeux démesurément ouverts sur la scène d'horreur qu'il avait devant lui.

Ils ne comprenaient pas. Qu'est-ce qu'il voulait ? Pourquoi avait-il tué la jeune fille ? Allaient-ils tous y passer les uns après les autres ?

Tout à coup, l'homme se redressa de toute sa hauteur, étira les bras vers l'arrière, gonfla le torse. Il inspira fort et à pleins poumons en levant la tête vers le plafond. Était-ce le signal d'une nouvelle tuerie ? Chacun se contracta, dans l'attente effroyable de ce qui allait suivre.

— Ah ! fit-il en expirant, une expression d'aise dans cette unique syllabe. Vous ne trouvez pas qu'on respire mieux avec une personne de moins ?

On sentait à sa voix qu'il souriait derrière son masque, qu'il prenait un plaisir sadique à les voir à sa merci, morts de peur, impuissants. Pour l'instant, aucun d'entre eux n'avait osé lui adresser la parole. La séquence où le courageux père de famille tente de raisonner l'agresseur en essayant de comprendre ses motivations, c'était bon pour les films au cinéma. En réalité, quand on tranchait la gorge d'une gosse innocente sous vos yeux, qu'on plantait un couteau sous le menton de votre plus jeune fils, la compréhension, on s'en foutait pas mal ! Tout ce qui comptait, c'était de ne pas énerver l'homme en face de vous, de se faire le plus silencieux et le plus petit possible pour que sa fureur s'abatte sur quelqu'un d'autre.

Claude Albert avait tellement honte ! Il se sentait si lâche devant ce monstre qui menaçait la vie des siens ! Mais il ne pouvait s'empêcher de penser qu'il ne voulait pas mourir ; il priait intérieurement pour que le couteau ne vienne pas déchirer sa propre trachée.

Il y eut un silence lourd, qui s'étira comme si les secondes de cette agonie étaient sans fin. Puis, le masque de chat se rapprocha du visage de Marie-Christine, dont la respiration se fit anarchique. Elle manqua s'étouffer dans ses sanglots alors que leur persécuteur la regardait se débattre contre sa peur irrationnelle.

Cette façon qu'il avait de ne rien dire pendant d'interminables minutes accentuait la tension. Un peu plus loin, sous le corps de l'adolescente assassinée, la flaque de sang s'étendait doucement. Victor, le benjamin de cette fratrie en péril, avait les yeux rivés sur cette masse écarlate et gluante qui s'étalait, avançait dans une lente progression jusqu'à lui. Il était figé, les membres aussi rigides qu'un morceau de bois, ses narines frémissantes, conscient de l'odeur qui remontait de son pantalon, comme si cela avait encore une quelconque importance...

— Dis-moi, maman, fit la voix atrocement douce de l'homme-chat, as-tu vu l'état de la nourriture dans ton frigo ?

Il s'accroupit juste en face d'elle et, sans attendre de réponse :

— Je suis navré de te dire ça, mais quand on a des gamins, il faut les assumer. Sinon, je t'informe qu'il existe un moyen efficace qui s'appelle la pilule. Et tu sais quoi ? C'est même remboursé par la Sécurité sociale.

L'on n'entendait que les reniflements de Victor et de sa sœur encore vivante, Mélissa. Tête baissée, Marie-Christine parvenait à peine à distinguer quelque chose à travers ses larmes, qui brouillaient tout. Elle sentit deux doigts se poser sous son menton et lui soulever le visage de façon qu'elle croise le regard de leur agresseur. Des yeux bleus dragée, si clairs qu'ils semblaient délavés.

La panique la gagna. Elle tenta de se débattre, ne réussit qu'à blesser son fils en tirant sur ses liens. Les prunelles étranges et froides ne la lâchaient pas, elle se sentit asphyxiée sous leur emprise maléfique.

— Mais je pense que tu préfères pondre des lardons et profiter des avantages généreusement versés par l'État. C'est-à-dire par les gens qui ont le bon sens de ne pas surpeupler cette bonne vieille Terre et qui payent pour que toi et ton engeance puissiez toucher vos allocs. Et tu en fais quoi, de tes allocs, d'ailleurs ?

La voix fit une courte pause, puis soudain, le ton changea. Il se saisit d'une poignée des cheveux de sa victime, qui se mit à gémir piteusement.

— Réponds ! Je t'ai posé une question !

Et, comme seuls des cris et des lamentations étouffées sortaient de sa bouche, la lame du couteau dessina un grand arc de cercle dans les airs, étincelante, puis s'abattit à toute vitesse, sectionnant la carotide gauche de la femme.

Les cris s'éteignirent dans un gargouillis effrayant, des jets d'hémoglobine éclaboussèrent tout à cinq mètres à la ronde. Jusqu'à ce que le cœur cesse de battre, le liquide chaud continua de gicler sur les murs, sur le sol, sur la chemise de nuit détrempée du corps inerte.

— Maman... Maman...

Au-delà du désespoir, Victor appelait sa mère, dont le sang recouvrait maintenant tout le côté droit de son visage et de son pyjama déjà souillé. Mélissa hoquetait de terreur. Claude, dos à la scène, avait des sueurs froides. Des gouttes coulaient le long de ses tempes et de son cou, ses cheveux étaient détrempés. Le salon commençait à ressembler à un étal de boucherie et cette maison allait devenir un mausolée.

Chapitre 6

Au lieu de se sentir humilié par son échec face à Agathe Delcourt, Louis décida que la difficulté pour la conquérir n'en était que plus excitante. Il se remémorait régulièrement les réactions de la jeune femme lorsqu'il avait ouvertement tenté de la séduire : ses sourires indulgents, ses silences mi-choqués, mi-amusés. L'air de rien, il l'avait bien observée. Il n'avait remarqué ni alliance ni bague de fiançailles à son doigt. Juste un anneau d'argent avec un pendentif au centre, comme c'était la mode en ce moment. Un bijou bon marché que portaient beaucoup de femmes et dont on voyait la publicité dans la plupart des magazines.

Elle lui résistait, mais il n'avait pas dit son dernier mot.

Toutes ces heures passées en voiture l'avaient un peu abruti, même si Maud prit le volant au retour. Il arriva en retard au rendez-vous avec Anne. Elle était furieuse d'avoir attendu, signe qu'elle allait beaucoup mieux que la dernière fois qu'il l'avait eue au bout du fil. Sa fille et elle, postées sur le trottoir avec sacs, cartons et valises, en avaient marre d'être un spectacle pour les passants.

Malgré tout, France-Alix était de bonne humeur.

Ses longs cheveux ondulés étaient détachés. Louis le remarqua parce qu'elle les portait tout le temps relevés en une sorte de chignon qu'elle faisait tenir avec une simple tige de métal ouvragé. Il la trouva un peu changée depuis la dernière fois qu'il l'avait vue. C'était peut-être simplement parce qu'elle était heureuse à l'idée d'aller habiter chez ses grands-parents, qui lui passaient tous ses caprices.

Décidément, Anne et lui devaient être de bien piètres parents pour que leur fille manifeste autant de joie à l'idée de vivre sans eux ! Mais quelque part, le fait qu'elle ne veuille pas continuer à cohabiter avec son ex constituait une petite vengeance pour Louis. Les mères obtenaient trop souvent tous les droits lors d'un divorce, au détriment des pères, qui n'étaient bons qu'à payer la pension alimentaire et à se taire. Il s'estimait heureux que sa fille ait consenti à continuer ses visites bimensuelles quand d'autres hommes dans la même situation se voyaient privés de leurs enfants à cause de femmes abusives et de juges complaisants.

Dès qu'il arriva à son tour, Vincent Salvant-Perret prit en charge France-Alix pendant que Louis installait Anne dans ses nouveaux appartements. Porter les valises et les cartons, ouvrir les compteurs, mettre en marche le réfrigérateur et la *box* internet occupa sa soirée. L'appartement, entièrement meublé, disposait de tout le confort possible, Anne ne manquerait de rien.

Pendant qu'il s'activait dans les différentes pièces, elle fit des confidences à Louis, avoua que sa nouvelle vie n'avait pas la saveur qu'elle avait escomptée. Les hommes manquaient de savoir-vivre, d'ambition, de fidélité aussi. Peut-être était-elle trop exigeante ?

Peut-être que leur mariage n'était pas si mal en définitive ?

Que cherchait-elle ? Qu'ils se remettent ensemble ? Louis préféra ne pas poser de questions. Il la laissa s'épancher sans donner son avis, maugréant des sons inintelligibles de temps en temps en hochant la tête quand il croisait son regard. Mieux valait ne pas s'éterniser, cela devenait dangereux.

À onze heures et quart, il refermait la porte de son domicile, exténué, mais avec le sentiment d'avoir accompli quelque chose de bien. Sa fille était entre de bonnes mains et son ex ne devrait plus lui poser de problèmes pendant un certain temps. Du moins, c'est ce qu'il espérait.

Malgré tout, pour la première fois depuis des mois, sa maison lui parut désespérément vide. Après avoir ingurgité les premières denrées qui lui tombèrent sous la main en ouvrant son réfrigérateur, le silence pesa sur lui comme jamais auparavant.

Il effectua les gestes du quotidien comme un fantôme : mettre les couverts dans le lave-vaisselle, se déshabiller, se doucher, se brosser les dents, enfiler une tenue de sport pour traîner. Une sorte de fatigue intérieure s'était emparée de lui. Même allongé sur son lit, la télévision allumée, il ressentait cette solitude qui se rappelait à lui avec obstination.

C'était une femme qui manquait dans cette maison, évidemment. Dès que ce constat fut établi, l'image d'Agathe Delcourt s'imposa d'elle-même. Il l'imaginait sans peine évoluant dans son intérieur un peu triste d'homme divorcé. Sa fraîcheur, son sourire, ses cheveux, ses jambes, son décolleté vertigineux...

Louis se ressaisit, se forçant à chasser ces pensées de son esprit. Pour cela, il appuya sur le bouton d'arrêt de la télécommande et prit un livre commencé un mois plus tôt, mais dont il n'avait lu que le premier chapitre. Cela s'appelait *Les Chiens de Belfast*, un polar écrit par Sam Millar, auteur irlandais au passé tumultueux dont il avait entendu parler par Jade, la femme d'Ismaël, amatrice de romans à *suspense* et de *thrillers*.

En tant que flic, il avait un regard assez critique sur ces livres qui fleurissaient partout dans les rayonnages des librairies. Certains auteurs ne connaissaient strictement rien au fonctionnement de la police et cela avait le don de l'agacer. Ou de le faire rire selon le degré d'ignorance. À côté de ceux-là, d'autres faisaient au contraire l'étalage d'acronymes, noyant le lecteur dans un foutoir alphabétique dont il n'avait sans doute que faire. Heureusement, il restait ceux qui vous offraient du rêve tout en vous faisant frissonner d'angoisse, ou vous embarquaient dans des enquêtes alambiquées à souhait.

Il dut reprendre sa lecture du début, ayant oublié de quoi il s'agissait. Mais lorsqu'il eut commencé, il ne lâcha l'ouvrage que fort tard dans la nuit, pris dans une intrigue qui le tenait en haleine. Le livre lui tomba des mains et il sombra dans le sommeil.

Le lendemain n'apporta rien de nouveau au sujet du massacre de la famille Lemonnier. Ismaël, Maud et lui furent mis sur une autre affaire pendant tout le reste de la semaine : un homicide dans le studio d'une étudiante, tuée à coups de couteau et défigurée à l'acide. Son petit ami avoua les faits rapidement, quelques heures après le début de sa garde à vue. La jeune fille n'était âgée que de dix-neuf ans, elle était très belle avant que l'acide ne fasse son œuvre. La jalousie maladive de son fiancé l'avait fauchée en plein cœur de sa jeunesse. Elle n'irait plus jamais illuminer les bancs de la faculté et son tortionnaire écoperait d'au moins quinze ans de réclusion. Deux destinées brisées.

Louis était en train de taper les dernières lignes d'un rapport lorsque le commissaire Amary fit irruption dans le bureau exigu qu'il partageait avec ses deux collègues :

— Bonnemort veut vous voir, annonça-t-il, un cure-dent au coin de la bouche.

Il avait arrêté de fumer cinq ans auparavant, mais ne parvenait pas à se défaire de ce petit bout de bois qui lui servait de substitut. Il le mâchouillait jusqu'à ce qu'il se désagrège complètement, avait développé une dextérité surprenante pour le faire passer d'un côté à l'autre de sa bouche tout en parlant.

— Bonne qui ? questionna Maud, qui semblait se réveiller d'une sieste derrière son écran d'ordinateur.

— La légiste, précisa Ismaël. Un nom pareil, ça ne s'oublie pourtant pas ! Surtout quand on fait ce métier ! On y va tous les trois ?

— Non, le prince et vous seulement. Cortès, j'ai besoin de vous pour une recherche. Ensuite, vous recevrez un certain Blanchard.

Maud ne se le fit pas répéter deux fois. Elle fut debout en un instant, au garde-à-vous.

— J'aurais bien aimé interroger ce Blanchard, intervint Louis, un peu contrarié. C'est moi qui ai demandé qu'il soit convoqué.

— Vous pensez que je ne suis pas au courant ? Vous n'aurez qu'à demander un compte-rendu à votre collègue. Ou mieux : vous lirez le procès-verbal d'audition. Et puis tant que je vous tiens, Salvant-Perret, vous me ferez le plaisir de passer un coup de fil à mademoiselle Delcourt, et au trot ! Il paraît que vous n'avez pas été très fin l'autre jour à l'institut Saint- Jean. Des excuses seraient les bienvenues. Qu'est-ce qui vous a pris ? Ça ne vous ressemble pas, ces façons de procéder. Si vous cherchez à vous recaser, inscrivez-vous sur Meetic, mais épargnez-moi ce genre de contrariété.

Agathe s'était donc plainte de lui auprès du commissaire Amary ? Il n'en revenait pas. Il était persuadé qu'elle avait pris son misérable numéro de charme à la rigolade, mais apparemment, il n'en était rien. Le rouge lui montant aux joues, il se leva pour aller décrocher son blouson du portemanteau.

— Désolé, commissaire, je veillerai à arranger ce malentendu, soyez tranquille.

— J'y compte bien ! Il ne faudrait pas qu'on se retrouve avec une plainte pour harcèlement sexuel.

— Ça n'arrivera pas.

L'avantage avec un homme comme Louis Salvant-Perret, c'était qu'il ne se départait jamais de ses bonnes manières. Jamais un mot plus haut que l'autre, un respect indéfectible de la hiérarchie, un sens inné de la politesse. En le regardant s'éloigner en compagnie d'Ismaël, le commissaire Amary était bien certain que le lieutenant présenterait ses plus plates excuses à la thérapeute.

À vrai dire, il avait un peu exagéré l'événement. Agathe Delcourt n'avait pas reproché le comportement de Salvant-Perret. Elle s'était simplement étonnée qu'un *gentleman* comme lui sorte de la réserve pourtant due à sa fonction, selon ses propres termes.

Le voir tout penaud, piquant un fard avait été un spectacle assez appréciable. Il repartit dans son bureau le sourire aux lèvres, content de son petit effet, Maud sur ses talons.

Chapitre 7

— Alors comme ça, on drague les petites psychologues ?

C'était à prévoir : Ismaël sauta sur l'occasion pour essayer de tirer les vers du nez à Louis. Au commissariat, tout le monde savait qu'il était divorcé. Mais nul ne l'avait jamais entendu parler de sa vie privée, encore moins d'une femme. Il aurait pu virer homosexuel ou adepte SM, il ne laissait rien filtrer. C'était son côté mystérieux — qu'il avait l'art de cultiver derrière ses airs de *dandy* qui s'ignore.

Il maintint un silence royal face aux piques du lieutenant Al Bakir en se concentrant sur son téléphone portable pendant tout le trajet jusqu'à l'institut médico-légal. De guerre lasse, Ismaël finit par se taire, les yeux fixés sur la route, mais bien décidé à obtenir le fin mot de cette histoire entre Louis et la psychologue.

Après tout, ils faisaient équipe, ils étaient comme des frères. Davantage que des frères, même. À son avis, Louis avait tendance à se renfermer sur lui-même depuis qu'il était seul. Son naturel introverti s'accentuait sérieusement. Il était de plus en plus difficile de le dérider, de le faire rire ou même de lui arracher une quelconque information sur son état de santé ou d'esprit.

La seconde rencontre avec la sémillante Françoise Bonnemort apporta son lot de révélations. Louis attendait beaucoup des résultats des autopsies, notamment de celle du père de famille soupçonné d'avoir assassiné tous les autres membres du clan Lemonnier, à part le petit dernier. Ismaël, ayant assisté aux autopsies durant la semaine qui venait de s'écouler, échangea un regard complice avec la femme dont Louis préféra ignorer la source.

La légiste, sur son terrain, se révéla très souriante et d'un tempérament jovial malgré la nature morbide de son activité professionnelle. Elle éclatait de rire pour un oui, pour un non, débitait les résultats de ses analyses comme si tout le monde était au fait du vocabulaire médico-légal et, avec son accent du Sud, l'on avait davantage l'impression d'assister à une parodie d'autopsie qu'à un compte-rendu soigneux.

Sans surprise, les causes de la mort chez madame Lemonnier étaient l'éviscération et, chez les deux enfants, une entaille létale à l'arme blanche au niveau du cou. En dehors de ces blessures mortelles, ils n'avaient pas reçu de coups.

– Quant à l'homme, continua la légiste, soudain très grave, il présente toutes les caractéristiques de la pendaison. Mais comme vous le savez, toute mort par pendaison est une mort violente et pouvant être suspecte. Je me suis donc attachée à chercher des indices d'un acte criminel. Sur les lieux, j'avais constaté une position incomplète : un des pieds du mort touchait légèrement le sol et il y avait une chaise renversée à sa droite. On peut supposer qu'il s'en est servi pour se pendre. L'analyse du nœud se fait en laboratoire, ce n'est pas de mon ressort. Mais à première vue, c'était un nœud coulant tout ce qu'il y a de plus classique. L'homme a attaché la corde en position latérale, il est monté sur la chaise et l'a rejetée sur le côté, ce qui a provoqué une élongation brutale de la moelle épinière cervicale ainsi que des traumatismes osseux rachidiens assez graves. J'ai noté des lésions sous-conjonctivales, une exophtalmie et une fracture de l'hyoïde. Tous les organes sont congestionnés. Vous êtes toujours avec moi ? s'inquiéta-t-elle en s'interrompant.

— On est au taquet, confirma Ismaël, qui tâchait de suivre ce charabia du mieux qu'il pouvait.

— Le sillon tracé par la corde est complet, ce qui confirme le nœud coulant et je n'ai pas constaté de marque moins profonde qui pourrait dissimuler une strangulation camouflée en pendaison.

Louis ne cacha pas sa déception :

— En somme, l'individu s'est bien pendu. C'est donc un suicide.

— Eh bien, en fait, peut-être pas.

L'effet de surprise se lut sur le visage des deux lieutenants.

— Comment ça ? Expliquez-nous ça, fit Ismaël tandis que Louis attendait la suite avec une sorte de fébrilité.

— Au cours de l'examen buccal, j'ai tout de suite remarqué qu'une de ses molaires avait été violemment arrachée. La gencive porte des lésions toutes récentes. Et figurez-vous que j'ai retrouvé cette dent dans son estomac. Il l'a avalée.

Elle se dirigea vers une étagère en inox derrière elle et revint avec une boîte de culture cellulaire dans laquelle se trouvait une molaire avec une partie de sa racine.

— Vous avez pu définir comment elle avait été arrachée ? questionna Louis.

— Sur le coup, à cause de la nécrose de la peau du visage liée à l'asphyxie, je n'ai rien remarqué de particulier. Mais après un examen plus poussé, il s'avère que l'homme a reçu un coup violent du côté gauche du visage qui a entraîné la chute de la molaire. J'ai donc ensuite cherché des marques de défense, des traces de lutte sur les poignets ou ailleurs : rien. Je peux vous dire deux choses avec certitude : *primo*, le coup n'a pas pu être porté ni par la femme ni par un des enfants. D'abord parce qu'ils n'en auraient pas eu la force, et ensuite parce qu'aucun d'entre eux ne présente d'ecchymoses aux jointures des poings. Un tel coup laisse des traces sur celui qui le donne. *Deuxio*, cela s'est passé quelques minutes seulement avant la pendaison.

— Ce qui prouve qu'il y avait une autre personne la nuit du drame, conclut Louis sans toutefois crier victoire.

— Cela prouve simplement que la victime a reçu une bonne droite, rectifia le docteur Bonnemort. Rien ne dit que le coup a été porté dans la maison. Pour ça, il faudrait retrouver le morceau manquant.

La légiste souriait d'un air malicieux en secouant légèrement la boîte où la dent se promenait en émettant un petit bruit agaçant.

— Regardez, continua-t-elle, leur présentant une loupe. La molaire s'est cassée ici et c'est tout frais. Or, le contenu de l'estomac n'a pas révélé le moindre bout de dent supplémentaire. Par conséquent, si vous dénichez le petit bout d'émail sur les lieux, vous pourrez alors considérer qu'il y avait effectivement quelqu'un avec eux au moment de la tuerie.

– Et que cette personne pourrait très bien en être l'auteur, termina Ismaël en se tournant vers Louis. Tu avais raison, putain ! C'est peut-être pas un simple « pétage » de plomb du père.

– Avez-vous trouvé des traces de marqueur noir sur les doigts du fils aîné ?

– Je n'ai rien remarqué à l'œil nu, mais je peux approfondir mes recherches dans ce sens si vous le souhaitez. Je vous recontacte dès que j'ai les résultats, ça vous va ?

– C'est parfait. Vous avez fait du bon boulot, la félicita Ismaël. Et vous entendre parler est un vrai bol d'air frais avec votre accent.

– Mon accent ? C'est vous autres qui avez un accent, pas moi ! se rebiffa-t-elle.

Et elle éclata d'un rire assourdissant qui se répercuta jusqu'aux entrailles de l'institut.

Chapitre 8

Durant la première semaine, Agathe n'avait pas sollicité Nathan Lemonnier. L'enfant avait intégré une chambre ordinaire dès son troisième jour à l'institut, car il était en bonne santé et ne présentait pas de danger pour lui-même ou quelqu'un d'autre.

En revanche, les soucis d'énurésie s'étaient aggravés, se manifestant à présent à certains moments de la journée, notamment en début de soirée, lorsque l'obscurité approchait. Son calvaire ayant eu lieu la nuit, cela n'avait rien d'étonnant.

La thérapeute allait lui rendre visite deux à trois fois par jour, mais n'avait pas encore commencé de séances à proprement parler. Cela n'allait pas tarder. Mais d'abord, elle s'était consacrée à son enquête préliminaire.

Pour commencer, elle avait obtenu un rendez-vous avec son enseignante, madame Fourcade, une femme d'une cinquantaine d'années bouleversée par ce qui était arrivé au petit Nathan. Elle demanda tout de suite s'il serait possible de le voir. Bien entendu, Agathe dut le lui refuser, mais elle lui assura qu'elle pourrait bientôt rencontrer son jeune élève si les choses évoluaient dans le bon sens. Il fallait être patient.

La maîtresse d'école ne tarit pas d'éloges au sujet de Nathan. Enfant précoce, il avait un an d'avance scolairement et l'on envisageait même de lui faire encore sauter une classe à la rentrée suivante. Cependant, à la suite de ces terribles événements, madame Fourcade redoutait que le garçon se retrouve pénalisé par son traumatisme, même si un enfant surdoué ne perdait jamais le bénéfice de son avance.

– Un élève attentif, intelligent, brillant, intéressé, intéressant, qui comprend tout du premier coup. J'appelle ces enfants-là des éponges à culture. C'est un tel plaisir de compter un élément de cette qualité dans sa classe ! Et ça souligne malheureusement le gouffre qui le sépare d'autres élèves moins gâtés intellectuellement.

– Je vois, marmonna Agathe tout en griffonnant sur sa feuille. Était-il souvent absent ? Pour maladie ou pour un autre motif ?

– Non, très rarement. Cette année, le pauvre a fait une méchante grippe, mais c'est tout.

– Et au niveau du comportement ? questionna Agathe, qui se faisait l'effet de mener un véritable interrogatoire.

– Eh bien, hésita madame Fourcade, étant donné le milieu dans lequel il évolue, il a quelques défauts de langage liés à ce qu'il entend autour de lui. Par exemple, il peut parfois se montrer très grossier dans ses propos. Je sais bien que vous n'avez pas pu connaître ses parents – paix à leur âme ! –, mais pour les avoir rencontrés, il faut que vous compreniez que c'étaient des gens à problèmes. Je ne les en blâme pas, loin de là, nous vivons une époque tellement difficile ! Mais ils subsistaient principalement des aides de l'État. Ils étaient au chômage tous les deux et je pense que la mère avait des soucis d'alcool. Son haleine était chargée lorsqu'elle venait déposer son fils à l'école. Les repas de la cantine sont souvent restés impayés, mais nous avons pallié. On ne laisse jamais un enfant le ventre vide. Surtout pas Nathan. Parce qu'il le méritait, ce pauvre chéri. Nous ne pouvions décemment pas exclure un gamin aussi brillant à cause de problèmes d'argent, vous comprenez ?

Agathe nota que l'institutrice parlait du garçon au passé, comme si lui aussi était mort, ou qu'elle n'allait jamais le revoir. Cela la dérangea quelque peu, mais elle n'en fit pas la remarque et continua :

— C'est une démarche très honorable, approuva la psychologue en souriant devant tant de bonté. Mais mis à part ces problèmes de langage dont vous parlez, est-il sociable ? A-t-il des camarades ? Peut-être a-t-il un copain qu'il côtoie davantage que les autres ?

— Nathan est un enfant introverti qui ne communique pas beaucoup ni avec ses camarades ni avec les adultes. Mais il est souvent fourré avec cette petite chipie d'Aurélie Duthil. D'ailleurs, ils partagent le même bureau. Ça m'a toujours épatée de les voir ensemble, ces deux-là ! Aurélie est aussi agitée que Nathan est calme et discret. Mais je crois qu'elle s'est prise d'affection pour lui parce qu'il est le plus petit de la classe, elle le protège comme une petite mère, c'est vraiment pas banal. Ce serait un cas d'étude fort intéressant pour une psychologue comme vous.

— Mais c'est justement pour étudier le genre de relations qu'il entretient avec son entourage que j'ai voulu vous voir. Tous les renseignements que vous me donnez sont précieux, croyez-moi. Pourrais-je juste jeter un coup d'œil à son bureau, s'il vous plaît ? Après je ne vous embêterai plus.

— Mais vous ne m'embêtez pas le moins du monde ! C'est tellement horrible ce qui vient d'arriver à Nathan. Suivez-moi.

Comme c'était l'heure de la pause déjeuner, les salles de classe étaient désertes. La totalité des élèves était dans la cour, où un vacarme de tous les diables vous agressait les oreilles. Même à l'intérieur, les cris suraigus se faisaient entendre. C'était la directrice de l'école qui lui avait arrangé ce rendez-vous entre midi et deux heures, de façon que l'enseignante et la thérapeute aient la paix — quoique relative.

Dans le couloir central, des dessins multicolores aux personnages simplifiés tapissaient les murs. Agathe aperçut les bureaux et les chaises miniatures de la salle des maternelles et des cours préparatoires, le dortoir où des dizaines de lits pliants s'alignaient, avec des couvertures aux motifs joyeux et des ours en peluche disposés dans des casiers. Il y régnait une odeur à la fois sucrée et aseptisée ; un mélange de détergent, de bonbons et d'encre.

Agathe ne se souvenait pas de l'odeur de sa propre école primaire, mais elle supposait que cela devait ressembler à ça. Elle avait eu l'occasion de visiter quelques établissements scolaires au cours de ses « enquêtes » et elle devait reconnaître que celle-ci était particulièrement bien aménagée, avec du mobilier et des équipements récents. Les peintures avaient été refaites, les tableaux étaient interactifs. Chaque enseignant disposait d'un PC sur son bureau. Et, comme ce matériel coûtait cher, il y avait un système de sécurité très performant, pourvu de caméras aux entrées et sorties, ainsi que dans la cour et les couloirs. La psychologue se demanda si elles étaient en fonction ou si ce n'était que de la poudre aux yeux afin de dissuader un éventuel voleur.

La table de travail de Nathan et Aurélie se trouvait au premier rang. Il était intéressant de noter que du côté du jeune garçon, les cahiers étaient impeccablement empilés sous le bureau alors que ceux d'Aurélie menaçaient de s'écrouler tant le rangement avait été fait à la va-vite, sans aucun soin. Pas de trace de stylo ou d'écorchures au compas sur la surface de travail, rien à signaler non plus sur les montants métalliques de la structure du bureau et de la chaise.

Madame Fourcade observait le manège un peu singulier d'Agathe avec curiosité. Elle n'aurait jamais imaginé qu'une psychologue pût se livrer à de telles investigations. Ce genre de praticiens restaient habituellement dans leur cabinet de consultation à écouter leurs patients, on ne s'attendait pas à les voir sur le terrain. Sans doute que la violence de ce qui venait d'arriver à Nathan réclamait des mesures exceptionnelles ? En tout cas, cette jeune femme fit une forte impression sur l'enseignante.

Devant le portail de l'école, alors que madame Fourcade avait raccompagné Agathe, celle-ci demanda encore :

— Une dernière question, si ça ne vous ennuie pas : savez-vous s'il est inscrit à un club de sport ?

— Oh, non ! Les parents n'avaient pas les moyens de payer une licence. Mais je sais qu'il est un membre assidu de sa bibliothèque de quartier. Ce gamin adore les livres. Surtout les histoires avec des magiciens, des dragons et toutes ces créatures fantastiques qu'il ne peut pas voir ni au cinéma ni sur écran à cause du manque d'argent. La bibliothèque est encore le seul endroit gratuit pour les moins de dix-huit ans. L'employée est l'une de mes amies. C'est d'ailleurs moi qui ai conseillé à Nathan d'aller voir Nina, c'est à deux pas de chez lui et du coup, nous discutons parfois du gamin entre nous. Allez lui parler, si vous voulez. Tenez, je vous note l'adresse.

– C'est très aimable, merci, dit Agathe en acceptant d'arracher une feuille de son carnet afin que l'enseignante y note les coordonnées.

La gentillesse de madame Fourcade et sa volonté de satisfaire Agathe dans ses démarches étaient touchantes. Le malheur qui frappait cet enfant était si horrible, si peu ordinaire que tous ceux qu'elle rencontra ce jour-là furent plus que désireux de lui apporter toute l'aide dont elle avait besoin pour cerner la personnalité de l'orphelin.

Nina, la bibliothécaire, était une magnifique brune vêtue tout de noir à la dernière mode, avec des yeux aux nuances d'ambre qu'elle maquillait savamment. Elle était bien plus grande qu'Agathe, qui pourtant était perchée sur des chaussures à talons de six bons centimètres. Au premier abord, elle avait l'air un peu froide, mais cette impression disparaissait dès qu'elle se mettait à parler, son sourire révélant des dents d'une blancheur éclatante.

Grâce à Nina, la thérapeute sut quels livres Nathan avait empruntés. Ainsi, elle put se faire une idée très précise de ses goûts. Une fois la phase d'étude terminée, elle saurait quel genre de lectures serait susceptible d'éveiller son intérêt.

Après son passage à la bibliothèque, elle décida de

retourner à l'institut. Il était déjà seize heures et, le temps de faire la route jusqu'en Normandie, la soirée serait bien entamée ; elle aurait voulu rentrer tôt pour une fois. Elle reviendrait un autre jour interroger les commerçants du quartier et éventuellement la petite Aurélie, avec l'autorisation de ses parents.

Elle recopia ses notes sur son ordinateur, puis dîna à la cafétéria en compagnie de Fanny. Enfin, elle rejoignit son petit immeuble de trois étages sans ascenseur où elle occupait un T 3 très *cosy* au second.

Il n'y avait pas de concierge comme dans certains bâtiments parisiens ni même de code pour entrer. Fatiguée d'avoir conduit une bonne partie de la journée, elle monta les escaliers avec lassitude et, lorsqu'elle posa les yeux sur son paillasson, elle poussa un hurlement en voyant le cadavre de ce qui ressemblait à un chat, les tripes à l'air, des mouches vrombissant autour de la plaie béante. Elle fit tomber ses clefs et son sac à main par terre, les deux mains devant la bouche, une envie de vomir la faisant chanceler jusqu'à la porte de son voisin de palier qui, alerté par son cri strident, venait d'ouvrir sa porte.

– Qu'est-ce qui se passe, ma p'tite dame ? En voilà un raffut à c't'heure !

Les larmes aux yeux, incapable de prononcer le moindre mot, Agathe désigna du doigt le corps de l'animal. Une odeur de charogne se répandait dans toute la cage d'escalier.

Depuis deux ans qu'elle habitait cet immeuble, à part les politesses d'usage, elle n'avait jamais adressé la parole à cet homme bourru qui maintenant lui posait une main réconfortante sur l'épaule :

– Allons, allons ! C'est rien, ça. Quelqu'un qui a

voulu vous faire une mauvaise blague. Y'a des gamins pas très nets qui traînent dans le village, ces jours-ci. M'étonnerait pas que ce soye un coup de ces vauriens.

Il disparut quelques instants dans la pénombre de son logement, puis revint avec un grand sac poubelle dans lequel il enferma le cadavre.

– Z'êtes bien délicate, fit-il, du reproche soudain dans la voix. M'en vais le mettre en bas au bourrier, z'en faites pas.

– M... Merci, bredouilla Agathe, dont tous les membres tremblaient.

– À vot' service, mademoiselle. Mais faudrait pas que ça devienne une habitude, hein ! Faut vous endurcir un peu. La vie, elle est pas tendre, vous savez. Allez ! Rentrez chez vous, oust ! Disparaissez !

Il avait quasiment hurlé ces derniers mots. Le changement de ton fit frissonner Agathe, qui prit peur. Cet homme n'avait pas l'air très équilibré. Même s'il était venu à son secours, quelque chose lui disait qu'il valait mieux ne pas trop chercher à le connaître.

Malgré les tremblements de sa main, elle ramassa ses clefs et parvint à ouvrir sa porte, les jambes écartées pour ne pas mettre les pieds sur le paillasson. Demain, elle le jetterait aux ordures et en achèterait un autre.

Une fois à l'abri dans le silence rassurant de son petit appartement, elle s'adossa à la porte, attendit que les battements de son cœur ralentissent.

Pourquoi avait-on déposé cet immonde cadavre de chat sur le pas de sa porte ? Et surtout, qui l'y avait mis ?

Ne pas céder à la panique.

Garder son calme.

Ne pas retourner dans le passé.

Avancer.

Il n'y avait aucune raison d'avoir peur. C'étaient sans doute des gosses, comme l'avait dit le voisin mal dégrossi. Elle se força à respirer à fond. Inspirer par le nez, expirer par la bouche. Elle ferma les yeux, prenant conscience des pulsations de plus en plus lentes de son cœur.

Ça va aller… ça va aller.

À peu près maîtresse d'elle-même, elle accrocha son sac à la patère de l'entrée en un geste machinal, puis alla s'échouer sur le canapé, allumant la télévision. Deux secondes plus tard, son cœur fit encore un bond lorsque la sonnette de la porte retentit.

L'angoisse et l'irritation se lièrent. D'un bond, elle se releva et atteignit l'entrée en vociférant :

— Quoi encore ?

— C'est pour une livraison, fit une voix de jeune homme. J'ai des fleurs pour vous.

— À cette heure du soir ?

— Je travaille pour une société privée, madame, nos horaires ne sont pas les mêmes qu'à la Poste.

À travers le judas, elle vit effectivement une silhouette derrière un énorme bouquet de fleurs. Elle eut un peu honte de s'être ainsi emportée et ouvrit, malgré une méfiance marquée, pour réceptionner cette livraison inattendue.

Une enveloppe était agrafée au papier d'emballage. À l'intérieur, une carte de visite très sobre avec le nom et les coordonnées du lieutenant Salvant-Perret. Au dos de la carte, il était écrit :

« En espérant que vous pardonnerez la plus

pitoyable tentative de séduction jamais enregistrée.

Je suis désolé. Je ne recommencerai plus sans votre permission.

L.S-P »

Agathe sourit, charmée par ce geste et ce petit mot qui, au lieu d'exprimer des remords, ne faisait que confirmer son désir de lui plaire.

Chapitre 9

Rien n'était plus rébarbatif qu'un compte-rendu écrit par un flic. Cependant, la prose réglementaire de Maud Cortès avait quelque chose d'agréable. Louis n'aurait su dire quoi au juste, mais la lecture de son entretien avec Christian Blanchard lui sembla aussi prenante qu'un roman de Lemaitre. Amary n'allait certainement pas apprécier, mais Cortès avait l'excuse de l'inexpérience, le commissaire passerait l'éponge.

L'automobiliste rapportait comment Fabrice Lemonnier s'était énervé après avoir constaté que son véhicule était bien plus endommagé que le sien, alors que le premier avait freiné sans raison. Lorsque Maud demanda pourquoi il avait donné ce fameux coup de frein, Blanchard déclara qu'il avait voulu s'arrêter sur le bas-côté de la route parce que son téléphone portable avait sonné et qu'il voulait répondre à l'appel. Il se mit à bafouiller lorsqu'on lui demanda ensuite s'il avait mis son clignotant pour signaler sa manœuvre. Il était clair que ce n'était pas le cas et que, par conséquent, Lemonnier avait toutes les raisons du monde d'être en colère, quand bien même il n'avait pas été maître de son véhicule. D'ailleurs, Blanchard opta pour cette défense :

— Oui, mais s'il m'est rentré dedans, c'est qu'il ne respectait pas les distances de sécurité. Il est en tort de toute façon, quoi qu'il en dise ! Et puis ce n'est quand même pas une raison pour me coller son poing dans la figure !

— Vous pouviez porter plainte, avait fait remarquer le lieutenant Cortès. Pourquoi ne pas l'avoir fait ?

— Avec ce genre de bonhomme, on ne sait jamais quelles vont être les représailles. J'ai préféré laisser courir.

— Vous lui en vouliez pour ce coup de poing ? C'est une vilaine balafre qu'il vous a laissée, dites-moi.

— Je l'avais mauvaise, ça, pour sûr !

— Vous n'avez pas eu envie de vous venger ?

— J'aurais pu.

— Vous aviez son adresse sur le constat. N'avez-vous pas cherché à lui rendre une petite visite, histoire de remettre les compteurs à zéro ?

À ce moment-là, l'homme ouvrit la bouche dans l'intention de répondre, puis la referma aussitôt, son esprit moulinant afin de trouver un sens à toutes ces questions. Il avait comme l'impression que cette flic voulait lui faire avouer une chose qu'il n'avait pas faite.

Il se rembrunit, sourcils froncés, et demanda :

— C'est quoi, ces questions ? Qu'est-ce que vous voulez ?

— Juste des éclaircissements sur les suites de cet accident, rien de plus. Il ne faut pas vous énerver.

— Il n'y a pas eu de suite, comme vous dites ! J'ai eu un arrêt de travail d'une semaine et point barre !

— Donc, vous n'êtes pas allé au domicile de

monsieur Lemonnier ? À aucun moment ?

— Mais qu'il crève, ce blaireau ! Arrêtez de me bassiner avec ce pauvre type !

— Eh bien, justement, il se trouve que monsieur Lemonnier est mort.

Blanchard devint livide, se leva d'un bond en renversant sa chaise, les bras en l'air en signe de reddition :

— Wow ! Wow ! Wow ! On se calme tout de suite, là ! C'est quoi, ça ? Je vous vois venir. J'ai pas touché à un cheveu de ce mec, OK ? Je sais même pas où il habite ni où il bosse. Et vous savez quoi ? Je n'ai rien fait, vous n'avez pas le droit de me retenir ici, je me tire !

Maud avait eu toutes les peines du monde à l'apaiser et à le faire rasseoir. Elle raconta cet épisode éprouvant pour elle alors qu'ils prenaient un verre au « Loup des Cévennes », leur QG, après leur journée de travail.

Louis fit remarquer qu'elle avait traité Blanchard comme un suspect alors que jusque-là, il n'y avait aucun soupçon sur lui. Ni sur personne d'autre, d'ailleurs.

— J'avais cru comprendre que vous n'écartiez pas l'hypothèse qu'il ait voulu se venger de s'être retrouvé à l'hôpital. J'ai été obligée de diriger l'entretien dans ce sens.

— C'est vrai, je ne vous reproche rien, Cortès, vous vous en êtes très bien sortie, la réconforta Louis.

— Oui, mais après ça, il s'est fermé comme une huître et je n'ai rien pu en tirer de plus. Le bon côté, c'est que maintenant qu'on a les conclusions de la légiste au sujet de Fabrice Lemonnier, on est presque sûrs qu'il y avait quelqu'un d'autre cette nuit-là. Alors pourquoi pas Christian Blanchard, malgré son numéro ?

— Il faut d'abord retrouver ce morceau de dent sur les lieux du massacre, fit remarquer Ismaël, qui soufflait patiemment sur son thé fumant. Amary n'était pas trop chaud pour faire revenir l'équipe technique, ça coûte cher. Il doit rappeler le juge d'instruction demain à la première heure pour obtenir son feu vert. La version du père qui pète les plombs et se suicide après aurait arrangé tout le monde. Y'a plutôt intérêt à ce qu'ils la trouvent, cette foutue dent, autrement on va se faire démonter, là-haut !

— Ils vont la trouver, je le sens, fit Louis avec la plus grande conviction. Et vous avez bien fait de pousser Blanchard dans ses retranchements, Cortès. Avez-vous eu l'impression qu'il jouait la comédie ? Qu'il pouvait mentir en affirmant ne pas être allé chez Lemonnier ?

— Je suis sûre que c'était sincère. N'importe qui au poste pourra vous le confirmer, la salle de travail était bondée, le commandant Fontaine est même intervenu pour m'aider à le calmer. Apparemment, ce monsieur a autant le sang chaud que feu Lemonnier. C'est pas étonnant qu'ils en soient venus aux mains. Mais de là à assassiner toute une famille pour se venger d'une simple droite, il y a un monde, vous ne croyez pas ?

— Une piste qui se refroidit, fit Ismaël pensivement. Pas comme ce thé brûlant !

— J'aimerais bien savoir ce que signifie la lettre en forme de « L » sur le matelas, dit à son tour Louis. Si on a affaire à un tueur, il s'agit soit d'un indice qu'il laisse volontairement afin que l'on comprenne son geste, soit d'une signature.

— Je préférerais que ce soit l'initiale de son prénom, parce que ce qui m'inquiète, moi, intervint Maud, c'est qu'une lettre en appelle une autre si l'on veut former un mot, ou une phrase. Il n'est donc pas impossible que l'on se retrouve avec d'autres corps sur les bras d'ici peu.

— Tu vas nous porter la poisse ! s'écria Ismaël en faisant semblant de cracher par terre pour éloigner le mauvais sort. Il ne manquerait plus qu'un tueur en série pour compléter notre carrière. Je suis sûr qu'Amary et Fontaine n'en ont jamais poursuivi un seul de toute leur vie et il faut que ça tombe sur nous !

— Il y a peut-être déjà eu d'autres cas similaires à cette affaire, avec le même mode opératoire. Dès qu'on en saura davantage, je contacte mon ami Yves Vidal, il est analyste au SALVAC, il pourra faire des recherches dans le fichier en priorité. Pour l'instant, il n'y a eu que ce cas-là.

— Oui, mais avec cinq cadavres quand même ! S'il remet ça, la cigale de la morgue ne va pas avoir assez de tiroirs pour garder les macchabées au frais.

— Espérons que ça n'arrivera pas. De toute façon, on va attendre de voir s'ils mettent la main sur le bout de molaire, on avisera à ce moment-là. Je serais d'avis d'aller interroger les gens du quartier pour savoir s'ils auraient vu quelqu'un rôder.

— L'enquête de proximité a déjà été faite, fit remarquer Maud.

— Certes. Mais on ne soupçonnait pas une tierce personne. Les gens ont été interrogés au sujet de la nuit du massacre. On ne leur a pas demandé si les

Lemonnier recevaient de la visite, si un inconnu traînait dans les parages les jours précédents, ou si un véhicule avait stationné plusieurs jours d'affilée dans la rue, par exemple.

– On s'y attelle dès demain, lança Maud avec son enthousiasme coutumier. J'aime aller à la rencontre de la population. Ça donne une image bienveillante de notre bonne vieille police.

– J'y crois pas : elle kiffe le porte-à-porte ! Tu as raté ta vocation, c'est représentante de commerce que tu aurais dû faire.

– Mon Dieu, non ! Quelle horreur ! Les gens n'ouvrent pas leur porte à ce genre de personnes et de toute façon, il n'y en a plus guère qui sillonnent les routes de nos jours. Non, une carte de police avec le bandeau tricolore ouvre bien plus de portes qu'un aspirateur ou une encyclopédie obsolète. Et qu'y a-t-il de mal à ne pas vouloir toujours être dans la répression ? Il y a de la bonté en chacun de nous. Je suis persuadée que si nous faisions preuve d'un peu plus de gentillesse au quotidien dans chacun de nos actes, le monde n'en serait que meilleur.

Maud avait souvent tendance à tenir ce genre de discours aussi fantaisiste qu'utopique. Si au moins elle avait la gentillesse silencieuse, mais non ! C'était à se demander comment elle avait réussi son concours pour passer lieutenant avec des idées pareilles ! Parfois, Ismaël avait l'impression qu'elle ne vivait pas dans le même monde que le reste de la population.

Elle trouvait toujours des excuses, ou tout au moins des circonstances atténuantes, aux pires malfaiteurs, distribuait des cadeaux à tous les membres du commissariat pour les anniversaires, et ne parlons pas de Noël ! Il la soupçonnait de se priver pour offrir des présents aux gens qui l'entouraient. Ou alors, elle avait touché un gros héritage et il n'était pas au courant.

Quand elle arrivait le matin, c'était des « Bonjour, mon petit lapin » ou « Coucou, mon chou à la crème ». Son seul défaut, c'était d'avoir la larme facile lorsqu'elle était confrontée à des gens hermétiques à son débordement de bonté. Et ça arrivait souvent dans leur métier. Mais elle savait faire la part des choses. Elle pouvait se montrer intransigeante quand il le fallait.

De fait, la plupart des personnes du poste l'adoraient, bien entendu. Comment ne pas l'aimer ? Seuls quelques esprits aigris trouvaient le moyen de la critiquer ; ils se comptaient sur les doigts d'une seule main. Le commandant Fontaine faisait partie de ceux-là. Mais cet homme semblait n'aimer personne, de toute façon.

Entre Louis Servant-Perret et Maud Cortès, leur trio était loin du cliché des flics qui en veulent, qui attaquent sur tous les fronts ou mènent leurs interrogatoires et leurs arrestations tambour battant. Même avec la pire des racailles, ils n'élevaient que très rarement la voix, ce qui déstabilisait les petits caïds aussi bien que les gros durs des banlieues.

Une autre semaine passa avant que l'équipe des techniciens ne mette la main sur le morceau de dent manquant que Louis espérait tant. Il s'était niché dans la terre d'un pot de fleurs dont la plante agonisait tristement faute de soins.

La légiste confirma qu'il s'agissait bien de l'élément qui prouvait que quelqu'un avait frappé Fabrice Lemonnier à son domicile, peu avant sa pendaison. Et ça changeait tout. Désormais, ils avaient un tueur dans la nature. Un individu capable d'égorger des enfants sans l'ombre d'un remords. La position dans laquelle les corps avaient été retrouvés démontrait une absence totale d'empathie ou de regret. Autant dire un monstre.

Le second passage dans le voisinage immédiat du domicile des Lemonnier n'avait rien donné de probant. Une vieille femme avait bien remarqué un homme louche qui avait squatté une entrée d'immeuble en face de chez elle, mais il s'avéra que c'était un sans domicile fixe inoffensif qui ne remit plus les pieds dans le quartier après cette dénonciation. Les gens de la rue aussi ont leur fierté, et le brave homme n'appréciait pas qu'on le confonde avec un malfaisant.

Ils vérifièrent les plaques d'immatriculation de toutes les voitures stationnées à deux pâtés de maisons à la ronde sans découvrir le moindre véhicule volé. À tous les trois, ils avaient interrogé tous les habitants vivants, il ne restait plus que le cimetière à deux rues de là, ou les quelques matous qui traînaient dans les coins sombres.

Tout ce qu'ils parvinrent à obtenir, ce furent des commérages au sujet de la mère Lemonnier qui sortait parfois en chemise de nuit pour amener son petit dernier à l'école, enfilant simplement un manteau par-dessus, en chaussons, pas coiffée ni maquillée, la démarche incertaine d'une ivrogne.

Françoise Bonnemort signala qu'elle n'avait pas trouvé de traces de marqueur sur les doigts des quatre cadavres. Aucun d'entre eux n'avait donc écrit la mystérieuse lettre « L » à l'envers du matelas. Elle avait également demandé que le labo lance des recherches d'ADN sur un prélèvement effectué sur la joue tuméfiée de Fabrice Lemonnier, sans résultat. En revanche, elle avait relevé la présence de phyllosilicate de magnésium – du talc en langage courant – qui devait avoir servi d'agent lubrifiant pour enfiler des gants de latex. Or, aucun gant de ce genre n'avait été retrouvé ni dans la maison ni dans les bacs à ordures, qui furent minutieusement fouillés après l'annonce de la présence d'un autre individu le soir de la tuerie.

Il y eut une conférence de presse, la nouvelle fit grand bruit dans les journaux télévisés et la presse écrite. On redoutait qu'un dangereux psychopathe coure les rues à la recherche d'une famille à trucider. Il était recommandé de bien vérifier que les portes et fenêtres étaient verrouillées à la nuit tombée, dans toute la capitale et ses banlieues, même éloignées. Rien ne prouvait que ce scénario se reproduirait, on pouvait encore moins prévoir où cela aurait lieu, mais sur ce coup, Amary avait eu confiance en l'instinct de Salvant-Perret : ce n'était pas fini. Il fallait prévenir la population du danger qui rôdait.

Ce vendredi soir, Louis s'installa à une table en terrasse d'un petit restaurant vietnamien de son quartier. L'agitation qui avait secoué le poste cette semaine l'avait lessivé, il n'avait aucune envie de se préparer à manger et de se retrouver seul avec un plateau devant la télévision.

Il tournait et retournait les derniers événements dans sa tête quand son portable se mit à vibrer sur la table où il l'avait posé. Il avala la dernière bouchée de son troisième rouleau de printemps – la serveuse, sachant qu'il en raffolait, lui en apportait toujours deux supplémentaires, à sa plus grande joie – et s'essuya les lèvres tout en vérifiant le nom de son correspondant. Il n'y en avait pas. Juste un numéro. Il se montra méfiant lorsqu'il répondit, mais son cœur fit un bond dans sa poitrine quand il reconnut la voix de la belle psychologue qui se présentait.

– Docteur Delcourt, dit-il en se rejetant sur le dossier de sa chaise, tout sourire.

– Comment savez-vous que je suis docteur ?

– Vous ne l'êtes pas ?

– Si. Mais j'aurais pu ne pas l'être. Tous les psychologues n'ont pas fait médecine.

– Mais vous, si. Que me vaut le plaisir de cet appel ?

– Je voulais vous remercier pour les fleurs. Elles étaient splendides. Je n'ai pas eu le temps de vous appeler avant, mais si ça vous intéresse : vous êtes pardonné.

Il se fit un court silence. Louis n'aurait su exprimer le bonheur que venaient de lui procurer ces trois derniers mots. Il avait espéré cet appel, ou un message de la part de la jeune femme. Mais presque deux semaines s'étaient écoulées sans qu'elle se manifestât. Il avait essayé de l'effacer de son esprit, de se consacrer aux enquêtes en cours en évitant de penser à elle.

Cela avait plus ou moins fonctionné et, à présent qu'il l'avait au bout du fil, il se sentait aussi timoré qu'un collégien boutonneux.

– Vous avez perdu votre langue ? relança la psychologue, sans doute un peu gênée de ce silence aussi.

– Non, non. C'est juste que je ne m'attendais pas à ce que vous m'appeliez directement sur mon portable.

— Vous avez laissé votre carte, lui rappela-t-elle.

— C'est juste. Et vous ne l'avez pas jetée à la poubelle, j'en suis heureux. Puis-je vous demander comment évolue le petit Nathan ? Le commissaire nous a fortement conseillé d'attendre que ce soit vous qui nous contactiez pour avoir de ses nouvelles, mais puisque vous avez fait le premier pas...

— Son état est stationnaire. Pas d'évolution pour le moment. Je dirais même qu'il est en pleine régression. Mais c'est une façon d'exorciser sa souffrance. Comme c'est le cas avec ce genre de traumatisme, les larmes sont en quelque sorte coincées, il faut alors évacuer d'une manière ou d'une autre.

— Il n'a toujours pas parlé ?

— Toujours pas. Cela dit, j'ai appris qu'il n'était pas d'un naturel très communicatif. C'est un enfant précoce, le saviez-vous ?

— J'avoue que je l'ignorais.

— Que faites-vous donc de vos journées dans la police si vous n'enquêtez pas ?

— Il s'agit d'une victime, mademoiselle Delcourt, et il a sept ans !

— Et alors ? le défia-t-elle. Toute personne, si jeune soit-elle, a une existence propre, un passé, une palette parfois complexe d'autres individus qui gravitent autour d'elle. Vous auriez beaucoup à apprendre des enfants, monsieur Salvant-Perret.

Elle avait prononcé son nom avec une insistance ironique, comme pour lui faire remarquer que se donner du « mademoiselle » et du « monsieur » était prétentieux.

— Vous pouvez m'appeler Louis, dit-il. Puis-je vous appeler Agathe en retour ?

Elle parut hésiter une fraction de seconde, mais finit par accepter.

— Vous savez, fit alors Louis, j'ai une fille : France-Alix. Quand elle était petite et jusqu'à ce qu'elle atteigne l'âge de douze ans à peu près, elle irradiait par son énergie et sa gaîté. C'était un véritable moulin à paroles aussi, pas moyen de l'arrêter ! À cette époque-là, elle et moi, on se comprenait rien qu'en se regardant.

Il fit une pause, gagné par la mélancolie qu'engendraient ces souvenirs.

— Qu'est-ce qui s'est passé ? demanda doucement Agathe.

— Elle a grandi. Il y a eu le divorce avec sa mère, et ce n'était plus la même personne.

— En êtes-vous sûr ?

Louis réfléchit un instant à cette question qu'il s'était si souvent posée :

— Je n'en sais rien. Peut-être que c'est moi qui ai changé.

— Souvent, les enfants font ressurgir l'enfant qui est en nous, adultes. Elle a su le faire apparaître chez vous lorsqu'elle était petite. Peut-être que c'est à votre tour, maintenant, de faire ressortir l'enfant qu'elle était. L'adolescence est une période de transition où l'on se perd un peu soi-même. On a parfois besoin qu'on nous rappelle quel enfant on a été pour savoir qui on est vraiment.

— Ça a du sens, ce que vous dites, approuva Louis. Je devrais peut-être envisager une thérapie avec vous ?

— Ne soyez pas ridicule, vous n'avez nul besoin d'une thérapie. Et puis je ne m'occupe que des enfants. Envoyez-moi plutôt votre fille.

— Vous êtes sérieuse ?

— Non.

Ils se mirent à rire. Cet échange détendit considérablement l'atmosphère entre eux.

— Pour en revenir à Nathan, reprit Louis, si j'ai bien compris, vous avez réussi à obtenir des informations sur lui ? Mais comment avez-vous fait ? Vous dites qu'il ne communique pas et il ne lui reste aucune famille vivante.

Agathe lui expliqua alors sa façon de procéder dès qu'un nouvel enfant lui était confié. Louis trouva son sérieux peu commun et admirable. Son implication allait plus loin que celle de n'importe quel autre thérapeute de sa connaissance. Il en ressentit d'autant plus de désir de mieux connaître une personne aussi dévouée aux causes qu'elle défendait. En revanche, il se garda bien d'exprimer ses sentiments à voix haute, de peur d'essuyer une réprimande de la part du commissaire si jamais il allait trop loin.

Le porc au caramel que la serveuse lui avait apporté était froid depuis bien longtemps quand il dit au revoir à Agathe. Ils avaient discuté pendant plus d'une heure. Le temps avait filé à toute allure, il n'avait rien vu. Elle s'était montrée absolument charmante, intelligente, spirituelle et d'un tempérament bien trempé.

Même froids, les morceaux de viande caramélisés lui parurent un délice. Il termina son assiette rapidement, paya et quitta la terrasse en se promettant d'amener la psychologue un jour prochain dans ce petit restaurant qu'il aimait tant.

Automne 2000

Claude Albert ne retenait plus ses larmes. C'était un véritable déluge. L'odeur dans la pièce était insoutenable, le spectacle du sang et des deux cadavres au-delà du supportable. Jusque-là, si son corps l'avait trahi, secoué de tremblements incontrôlables, son mental avait miraculeusement résisté. Il essayait de sauver les apparences en refoulant les sanglots qui menaçaient de l'étouffer. Mais les digues avaient cédé d'un coup. Il n'avait plus pleuré comme ça depuis qu'il était enfant. Ils allaient tous y passer, c'était certain.

Derrière son masque de chat, l'homme gardait le silence depuis de longues minutes. À pas lents, il tournait autour de leur cercle morbide en prenant soin de ne jamais marcher dans les énormes flaques brunes qui s'étalaient tout doucement sur le linoléum.

L'on n'entendait plus que le déclic du couteau à cran d'arrêt qu'il enclenchait toutes les dix secondes, un son métallique entêtant lorsqu'il repliait la lame dans son logement avec un soin maniaque.

La plaie sur le cou de Victor le faisait souffrir, mais il n'avait plus de larmes pour extérioriser sa douleur. Le corps de sa mère s'était lentement affaissé, sa tête sans vie reposait sur les genoux du garçon tétanisé à la vue du gouffre béant qu'était la gorge de la femme. Il ne parvenait pas à détacher son regard de la déchirure monstrueuse, des yeux révulsés qui ne voyaient plus rien, de la bouche tordue en un cri muet et de la langue qui pendait sur le côté en une grimace burlesque qui n'avait rien de drôle.

L'homme, en revanche, avait l'air de se délecter de cette scène d'épouvante, même si l'on ne pouvait pas voir l'expression de son visage. Il finit par s'arrêter devant Claude. Immobile, les jambes écartées, il penchait vers lui ses traits de chat où le bleu de ses yeux semblait luire d'une menace latente.

Claude avait l'odieuse sensation de n'être qu'une pauvre merde face à ce monstre de cruauté planté devant lui. Il se laissait aller sans aucune retenue à présent, parce qu'il savait que ce serait bientôt son tour.

— Allons, allons ! fit la voix doucereuse de leur persécuteur, presque apaisante malgré la situation. C'est à cause de ta femme que tu pleures ? À quoi elle servait, franchement ? Regarde autour de toi, c'est une véritable porcherie, ici. Ça fait combien de temps que le torchon à poussière n'a pas été passé sur ces meubles, hein ?

Était-ce une question à laquelle Claude devait répondre ? Ou bien devait-il garder le silence ? Comment savoir ce que ce détraqué attendait de lui ? Malgré les larmes qui brouillaient sa vision, il leva la tête, cherchant dans ce regard froid un signe qu'il ne vit pas.

— Trois enfants ! reprit l'homme. Tu te crois sans doute viril parce que tu as planté tes saloperies de

petites graines dans le ventre de ta pathétique jument ? Tu sais combien on est sur cette Terre ? Est-ce que tu as une idée du nombre d'inconscients dans ton genre qui flattent leur ego *en se reproduisant, en engendrant des parasites qui pillent les dernières ressources de la planète ? Non, bien sûr ! Ça te dépasse, tout ça. Jamais tu ne te demandes si tes petits-enfants auront la moitié de tout ce que tu as gaspillé durant ta misérable vie de cloporte reproducteur.*

Ce n'était pas du reproche dans le ton de la voix, mais un profond mépris.

— Dans cinquante ans, à ce rythme, il n'y aura plus d'eau ni de nourriture suffisante pour tout le monde. Les déchets s'entassent, débordent. Les océans sont des poubelles. Il y a des surfaces aussi grandes que des continents saturées de plastique. Ils commencent enfin à prendre conscience de l'ampleur de la catastrophe qui nous pend au nez. Mais est-ce que ça t'inquiète, toi ? Est-ce que tu as réfléchi une seconde à toute la merde que tes enfants allaient produire ?

Claude ne comprenait son discours qu'à moitié. Il ne savait pas où il voulait en venir ni pourquoi il s'en prenait à lui et à sa famille en particulier. Cela n'avait aucun sens.

— Je n'ai rien fait, parvint-il à articuler.

Sa langue restait collée à son palais, il avait la gorge sèche, sa tête tournait, son esprit ne fonctionnait plus.

— Quoi ?

L'homme-chat s'était accroupi. Claude sentit qu'il ne pourrait plus en supporter davantage, il allait craquer, il devenait fou tellement il avait peur. Les gémissements de Mélissa lui parvenaient, mais il avait l'impression qu'elle était loin, si loin !

— Qu'est-ce que tu as dit ? insista l'homme avec plus de véhémence.

— Je n'ai rien fait, répéta Claude, qui s'enhardissait en dépit de sa terreur. Laissez-nous tranquilles, on ne dira rien, je vous le jure !

Le couteau vint se planter dans sa cuisse avec une telle rapidité que le père de famille ne sentit pas tout de suite la douleur. La lame n'avait pas pénétré profondément, mais suffisamment pour qu'il se mette à perdre son sang abondamment lorsque l'homme retira le couteau.

Aucun cri ne sortit de sa bouche. Il poussa juste un gémissement qu'il essaya de toutes ses forces d'étouffer pour ne pas déclencher davantage de fureur chez leur tortionnaire. Ses traits se tordirent en un masque de souffrance tandis que la voix reprenait, pleine de colère, cette fois :

— Comment oses-tu dire que tu n'as rien fait ? Tu es comme tous les autres de cette race humaine : inconscient, égoïste, destructeur, lâche et faible ! Regarde-toi ! On dirait une loque. Tu pleures et tu transpires. Ta crasse sort par tous les pores de ta peau. Vous me dégoûtez !

Claude sentait que la tension était montée d'un cran. De sa main gauche, il tâchait de faire pression sur sa blessure à la cuisse, comme on le lui avait appris aux cours de premiers secours obligatoires dans son entreprise, afin de stopper l'hémorragie. Son bras droit était entraîné vers l'arrière par le poids du corps de sa femme gisant à moitié sur son plus jeune fils.

— Vous ne comprenez pas. Personne ne réalise la

gravité de la situation. D'ailleurs, ça ne vous intéresse même pas. Vous ne pensez qu'à vous-mêmes, vous ne voyez pas plus loin que le bout de vos chaussures !

Qu'est-ce que c'était que ce charabia ? Qui était ce détraqué ? Claude avait beau essayer de se concentrer, sa voix ne lui disait rien, son allure non plus. Il était certain de n'avoir jamais rencontré cet homme avant. Avant, pensa-t-il, le cœur près de lâcher tellement son désespoir était immense, sa douleur à la cuisse lancinante. Il y avait un avant, mais y aurait-il un après ? Rien n'était moins sûr et cette perspective anéantissait tout désir de lutte. C'était perdu d'avance, leur destin était scellé, leur mort annoncée. Et ça continuait :

– Tu fais partie de ce troupeau beuglant qui s'entasse dans les transports en commun, qui fait la queue aux Allocations familiales. Vous copulez, vous vous reproduisez comme des rats sans vous rendre compte que si l'État vous donne des aides, c'est qu'il a besoin de vos gosses pour les asservir. Tu as mis au monde des esclaves destinés à consommer pour enrichir ces mêmes gouvernements qui t'aident à les nourrir ! Ces gouvernements qui souillent la planète et qui s'en foutent parce qu'ils ne seront plus là quand la Terre vomira sa colère. Vous pensez être libres, mais vous n'êtes que des moutons décérébrés. Vous, ces couples qui faites des gosses, je vous hais, vous entendez ! On devrait stériliser toute la population jusqu'à ce que la race humaine soit exterminée ! Les scientifiques devraient lâcher un virus pour tous vous tuer. Un génocide à l'échelle mondiale, oui !

Il était complètement dément ! Il s'exaltait lui-

même. Les mots sortaient de sa bouche derrière le masque comme s'il les vomissait. Une excitation malsaine le secouait. Il s'était redressé, le couteau maculé de sang toujours dans sa main, ses yeux glacials lançaient des éclairs de folie meurtrière.

Enfin, d'un coup, il se calma. Ses bras retombèrent le long de son corps et il déclara d'une voix presque solennelle :

— Je vais te laisser le choix : un seul de tes enfants aura le droit de rester en vie. À toi de choisir lequel.

Chapitre 10

Le *week-end* s'annonçait pluvieux. Au-dessus de la verdoyante campagne normande, le ciel était plombé de gros nuages sombres qui menaçaient d'éclater d'un moment à l'autre.

Arrivé la veille au soir chez ses parents, Louis Salvant-Perret s'était levé aux aurores alors qu'il aurait pu profiter du calme du domaine et faire une grasse matinée bien méritée.

Comme il avait débarqué un peu tard, il n'avait pas eu l'occasion de voir sa fille. Celle-ci était partie au cinéma avec une amie qu'elle venait de se faire dans son nouveau lycée. Une certaine Léa, une jeune fille de sa classe.

Installé dans le jardin d'hiver, il aperçut sa mère un peu plus loin dans la serre, déjà occupée à couper les fleurs fanées de la végétation luxuriante dont les cimes touchaient le plafond de verre. C'était son endroit à elle, son havre de paix, son refuge. Depuis qu'elle avait pris sa retraite, elle y passait le plus clair de son temps. Soit elle prenait soin de ses innombrables plantes, soit elle lisait, à l'endroit même où Louis était en train de prendre son petit déjeuner.

– Pourquoi tu te lèves si tôt, mon chéri ? avait

demandé Hélène, un seau vert pomme dans une main, des sécateurs dans l'autre.

— Tu sais bien que je suis du matin. J'ai les idées claires et l'esprit bien éveillé. Et puis j'aime bien te voir déambuler dans la verdure au lever du jour.

Hélène sourit avec attendrissement :

— C'est bien, fit-elle d'une voix un peu lointaine. Promets-moi une chose, Louis, veux-tu ?

— Oui ?

— Promets-moi que tu t'occuperas de mes plantes quand je ne serai plus là.

Louis manqua s'étouffer avec son café :

— Qu'est-ce qui te prend de parler comme ça ?

Puis, soudain inquiet, il ajouta :

— Tu n'es pas malade, n'est-ce pas ?

Tout à coup, il n'avait plus du tout d'appétit. Il était incapable d'avaler quoi que ce soit à la pensée que sa mère pouvait lui avoir caché qu'elle souffrait d'une maladie et qu'elle puisse disparaître. Il devait bien avouer qu'il n'avait encore jamais imaginé un instant que ses deux parents mourraient un jour, comme s'ils étaient éternels. Il avait beau côtoyer la mort presque quotidiennement, il n'arrivait pas à admettre que cela pouvait les toucher eux.

Comme elle ne répondait pas, Louis l'appela, la voix transformée par l'angoisse.

— Non, non, je vais bien, le rassura-t-elle. Mais vois-tu, parfois, je me demande qui prendra soin de la serre quand je ne pourrai plus m'en occuper. Je vieillis, tu sais.

— Ne dis pas de bêtises, tu es en pleine forme et tu fais dix ans de moins que ton âge !

— Avoir l'air plus jeune ne signifie pas que l'on se sente plus jeune, Louis. Il y a des choses que je fais moins facilement. Quand je me lève, il me faut dix bonnes minutes avant de pouvoir marcher correctement tant mes articulations sont douloureuses. Dans ces moments, je t'assure que j'ai plutôt l'air d'une mamie de quatre-vingt-dix ans !

C'était la première fois que Louis entendait sa mère parler de cette façon. D'une nature plutôt discrète, tout comme lui d'ailleurs, elle ne se plaignait que rarement – pour ne pas dire jamais –, ce qui ne manqua pas d'alerter le lieutenant.

Elle avait quitté ses gants de travail, s'assit à la table de jardin face à son fils, à qui elle adressa un sourire empli de douceur, voyant à quel point ses paroles l'avaient affecté.

– Ne t'inquiète pas, je ne voulais pas te faire peur. Tout va bien. Parle-moi plutôt de toi : ton père m'a dit que tu étais sur l'affaire de cette famille assassinée dont tous les journaux parlent. As-tu vu ce pauvre garçon qui a survécu ? Quelle horreur ! Comme il doit être malheureux, cet enfant.

– Il est entre de bonnes mains, rassure-toi. Il a été placé à l'institut Saint-Jean, dans un service spécialisé.

– Parce qu'il y a des services spécialisés pour les enfants dont on a tué toute la famille ? Dans quel monde on vit, tout de même !

– C'est un service spécialisé grand trauma de l'enfant. Mais ça ne concerne pas forcément des cas de meurtres. Il y a des victimes de pédophilie, d'inceste ou de violence parentale. C'est d'ailleurs la majorité des cas, heureusement. Enfin, si j'ose dire, ajouta Louis en voyant le visage horrifié de sa mère.

– Comment s'appelle-t-il ? Les journaux ne l'ont pas précisé, il me semble.

— Il s'appelle Nathan. Et il est préférable que le public en sache le moins possible pour la sécurité et le bien-être de l'enfant.

— Comment ça ? Je ne te suis pas. Puisque c'est le père du petit qui a fait une crise de démence meurtrière et qu'il s'est tué après, je ne vois pas comment ce gamin serait encore en danger.

— Maman, les journalistes ne savent pas tout et peut-être qu'il serait préférable que toi non plus.

— Oh ! fit-elle, offusquée. Depuis quand as-tu des secrets pour ta mère ? Tu sais pourtant que tout ce que tu me dis reste strictement entre nous.

— Je sais bien, mais là, c'est un peu différent. Je n'ai jamais eu affaire à un cinglé qui tue des enfants et leur mère sans le moindre état d'âme.

— Si je comprends bien, tu es en train de dire que ce serait quelqu'un d'autre qui aurait tué cette famille ? Le père ne s'est donc pas suicidé. Mais pourquoi ? Qui pourrait être assez malveillant pour assassiner des enfants ? Et pourquoi ne pas avoir tué Nathan ? C'est incompréhensible. S'il parle, le petit pourrait reconnaître le meurtrier.

— Sauf s'il ne l'a pas vu, dit Louis, que cette idée venait de frapper.

Il se leva d'un bond, soudain pressé, termina son café d'une longue lampée et embrassa sa mère sur la joue avant de quitter le jardin d'hiver en toute hâte, comme s'il avait le diable aux trousses.

Ce n'était pas la première fois que son fils trouvait la solution à un problème rien qu'en discutant avec elle des affaires qui l'occupaient. Aussi le regarda-t-elle disparaître sans sourciller, un demi-sourire aux lèvres, comme si c'était une attitude parfaitement normale qu'il s'échappe à toute vitesse en plein milieu d'une conversation.

Louis avait toujours supposé que Nathan avait assisté aux meurtres de ses parents et de ses frères et sœur. Mais si ça n'était pas le cas ? S'il s'était caché quelque part pendant le massacre et n'était reparu qu'une fois le danger passé ?

Certes, il avait été retrouvé couvert du sang de sa famille, mais il pouvait parfaitement être sorti de sa cachette et avoir tenté de secouer sa mère et les autres dans son affolement. Ce qui expliquait l'hémoglobine sur lui.

Il appela Ismaël. Comme celui-ci était de permanence ce samedi, il répondit aussitôt. Il était en route pour le commissariat. En quelques mots, Louis lui exposa l'idée qui venait de lui traverser l'esprit.

– OK, fit Ismaël, admettons qu'il n'ait pas assisté à la scène. Et après ? C'est quoi, ton plan ? Qu'est-ce que ça change ?

– Je ne sais pas encore, mais j'aimerais en avoir le cœur net. Il faut qu'on retourne dans la maison, qu'on cherche où le gamin aurait pu se cacher. Si on part du principe que le tueur n'est pas un des membres de la famille, il n'est pas logique qu'il ait épargné le gosse, si jeune soit-il. À sept ans, on est parfaitement capable de décrire quelqu'un. C'est un énorme risque. Et si ce tueur lit les journaux et que j'ai raison, il sait forcément qu'il a laissé un témoin derrière lui. Tu vois mieux ce que ça change, maintenant ?

– Tu as peut-être raison. Mais pour l'instant, tout ça, ce ne sont que des suppositions.

– Je passe te prendre pour déjeuner à midi. On retourne à la maison des Lemonnier. Je réserve une table aux *Cévennes*, à tout à l'heure.

Tout en remontant à l'étage pour se doucher et s'habiller, il réalisa qu'il n'aurait même pas eu l'occasion de voir sa fille alors qu'elle était là depuis bientôt deux semaines. Il se sentait coupable, se reprochait de ne pas être disponible pour elle, mais cette nouvelle affaire accaparait son esprit. Une fois la lumière faite sur cette enquête, il se promit de faire l'effort de se rapprocher de France-Alix.

Après tout, maintenant qu'elle n'était plus entre les griffes de son ex-femme, elle ne subirait plus son influence. C'était une chance qui lui était offerte, peut-être la dernière, il ne fallait pas qu'il la laisse filer entre ses doigts. Même s'il avait l'impression que sa fille lui échappait, les paroles de Vincent Salvant-Perret lui revenaient en mémoire : France-Alix l'aimait. Elle ne savait simplement plus comment le lui montrer parce qu'ils s'étaient éloignés au moment de la séparation avec Anne. À lui de renouer les liens maintenant que la jeune fille vivait chez ses grands-parents.

Fraîchement rasé, un pantalon de lin noir et une chemise assortie qui lui donnaient fière allure, Louis se retrouva nez à nez avec sa fille sur le palier alors qu'elle sortait de sa chambre en bâillant à gorge déployée.

— Bonjour, lui dit-il simplement, ne sachant pas quoi ajouter.

— Salut, répondit-elle sans même lui jeter un regard, le ton glacial.

Au temps pour lui et l'espoir qu'il restait un semblant d'amour entre eux ! Dans son pyjama en tissu polaire beige où un ours gambadait joyeusement sur le devant, elle avait l'air d'une grande enfant – ce qu'elle était, en réalité. On ne lui voyait pas la moitié du visage à cause de la masse de ses cheveux détachés qui le recouvrait.

Louis eut envie de la prendre dans ses bras, comme lorsqu'elle était petite et qu'il l'accueillait ainsi au saut du lit le dimanche matin. Comme cela aurait été bon ! Mais elle était déjà en train de descendre les marches, l'ignorant complètement. L'instant était perdu, c'était trop tard.

Il aurait dû lui demander comment s'était passée sa soirée, quel film elle était allée voir, avec qui elle était sortie. Au lieu de ça, il était planté en haut de la cage d'escalier, à la regarder disparaître sans oser la rappeler.

Lorsqu'il fut sur le périphérique, il passa un coup de fil à Ismaël. Ce dernier avait plaidé leur cause auprès du commissaire Amary, ils auraient une réponse avant quatorze heures. Ils décidèrent de se retrouver au « Loup des Cévennes » directement. Le trafic était chargé, Louis perdrait du temps s'il passait par le poste de police.

Contre toute attente, il arriva à bon port avant son collègue, qui apparut tout sourire, vingt minutes après que Louis se fût attablé.

– C'est un garçon ! claironna-t-il avec des étincelles dans ses pupilles noires.

Il était fou de joie, il rayonnait littéralement. Louis se leva, heureux pour lui, et lui donna une accolade chaleureuse, le félicitant avec sincérité.

– Jade a fait une écho ce matin. Comme j'étais de permanence, c'est sa mère qui l'a accompagnée. J'arrive pas à croire que je vais être papa ! Un petit gars, en plus, tu te rends compte ?

— Tu aurais été aussi heureux si ça avait été une fille, tu sais. C'est un peu tôt pour être sûr du sexe de l'enfant.

— Il était bien placé, aucun doute possible, c'est un mini-Ismaël !

— Vous avez réfléchi à des prénoms ?

— Secret défense, désolé ! Si je t'en parle, Jade m'étripe.

Ils plaisantèrent encore quelques minutes, partageant le bonheur du futur papa autour d'un verre. Ismaël étant en service, il n'avait pas le droit de boire de l'alcool. Louis fut solidaire, se contentant de trinquer avec un soda.

L'appel du commissaire Amary arriva alors qu'ils commandaient leur café. Par le biais d'Ismaël, il prévint le lieutenant Salvant-Perret que plus aucune équipe de la police technique et scientifique ne serait dépêchée, il ne fallait tout de même pas exagérer !

— Il te connaît bien, fit remarquer Ismaël après avoir coupé la communication.

— Je fais mon boulot, répliqua Louis, fort peu perturbé par les avertissements du taulier.

Ils expédièrent le café et l'addition, Louis était pressé de vérifier ses suppositions. Bien qu'ignorant où cela le mènerait, il pressentait que le tueur ne pouvait pas avoir pris le risque de laisser un témoin derrière lui.

Alors qu'ils venaient de bifurquer dans la rue où se situait la maison des Lemonnier, Louis, qui regardait en direction des commerces occupant le rez-de-chaussée des immeubles alentour, aperçut la silhouette à présent familière de la jeune psychologue. Elle n'était pas seule. Un homme était en train de lui parler en gesticulant.

Sans savoir pourquoi, les sens de Louis furent en alerte.

— Fais demi-tour, demanda-t-il dans un souffle à l'intention d'Ismaël.

Rien qu'au ton de sa voix, celui-ci ne chercha même pas à discuter. Il manœuvra dans une allée et rebroussa chemin en direction d'Agathe Delcourt, qui se trouvait face à ce journaliste minable, celui avec qui ils avaient eu une altercation le jour du massacre des Lemonnier.

Ismaël suivit le regard de Louis. Il ne lui fut pas difficile de reconnaître aussi l'individu :

— Ça serait pas l'autre demeuré de journaliste avec la psy ?

Louis voyait bien que plus la jeune femme reculait, plus le journaliste tentait une approche que le lieutenant considéra comme franchement lourde. Non seulement il affichait un sourire de dragueur de minettes qui allait très mal avec son allure un peu efféminée, mais en plus, il semblait aveugle au fait qu'Agathe affichait une gêne non dissimulée devant son manège. Sa posture laissait clairement supposer qu'elle cherchait à se débarrasser de l'homme.

— Ralentis, s'il te plaît.

Louis baissa sa vitre entièrement, prêt à en découdre avec le journaliste. Dès qu'il aperçut la voiture et ses occupants, ce dernier cessa ses mouvements de bras et se recula sensiblement d'Agathe, qui ne cacha pas son soulagement de les voir.

— Un problème, mademoiselle Delcourt ? demanda Louis, les yeux rivés sur le journaliste, qui choisit de déguerpir en maugréant des paroles incompréhensibles.

— Vous tombez bien, soupira la jeune femme. J'ai cru que je n'allais jamais m'en défaire.

Avant d'ouvrir sa portière pour descendre, Louis se tourna vers Ismaël, à qui il n'eut pas à expliquer quoi que ce soit.

— Je vais me garer devant la maison, je t'attends là-bas.

Louis sourit discrètement, reconnaissant, il n'en aurait pas pour longtemps. Tandis que la voiture s'éloignait, le lieutenant Salvant-Perret se retrouva face à cette délicieuse psychologue, à qui il tendit la main pour la saluer.

— Vous le connaissez ? questionna-t-il en désignant d'un mouvement du menton le bout de la rue par lequel le journaliste avait disparu.

— Il a téléphoné plusieurs fois à l'institut pour m'interviewer. Il s'est même posté au portail pour m'attendre, mais j'avais réussi à lui échapper.

— Vous avez très bien fait. Vous passiez par hasard dans le quartier ou vous jouez encore les Miss Marple ?

— Ce que je fais n'a rien d'un jeu, Louis.

Le lieutenant ne put se retenir de sourire en entendant son prénom dans sa bouche. Et il sut à son regard qu'elle en avait parfaitement conscience. Dès le premier instant, leurs échanges avaient été remplis de non-dits, de sous-entendus qui laissaient présager quelque chose de profond. Louis la sentait proche et lointaine à la fois, c'était une drôle de sensation, il était un peu perdu.

— C'était une façon de parler, ne le prenez pas mal, Agathe.

Rêvait-il ou avait-il aperçu une légère rougeur colorer ses joues ? Cela ne dura qu'un bref instant, car elle se reprit très vite. En quelques mots, elle lui expliqua qu'elle était allée interroger les commerçants au sujet de Nathan et de sa famille. Malheureusement, l'enfant ne venait jamais dans ces magasins.

Un buraliste voyait régulièrement la mère, qui venait lui acheter des jeux à gratter. Il l'avait vue à maintes reprises avec le gamin, de loin, sûrement lorsqu'elle l'accompagnait à l'école. Mais il n'avait pas sans arrêt le nez collé à sa vitrine, il avait un commerce à tenir, des clients à satisfaire. Et dans ce quartier, ça n'était pas une sinécure ! Il ne pouvait pas la renseigner sur les relations qui pouvaient exister entre la mère et son jeune fils.

– C'est dingue comme les gens peuvent se montrer indifférents au malheur des autres, remarqua-t-elle avec tristesse. Il était évidemment au courant de ce qui est arrivé à cette famille, mais cela ne l'intéressait pas le moins du monde de savoir ce que ce pauvre gamin allait devenir. Un petit garçon qu'il voyait tous les jours pratiquement ! Et qui vivait à deux pas !

– En ce qui me concerne, plus rien ne m'étonne sur la nature humaine, répliqua Louis.

– On dirait une chanson, fit Agathe en riant. Et vous, qu'est-ce qui vous amène par ici ?

– Une intuition.

– Oh ! J'espère qu'elle sera bonne. Merci, en tout cas, d'être passé par là au bon moment. Je vous tiens au courant en ce qui concerne Nathan. Bon *week-end*, lieutenant.

Ce retour à la mention de son grade le contraria quelque peu, mais le sourire qui l'accompagna adoucit la déception. Elle le provoquait gentiment.

Ce fut le cœur léger que Louis rejoignit Ismaël, qui avait pris les devants, déjà occupé à faire le tour de la maison. Connaissant son collègue, ce dernier ne lui posa pas de question ; il n'obtiendrait qu'un regard noir au mieux, une réponse laconique au pire. Vu son air dégagé, il n'était pas interdit de penser que son entretien avec la jolie psychologue avait été satisfaisant.

Sans plus échanger de paroles, ils se séparèrent, chacun partant d'un côté opposé. Dans le salon, il n'y avait aucune cachette possible, même pour un enfant. Pas de placard. Le meuble pour la télévision était constitué d'étagères. Le canapé n'avait pas de pieds, personne n'aurait pu se glisser en dessous. Dans le minuscule hall d'entrée non plus, il n'y avait rien à part des portemanteaux fixés au mur où un amoncellement de blousons et de parkas s'entassait.

Pas d'escalier sous lequel se camoufler, la maison était de plain-pied. Ismaël signala que la cuisine n'offrait pas davantage de possibilités. Un seul des lits, dans la chambre des enfants, aurait pu servir de refuge en rampant dessous. Ils soulevèrent le matelas ainsi que la structure, mais étant donné la couche de poussière qu'il y avait là, un corps s'y serait forcément incrusté et il n'y avait rien. En plus, c'est le premier endroit où on irait chercher quelqu'un qui se cache.

— Rien ne dit que le tueur savait de combien de membres était composée la fratrie, pensa Louis à voix haute. Je n'ai vu aucune photo de famille nulle part. Si le gamin n'a fait aucun bruit, il aura pu passer inaperçu.

Il ne restait plus que la salle de bains. Une pièce exiguë et malodorante dans laquelle ils étaient déjà venus plusieurs fois lors de leurs précédentes visites. Louis scruta l'endroit avec attention, tourna sur lui-même en détaillant la baignoire crasseuse à demi cachée par un rideau maculé de taches de moisissure, l'armoire à pharmacie ouverte au-dessus du lavabo dont les étagères dégueulaient de boîtes et de tubes en tout genre. L'odeur qui imprégnait même les murs vous prenait à la gorge, vous empêchait d'avoir les idées claires.

Tandis qu'Ismaël entrouvrait la minuscule fenêtre pour respirer un peu d'air frais, le regard de Louis se posa sur la panière à linge débordant de vêtements :

— Si ma mémoire est bonne, Nathan est un petit gabarit pour son âge ? Il rentrerait facilement au fond de cette panière. Avec des habits par-dessus, on ne le verrait pas.

Ismaël approuva d'un hochement de tête pendant que Louis se saisissait de l'objet avec tout le linge à l'intérieur et se dirigeait vers la sortie.

— Allez, viens ! Je crois qu'on a trouvé ce qu'on cherchait. Si le gamin était là-dedans, sachant ce qui était en train de se passer dans l'autre pièce, il a dû pleurer. Il y aura des traces de larmes partout. On l'apporte aux techniciens.

Chapitre 11

Comme il voulait éviter le trafic de la fin d'après-midi, Louis ne prit la route de sa chère Normandie que tard dans la soirée. Sa mère prévenue, elle resta éveillée, incapable de trouver le sommeil tant qu'il ne serait pas arrivé à bon port.

Louis se rendait compte de sa chance d'avoir une mère comme Hélène. Elle était la bonté incarnée. On ne pouvait pas rêver d'une femme plus maternelle. C'était peut-être pour cette raison que son ex avait éprouvé tant de mal à l'aimer. Les qualités de la première suscitaient l'envie, voire la jalousie de la seconde. En tout cas, il était difficile de rivaliser avec elle et Anne avait souvent critiqué ce côté trop parfait chez Hélène. Ça l'agaçait de voir toute cette tendresse qu'elle déversait sur Louis et sur France-Alix. Elle avait eu le sentiment d'être exclue parce qu'elle n'était pas du même sang. Elle avait eu l'impression de n'être qu'une pièce rapportée. Pourtant, Hélène s'était toujours montrée aimable, aux petits soins. Mais c'était justement cet aspect irréprochable qui irritait Anne.

Quant à Louis, après s'être senti coupable d'avoir grandi dans une famille aimante, il était à présent libre d'apprécier les siens à leur juste valeur, sans subir les reproches acerbes de son ex. Il s'était bien promis de ne plus jamais laisser quiconque porter un jugement sur ses parents. Il s'était montré bien trop coulant avec Anne, considérant qu'il aurait été mal placé pour critiquer sa femme alors qu'il n'était que très peu présent pour les tâches du quotidien.

À présent qu'il vivait seul, il n'aspirait qu'à la paix, sans rien demander d'autre à la vie que de pouvoir bien faire son travail et de n'entrer en conflit avec personne. En somme, il n'avait pas de grandes ambitions. Quant à l'amour avec un A majuscule, c'était bon pour le cinéma. Pour être tout à fait honnête, il n'y avait jamais vraiment cru, même jeune. Il avait aimé sincèrement la mère de France-Alix, mais la vie de couple lui avait rapidement pesé sur les épaules. C'était un fardeau dont il ne voulait pas. Ou peut-être n'avait-il pas déniché la perle rare. Toujours est-il qu'il ne la cherchait pas. Encore moins aujourd'hui qu'hier. Vivre au jour le jour lui convenait parfaitement. S'engager, faire des projets à long terme l'assommait.

La seule ombre au tableau était France-Alix. Car si tout le reste glissait sur lui, l'attitude méprisante qu'elle adoptait envers lui le rendait vraiment malheureux.

Il fut un temps où elle le regardait comme son héros. Dans ses yeux, il avait eu l'impression d'être fort, juste et beau. C'était il y avait longtemps. Maintenant, elle ne le voyait même plus. Cette situation devenait de plus en plus intolérable et, après sa discussion avec la psychologue à ce sujet, il avait décidé de ne pas laisser les choses en l'état. Après tout, il n'était certes pas un père parfait, mais il ne l'avait jamais maltraitée ni frappée ! Il n'avait même jamais élevé la voix contre elle. Et plus important : il l'aimait.

En ce dimanche matin, il voulut faire une surprise à sa fille en allant au village acheter un *kouglof.* Quand elle était enfant, elle raffolait de ce gâteau, qu'ils dévoraient assis tous les trois autour du petit déjeuner.

Il n'avala qu'un café noir afin de partager un moment privilégié avec elle dès qu'elle se lèverait. En attendant, il s'installa dans la bibliothèque avec son ordinateur portable. C'était une pièce stratégique, située juste au pied des escaliers. De là, il ne pourrait pas la manquer.

L'heure tournait. Pas de France-Alix à l'horizon. Ses parents étaient partis de bonne heure au marché, ils ne rentreraient pas avant onze heures. Allait-elle rester au lit toute la journée ? Maintenant qu'elle était jeune fille, il ne se serait pas permis d'entrer dans sa chambre, mais il fut tenté. Il commençait à vraiment s'impatienter lorsqu'il entendit le bruit de la porte d'entrée.

Il regarda l'heure au cadran de l'horloge à balancier : onze heures moins le quart. Étaient-ce ses parents qui revenaient ? Il se leva, déposa l'ordinateur sur le fauteuil qu'il venait de quitter et se dirigea vers des bruits de clefs qu'il percevait du côté de la cuisine.

Arrivant sans faire de bruit, il vit avec étonnement qu'il s'agissait de France-Alix qui, de toute évidence, n'avait pas passé la nuit dans sa chambre mais revenait de Dieu sait où ! Son sac sur le bras, elle se tenait immobile devant la table que Louis avait arrangée avec deux bols, des verres pour le jus d'orange, du miel et le gâteau qui trônait au milieu, dans son emballage de carton. Il n'apercevait que son profil, mais il distingua clairement un sourire se dessiner sur les lèvres de la jeune fille, qui pencha légèrement la tête de côté.

Au moment où elle se tournait pour voir si quelqu'un était là, comme alertée par un sixième sens, Louis se plaqua contre le mur, osant à peine respirer de peur qu'elle le surprenne à l'observer.

Il attendit quelques secondes, puis risqua un œil. Elle était en train de soulever le couvercle et se penchait pour humer l'odeur de la pâtisserie.

À ce moment-là, Louis sut qu'elle avait compris d'où venait le gâteau. Il retourna à pas de loup jusqu'à la bibliothèque en attendant qu'elle passe par là, content de son petit effet. En revanche, le fait qu'elle ait dormi ailleurs ne manquait pas de l'inquiéter. Il réfléchit. Si elle avait fait le mur, elle ne serait certainement pas revenue par la porte d'entrée. C'était donc une sortie autorisée. Restait à savoir avec qui elle se trouvait.

Il ne le montra pas, mais une certaine appréhension le taraudait lorsqu'il l'interpella à son passage :

— Tu as découché ? lança-t-il le plus diplomatiquement possible.

France-Alix stoppa au bas de la cage d'escalier, baissa la tête quelques secondes sans répondre, comme si elle réfléchissait à ce qu'elle allait dire, puis fit un mouvement gracieux pour dégager ses longs cheveux bouclés vers l'arrière avant de le regarder. Elle avait les yeux verts de sa mère et il la trouva très belle du haut de ses quinze ans.

— J'étais chez Léa.

— J'ai entendu parler de cette Léa. Une amie du

lycée ?

Elle haussa simplement les épaules. Il sentait qu'elle allait encore lui échapper, il fallait la retenir :

– J'avais pensé qu'on pourrait prendre le petit déjeuner ensemble. Je suis allé chercher un *kouglof* exprès.

– J'ai déjà déjeuné.

Pour une fois, elle ne mit aucune agressivité dans sa réponse. Il crut même déceler une pointe de regret. Elle s'éloigna néanmoins en ajoutant à mi-voix :

– Désolée, papa.

Ça s'était plutôt bien passé.

Même depuis le fond de la bibliothèque où il se trouvait, Louis renifla une odeur de tabac qui flottait dans le sillage de France-Alix. Il ne l'avait jamais vue en train de fumer, elle s'arrangeait pour ne pas être prise, sachant que son père n'appréciait pas, mais tous ses vêtements étaient imprégnés, ses cheveux aussi.

Quel dommage ! songeait Louis. Elle ne se rend pas compte qu'elle est en train de forger les barreaux de sa propre prison. Mais ce n'était pas le moment d'entamer une discussion sur ce sujet-là. Plus tard peut-être, quand ils auraient franchi toutes les barrières qui s'étaient dressées entre eux. Dans l'immédiat, ce premier échange, si modeste soit-il, était une petite victoire pour Louis : elle l'avait appelé papa. D'habitude, elle évitait soigneusement de prononcer ce mot comme s'il allait lui brûler la langue.

Au cours du repas dominical, Louis eut l'agréable surprise d'entendre sa fille converser presque normalement avec ses grands-parents. À lui, elle ne lui adressa pas la parole et il fit de même. Mais il apprit qu'en seulement deux semaines, les notes de France-Alix avaient sensiblement remonté, son attitude envers ses nouveaux professeurs était satisfaisante et elle n'avait encore séché aucun cours.

Plus tard, Hélène lui confia que tous ces progrès étaient dus à ses nouvelles fréquentations. La fameuse Léa avec qui France-Alix passait le plus clair de son temps était une excellente élève, très studieuse malgré un *look* gothique qu'on lui passait aisément étant donné ses résultats scolaires.

Au lieu de traîner dans les cafés comme c'était le cas quand elle vivait avec sa mère, l'adolescente fréquentait à présent les bibliothèques et les librairies. De plus, Hélène connaissait bien la famille Redon, dont Léa était une petite-fille. Elle avait été l'enseignante de sa mère dans ce même lycée.

Tout ce que Louis espérait, c'était que cet état de grâce dure le plus longtemps possible.

Il put attaquer une nouvelle semaine avec sérénité après ce *week-end* normand. Et elle commença dès le lundi matin sur les chapeaux de roue avec la découverte d'une autre famille décimée dans la commune de Corbeil-Essonnes.

Comme il y avait pas mal de similitudes avec la tuerie de la famille Lemonnier trois semaines plus tôt, le service d'Amary fut appelé sur les lieux.

Cette fois, pas de survivant. Trois enfants égorgés de la même façon qu'à Aulnay-sous-Bois et les parents étranglés. Selon les premières constatations relevées sur place par les deux officiers de PJ qu'Ismaël et Louis rejoignirent, on s'était servi du cordon électrique d'un sèche-cheveux. L'appareil gisait à côté du corps de la mère de famille, l'assassin n'avait même pas pris la peine de l'éloigner ou de s'en débarrasser.

Fred et Stan avaient été prévenus de l'arrivée de leurs collègues quelques minutes avant que ceux-ci ne débarquent, sans tambour ni trompette, comme s'ils étaient de simples visiteurs sur une bien macabre scène. On leur demanda de montrer leur carte à deux reprises avant qu'ils accèdent au salon où les corps jonchaient le sol moquetté imbibé du sang des trois enfants.

Un spectacle qui se répétait un peu trop souvent au goût de Louis. Maud Cortès avait déclaré forfait, elle ne pouvait supporter d'affronter encore une telle abomination à si peu de temps d'intervalle. Elle avait les larmes aux yeux lorsqu'elle avait appris la nouvelle découverte des jeunes corps.

— La PTS a terminé les prélèvements, on a fait un premier tour à l'intérieur, informa Stan, le plus grand des deux officiers.

— Vous avez regardé dans toutes les pièces ? demanda Louis.

— On a fait le tour en arrivant, mais on ne s'est pas attardés.

Louis jeta un coup d'œil à Ismaël tout en enfilant ses gants de latex. Il évitait soigneusement de laisser son regard se poser sur les corps des victimes, c'était trop éprouvant, même pour un flic qui en avait vu d'autres. Son coéquipier comprit ce qu'il avait l'intention de faire. D'un seul mouvement, les deux lieutenants se dirigèrent vers le couloir étroit donnant sur les chambres. Quatre en tout. Chacun des frères et sœurs avait donc la sienne en plus de celle du couple. C'était celle de l'aînée qui les intéressait.

D'après les explications de Fred et Stan, la plus grande de la fratrie se prénommait Emma, elle était âgée de dix-sept ans. Les deux autres, Lucas et Tiffany, avaient respectivement treize et huit ans.

En parcourant l'appartement, il n'était pas difficile d'en déduire que la famille Aubry ne roulait pas sur l'or. Cependant, contrairement au domicile des Lemonnier, qui ressemblait à un taudis, ce logement était plutôt bien entretenu malgré un mobilier de seconde main et les dégâts sur les ouvertures et les murs liés à la vétusté. L'humidité occasionnait des auréoles noirâtres au plafond et sur les cloisons, l'état de décrépitude des fenêtres les empêchait de fermer correctement. L'hiver, ce devait être un cauchemar pour parvenir à chauffer un endroit pareil !

Il leur fut aisé de repérer la chambre de l'aînée : son prénom était inscrit sur la porte en lettres de strass. À l'intérieur, une collection de livres *manga* occupait tout un pan de mur et des *posters* de personnages colorés japonisants décoraient la pièce.

Ils allèrent droit en direction du lit consciencieusement fait dont ils retournèrent le matelas, chacun d'un côté. Là, encore une lettre dessinée au marqueur noir : un « A », cette fois. Louis n'aurait pas su dire s'il était mortifié parce que le même meurtrier venait de sévir à nouveau ou s'il était soulagé de ne pas avoir deux tueurs d'enfants qui frappaient au même moment dans la même région.

L'imposante stature de Stan se découpa dans l'encadrement de la porte :

— Alors, vous avez quelque chose ?

— Une lettre écrite au marqueur sur l'envers du

matelas, comme chez les Lemonnier, répondit Louis.

L'officier de police souleva lui-même le matelas, il voulait voir ça de ses propres yeux.

— J'ai entendu parler de cette histoire de lettre. Un « L », c'est ça ? Et là, on a un « A ». Le mec veut faire une partie de Scrabble avec les flics. Si on le chope, ça lui fera une peine de prison compte triple, à cet enfoiré ! Égorger des gosses, sans déconner, même en taule, les gars vont pas le louper quand il se fera serrer.

Louis ne releva pas, jugeant que puisqu'ils étaient au courant pour les lettres au marqueur, ils auraient pu avoir la présence d'esprit d'en chercher la trace sur les lieux. Il n'avait pas très envie d'échanger avec des officiers venant d'un autre groupe au sujet de leur affaire. Comme ils étaient arrivés en premier, il ne leur demanda pas de quitter les lieux et de leur laisser le champ libre. De toute façon, les techniciens se chargeraient d'analyser tout ce qu'ils venaient de prélever et il avait vu ce qu'il était venu chercher : cette seconde lettre qui ne les avançait pas beaucoup. De plus, le groupe de Stan et Fred serait dessaisi de l'affaire très vite.

Leur seule certitude pour l'instant, c'est que le « L » n'était pas cinquante en chiffre romain.

— LA, fit Ismaël en réfléchissant tandis qu'ils retournaient dans la pièce principale. LA poisse. LA chienlit.

— C'est pas un déterminant. Ça doit être un nom commun ou un nom propre.

— Alors quoi ? Laurent, Lalie, Laurence, Laura, Laure, Lara ?

— Laetitia, ajouta Louis sans conviction.

— Y'en a des tas, des prénoms qui commencent

par LA, fit remarquer Ismaël, qui se creusait la cervelle pour en trouver d'autres, sans succès.

— Quant à des noms communs qui commencent aussi par LA, on n'est pas sortis de l'auberge !

— Dis donc, t'es calé en français, toi ! Déterminants, noms communs, noms propres, tout ça... Et ça pourrait tout aussi bien être un nom de famille, tu crois pas ?

— On n'a pas assez d'éléments pour l'instant, maugréa Louis, à qui cette nouvelle tuerie offrait davantage de questions que de réponses à la première.

Il avait pressenti qu'il y aurait un autre acte de barbarie, il l'avait su dès qu'il avait vu cette lettre qui en appelait forcément d'autres. Ils se retrouvaient avec pas moins de dix corps sur les bras en trois semaines, deux familles entières décimées, et pas l'ombre d'un suspect.

Le commissaire Amary, rasé de près, costume couleur crème impeccable qui donnait au teint sombre de sa peau des tons caramélisés, aidait le substitut du procureur de la République à enfiler ses surchaussures en lui servant d'appui. À la vue de Louis et Ismaël entrant dans la pièce, il leur lança un regard presque désespéré. Sack, le substitut du procureur, n'était pas réputé pour sa gentillesse. C'était un esprit revêche dans un corps long et maigre, aussi sec que son nom quand on le prononçait. Même sans distinguer ses paroles, le ton de sa voix indiquait qu'il était d'une humeur de chien H 24.

— Il faudrait voir à s'enlever les doigts de là où je pense, était-il en train de dire à Amary, qui n'en menait pas large. La presse va s'en donner à cœur joie : six gosses égorgés en même pas vingt jours et la police qui patauge dans sa propre incompétence, c'est racoleur, vous ne trouvez pas ? On passe pour des incapables et le coupable doit bien rigoler en préparant son prochain numéro. Vous devriez lui dérouler un tapis rouge, tant que vous y êtes !

— Mon équipe est sur le pont depuis le début...

— Eh bien, mettez-y une autre d'équipe, si ce n'est pas suffisant ! Débrouillez-vous comme vous voulez, mais sortez-nous de ce merdier !

Malgré l'agressivité dont il faisait preuve, Sack parlait suffisamment doucement pour n'être entendu que du commissaire et des deux ou trois personnes qui se trouvaient à proximité. La peau noire d'Amary s'assombrit encore davantage tant il contenait sa colère.

— On va en prendre plein la tête, murmura Ismaël à l'oreille de Louis. On a intérêt à dégager vite fait avant qu'ils nous tombent dessus.

Ismaël avait entraîné Louis dans un coin du salon d'où ils purent observer l'opération de rangement des équipements des techniciens de la PTS, ainsi que l'arrivée fort remarquée de la légiste haute en couleur. À chacune de ses apparitions, Ismaël s'attendait à une prestation digne d'un *one woman show*. Il souriait déjà rien qu'à l'idée qu'elle allait ouvrir la bouche. Et en effet, quand le substitut eut la mauvaise idée de demander au médecin ce qu'elle avait fichu pour arriver si tard sur une scène de crime, il en prit pour son grade.

Françoise Bonnemort, loin de se démonter devant la fatuité du bonhomme, sembla gonfler sa poitrine et grandir de dix bons centimètres lorsqu'elle rétorqua avec son accent du Sud-Ouest :

— S'il n'est pas content, il n'a qu'à faire une réclamation pour me procurer un véhicule de fonction, parce que je lui signale que ça fait des semaines que c'est avec *ma* voiture personnelle que je me déplace sur *ses* scènes de crime ! Alors faudrait voir à pas trop me courir sur le haricot, hein !

Sack devint cramoisi. Un grand silence s'était abattu dans la pièce, où tous attendaient sans oser respirer la réaction du substitut du procureur. Personne ne s'adressait jamais à lui de cette façon, encore moins une femme. Dans tous les esprits, il était clair que Bonnemort allait se faire laminer. L'atmosphère ne pouvait pas être plus tendue.

Et, contre toute attente, Sack eut une sorte de tic nerveux à la Sarkozy, un tressautement d'épaule accompagné d'une tension du cou. Il remit sa cravate en place, se racla la gorge et déclara d'une voix forte et claire :

— Allons, messieurs et mesdames ! On se remet au travail !

Ismaël, qui esquissa un sourire en coin, se fit reprendre sévèrement :

— Qu'est-ce qui vous fait rire, officier ? Vous n'avez pas une enquête de voisinage à effectuer plutôt que de rester planté là ?

Instinctivement, Ismaël avait serré les fesses à l'interpellation. Il ne s'aventura pas à émettre une quelconque observation et se dirigea vers la porte de sortie la plus proche. Mais décidément, cette légiste ne manquait pas d'aplomb ! Parvenir à clouer le bec de Sack était un exploit inédit dans l'histoire du service d'Amary. Rien que pour ça, il lui voua une admiration qui ne fit que se confirmer plus tard.

— Pourquoi Maud n'est-elle pas là ? questionna

soudain le commissaire Amary, qui les avait suivis à l'extérieur.

Le « taulier », comme ses subordonnés avaient coutume de l'appeler, s'épongeait les tempes et le cou à l'aide d'un mouchoir en papier qu'il garda ensuite dans son poing serré. Il ne fallait pas être devin pour voir que lui aussi avait besoin d'un peu d'air frais après l'épisode Sack.

— Je l'appelle, proposa Louis, téléphone en main.

Il avait couvert l'absence de leur collègue jusque-là, mais il n'avait pas d'autre alternative que de lui dire de venir. Au moins ne serait-elle pas obligée de voir la scène de crime puisqu'ils étaient déjà passés par là.

— J'ai pourtant dit tout le monde sur le pont, c'est pas le moment d'être en sous-effectif ! Vous lui dites de rappliquer en quatrième vitesse et vous commencez à interroger les voisins. C'est un immeuble HLM, tout s'entend d'un appartement à l'autre.

Un groupe de badauds s'était attroupé devant l'entrée du bâtiment. Les vacances de printemps n'étant pas encore terminées, il y avait quelques adolescents que l'événement hors du commun réjouissait. Ils fumaient sans doute autre chose que de simples cigarettes, mais ce jour-là, la police ne s'était pas déplacée pour coincer des consommateurs d'herbe.

Leurs rires se calmèrent lorsque le défilé des corps emportés dans des sacs mortuaires commença. Là, les visages exprimèrent la stupéfaction, puis l'incompréhension devant le nombre de cadavres que l'on extirpait de ce hall d'entrée.

Les véhicules de la presse ne tardèrent pas à

débarquer aussi. Des journalistes installèrent caméras et micros, interrogeant les curieux rassemblés, cherchant à récolter des informations sur ce qu'ils avaient vu ou entendu. Mais Louis et Ismaël venaient de battre le pavé, ces gens habitaient les immeubles voisins, ils ne savaient rien.

Pendant qu'il essayait de joindre Maud, tombant systématiquement sur son répondeur, Louis regarda parmi les journalistes si le malotru qui tournait autour d'Agathe Delcourt ne se trouvait pas dans le lot. Il ne le vit pas. Mais cela ne voulait pas dire qu'il n'apparaîtrait pas à un moment ou à un autre. L'affaire était de taille, un sujet en or pour tout bon journaliste.

Stan et Fred furent chargés de les seconder dans l'enquête de voisinage. Ils se distribuèrent donc les étages et firent le point deux heures plus tard dans un bar PMU, devant des tasses de café.

Maud avait fini par se manifester : elle avait eu les messages vocaux de Louis, mais tombée en panne de voiture à un endroit où elle n'avait aucun réseau, elle avait été obligée de marcher plusieurs kilomètres avant de trouver une habitation où on l'avait laissé utiliser une ligne fixe afin qu'elle soit dépannée et qu'elle les prévienne de ce contretemps qui, finalement, l'arrangeait bien.

— Le garagiste me prête un véhicule de courtoisie, je suis là d'ici une heure. Vous me dites ce qui se passe ?

Louis résuma rapidement la situation, Ismaël le menton sur son épaule qui le harcelait pour qu'il raconte l'épisode Bonnemort *versus* Sack. Agacé autant qu'amusé, Louis relata l'altercation, qui fit beaucoup rire la jeune lieutenant.

Ils convinrent qu'étant donné l'heure, ce n'était plus la peine qu'elle vienne les rejoindre, ils se retrouveraient plutôt au commissariat, où il y aurait du pain sur la planche. Les deux lieutenants de l'autre brigade enverraient la procédure initiale dès le lendemain pour compléter celle de Louis et d'Ismaël.

Ces derniers avaient réussi à apprendre qu'il y avait eu des bruits de pleurs, tard dans la nuit, chez les Aubry. Leur voisin du dessous les avait entendus, mais comme c'était monnaie courante dans ce genre d'immeubles où des drames se déroulent chaque jour, il n'y avait pas prêté attention plus que cela.

Louis ne put s'empêcher de penser que si Maud avait été là, elle aurait ressenti une douleur immense devant l'indifférence d'un homme face aux larmes d'un de ses voisins.

— Vous savez, ça fait trente ans que j'habite ici. J'en ai vu défiler, des familles, dans cet appartement du cinquième. Ça se dispute souvent, ça crie et ça pleure. La vie, quoi ! Si j'avais dû monter à chaque fois qu'ils s'insultaient ou se mettaient sur la gueule ! conclut le vieil homme sans paraître affecté le moins du monde.

Louis remarqua qu'aucune des portes de l'immeuble n'était pourvue d'œilleton. Si un étranger pénétrait dans les étages, il pouvait déambuler en toute liberté sans être vu. Et de fait, nul n'avait aperçu d'inconnu la veille. De toute façon, personne ne faisait attention à personne dans ce genre de cité. Il n'était pas rare de retrouver un locataire mort depuis des semaines dans un appartement sans qu'aucun voisin s'en soit rendu compte. Le plus souvent, c'était l'odeur qui alertait les esprits.

Chapitre 12

De retour au commissariat, Louis reçut un appel de Françoise Bonnemort. La légiste les avait cherchés après ses premières conclusions dans l'appartement des Aubry mais, ne les trouvant nulle part, elle était repartie en en disant le moins possible au duo Stan et Fred, qu'elle ne connaissait pas. C'était à Ismaël et lui qu'elle donnerait ses analyses, à personne d'autre. Le substitut du procureur pouvait bien aboyer tant qu'il pouvait, elle n'en avait cure. Tant de loyauté attendrit Louis, qui la remercia.

— Il y a quelques différences entre les meurtres de la famille Lemonnier et ceux-ci, commença-t-elle. D'abord, je suppose que vous avez noté que le meurtrier n'a pas cherché à maquiller cette tuerie en un pétage de plomb du chef de famille qui se suicide après.

— J'avais bien noté, oui, confirma le lieutenant. Ensuite ?

— Ensuite, il y a des traces d'adhésif sur les poignets de tous mes cadavres, du plus petit au plus grand. Il s'est servi de scotch épais pour les immobiliser. Et la fille aînée a été violée.

— Vous êtes sûre ?

— Mon chéri, bien sûr que je suis sûre ! Et je peux

vous dire qu'il n'a pas fait ça en douceur. Je n'ai pas encore étudié les lésions internes, mais elle présente des déchirures importantes non seulement au niveau vaginal, mais également au niveau anal. D'après moi, il s'est servi d'un instrument encore indéterminé pour la pénétrer sauvagement.

— Autre chose ?

— C'est à peu près tout pour le moment. Je vous envoie mon rapport préliminaire le plus vite possible, mais j'ai pensé que ces éléments pourraient vous aider un peu.

Louis raconta ce qu'il venait d'apprendre à Maud et Ismaël.

— Il est en pleine escalade, fit ce dernier gravement.

— Oui, il est de plus en plus violent.

— C'est peut-être pas le même, hasarda Maud. Et qui nous dit que c'est un homme ? Bonnemort a bien dit qu'il s'était servi d'un objet pour violer la gamine. Peut-être que c'est une femme qui tue toutes ces familles ?

— Une femme qui tue des gosses, franchement, j'ai du mal à y croire. Quant à un autre assassin qui laisserait aussi des lettres sur l'envers des matelas du premier né des familles, c'est carrément impossible.

Maud fut forcée de reconnaître qu'il avait sans doute raison. Mais elle ne repoussait pas l'idée qu'il puisse s'agir d'une femme, même si le taux de probabilité était très faible.

— Un imitateur, alors ? insista-t-elle encore.

— La presse ne sait rien des lettres, il n'y a que les flics sur l'affaire qui soient au courant. Non, je n'y crois pas. Surtout à un intervalle si court entre les deux séries de meurtres.

— Moi non plus, appuya Ismaël.

— On dirait qu'il est en colère, dit Louis, qui réfléchissait à la signification de ce changement dans le *modus operandi*. Qu'il a agi sous une impulsion.

— Un drogué ? s'interrogea Maud.

— Rien n'a été volé. Pas plus que chez les Lemonnier. Un camé, même défoncé, pense à son prochain *shoot*. Il vole tout ce qui peut se vendre dans la rue. Et Stan et Fred ont dit que rien ne manquait. Les cartes de crédit se trouvaient dans les portefeuilles des parents et les gosses avaient de l'argent dans leur chambre qui n'a pas bougé.

Ismaël savait de quoi il parlait, il avait travaillé quatre ans chez les stups avant d'atterrir aux côtés de Louis Salvant-Perret.

Ils avaient beau tourner ça dans tous les sens, ils n'avaient aucune idée du mobile de tous ces meurtres. Il fallait qu'ils creusent dans l'entourage de chacun des membres des deux familles. Cette fois, il s'agissait d'avancer de façon significative et Amary ne mâcha pas ses mots pour les engager à mettre les bouchées doubles.

Ils passèrent donc à la vitesse supérieure. À la décision du substitut, le service de Stan et Fred fut dessaisi de l'affaire au profit de celui du commissaire Amary. Durant les deux semaines qui suivirent, ils convoquèrent une cinquantaine de personnes plus ou moins proches de chacun des membres des deux familles, enfants ou adultes. Du médecin de famille au boucher du coin de la rue, ils interrogèrent un échantillon si vaste de la population que c'était un défilé d'individus tous plus différents les uns que les autres.

Ils s'attachèrent à chercher un point commun

entre les Lemonnier et les Aubry. Un opérateur téléphonique ou Internet dont un technicien aurait pu pénétrer dans les deux maisons. Quelqu'un prétendant faire une enquête ou un faux témoin de Jéhovah, qui sait ?

Cela ne donna rien. Ils n'avaient pas le même et dans la seconde famille, c'était Franck Aubry qui s'occupait de l'informatique, sa sœur le confirma. Ils regardèrent alors du côté d'une école commune aux enfants, d'un psy, d'un club sportif, d'un supermarché. Rien ne collait.

Le point positif avec les Aubry, c'était qu'ils laissaient derrière eux des oncles, tantes et grands-parents que le trio de lieutenants put interroger. Ce qui n'était pas le cas pour les Lemonnier.

La piste Christian Blanchard s'était refroidie. Si le conducteur accidenté avait un mobile éventuel pour Lemonnier, il n'avait aucun lien avec la famille Aubry. Quand il fut convoqué pour la deuxième fois, il fallut toute la diplomatie du prince du central afin de calmer sa fureur d'avoir encore à s'expliquer sur cet événement dont il se clamait la victime. Il menaça de porter plainte, c'était du harcèlement policier !

La première semaine du mois de mai, ils reçurent enfin les résultats des analyses effectuées sur les vêtements contenus dans la panière à linge de chez les Lemonnier. Des traces conséquentes de larmes confirmaient que Nathan s'était dissimulé dedans, sûrement pendant tout le temps qu'avait duré la tragédie. Ce qui expliquait qu'il ait survécu. Il n'était pas question de pitié. Étant donné la sauvagerie des derniers meurtres perpétrés, le coupable n'avait pas l'air du genre à se laisser attendrir par des considérations d'âge. Il ne manifestait aucune empathie, agissait même avec barbarie.

Vers le milieu du mois, n'ayant aucune nouvelle de la psychologue, Louis se décida à la contacter, histoire de la tenir informée de ses dernières découvertes. Évidemment, l'idée d'avoir une bonne excuse pour lui parler le réjouissait, mais il se montra très professionnel lorsqu'il l'eut au bout du fil.

À la vérité, il ne savait jamais trop comment aborder la jeune femme. Il ne savait même pas ce qui le poussait à lui faire un numéro de charme à chaque fois qu'il la rencontrait. C'était comme si une force extérieure le persuadait qu'il fallait lui plaire alors que de son côté, elle gardait une certaine distance. C'étaient peut-être justement ces barrières qu'elle érigeait entre eux qui excitaient sa convoitise. Parce qu'il faut bien avouer que jusqu'à présent, aucune femme ne l'avait suffisamment intéressé pour qu'il envisage une opération séduction.

Quand il se fut présenté, il lui trouva une drôle de voix. Elle avait appris par les journaux qu'une autre famille avait été supprimée et cela semblait l'atteindre comme si ce drame la touchait de près.

— Quel âge avait le plus jeune, cette fois ? demanda-t-elle.

— Huit ans. C'était une petite fille : Tiffany.

— Je vous en prie, évitez de citer des prénoms, c'est encore plus affreux. Je change de chaîne à chaque fois qu'il est question de ça aux informations. Ce monstre n'a même pas laissé la vie sauve au plus jeune, comme l'autre fois.

— Agathe, commença à expliquer Louis, en fait, nous avons à présent la preuve que le petit Nathan n'a pas été choisi volontairement par le tueur pour survivre à sa famille. Il s'était caché dans la salle de bains.

— Comment pouvez-vous le savoir ? s'étonna-t-elle.

— On a fait analyser la panière à linge sale et on a retrouvé des traces de sécrétions lacrymales en abondance. Ce sont les larmes du gamin, aucun doute là-dessus. Il s'était caché. D'après moi, il n'a rien vu de ce qui s'est passé. Mais il a dû entendre, par contre. Ce qui est peut-être pire, je ne sais pas.

Il y eut un silence assez long que Louis n'interrompit pas, car il sentait que cette révélation avait secoué Agathe.

— Vous voulez dire que Nathan serait mort comme les autres s'il ne s'était pas caché ?

Elle paraissait si désemparée que Louis ne savait pas trop comment la réconforter. Surtout au téléphone, ce n'était pas chose facile.

— Je le crains, oui. On n'a pas affaire à un individu qui raisonne comme vous et moi. Je pense qu'il est sérieusement dérangé.

— Vous pensez que c'est le même homme qui s'en est pris à ces deux pauvres familles ?

Louis hésita. Elle s'en rendit compte :

— Vous avez des éléments qui désignent un même coupable ?

Finalement, il se lança, lui parla des deux lettres qu'ils avaient retrouvées sur l'envers des deux matelas, détail que seuls les enquêteurs connaissaient.

— Le plus étrange, c'est que les deux fois, les lettres ont été tracées sous le matelas de l'aîné de la fratrie.

— Vous pensez que cela a une signification ? questionna-t-elle.

— Je le pense, oui. Pas vous ? En tant que psy, vous devez bien avoir une petite idée de ce que ça révèle sur la personnalité de l'assassin.

— Il peut y avoir des dizaines d'explications possibles il faudrait creuser de ce côté-là. Mais mon travail consiste à m'occuper en priorité des victimes, pas des bourreaux.

— Ce sont souvent les mêmes, fit remarquer Louis. Un coupable n'est-il pas presque toujours une ancienne victime ?

Sa question resta sans réponse. D'ailleurs, il n'en attendait aucune. La psychologue revint sur un point qui l'interpellait :

— Quelles sont ces lettres qui ont été écrites ?

— J'aimerais que ça reste entre nous, la mit-il gentiment en garde.

— Vous pouvez compter sur ma totale discrétion, affirma la jeune femme d'une voix ferme.

— On a d'abord eu un « L ». Et cette fois, c'était un « A ». Ça vous parle ?

La psychologue réfléchit un instant, mais bien sûr, elle n'avait aucune idée de ce que cela pouvait signifier. Néanmoins, son silence s'éternisant un peu, Louis ressentit de la gêne et reprit la parole, changeant de sujet :

— On ne peut toujours pas interroger Nathan ? Avez-vous réussi à communiquer avec lui ?

— Il est moins agité, admit Agathe en se radoucissant. Mais vous pourriez peut-être venir juger par vous-même si vous promettez de ne pas le brusquer. En aucun cas il ne s'agit de l'interroger comme vous le feriez avec un autre témoin. C'est un enfant et, même si ce que vous dites est vrai, qu'il n'a rien vu de ce qui est arrivé à ses parents, il demeure extrêmement fragile.

Un sourire s'épanouit sur le visage du lieutenant, détendant ses traits tirés par ces derniers jours d'intense activité. Il n'était pas retourné en Normandie depuis trop longtemps, enfermé dans le bureau du commissariat chaque jour de la semaine entre recherches, lectures de rapports et interrogatoires. Il avait besoin de prendre l'air.

— Quand ? fit-il un peu brusquement, il s'en rendit compte après coup.

— Demain après-midi, si ça vous convient ?

— Parfait. Je serai là à quatorze heures.

Si le temps semblait long depuis le dernier drame lié à leur meurtrier, il s'éternisa encore davantage à la perspective de revoir la jolie psychologue. Dans leur bureau étroit, Maud perçut la nervosité grandissante de son collègue, mais elle mit cela sur le compte du commissaire Amary, qui ne les lâchait pas de la journée.

Il voulait des résultats. Tous les matins, c'était une séance de *débriefing* sur les avancées de la veille et le programme du jour à venir.

Heureusement, les journaux finirent par se lasser, d'autres événements ayant pris le devant de la scène. Cette année 2015 était ponctuée de deux ou trois attaques terroristes par mois, revendiquées par l'État islamiste, ce qui réduisait les effectifs pour d'autres affaires, mais avait l'avantage de détourner l'attention des médias.

Le lendemain, Louis Salvant-Perret prévint qu'il s'absentait. Lui qui croyait pouvoir s'éclipser sans rendre de comptes en fut pour ses frais, Amary ordonna que Cortès l'accompagne. Il estimait que pour faire parler un gamin, une femme était plus indiquée.

Maud fut donc encore une fois la compagne discrète du lieutenant, qui s'en accommoda. Armée de ses aiguilles à tricoter, qu'elle traînait partout, elle s'absorba dans son tricot comme on plonge dans un livre.

Du coin de l'œil, Louis s'aperçut que le pull qu'elle avait commencé lors de leur dernier périple était quasiment terminé. De plus, il devait le reconnaître, le vêtement était plutôt joli.

— Vous savez faire autre chose que des pulls ? questionna Louis pour discuter un peu.

— Pourquoi, vous voulez des moufles ?

— C'est ça, avec un bonnet assorti, continua-t-il sur le ton de la plaisanterie. Et tant que vous y êtes, un holster pour mon 9 mm, en poil angora si possible.

Ils éclatèrent de rire. Le côté vieille France de Maud Cortès instaurait toujours une atmosphère bienveillante où qu'elle aille, comme une *aura* de légèreté qui enveloppait chaque personne qu'elle croisait. Cela fonctionnait à merveille avec Louis, qui s'estimait chanceux de travailler avec des coéquipiers aussi paisibles. Ismaël faisait figure de dur à cuire au sein de leur trio et pourtant, il était loin du cliché du méchant flic des feuilletons américains. Mais ils s'entendaient bien et jusqu'à présent, leur collaboration était couronnée de succès.

— Vous savez, je pourrais aller fouiner du côté de la cafétéria pendant que vous discutez avec mademoiselle Delcourt.

— Pourquoi feriez-vous ça ?

— Pour vous laisser le champ libre.

Louis fit l'innocent. De quoi parlait-elle ?

Maud se contenta de hausser les épaules avec un sourire équivoque. Si le prince du central n'avait pas envie de se confier à elle, libre à lui. Mais elle n'avait pas été la dernière à remarquer son empressement à se rendre à l'institut où travaillait la psychologue à chaque fois qu'une occasion se présentait. D'ailleurs, tout le monde s'en était rendu compte et les paris étaient ouverts au commissariat : allait-il conclure avant que l'affaire soit bouclée ou attendrait-il le dénouement pour déclarer sa flamme ? Car ce n'était un secret que pour Louis : il en pinçait sérieusement pour Agathe Delcourt.

Ismaël avait parié cinquante euros que le lieutenant ne ferait rien avant d'avoir trouvé l'assassin des deux familles. Il le connaissait suffisamment pour savoir qu'Agathe étant plus ou moins impliquée dans leur affaire, Louis préférerait attendre d'être sûr que cela n'empiéterait pas sur leur enquête en cours.

Amary était partagé. Il n'avait aucun doute sur l'intégrité de Salvant-Perret, mais il savait aussi qu'il était célibataire depuis des mois. Même si Louis était discret au sujet de sa vie privée, il doutait que ce dernier eût beaucoup d'aventures sentimentales. Il était donc susceptible de succomber facilement au charme indéniable de la jeune femme. Cinquante euros qu'il allait craquer.

Quant à Maud, elle ne paria pas, c'était contraire à sa philosophie. Cependant, elle était convaincue que Louis agirait selon sa raison. Vingt fois, elle avait été tentée de lui avouer qu'il faisait l'objet de paris stupides dans son dos, et puis elle avait renoncé. Si ça se trouve, il s'en serait moqué et elle aimait autant ne pas le contrarier, ce qui était une bonne manière de conserver des relations saines.

Chapitre 13

Le mercredi, Agathe Delcourt tâchait de proposer aux enfants des activités aussi ludiques qu'artistiques. Lorsque Louis se présenta à l'entrée de la grande salle de jeux où elle se trouvait, une musique enregistrée déroulait ses notes tandis que deux petits garçons et une fillette dessinaient, assis autour d'une table en forme de croissant de lune.

La psychologue adressa un petit signe à Louis l'autorisant à entrer. Penchée au-dessus de Nathan, elle semblait particulièrement attentive à ce que le garçon était en train de dessiner.

Il n'utilisait pas les feutres ni les crayons de couleur comme les deux autres, mais des bâtons de pastels qui jonchaient sa partie de table, étalés là comme un arc-en-ciel en vrac.

Louis avait pénétré dans la pièce sans faire de bruit, soucieux de ne pas effrayer les têtes blondes tout à leurs chefs-d'œuvre. Il fit le tour, longea des étagères où toutes sortes de jouets et d'instruments dont il ne connaissait même pas l'usage étaient rangés. Aux murs, des lettres en forme de personnages ou d'animaux, des dessins, productions d'anciens pensionnaires que la vie avait fait s'échouer là pour un temps.

À moitié camouflé par des tapis de sol et des couvertures qui devaient servir aux siestes, un piano retint son attention. Le tabouret était occupé par un énorme crocodile en peluche vert fluo. Louis se mit à débarrasser l'instrument de tout ce qui l'encombrait. Il fit une pile par terre avec le crocodile qui trônait par-dessus, et s'assit sur le tabouret au moment où la musique dans les haut-parleurs s'arrêtait.

Il y eut un craquement sinistre lorsqu'il souleva le couvercle qui fermait le clavier. Il y avait tellement longtemps que personne ne l'avait ouvert que le bois avait joué. Louis rentra la tête dans les épaules en serrant les dents, craignant qu'Agathe ne le réprimande pour avoir fait peur aux jeunes patients. Mais quand il jeta un coup d'œil dans sa direction, il s'aperçut qu'elle ne le regardait même pas, toujours absorbée par le dessin de Nathan.

Alors il appuya sur une touche.

Un la.

La note résonna dans la grande salle, un peu fausse, irréelle, mais passable pour un instrument de cet âge.

Puis un do.

Cette fois, ça sonnait juste.

Il prit une inspiration, ajusta ses mains au-dessus des touches, écarta les jambes, et se mit à jouer un morceau de Yann Tiersen intitulé *La Plage* qu'il jouait souvent à sa fille quand elle était petite.

Il commença doucement, ralentissant volontairement le tempo original de l'air. Le son du piano avait quelque chose de fantastique, comme une vieille boîte à bijoux à la musique désuète que l'on fait jouer et rejouer pour la saveur des souvenirs qu'elle recèle. Puis, petit à petit, le rythme s'accéléra. Il prenait plaisir à rejouer ce morceau que ses doigts se rappelaient au point qu'ils filaient tout seul sur le clavier, comme s'ils étaient dotés d'une vie propre.

D'ordinaire, cette pièce était plutôt courte, elle ne durait pas plus de trois minutes. Emporté par le bonheur de la musique, Louis la prolongea de cinq bonnes minutes supplémentaires et, lorsque la dernière note s'éleva, il était entouré d'Agathe et des enfants, Nathan assis sur le tabouret près de lui. Ils se mirent à l'applaudir. La fillette arborait un sourire qu'elle avait perdu depuis longtemps et Nathan fixait les touches, comme fasciné.

Quand ils cessèrent de taper dans les mains, Louis entendit une petite voix à côté de lui qui disait :

— Encore.

Automatiquement, le lieutenant se tourna vers Agathe. Avait-elle entendu comme lui ? L'expression de son visage lui dit que c'était le cas. Elle l'encouragea du regard. Louis replaça ses mains et vit que le petit garçon faisait de même, mimant chacun de ses gestes. Comme il n'était pas au-dessus des bonnes touches, le lieutenant prit doucement les doigts de son voisin, qu'il dirigea au bon endroit. Puis il commença un air très simple, jouant une dizaine de notes et s'arrêtant. Nathan reproduisit exactement les mêmes notes, deux octaves plus haut.

Louis sourit au garçonnet, qui ne quittait pas ses mains des yeux, et recommença. L'enfant exécuta la suite encore mieux que la première fois. Au bout de quatre reprises, Louis se tourna vers le petit, lui faisant comprendre par son regard qu'ils pouvaient jouer en même temps.

Et ce fut magique. Les quatre mains se mirent à courir en rythme sur le clavier devant un modeste public conquis. Leur performance fut applaudie avant qu'Agathe n'encourage les deux autres jeunes patients à retourner à leur coloriage. Quant à Nathan, il resta assis à côté de Louis, qui tenta une approche :

– Tu avais déjà joué avant ?

Le garçon secoua la tête négativement.

– Tu aimes ?

Cette fois, un petit « oui » s'échappa de ses lèvres.

– Tu as l'air dégourdi, je peux t'apprendre les gammes, si tu veux. Et si tu t'entraînes tous les jours, après, tu pourras jouer des morceaux. Ça te dit ?

L'enfant acquiesça d'un mouvement de tête et, pendant plusieurs minutes, le lieutenant lui apprit à placer ses doigts et à répéter les notes sur le clavier. Nathan comprenait vite, on pouvait même dire qu'il avait des prédispositions pour la musique.

Lorsque le garçon eut bien assimilé les gammes, Agathe l'invita à se rasseoir avec les autres enfants tandis qu'elle entraînait Louis un peu à l'écart pour lui montrer les dessins que Nathan avait faits durant les jours précédents.

Il ne s'agissait pas de dessins figuratifs comme les gamins ont l'habitude d'en produire, mais plutôt d'un assemblage de couleurs à dominantes grises, noires et rouges. Le dernier ressemblait à une sorte de gigantesque tourbillon de boue mêlée de sang qui attirait le regard dans un gouffre sans fond au centre de la feuille surchargée de couleurs sombres. L'ensemble était à la fois beau et terriblement déprimant.

– Si ça reflète son état d'esprit, remarqua Louis, je n'aimerais pas être dans sa tête.

– C'est bien qu'il exprime sa noirceur à travers le

dessin. Il a fait des progrès depuis qu'il est arrivé. Mais j'avoue qu'avec votre intervention au piano aujourd'hui, on a franchi un cap. Pour la première fois, il a parlé et je l'ai vu éprouver du plaisir. C'est grâce à vous.

— Si je peux être utile, répondit Louis, un peu gêné.

— Comme vous vous êtes montré patient, je tenterai de le questionner ce soir à propos de la nuit du drame. En douceur.

Si elle disait au garçon que l'homme qui lui avait appris à jouer du piano avait besoin qu'il se rappelle des choses, même désagréables, il se pouvait bien qu'il accepte de rendre ce service à quelqu'un qu'il semblait avoir apprécié. C'était une chance à prendre.

Alors que la psychologue avait tiré une chaise pour s'asseoir, Louis se posta un peu devant elle, à demi assis sur la table :

— Qu'est-ce qu'il va devenir une fois qu'il aura quitté cet établissement ? demanda-t-il, la voix préoccupée. Où est-ce qu'il va aller s'il n'a plus la moindre famille ?

— Ça vous inquiète ? fit Agathe, insondable.

— Après ce qu'il a vécu, être trimballé d'une famille d'accueil à une autre, je ne pense pas que ça contribuera à ce qu'il retrouve un équilibre émotionnel. Je n'imagine même pas ce qu'il doit ressentir. Il doit être terrifié. Non seulement par ses souvenirs, mais à la perspective d'un avenir sans personne.

— Ça ne sera pas facile de se reconstruire, c'est sûr. Mais j'ai l'audace de croire que ce n'est pas impossible.

Puis, après un très court silence, elle reprit :

— Vous semblez être quelqu'un de très attaché à votre famille, je me trompe ? Je suppose que vos parents sont très proches de vous ?

— J'ai la chance d'avoir encore mes deux parents, oui. Et même une grand-mère, si vous voulez tout savoir. Elle a dépassé allègrement les quatre-vingt-quinze ans, mais elle a encore toute sa tête.

— C'est merveilleux. Ce doit être enrichissant de passer du temps avec un parent qui a une telle expérience de la vie.

— Et vous ? Vous avez votre famille ?

À ce moment, les premières notes du film d'Harry Potter se firent entendre. C'était le téléphone d'Agathe, qu'elle extirpa de la poche de sa blouse blanche en s'excusant. Louis remarqua que son visage se ferma lorsqu'elle regarda l'écran.

— Vous ne répondez pas ? s'enquit-il.

— Le numéro est masqué.

— Ça a l'air de vous contrarier.

— C'est que ça arrive souvent depuis quelques semaines, confia-t-elle. Et quand je décroche, il n'y a personne au bout de la ligne.

— Vous n'avez pas bloqué le numéro ?

— C'est un numéro masqué. Je l'ai fait, mais je pense qu'il le change constamment.

— Vous n'en avez pas parlé à la police ?

— C'est ce que je suis en train de faire, il me semble, non ? rétorqua-t-elle en regrettant aussitôt son ton un peu agressif.

Heureusement, l'homme qu'elle avait en face d'elle ne lui en tint aucunement rigueur.

— Ces appels vous effraient ?

Louis sentait que la jeune femme était sur la

défensive. Elle avait éteint son téléphone d'un geste plein de nervosité. Sa pâleur trahissait son angoisse.

— Au début, je pensais que c'était une erreur, quelqu'un qui ne faisait pas attention et composait un mauvais numéro. Ou bien une de ces plateformes de vente qui appellent automatiquement. Mais ça s'est reproduit à intervalles réguliers. À chaque fois, je me dis que je vais aller porter plainte, et puis j'ai mille choses à faire et j'oublie jusqu'à ce que ça recommence.

— Je comprends. Et vous avez eu d'autres soucis en dehors de ces coups de fil ?

Agathe fit une petite moue, réfléchit, puis ses yeux s'agrandirent :

— Il y a un mois, un soir que je rentrais chez moi, j'ai trouvé un chat mort sur mon paillasson. C'était horrible ! On lui avait ouvert le ventre, ses tripes pendaient.

— Quelqu'un vous en veut ? Un ex, un amant éconduit ?

— Non, répondit-elle en secouant la tête.

— Si vous me confiez votre téléphone, je pense pouvoir trouver quelqu'un qui saura démasquer votre harceleur. Ça ne prendra que quelques heures.

— Et après ? Si vous trouvez qui s'amuse à passer ces coups de fil, qu'est-ce qui arrivera ? Vous irez l'arrêter ?

Louis fut un peu désarçonné par ses réactions, qu'il jugeait anarchiques.

— Eh bien, dans un premier temps, je me ferai un devoir de le convoquer au poste et, selon à qui j'aurai affaire, nous aviserons. Vous avez envie que ça s'arrête, non ?

— Bien sûr, oui. Pardonnez-moi, mais ces appels

me mettent les nerfs à vif.

– D'après moi, c'est justement le but de la manœuvre. Alors, j'ignore pourquoi on s'en prend à vous, mais vous avez bien fait de m'en parler.

Et, comme elle n'avait pas esquissé le moindre geste :

– Vous me le donnez, ce téléphone, ou on attend le prochain appel ?

Le sourire encourageant que le lieutenant adressa à Agathe la détendit. Elle finit par lui tendre l'appareil, qu'elle ralluma afin qu'il puisse accéder à ses données. Elle nota son code sur un *post-it* pour plus de facilité, puis elle regarda Louis empocher son téléphone avec une sorte de tristesse qu'il détecta :

– Allons, allons ! Je vous le rends au plus vite, n'ayez pas peur. Je l'apporte dès mon retour à Paris à mon collègue Mespouille et je vous contacte quand j'ai un résultat. Par la même occasion, vous pourrez me dire si vous avez pu tirer quelque chose de Nathan.

Agathe accepta. Entre-temps, Maud Cortès avait reparu. Elle attendait discrètement à la porte de la salle, mobile en main. Qui sait depuis combien de temps elle était là ? Louis, absorbé par la présence de la psychologue, n'avait pas jeté un seul regard ailleurs que dans l'espace où elle évoluait.

Il était temps de partir et Louis était obnubilé par l'envie d'inviter la jeune femme à dîner, sans se décider à ouvrir la bouche. Après tout, que savait-il d'elle ? Elle avait peut-être un petit ami. Même s'il avait pris note de l'absence d'alliance à son annulaire gauche, cela ne signifiait pas que son cœur soit libre. La peur d'un refus l'empêcha de sauter le pas et il quitta l'institut en se maudissant. Il se dit qu'il pourrait tenter sa chance lorsqu'il la rappellerait pour lui donner les résultats des recherches sur son téléphone.

Le portable de la jeune femme dans sa poche était une source de tentation. Il aurait pu le fouiller et ainsi, grâce au journal d'appel et aux SMS, savoir si un homme en particulier figurait dans ses favoris. Par respect, il s'abstint.

Après avoir déposé Maud au commissariat, il se rendit dans les locaux où Mespouille officiait. Il lui confia le téléphone en précisant qu'un examen rapide serait le bienvenu.

Le dénommé Daniel Mespouille, un grand gaillard au visage carré, marmonna dans sa barbe avec un air peu engageant. Louis connaissait le loustic : il grognait beaucoup, mais ne mordait pas. Enfermé dans son laboratoire, il ne voyait que très peu de monde et ne s'en plaignait pas, misanthrope sur les bords. Aussi, lorsqu'il avait de la visite, il exprimait toujours un certain mécontentement auquel Louis ne prenait plus garde depuis longtemps.

Le colosse fit même preuve de compassion envers la propriétaire du téléphone lorsque Louis lui eut expliqué qu'elle était victime de harcèlement. Quelques années plus tôt, sa propre sœur avait subi le même type d'agression morale et cela s'était malheureusement soldé par un suicide. Il ne prenait donc pas la chose à la légère, ce genre de détraqués le rendaient fou, il ferait tout son possible pour débusquer celui qui s'en prenait à Agathe.

— J'ai déjà un truc urgent sur le feu, dit Daniel de sa voix de baryton, mais je m'y mets dès que j'ai fini avec ça.

— Tu m'appelles, je compte sur toi, hein ?

L'homme poussa un soupir exaspéré sans regarder le lieutenant.

— Tu crois que ce sera bon pour demain ?

— Tire-toi, petit prince, me pompe pas l'air si tu veux qu'on reste en bons termes.

— OK.

Mieux valait s'éclipser sans demander son reste.

En prenant la direction de la sortie, il croisa le capitaine Hébrard, qui sembla étudier les traits de son visage avec une attention non dissimulée avant de déclarer en riant :

— Toi, tu viens de rendre visite à Mespouille ou je ne m'appelle plus Hébrard ! Il t'a renvoyé dans tes pénates, c'est ça ?

— Je m'en remettrai, merci, capitaine. Et toi, qu'est-ce que tu fais là ? Toujours après la petite secrétaire du troisième ?

— J'y suis presque. Encore deux ou trois cafés le matin quand elle embauche et c'est marre. Elle est en train de fondre.

Hébrard devait avoir essayé de mettre dans son lit la moitié du personnel féminin de la police d'Île-de-France. Toujours sur le point de conclure, rarement capable de davantage. Mais il persévérait, convaincu qu'aucune de ces dames ne pouvait résister à son pouvoir de séduction. Évidemment, la gent féminine s'était donné le mot, on le voyait venir à des kilomètres. Mais le bougre n'était pas méchant et il était généreux. Aussi était-ce devenu un jeu entre les femmes de savoir laquelle d'entre elles recevrait ses faveurs le mois suivant.

De retour au commissariat, Ismaël informa Louis que l'analyste du SALVAC à qui il avait fait appel quelques semaines plus tôt avait tenté de le joindre.

— Tu n'as pas pris l'appel ? s'étonna Louis.

— Il voulait te parler à toi.

— Je vais le rappeler. On en est où avec les convocations de la famille Aubry ?

— Maud est en train de cuisiner un ex-petit ami de la fille aînée. Un certain Adam Couderc. Il n'a aucun alibi pour la nuit des meurtres et Fontaine vient de nous sortir ses antécédents. Regarde-moi ça.

À peine âgé de vingt et un ans, le dénommé Couderc avait déjà une collection de condamnations longue comme le bras à son actif. Les délits allaient du vol à l'étalage aux coups et blessures, en passant par la détention et la vente de stupéfiants, ainsi que plusieurs arrestations pour conduite en état d'ivresse.

— On pourrait ajouter détournement de mineur, fit remarquer Ismaël. Emma Aubry n'avait que seize ans lorsqu'ils sont sortis ensemble. Et j'imagine qu'ils ne passaient pas leur temps à lire des *Corto Maltese*.

— Si tu veux mon avis, les *Corto Maltese* sont même d'un trop haut niveau pour l'énergumène. Si j'en crois son parcours résumé ici, il a quitté les bancs de l'école après le collège et apparemment, il n'a occupé aucun emploi depuis. Ce qui ne l'empêche pas de rouler en Mercedes.

Les deux lieutenants récoltaient leurs informations sur l'ordinateur que le commandant Fontaine avait laissé en fonction avant de sortir, appelé sur une autre affaire. Il avait lancé les recherches auprès des différents services administratifs, Louis et Ismaël n'avaient plus qu'à ouvrir les fenêtres reléguées au bas de l'écran.

— Il faut voir s'il a un lien avec les Lemonnier et

on le colle en garde à vue.

— Ah ! j'oubliais : la fille de l'institut Saint-Jean a appelé aussi, il y a une petite heure de ça.

— Ah, bon ? Je viens de la quitter. Pourquoi n'a-t-elle pas essayé de me joindre sur mon portable ? s'étonna Louis en attrapant son appareil dans la seconde.

— Elle l'a fait. Elle t'a laissé un message. Tu devais être sur la route à un endroit où il n'y avait pas de réseau, je suppose.

En effet, Louis vit clignoter le symbole des messages vocaux qui s'affichait quand il appuya sur la touche d'allumage de l'écran.

S'éloignant de quelques pas, il écouta la voix d'Agathe lui annoncer que Nathan lui avait révélé quelque chose qui pourrait peut-être l'intéresser. Alors qu'ils étaient dans le parc après le départ de Louis, l'enfant avait remarqué une odeur provenant d'un couple qui passait à côté d'eux. Il avait d'abord fait la grimace, puis avait fondu en larmes, pour la première fois depuis qu'il était interné. Agathe avait identifié l'odeur en question comme étant du haschisch. Lorsqu'elle avait demandé au garçon pour quelle raison cette odeur le rendait si malheureux, il dit que cela lui rappelait les cigarettes que son frère Enzo fumait en cachette.

Rapidement, Louis résuma ce qu'il venait d'apprendre à Ismaël. Devaient-ils en conclure que ces meurtres étaient liés à une simple histoire de drogue, comme l'avait suggéré Maud ? Ce Couderc était-il en contact avec l'un ou l'autre des membres de la famille Lemonnier ?

— On va faire des tirages de la photo de Couderc et les mettre en circulation au collège du frère de

Nathan.

Louis se dirigeait déjà vers l'imprimante quand Ismaël intervint :

— On est mercredi, il n'y aura aucun élève, surtout à cette heure de la journée. Demain, on aura plus de chance de trouver du monde.

— On n'a pas jusqu'à demain. Le type va nous filer entre les doigts.

— On peut le coincer en faisant fouiller son appart. On devrait trouver des produits intéressants, là-dedans. Il nous faut juste une commission rogatoire. Avec un peu de chance, Couderc fournit le quartier des Lemonnier.

— Mmm, grommela Louis, peu convaincu. On n'a pas trouvé de drogue chez les Lemonnier, comment on va faire le lien avec Couderc ? Et puis je demande à voir la tête du gars. Je monte au premier, tu continues ici ?

Même si Louis voyait bien que son coéquipier avait l'impression d'avoir avancé, lui doutait qu'un gamin à peine majeur eût assassiné deux familles pour une misérable histoire de H. Ça ne tenait pas la route.

Il fut happé dans le bureau d'Amary devant lequel il passait, celui-ci bien décidé à dénicher un suspect quel qu'il soit. Le commissaire assura qu'il obtiendrait une commission rogatoire dans l'heure. Al Bakir, Cortès et lui avaient plutôt intérêt à se bouger et à trouver de quoi mettre ce margoulin à l'ombre pour calmer les esprits. Louis dut s'incliner, non sans penser que c'était comme ça que des innocents se retrouvaient derrière les barreaux. Certes, ce Couderc était loin d'être irréprochable, mais il était bien parti pour porter le chapeau jusqu'à ce que les soupçons se portent sur quelqu'un d'autre. Et ça pouvait prendre du temps, surtout si le jeune *dealer* n'avait aucun alibi pour les meurtres des deux familles.

Automne 2000

Claude ne se rappelait pas la dernière fois qu'il s'était fait dessus, mais le liquide chaud imbibant son caleçon et dégoulinant dans son entrejambe le fit se sentir comme un enfant sans défense qui vient de faire une bêtise monumentale et attend la sentence.

— Un, deux, trois, trois p'tits chats, trois vilains petits fripons...

L'homme s'était mis à chantonner cette comptine, répétant toujours les mêmes notes, les mêmes paroles, jusqu'à vous rendre dingue.

Deux corps gisant dans leur sang, trois petits chats entrant dans une maison.

Un bol de lait pour les chatons.

De la farine par terre.

Et tout ce sang qui se mélange, qui forme des grumeaux dégoûtants.

Les chats qui se roulent dedans.

Et ressortent tout blanc.

Claude avait l'impression que sa tête allait exploser. Tout se mettait à tourner et à tanguer devant lui, en lui. Un vertige qui se répercutait à l'intérieur de tout son être, faisant monter la nausée.

— Il faut que tu te décides, papa, reprit l'homme

de sa voix la plus calme, cette fois. On n'a pas toute la nuit, malheureusement. Et puis tu sais, ça ne m'amuse pas d'avoir à faire ça.

Il y eut un court moment de silence. Ces passages de la fureur à un discours presque normal ne présageaient rien de bon. On ne savait pas sur quel pied danser. Toute parole inconsidérée pouvait s'avérer fatale. Claude tenta quand même de le raisonner :

— Alors pourquoi le faites-vous ?

Derrière le masque, les yeux s'agrandirent, menaçants, une lueur de folie malsaine perça.

— Mais c'est ta faute. C'est toi qui t'es mis tout seul dans cette situation. Et le pire, c'est que tu ne t'en rends même pas compte, comme les milliers de gens dans ton genre que je vois défiler chaque jour à mon guichet.

Claude n'était pas un spécialiste des agissements des psychopathes, mais il avait vu suffisamment de films policiers pour savoir que si un tueur commençait à vous révéler des détails de sa vie, c'est qu'il ne donnait pas cher de la vôtre. Son cerveau se mit en branle dès qu'il eut enregistré l'information du guichet. Une banque ? Une gare ? Non, il ne prenait jamais ni le train ni le RER. La Poste peut-être ?

Il avait mentionné les allocations familiales à plusieurs reprises. Sa femme, sans emploi, allait chaque mois recevoir l'argent des allocations directement dans les locaux de la CAF. Se pourrait-il que cet homme en fût un employé ? Cela expliquerait une partie de son discours et le fait qu'il connaissait leur mode de vie.

Fallait-il qu'il questionne ce monstre afin de

confirmer ses soupçons ? Et après ? À quoi ça l'avancerait ? Cela ne ferait pas revenir les morts à la vie et cela ne les sauverait pas, ses deux enfants restants et lui.

— Alors je vais te poser la question encore une fois.

Tout en parlant, l'homme-chat se dirigea vers Mélissa et Victor, dont il dénoua les liens. Mélissa se mit à pousser des cris suraigus qui vous transperçaient les tympans et vous déchiraient le cœur. Elle reçut une gifle magistrale du plat de la monstrueuse main de l'homme. Elle s'écroula à terre, aussitôt harcelée :

— Lève-toi ! Arrête de pleurnicher et debout !

Claude était au-delà du choc. Son esprit n'était plus qu'une plaie qui suppure. Que pouvait-il faire ?

Mélissa se releva, un élancement brûlant sur sa joue, comme marquée au fer rouge. Elle respirait tant bien que mal, retenait les hurlements qui se bousculaient au fond de sa gorge. Est-ce que personne n'allait venir la sauver ? Ses cris de tout à l'heure n'avaient-ils pas alerté un voisin, un passant ?

Leur bourreau les avait agrippés par les cheveux, Victor et sa sœur, puis il les avait fait avancer jusque devant Claude, qu'ils eurent de la peine à reconnaître avachi là, par terre, le caleçon trempé de sa propre urine, le visage ravagé par la peur, la honte, le chagrin. Il n'osait pas les regarder, gardait obstinément les yeux baissés.

— Lequel des deux ? demanda l'homme, un bras passé autour du cou de chacun des deux enfants, son couteau flirtant dangereusement avec le dessous de l'œil de Mélissa.

— Je ne peux pas, fit la voix faible de Claude.

— Comme dit l'adage, c'est un cruel dilemme. Mais tu dois choisir. Autrement, ils vont mourir tous les deux, et toi avec. La vie de tes enfants est entre tes mains.

— Je ne peux pas. Je ne peux pas…

Claude répétait ces mots sans pouvoir s'arrêter alors que son fils et sa fille se tenaient devant lui, morts de peur, tremblants, espérant que ce cauchemar allait enfin se terminer. Il n'osait pas lever les yeux sur eux, gardait la tête obstinément baissée vers le sol, qu'il ne voyait pas. Les mots qu'il prononçait n'avaient plus aucun sens, plus rien n'était cohérent. Il voulait que ça s'arrête, il ne pouvait en supporter davantage.

S'il prononçait le nom de Mélissa, alors Victor mourrait. Et s'il optait pour Victor, c'est sa fille qui perdrait la vie. Et tout ça pour quoi ? À quoi ça rimait d'imposer un tel dilemme à un père de famille ? L'homme avait-il déjà joué à ce jeu immoral, inhumain ? Prenait-il du plaisir à voir le désespoir le plus absolu dans les yeux de ses victimes ?

Il ne vit qu'un corps s'effondrer devant lui comme une poupée de chiffon. Il reconnut les chaussons en forme de petits moutons de Mélissa, mais il n'eut pas le courage de regarder la longue plaie profonde qui lui entaillait le cou de l'oreille gauche à la glotte.

Il ferma très fort les yeux, car il savait à présent que c'était terminé.

Il n'avait pas pu choisir.

Leur sort était scellé.

De toute façon, il aurait été incapable de vivre

avec le poids de toutes ces morts sur la conscience. Il souhaitait que ça se termine.

Vite.

— Regarde ce que tu as fait, dit la voix glaciale du monstre.

La Mort personnifiée. Était-ce elle qui s'adressait à lui ? Il semblait à Claude que tous les sons étaient étouffés, comme si une couche épaisse de coton obstruait ses oreilles. Ou comme ces bruits que la neige atténue quand elle recouvre tout.

Quand Victor s'écroula à son tour, dans un frémissement, Claude n'était plus qu'une coquille vide. Un corps sans esprit, sans âme. Il avait tué ses enfants sans même avoir le courage de les regarder.

Chapitre 14

– Bonne pêche ! s'écria Ismaël en brandissant une liasse de billets de vingt euros qu'il venait de dégotter sous le matelas. Pas très original, comme planque.

– C'est sa grand-mère qui a dû lui filer le tuyau, plaisanta Maud. Quoique, la mienne préférait les glisser entre les piles de draps dans l'armoire. Quand elle est morte, on a même trouvé des pièces dans les chaussettes de mon grand-père, qui était parti bien avant elle. Il y en avait pour une petite fortune ! Je crois que mes parents s'en sont servi pour payer les funérailles.

On sentait une certaine amertume poindre dans ces dernières paroles.

– Si c'était moi qui les avais trouvées, j'en aurais fait cadeau à mes enfants. Mais bon, chacun est différent.

– Ça dépend des grands-parents en question, releva Ismaël. Du côté de mon père, ils étaient mauvais comme des teignes ! On n'y mettait jamais les pieds, même pas pour *l'aïd*.

– Bingo ! fit soudain Louis, le nez dans les livres d'une bibliothèque bien fournie.

Il brandit un gros bloc de résine de cannabis qu'il

avait extirpé d'un volume factice.

— Les techniciens du labo ne nous ont encore rien dit des analyses toxicologiques, n'est-ce pas ? questionna Ismaël.

— Ils doivent nous faire parvenir leur rapport dans la semaine. Avec tous les homicides qu'on a eus sur les bras, on ne peut pas s'attendre à ce qu'ils fassent des miracles non plus ! les défendit Maud, toujours solidaire.

— S'ils ne trouvent aucune trace de stupéfiants dans l'organisme des gamins, on n'aura que dalle !

— Ne sois pas si négatif, temporisa Louis. Et rappelle-toi que le petit Nathan a vu son frère fumer du cannabis. Donnons d'abord tout ça à analyser et on verra plus tard.

— Plus tard, plus tard… Amary ne va pas aimer ça.

— Amary sait très bien comment ça fonctionne. C'est Sack qui lui met la pression. Il saura le calmer si besoin est.

— Ou alors il enverra Bonnemort ! lança Ismaël.

Les deux lieutenants se mirent à rire tandis que Maud les considérait sans comprendre.

— Rappelle-toi de quelle manière notre nouvelle légiste de compétition a mouché Sack ! fit Ismaël. C'est dommage que tu aies raté ça, crois-moi !

Pendant qu'ils riaient au souvenir de l'épisode, Louis passa dans les toilettes, d'où on ne le vit plus ressortir. On entendit alors sa voix qui appelait ses coéquipiers, mais elle avait l'air de venir de très loin.

Maud pénétra dans le réduit qui faisait office de lieu d'aisance. Il n'y avait personne, mais devant elle, une petite fenêtre était ouverte, donnant sur un mur gris. Elle s'approcha, se pencha, se tordit le cou pour lever la tête, et vit des marches de fer qui montaient jusqu'au toit par cet étroit conduit.

Le visage de Louis apparut tout en haut, puis un paquet dégringola que Maud réceptionna. D'autres blocs de résine de cannabis suivirent le même chemin, ainsi qu'un sac rempli de cachets blancs, probablement de l'ecstasy. C'était une pluie continue de paquets bien emballés qui tombaient dans les bras de Maud. Ismaël était en bout de chaîne, dans la cuisine, il mettait la récolte dans un grand sac de sport qu'il avait déniché dans un placard.

— Vous voyez qu'il n'est pas si bête ! C'est l'endroit idéal pour cacher de la *came*, là-haut, dit Louis une fois redescendu.

— Bon, je crois qu'on a fait le tour, fit Ismaël, prêt à plier bagages. En tout cas, on a de quoi mettre le lascar à l'ombre un bon bout de temps avec ce qu'on a là.

Louis se chargea de refermer l'appartement à clef derrière eux.

— Vous aviez réussi à en tirer quelque chose, Cortès ? On a d'autres arguments que la détention de drogue ?

— C'est un frimeur, il se la pète, répondit Maud, qui avait procédé à l'interrogatoire d'Adam Couderc. Il n'a pas résisté au besoin de dire qu'il couchait avec Emma Aubry. Et quand je lui ai demandé pourquoi leur histoire s'était terminée, il a prétendu que c'est lui qui en avait eu marre *de cette gamine*, je cite.

— Vous lui avez fait remarquer qu'il s'agissait de détournement de mineur ?

— Ça l'a fait rire. La fille n'est plus de ce monde pour témoigner qu'ils avaient eu des rapports sexuels, ce sera difficile à prouver. Ce en quoi il n'a pas tort.

— Mais on a des aveux.

— Mais on a des aveux, confirma Maud en souriant. Tout a été filmé. En revanche, je doute que ça constitue un mobile pour les meurtres dont on veut le charger. Il n'y a eu aucune plainte déposée contre lui de la part d'Emma ou de ses parents, j'ai vérifié.

— Et on n'a toujours pas de lien entre lui et les Lemonnier.

— Tout vient à point à qui sait attendre, philosopha Louis en sortant la carte électronique de leur voiture en même temps que son téléphone, qui sonnait.

Il lança la carte à Ismaël et s'éloigna de quelques pas sur le trottoir pour répondre à l'appel.

C'était Yvan Duval, l'analyste du SALVAC à qui il avait fait appel quelques semaines auparavant pour vérifier si d'autres affaires de tueries familiales leur avaient échappé.

— Putain, Louis ! Ça fait vingt fois que j'essaie de te joindre au poste et que je laisse des messages pour que tu me rappelles. Personne t'a rien dit ?

— Si, si, désolé, Yvan, s'excusa le lieutenant. J'allais te rappeler. On a pas mal de cadavres sur les bras et pas de suspect sérieux. Alors, tu imagines l'ambiance, je ne vais pas te faire un dessin. Tu as du nouveau pour moi ?

— Ben d'après toi ? Sinon, je ne t'aurais pas rappelé et couru derrière depuis trois plombes !

— Raconte.

— Alors voilà : j'ai un cas qui pourrait se rapprocher de tes petits meurtres en famille. Ça s'est passé en novembre dernier, à Argenteuil. J'ai eu du mal à faire le recoupement avec ton affaire d'Aulnay-sous-Bois parce que la famille en question n'a pas été victime d'un tueur extérieur. Du moins, ça a été la conclusion des enquêteurs. C'est le père qui a massacré tout le monde et s'est suicidé après. Il s'est pendu. C'est ce qui m'a mis la puce à l'oreille. Mais si ça se trouve, il n'y a aucun rapport.

— Le nom de la famille, s'il te plaît ?

— Je t'envoie tout ça par *mail*. Je voulais juste savoir si ça t'intéressait.

— Bien sûr que ça m'intéresse, merci.

Louis allait couper la communication lorsque son ami le rappela :

— J'ai pas fini.

Le lieutenant ne cacha pas son étonnement. Dans la voiture où ils étaient montés, Ismaël et Maud le regardaient à travers le pare-brise, trouvant le temps long. Il leur fit un petit signe destiné à les faire patienter en leur faisant comprendre que c'était important. Depuis le temps qu'ils travaillaient ensemble, les deux lieutenants avaient développé une sorte de langage corporel et de signes qu'ils comprenaient parfaitement. Si Maud avait un peu plus de mal, Ismaël se chargeait de traduire.

— Ça n'a peut-être rien à voir, mais je suis remonté jusqu'à vingt ans en arrière pour être sûr de ne rien louper. Il se trouve qu'en novembre 2000, encore à Argenteuil, la famille Albert a été découverte assassinée. On n'a jamais retrouvé le meurtrier, mais d'après mes renseignements, il y a eu un survivant.

— C'est un des enfants qui a survécu ?

— Aucune idée. Je n'ai pas accès à son identité de l'époque ni à celle qu'il ou elle a aujourd'hui.

— Tu m'envoies aussi tout ça ?

— C'est fait. Sur ton adresse pro.

— T'es le meilleur, Yvan, je te l'ai déjà dit ?

— Non, mais c'est gentil de le reconnaître, plaisanta l'analyste.

Lorsque Louis rangea son portable dans sa poche, il se sentit à la fois submergé par ce flot d'informations et léger à l'idée de partir sur de nouvelles pistes.

Une fois dans le véhicule, installé côté passager, il relata ce qu'il venait d'apprendre aux deux autres. L'impatience de plonger dans les fichiers qu'Yvan Duval lui avait transmis n'avait d'égal que son désir de trouver un lien entre toutes ces affaires pourtant très éloignées dans le temps puisque la plus ancienne remontait à quinze ans en arrière.

En tout, ils se retrouvaient donc avec quatre familles dont tous les membres avaient été assassinés dans des circonstances incertaines. Cela ne pouvait pas être un hasard, Louis en était convaincu.

Quand ils se garèrent dans le parking réservé aux membres des forces de l'ordre, il se dirigea vers la porte d'entrée du commissariat, mais se rendit rapidement compte que les autres ne le suivaient pas. Il se retourna.

Alors seulement, il réalisa que la nuit était tombée. Les lampadaires de la rue étaient allumés, les agents et le personnel d'entretien se croisaient sur le perron, où Louis gênait.

— Il est tard, lui dit Ismaël, qui vit bien son désarroi. Je serai là demain à la première heure, mais là, il faut que je rentre. Jade m'attend, tu comprends...

Il laissa sa phrase en suspens, fit un geste d'au

revoir de la main et rejoignit son propre véhicule un peu plus loin.

— Allez-y aussi, Cortès, votre famille doit avoir hâte de vous voir rentrer.

Le visage de la jeune femme s'assombrit lorsqu'il prononça ces paroles. Elle prit conscience que personne n'attendait Louis Salvant-Perret chez lui et qu'il devait se sentir bien seul.

— Vous voulez venir dîner à la maison ? proposa-t-elle, soudain joviale. J'ai prévu du gratin de courgettes avec un bon steak.

— Non, non, c'est gentil. J'ai besoin d'être seul pour faire un peu de ménage dans tout ce qu'on a récolté aujourd'hui. Ne vous en faites pas pour moi, je vais mettre cette soirée à profit. À demain.

Et il disparut par la grande porte cochère sans se retourner, le sac de sport rempli de drogue à bout de bras qui allait rejoindre la pièce prévue à cet effet.

Chapitre 15

Plus elle apprenait à connaître le lieutenant Salvant-Perret, plus elle baissait sa garde. Son intervention au piano ce jour-là avait illuminé l'après-midi des enfants, et la sienne par la même occasion.

Sous ses airs de flic de salon, il cachait une personnalité pleine de sensibilité en plus d'une âme de mélomane. Elle le devinait honnête et gentil à défaut d'être beau. Il avait certes beaucoup de charme, mais ce côté aristocratique que l'on sentait chez lui, et qu'il se donnait tant de mal à dissimuler, rendait le personnage un peu faux. Ou superficiel, elle n'arrivait pas à se décider.

En tout cas, elle était ravie qu'il ait abandonné ses tentatives de séduction puériles. Elle avait enfin le sentiment de l'avoir vu sous son véritable jour, ou du moins d'avoir découvert une des facettes de sa personnalité.

Agathe rangea les papiers épars sur son bureau, dont elle fit un tas parfaitement symétrique avant de s'apprêter à quitter l'institut. Par automatisme, elle tâta la poche droite de sa blouse avant de l'enlever pour enfiler sa veste, à la recherche de son téléphone. Ne le trouvant pas, elle se rappela l'avoir confié au lieutenant. C'est inouï comme cet objet était devenu indispensable. Non seulement pour elle, mais pour tout individu normalement constitué vivant avec son temps. Elle se sentait démunie sans son *smartphone*.

D'un côté, elle se disait qu'elle avait bien fait de le confier à Salvant-Perret. Peut-être qu'ainsi, les appels anonymes cesseraient. Mais d'un autre côté, elle avait conscience de s'exposer aux regards d'un homme qu'elle connaissait à peine. Avait-elle envie de se livrer à lui ? Rien n'était moins sûr. Malheureusement, elle n'avait pas trop le choix. Le danger rôdait autour d'elle, ombre silencieuse, insidieuse.

Il lui avait fallu tant d'années pour réapprendre à vivre ! Elle s'était crue à l'abri. Même seule, elle s'était sentie en sécurité. Du moins avant l'épisode du chat crevé et des coups de fil à répétition.

Depuis qu'il l'avait débarrassée du cadavre de l'animal, son voisin de palier se sentait obligé de lui faire la conversation à chaque fois qu'ils se croisaient. Et ça arrivait souvent, ces derniers jours. On aurait dit qu'il la guettait, car si auparavant, elle ne le rencontrait que rarement, cela devenait un peu trop régulier. Et sa conversation avait tendance à tourner à la leçon de savoir-vivre, si bien qu'Agathe partait plus tôt le matin et rentrait très tard le soir pour ne pas tomber sur lui. Ça avait l'air de fonctionner.

Sept heures du soir venaient de sonner au clocher de la petite chapelle Saint-Jean lorsqu'elle salua de loin le père Pondillac, qui accueillait les religieuses pour la messe quotidienne. Elles étaient une petite vingtaine, d'âges divers, leurs robes et leurs voiles flottant au vent. Elles se pressaient pour se mettre à l'abri à l'intérieur de la petite église.

La jeune psychologue avait de l'affection pour ces femmes de Dieu. Elle les connaissait bien. Mais sa préférée restait sœur Constance, la plus jeune d'entre elles, et assurément la plus douce des créatures vivantes. Avant de monter dans sa voiture, elle tâcha de la reconnaître parmi ses pairs. Comme si elle avait senti le regard d'Agathe, Constance tourna la tête dans sa direction et, la voyant, lui adressa un sourire radieux.

Au lieu de rentrer directement à son appartement, la jeune femme fit un détour par un restaurant de spécialités italiennes qu'elle fréquentait. Encore une fois, l'absence de son portable se fit cruellement sentir. D'ordinaire, elle jouait au *sudoku* tout en dînant mais ce soir-là, elle fut contrainte de garder le nez dans son assiette.

Autour d'elle, quelques tables étaient occupées par des couples. On était en plein milieu de semaine, c'était plutôt calme. L'endroit était chaleureux. Le chef cuisinier, un homme bedonnant et jovial proche de la retraite, faisait sauter et virevolter ses pâtes à *pizza*, trônant derrière un comptoir où lui seul avait le droit de circuler. Les joues rouges à cause de la proximité du four qu'il ouvrait et refermait sans arrêt, c'était un véritable Italien du sud et, lorsqu'il appelait sa serveuse parce que les plats étaient prêts, on entendait un *PIZZE !* tonitruant s'élever au milieu des conversations feutrées.

Un peu tendue quand elle était arrivée, Agathe se détendit peu à peu, aidée par la chaleur qui régnait dans le restaurant, le verre de vin qu'elle venait de siroter et la bienveillance du personnel, qui la chouchoutait parce que ce n'était jamais drôle de dîner tout seul.

Ici, tous les plats étaient de qualité, les produits utilisés de première fraîcheur, la pâte travaillée avec soin et savoir-faire. Rien à voir avec ces tartes à la tomate vendues dans les camions qui fleurissaient au coin des rues les plus passantes.

Sa *pizza* lui parut encore meilleure que d'habitude. Elle avait demandé une *calzone* avec un œuf à l'intérieur. Le patron avait d'abord grommelé qu'on ne mettait jamais d'œuf dans une *calzone* puis, par sympathie pour cette jeune femme solitaire, il avait cédé à sa demande. Agathe ne put qu'honorer le restaurateur en finissant son assiette jusqu'à la dernière miette.

Elle était repue.

Lorsque la serveuse vint débarrasser, elle se recula contre le dossier de la banquette en soupirant d'aise.

— Eh bien ! Ça a l'air de vous avoir plu ! déclara l'employée avec un large sourire.

— Ça devrait être interdit de faire des *pizzas* aussi bonnes ! Depuis que je viens ici, j'ai dû prendre trois kilos.

— Franchement, si c'est le cas, je ne vois pas bien où vous les mettez. Moi, je prends tout dans les hanches.

Et elle se dandina en montrant ses rondeurs, qui n'avaient rien de laid, au contraire. Agathe la trouvait même très jolie avec ses formes généreuses. Elle, en comparaison, était filiforme, plutôt grande et aurait aimé avoir un peu plus de courbes, notamment au niveau de sa poitrine, qu'elle jugeait fort modeste.

— En même temps, après deux accouchements, faut pas rêver. Quoiqu'il y ait des femmes qui ne bougent pas, même après avoir eu des enfants. Quelle chance ! Vous en avez eu, vous ?

— Pas encore, non.

— Excusez-moi, je suis peut-être indiscrète.

— Non, non, ça va. Et puis ça commence à faire un petit moment que je viens maintenant, on peut faire les présentations. Je m'appelle Agathe.

La serveuse parut tout à fait enchantée de cette marque d'attention.

— Lou, annonça-t-elle à son tour en tendant une main franche qu'Agathe serra.

— Quel joli prénom, c'est ravissant !

— Le vôtre est très joli aussi. Vous habitez par ici pour venir aussi souvent ?

— Oui, à deux rues de là, dans les bâtiments neufs.

— Ah, oui ! Ceux de trois étages, je vois très bien où c'est. J'avais fait une demande pour louer là-bas, mais c'était déjà trop tard. Tout était réservé six mois avant la fin des travaux. Vous avez dû vous y prendre drôlement tôt pour obtenir un appartement.

— J'ai eu la chance de connaître un des propriétaires, qui m'a mise sur le coup. Si un appartement se libère, je peux vous en informer, si vous voulez.

— Je ne dis pas non, c'est gentil. J'ai une heure et demie de route pour venir jusqu'ici. Ça m'arrangerait bien si j'habitais un de ces appartements. En plus, ils ont l'air vraiment super. Vous en êtes contente ?

La conversation entre les deux jeunes femmes se prolongea après que la plupart des clients furent partis. Même le patron vint se joindre à elles et offrit un *limoncello* qui fit légèrement tourner la tête d'Agathe.

Comme il était assez tard et que son service était terminé, Lou lui proposa de la déposer devant chez elle si elle pouvait patienter juste dix petites minutes pour qu'elle nettoie les tables. Par les temps qui couraient, une femme seule dans les rues à la nuit tombée, ce n'était pas très prudent. La psychologue se laissa convaincre.

Alors qu'elle ouvrait la portière de la Clio pour en sortir, Lou lui demanda si elle viendrait au restaurant le lendemain.

— Comment refuser ? répliqua Agathe aimablement.

— À demain, alors ?

— À demain.

Agathe resta quelques secondes immobile sur le trottoir devant la porte d'entrée de son petit immeuble, faisant un signe de la main à la voiture qui s'éloignait dans la nuit.

Lou lui était sympathique. Elle aurait pu envisager de s'en faire une amie. Elle songea même que ce n'était peut-être pas très poli de sa part de ne pas l'avoir invitée à monter chez elle, histoire de lui montrer à quoi ressemblaient les appartements qu'elle convoitait tant. Mais cela se faisait-il entre personnes du même sexe ? Lou ne se serait-elle pas imaginé qu'elle était en train de la draguer, ou quelque chose comme ça ?

Ridicule !

Elle avait bien fait de la laisser repartir et chassa très vite ses doutes pour monter jusque chez elle.

Depuis l'épisode du cadavre du chat sur son paillasson, elle ralentissait toujours en atteignant son étage, jetant un coup d'œil inquiet sur le pas de sa porte, où il n'y avait plus de paillasson du tout.

Rien de suspect en vue.

Clefs en main, elle gravit les dernières marches en direction de la porte d'entrée, qu'elle ouvrit et referma derrière elle rapidement, de peur que son voisin bizarre ne l'entende et vienne lui parler. Quoiqu'à cette heure-ci, le bonhomme dût être dans son lit, c'était le genre à se lever aux aurores et à se coucher avec le soleil.

Inconsciemment, elle respira mieux une fois chez elle. Sans se préoccuper de l'endroit où elles allaient atterrir, elle envoya valser ses chaussures, suspendit sac et veste au portemanteau de l'entrée, puis se dirigea vers la cuisine, où elle se servit un verre d'eau. Ce *limoncello* lui avait donné soif en plus de l'avoir éméchée.

Après avoir déposé son verre dans le lave-vaisselle, elle entendit un bruit léger qu'elle ne parvint pas à identifier. Elle se redressa, aux aguets, immobile.

Le bruit recommença. Un grattement derrière elle, à la fenêtre. Elle s'approcha, tourna la poignée pour laisser entrer un énorme matou au poil angora tigré qu'elle accueillit dans ses bras.

— Sherlock, te voilà enfin ! Ça fait des jours que tu n'es pas venu me rendre visite. Tu boudais ou tu as trouvé un autre appartement où t'incruster ?

Le chat errant se mit à ronronner, enfouissant son museau dans le cou d'Agathe. Elle ignorait si l'animal avait un maître, mais elle en doutait. Ou alors, c'était une personne bien peu scrupuleuse, car le chat passait son temps chez les uns et les autres, au gré de son humeur et du contenu des placards des habitants du quartier, surtout. Agathe l'avait baptisé Sherlock parce qu'il avait l'air d'avoir un monocle à un œil et que cela lui rappelait la loupe avec laquelle on avait coutume de représenter le célèbre détective de Baker street.

Elle ouvrit le placard où elle rangeait des boîtes pour chat qu'elle achetait spécialement pour lui. Ses visites la ravissaient toujours. Elle adorait les animaux, mais avec ses horaires de dingue, il lui était impossible d'en avoir. Sherlock était parfait. Indépendant, affectueux, peu envahissant, mais présent quand il le fallait. Ça valait bien qu'elle se fende de quelques euros pour de la nourriture.

Lorsqu'elle avait vu le cadavre du félin l'autre jour, elle avait craint un instant que ce fût celui de Sherlock. Mais la corpulence et le poil du malheureux ne correspondaient pas.

Pendant qu'elle vidait le contenu du sachet dans une gamelle qui lui était également destinée uniquement, le matou se frotta contre ses jambes en miaulant comme s'il n'avait pas mangé depuis des jours ; ce qui était fort probable. Elle faillit renverser tout le contenu du récipient au moment où l'animal donna un coup de tête sur son poignet alors qu'elle se penchait pour le déposer sur le sol.

Le temps qu'il mange, elle passa dans la salle de bains se brosser les dents, puis entra dans sa chambre afin d'enfiler un vêtement de nuit.

À peine entrée, elle se figea. Face à elle, au-dessus de son lit, sur le mur sobrement peint en blanc, on avait écrit en grosses lettres noires :

JE SAIS QUI TU ES

Chapitre 16

Un grand *mug* de café en main, Louis Salvant-Perret alla s'installer dans le bureau que le commissaire Amary venait de quitter quelques minutes auparavant pour rentrer chez lui. Avec sa bénédiction, bien entendu. Étant donné l'heure tardive, il restait peu d'officiers au poste et l'un des agents d'entretien travaillait à dépoussiérer son bureau lorsque Louis avait voulu s'y rendre. Voyant sa déconvenue, Amary, sur le départ, lui avait proposé le sien.

Le fauteuil était le plus confortable du commissariat. Il avait coûté une blinde, comme disait Ismaël. Le plan de travail était vaste, dégagé de tout dossier ou papier volant ; Amary aimait l'ordre. Tout était rangé à sa place, rien ne traînait.

Louis mit l'ordinateur en fonction, puis accéda à sa boîte *mail,* où il cliqua sur le message d'Yvan Duval avec ses deux pièces jointes. L'une concernait la famille Prudhom, dont les corps avaient été retrouvés en novembre 2014, l'autre celle de la famille Albert, en novembre 2000.

Même si ces deux affaires étaient éloignées dans le temps, Louis y voyait des liens qui lui parlaient. Le lieu, par exemple : Argenteuil. La période de l'année :

novembre. Et enfin, le fait que les pères de famille avaient été retrouvés pendus.

En novembre 2000, c'était le commissaire Dupontet et son équipe qui avaient mené l'enquête. Une courte recherche indiqua à Louis que l'officier était à présent à la retraite.

Yvan Duval avait dit qu'il y avait eu un survivant à cette époque. Mais Louis eut beau éplucher le dossier, il était écrit que cinq cadavres avaient été sortis du domicile et la famille comptait bel et bien cinq membres. Avait-il loupé quelque chose ? L'analyste se serait-il trompé ? Ou alors, cette information ne figurait pas dans le dossier. Qu'est-ce que cela signifiait ?

Dans son calepin ouvert sur le bureau, il griffonna le nom du commissaire à la retraite, bien décidé à le contacter au sujet de ce mystère. Il n'eut aucun mal à dénicher les coordonnées de l'ancien enquêteur, il l'appellerait dès le lendemain.

Son café était avalé depuis bien longtemps lorsqu'il termina la lecture du dossier Albert, qu'il réduisit sur l'écran. Il fit une courte pause, en profita pour aller s'en chercher un autre et se replongea tout de suite dans l'étude du dossier Prudhom, cette fois.

On avait le même schéma de structure familiale avec les deux parents et trois enfants : Paul, Camille et Noa. Avec Cortès et Ismaël, ils avaient pourtant cherché si un cas similaire à celui de la famille Lemonnier s'était produit, mais comme l'enquête avait conclu au suicide du père meurtrier présumé, cette affaire ne figurait pas dans la catégorie des homicides non élucidés.

En revanche, les assassinats de la famille Albert constituaient une affaire non résolue. Ce qui n'avait pas été révélé aux médias de l'époque, qui avaient titré les unes de journaux avec des accroches racoleuses telles que :

« Folie meurtrière d'un père. Il tue femme et enfants avant de se pendre. »

Alors qu'en réalité, en novembre 2000, si Claude Albert avait effectivement été retrouvé pendu à la rampe d'escalier avec sa ceinture, laissant croire à son suicide, des blessures sur le cou du plus jeune et sur la cuisse du père contredisaient cette hypothèse. De plus, une marque de semelle de chaussure sur la joue de la fille aînée avait fait penser à la présence d'une tierce personne la nuit du drame. Cette empreinte ne correspondait à aucune des chaussures des membres de la famille. Mais ces informations n'avaient jamais été révélées au public.

Il était écrit dans le rapport du lieutenant Christophe Gaillard qu'on avait l'impression que le meurtrier avait voulu écraser le visage de la pauvre fille. Fait confirmé par le compte-rendu du médecin légiste, qui précisait que l'acte avait eu lieu post mortem.

Cela ressemblait à une manifestation de rage comparable au viol d'Emma, la fille aînée des Aubry. À chaque fois, il y avait un lien avec le premier né des fratries. C'était forcément une piste à suivre, mais pour aller où ?

S'il s'agissait du même tueur qui avait sévi en 2000 et en 2015, il devait être âgé d'au moins quarante-cinq ans. Ce qui disculpait d'office le jeune Adam Couderc puisqu'il n'avait que vingt et un ans. De plus, pour quelle raison le délinquant aurait-il violé une fille qui avait été d'accord pour avoir des relations sexuelles avec lui quelques mois plus tôt ?

Et en se servant d'objets de substitution par-dessus le marché ! De la part d'un jeune mâle en pleine forme, cela n'avait aucun sens. Juste avant de monter dans les bureaux, il était allé voir par lui-même à quoi il ressemblait. Ce n'était encore qu'un gamin, le front couvert de boutons d'acné, le visage percé à plusieurs endroits et les bras tatoués. Il jouait au dur, mais il n'en avait ni la carrure ni les tripes.

Non, l'homme qu'il soupçonnait d'être l'auteur de toutes ces tueries avait un ou plusieurs comptes à régler. S'en prendre de la sorte à des familles entières, cela n'avait rien d'anodin, ça voulait forcément dire quelque chose. Massacrer des enfants, c'était innommable, mais aucun d'entre eux n'avait été torturé. La mort avait été rapide. Néanmoins, seul un monstre dénué d'humanité pouvait ôter la vie à des êtres innocents. Un tel degré de cruauté dépassait son entendement.

Cortès éprouvait beaucoup de répugnance dès qu'il s'agissait de cette affaire. Depuis le début de l'enquête, Louis s'était aperçu qu'elle s'arrangeait pour éviter de se rendre sur les lieux des découvertes macabres, préférant rester au poste à faire des recherches ou à interroger les différents témoins. D'un tempérament profondément humain et généreux, elle avait du mal à s'accommoder de ces meurtres immondes. Cela dit, il le vivait mal aussi, mais le désir de coincer le malade derrière tout ça lui permettait de tenir le choc. Seul Ismaël paraissait peu affecté par la barbarie de ces dernières semaines. Mais cela changerait certainement dès que son enfant viendrait au monde. Pour l'instant, il avait un peu l'esprit ailleurs, tout à l'euphorie de la naissance à venir, et c'était compréhensible.

En revenant sur l'affaire Prudhom, Louis apprit que le petit pavillon que la famille occupait avait brûlé peu après la tragédie. L'incendie s'était déclaré dans la cuisine de la maison voisine et s'était propagé aux deux habitations mitoyennes, dont la leur.

Si Louis voulait vérifier si une lettre avait été tracée sur le matelas de l'aîné des enfants, c'était compromis. En 2000, il n'était fait aucune mention d'une telle signature chez les Albert et trop de temps s'était écoulé pour espérer s'assurer qu'il y avait eu une telle trace sur un des matelas à l'époque. Mais plus il y réfléchissait, plus il se disait qu'il fallait absolument qu'il sache si une lettre avait été laissée chez les Prudhom. Après tout, six mois s'étaient écoulés depuis le massacre de cette famille, c'était jouable.

Retrouver les meubles. Voilà ce qu'il devait faire. Comme le feu n'était pas parti de ce pavillon-là, peut-être que le mobilier n'avait pas trop été endommagé. Il existait des sociétés spécialisées dans le nettoyage des lieux ayant subi des dégradations importantes. Il était trop tard pour tenter de les joindre, mais il nota sur son carnet de les contacter dès le lendemain. Il n'y en avait pas cinquante dans la région, il trouverait rapidement.

Dans les divers rapports, il n'était mentionné nulle part qu'une lettre de l'alphabet suspecte avait été repérée sur l'envers d'un matelas. Mais cela ne voulait pas dire qu'elle ne s'y trouvait pas au moment où la famille avait été retrouvée morte. Comme le père avait tout de suite été désigné comme suspect, la maison n'avait peut-être pas été passée au peigne fin. Il n'y avait aucune raison.

Louis jeta un œil à l'horloge numérique au bas de

l'écran. Il était presque une heure du matin. Il bâilla, s'étira et laissa retomber ses bras le long du corps, harassé par toutes les informations qu'il venait d'ingurgiter, dépassé par les nombreuses interrogations que cela soulevait.

C'était un peu le chaos dans sa tête. Mais la question qui revenait sans arrêt était de savoir pourquoi le tueur des deux dernières familles laissait ces lettres sous les matelas des aînés. Il n'y avait certes que deux cas, mais comment ne pas y voir un message. Le problème, c'est qu'il ne détenait pas la clef du code. Ces lettres formaient un mot, mais lequel ? Voulait-il désigner quelqu'un en particulier ? Qui ?

Il tournait les éléments dans tous les sens, forgeait cinquante hypothèses toutes plus improbables les unes que les autres. Ce qui lui paraissait solide, c'était que deux affaires s'étaient déroulées durant la même période de l'année et au même endroit. Comme si le massacre de novembre 2014 faisait écho à celui de novembre 2000. Était-ce une sorte d'anniversaire macabre ? Et pourquoi tuer des enfants ?

Il resta là, assis devant l'écran qui s'était mis en veille, à se demander quelles pouvaient être les motivations d'un homme qui s'attaquait à des créatures sans défense. Mais il n'en trouvait aucune. Rien ne pouvait justifier cela.

La fatigue finit par avoir raison de lui. Il se réveilla en sursaut, regarda la pendule murale. Il avait dormi une heure.

La bouche pâteuse, Louis éteignit l'ordinateur, quitta le bureau pour rejoindre l'accueil, où il laissa un message pour la secrétaire. Il voulait les deux dossiers imprimés en six exemplaires pour le *débriefing* du lendemain matin. Lire sur papier était plus facile que sur un écran et, en réunion avec ses coéquipiers, ce serait plus pratique.

Le lendemain, il aurait du pain sur la planche. En attendant, comme son ventre criait famine, il sortit du poste. Une halte à l'épicerie arabe du quartier s'imposait. Il dévora un *chiche-kebab* dans la petite salle déserte où le propriétaire laissait son téléviseur branché sur une chaîne orientale dont la musique vous envoûtait comme dans un conte des *Mille et une Nuits*. Le commerçant restait jusqu'au milieu de la nuit et son fils prenait le relais au petit matin. Ainsi, l'épicerie était ouverte vingt-quatre heures sur vingt-quatre.

Une fois rassasié, Louis rentra chez lui et se jeta sur le lit tout habillé. Il n'ôta que ses chaussures avant de se rouler dans la couette, sombrant la seconde suivante dans un sommeil agité.

Chapitre 17

Les trois lieutenants, le capitaine Hébrard, le commandant Fontaine et le commissaire Amary se dirigeaient d'un pas martial vers la salle de réunion au premier étage. En les voyant défiler devant son bureau comme au 14 Juillet, la secrétaire d'Amary se dit qu'il devait y avoir une crise pour qu'ils affichent tous ces têtes d'enterrement.

Elle avait reçu les tirages que Salvant-Perret avait commandés à sa collègue de l'accueil et c'est elle-même qui avait préparé la salle comme si des ministres allaient tenir conseil. Elle avait installé des petites bouteilles d'eau pour chacun, du jus d'orange pour le commissaire, qui ne buvait que ça le matin, du café et des mini-viennoiseries qui furent englouties dès la troisième minute.

— Votre Isabelle nous gâte, fit remarquer Louis, qui en était à son deuxième pain au chocolat.

— Ne rêvez pas, petit prince, elle ne fait pas ça pour vos beaux yeux. C'est l'association de l'amicale de la police qui paye, répliqua Amary.

— Elle en est bien la présidente, non ?

— Qu'est-ce que ça change ? intervint Hébrard, la bouche pleine. Le fait est qu'Isabelle a été bien inspirée, ce matin.

— De toute façon, vous avez toujours faim, vous ! lança le commandant Fontaine avec un certain dédain.

— C'est que je me lève très tôt. Mon petit déjeuner est déjà de l'histoire ancienne. Et puis je ne résiste pas aux petites gâteries.

— Oui, ça, on sait, ironisa Ismaël, le ton chargé de sous-entendus.

— Bon, messieurs ! les rappela à l'ordre Amary.

Maud se racla discrètement la gorge, histoire de rappeler qu'elle n'était pas un homme.

— Pardon, Cortès, je ne vous oublie pas. Mais comme c'est encore vous la plus discrète, je ne vous inclus pas dans les éléments perturbateurs.

Les deux assiettes de viennoiseries avaient été pillées, le jus d'orange achevé. Le capitaine Hébrard se tenait avachi sur sa chaise, les deux mains sur sa panse distendue, la mine un peu béate, les paupières prêtes à se fermer après s'être goinfré. Il n'était pas rare de le surprendre endormi à son bureau dans la journée, la tête dodelinant au-dessus de sa poitrine au gré de ses rêves. En général, personne ne le réveillait, pas même le commissaire, qui était sensiblement du même âge et qui, pour dire la vérité, aurait bien aimé pouvoir somnoler ainsi ; mais il avait un grade à honorer.

De son côté, le commandant ne voyait pas d'un très bon œil ces siestes intempestives. Combien de fois était-il venu se plaindre auprès d'Amary, accusant le capitaine de laisser tout le travail aux collègues ? Mais Amary connaissait Hébrard. Il savait surtout que quand il le fallait, le capitaine était un des meilleurs dans son domaine. Aussi laissait-il le bonhomme prendre ses aises. L'un dans l'autre, leur petit groupe fonctionnait plutôt bien, tout le monde savait ce qu'il avait à faire et l'entente était cordiale la plupart du temps. Plus important encore : l'équipe faisait du très bon boulot et obtenait d'excellents résultats. De plus, étant donné son ancienneté, Louis ne tarderait pas à passer capitaine.

Ce dernier, qui avait avisé les six chemises bien épaisses au milieu de la table, se chargea de les distribuer à tous les membres présents. Il expliqua en détail le contenu des deux affaires en tâchant de démontrer les liens entre les tragédies.

Tous l'écoutèrent avec la plus grande attention, sans l'interrompre, feuilletant les divers dossiers au fur et à mesure que Louis exposait les faits.

– Duval, du SALVAC, m'a affirmé qu'il y avait eu un survivant en novembre 2000. Mais il n'a pas su me dire de qui il s'agissait. Ça sent pas très bon, tout ça, parce que si vous lisez les rapports, vous verrez que la famille comptait cinq membres et qu'il a été amené cinq corps à la morgue. Alors je me pose la question : qui est le survivant ?

– Je vous dirai ça demain au plus tard, fit le commissaire Amary, le seul à avoir suffisamment d'ancienneté pour avoir des relations dans beaucoup de services. Mais qu'est-ce qui vous fait croire qu'il s'agit du même suspect qui aurait sévi à quinze ans d'intervalle ?

– Absolument rien, reconnut Louis avec un naturel déconcertant. Je dis juste qu'il y a des concordances entre les deux cas. Il y a quelque chose qui lie ces deux affaires et les dernières sur lesquelles on travaille. À chaque fois, le tueur s'évertue à faire croire que c'est le père qui élimine sa famille et se suicide après.

— Sauf dans le cas de la famille Aubry, objecta Maud Cortès.

— C'est vrai, mais il y avait une lettre à l'envers du matelas de la fille aînée, comme chez les Lemonnier.

— Vos foutues lettres ne nous servent à rien, Salvant-Perret, si on ne sait pas ce qu'elles signifient, intervint le commandant Fontaine du ton fort peu aimable qui le caractérisait. Et que je sache, aucune autre de ces lettres n'a été retrouvée dans les deux affaires que vous nous mettez sous le nez.

— Si vous permettez, le domicile des Prudhom a partiellement brûlé après leur disparition. Et les lieux n'ont pas été retournés comme s'il s'était agi d'un homicide classique. Je compte bien me lancer à la recherche des matelas de cette famille.

Fontaine se mit à rire, entraînant le regard courroucé de Maud dans sa direction.

— Je ne vois pas ce qu'il y a de drôle. Si vous avez une meilleure idée, on vous écoute, lança Ismaël, muet jusque-là.

— Vous perdez votre temps, ajouta le commandant en se renfrognant devant le mécontentement général face à ses réactions. On ferait mieux de s'occuper de notre suspect. Celui-là, on l'a sous la main, au lieu de partir sur des affaires non élucidées qui datent d'il y a quinze ans !

S'ensuivit une prise de bec où chacun y allait de son commentaire pour défendre son point de vue. Une chose était sûre, c'est que Louis avait éveillé l'intérêt de ses collègues en mettant au jour ces anciennes affaires.

Le commissaire finit par calmer tout le monde en tapant du poing sur la table. Le capitaine Hébrard, qui avait assisté aux débats sans sortir de son état comateux, sursauta.

— Françoise Bonnemort a envoyé son rapport au labo et on a du nouveau. Ils ont comparé les résultats des analyses du cannabis que vous avez saisi chez Couderc avec les traces présentes dans le sang d'Enzo Lemonnier. Ce n'est pas le même.

— De mon côté, intervint Ismaël, j'avais envoyé quelques hommes dans les environs du lycée du gamin avec le portrait de Couderc : ça n'a rien donné. Personne ne l'a vu traîner dans le coin. Notre suspect n'a donc aucun lien avec la famille Lemonnier, désolé commandant. Sack ne va pas être content non plus, d'ailleurs.

— Je ne vous le fais pas dire. Raison de plus pour mettre les bouchées doubles et arrêter ce massacre. La presse ne nous ratera pas si un autre cas nous tombe dessus. Des têtes vont sauter, je vous le dis ! Salvant-Perret, je vous tiens informé au sujet de votre mystérieux survivant. Où en est mademoiselle Delcourt, avec Nathan Lemonnier ? Des nouvelles ?

Il y eut des échanges de regards en coin auxquels Louis ne fit pas attention. Il les informa des avancées à propos de cet enfant qui, en réalité, s'était caché dans la salle de bains et n'avait probablement rien vu de ce qui s'était passé. À la rigueur pouvait-il passer pour un témoin auditif, mais d'après ce que Louis savait du garçon, celui-ci n'était pas près de parler avant un bon bout de temps. Le traumatisme était trop grand.

À ce moment-là, Isabelle passa discrètement la tête par la porte qu'elle avait entrouverte après avoir frappé tout doucement. Elle attira l'attention de Louis en lui faisant signe qu'il y avait un appel pour lui.

— De toute façon, on a terminé, annonça Amary en se levant, le dossier sous le bras. Au travail, messieurs, dame, je vous souhaite une bonne journée.

Tandis que le commissaire sortait le premier, Fontaine le talonna, échangeant des propos qu'il s'efforçait de rendre inaudibles pour les autres. Le capitaine Hébrard émergea de sa léthargie à regret. Il quitta la salle le dernier, pensant qu'il aurait bien repris de ces délicieux petits croissants.

La ligne 2 clignotait sur le standard, qui datait d'un autre temps. Louis appuya sur le bouton en mettant le combiné à l'oreille. La voix de Daniel Mespouille se fit entendre. L'expert n'avait pas réussi à découvrir l'identité de la personne qui appelait sans arrêt Agathe Delcourt. À chaque fois que l'individu s'était manifesté, il s'agissait d'un numéro provenant d'un téléphone prépayé et ce n'était jamais le même. La seule certitude, c'est qu'il ne s'agissait pas d'appels provenant d'une plateforme, mais bel et bien d'un particulier anonyme.

La déception de Louis fut immense. Il aurait bien aimé pouvoir annoncer une bonne nouvelle à la jolie psychologue.

Il remercia Mespouille en lui promettant une bouteille de bon vin, dont il savait qu'il était amateur. En revanche, il n'eut pas le courage de téléphoner à Agathe tout de suite et repoussa cet appel à plus tard. De toute façon, il devait d'abord aller récupérer le portable au laboratoire de Mespouille pour le lui rapporter en personne.

En attendant de s'en occuper, il chargea Maud de se mettre en relation avec les diverses sociétés de nettoyage afin de savoir si l'une d'entre elles avait travaillé dans le logement brûlé de la famille Prudhom.

De son côté, Ismaël contacta les deux sites Emmaüs les plus proches, à la recherche du mobilier qui avait peut-être été récupéré. Quant à lui, il appela le commissaire Chaubet, qui était à la tête de l'équipe ayant découvert les corps sans vie des Prudhom.

L'homme qu'il eut au bout du fil était bourru et soupe au lait. Sa première réflexion fut qu'il n'avait pas pour habitude de bâcler une affaire dont on le chargeait et qu'il ne voyait pas très bien en quoi il pourrait contredire ses conclusions.

— Je veux simplement savoir si quelqu'un était retourné sur place après l'incendie de la maison.

— Non. Pour quoi faire ? Cette baraque ne présentait plus aucun intérêt, elle est restée ouverte aux quatre vents après que le feu a été éteint. Et je n'ai pas souvenir qu'il y ait eu quelque chose de suspect dans aucune des chambres qu'on a fouillées. J'ai entendu parler de vos mots croisés sous les matelas. Vous avez l'air de bien vous amuser dans votre coin, dites donc ! En tout cas, la prochaine fois qu'on a un mec qui pète les plombs et se pend après, on vous sonne...

Et il raccrocha au nez de Louis, qui eut un mouvement de recul de la tête devant la brutalité de la manœuvre.

— Quelque chose ne va pas ? s'inquiéta aussitôt Maud.

— C'est rien. Un flic mal embouché, c'est tout. Vous en êtes où, tous les deux ?

Maud était toute rouge, ses cheveux un peu en bataille après avoir passé presque une heure derrière son écran d'ordinateur, le téléphone coincé entre son épaule et sa joue. Elle n'était pas loin du torticolis.

— Ces satanées sociétés vous font poireauter un temps infini avec une musique insupportable et finissent par vous raccrocher au nez ! se plaignit-elle.

— Bienvenue au club, ne put s'empêcher de répondre Louis en souriant de leurs déconvenues communes. Vous avez quand même réussi à trouver la société susceptible de nous intéresser ?

— Oui, Net Pro Excel. Ils ont été appelés pour le nettoyage de la maison des Prudhom, mais ils m'ont dit que des squatteurs s'étaient installés entre le moment où le feu avait été éteint et celui où ils devaient intervenir. De toute façon, ils ne se sont finalement pas occupés de ce chantier, il y avait trop de dégâts, il fallait carrément des ouvriers du bâtiment. Emmaüs est venu chercher les meubles encore en état, mais pas mal de choses ont dû être volées et ce qui était trop brûlé est parti en déchetterie.

— Les Emmaüs du coin n'ont reçu aucun matelas provenant de cette adresse, je viens de parler au responsable du site de La Garenne-Colombes. Ce sont eux qui ont récupéré ce qui était récupérable. Ça a pris du temps avant que celui qui m'a répondu trouve les gars qui se sont rendus sur place, mais ils ont affirmé qu'il n'y avait plus aucun matelas dans la maison quand ils sont intervenus.

Louis resta un moment dubitatif. Si la maison était restée ouverte, n'importe qui avait pu y entrer et se servir. Les squatteurs eux-mêmes, voyant qu'ils allaient être chassés, étaient susceptibles d'avoir embarqué les matelas pour s'en servir ailleurs. Autant chercher une aiguille dans une botte de foin.

— Qu'est-ce qu'on fait ? demanda Maud d'une

toute petite voix.

— J'ai encore un coup de fil à donner, répondit Louis.

Sans en dire davantage, il prit son blouson d'un geste et se dirigea vers la sortie, laissant les deux autres un peu surpris.

Une fois sur le parking, où une demi-douzaine de voitures de police stationnaient, il attrapa la carte du numéro direct d'Agathe Delcourt à l'institut Saint-Jean. Son cœur battit un peu plus fort lorsqu'il entendit sonner. Après plusieurs secondes durant lesquelles elle aurait dû décrocher, il y eut une infime interruption, puis la sonnerie reprit, sur un timbre légèrement différent. L'appel venait d'être transféré.

Une voix de femme, rauque et désagréable, répondit en récitant à toute vitesse :

— Accueil-de-l'institut-Saint-Jean-bonjour-que-puis-je-faire-pour-vous ?

Cette phrase devait être répétée tellement souvent qu'il n'y avait plus rien d'accueillant dedans. Juste une suite de mots vides de sens balancés sur un ton blasé et inhospitalier.

— Bonjour, lieutenant Louis Salvant-Perret à l'appareil. Je pensais avoir composé le numéro du cabinet de mademoiselle Delcourt. Pouvez-vous me la passer, s'il vous plaît ?

— Le docteur Delcourt est absente, monsieur, je suis désolée. Vous voulez laisser un message ?

Sa façon de parler avait quelque chose de vraiment irritant. Ou bien était-ce la déception de ne pas pouvoir parler à la psychologue ?

— Elle attendait mon appel, pourtant. Vous savez à quel moment elle sera joignable ?

— Je ne peux pas vous renseigner, je ne suis que

l'hôtesse d'accueil.

— Très bien, alors passez-moi la personne responsable, s'il vous plaît.

— Vous voulez parler à madame Bosquet ?

Silence. Louis ignorait qui était cette madame Bosquet.

— C'est la directrice de l'institut, finit par préciser la femme qui, finalement, n'était pas si cruche.

— Je veux bien, oui, merci.

Sans autre formule de politesse, une musique de supermarché trop forte remplaça la voix agaçante de la réceptionniste.

Une pluie fine commençait à tomber, Paris était sous la grisaille. Dans la rue, des bruits de klaxons et de moteurs à l'arrêt se faisaient entendre ; la circulation devait encore être bloquée par les camions de livraison ou les véhicules garés en double file. Louis alla s'abriter sous l'avant-toit du parking à vélos en attendant qu'on lui passe la directrice.

Celle-ci répondit au bout de cinq bonnes minutes de supplice musical. Elle se confondit en excuses pour la longueur de l'attente, elle était en ligne avec un ancien patient. Comme la femme de l'accueil lui avait communiqué son identité et qu'elle ne voulait pas faire attendre la police, elle avait abrégé au maximum son échange téléphonique.

— Je suis contente que vous appeliez, justement, dit tout de suite la directrice après les salutations d'usage. Agathe n'est pas venue travailler ce matin et elle n'a pas prévenu. Cela ne lui ressemble pas du tout. Et ce qui m'inquiète le plus, c'est que je tombe sans arrêt sur son répondeur.

— Pour le téléphone, c'est normal, c'est moi qui l'ai. Enfin, c'est un de mes collègues, plus exactement, mais c'est un peu long à expliquer. Elle me l'a confié hier et je comptais le lui rapporter. N'a-t-elle pas une ligne fixe où on peut la joindre ?

— Je ne crois pas, non. En tout cas, si elle en a une, elle ne nous l'a pas communiquée. Depuis cinq ans qu'elle travaille chez nous, elle n'a jamais été absente.

— Peut-être est-elle souffrante ? suggéra Louis, sans conviction toutefois.

L'inquiétude qu'il décelait dans la voix de la directrice ne lui disait rien qui vaille. Son instinct lui soufflait que quelque chose était arrivé.

— J'irai jusqu'à chez elle pendant ma pause déjeuner si elle n'a pas réapparu d'ici là, proposa madame Bosquet.

— Je vais vous laisser mes coordonnées personnelles. Vous pourrez me tenir informé si jamais vous ne la trouvez pas ? Et dans le cas contraire, dites-lui de m'appeler au poste ou sur mon portable. À toute heure.

C'était peut-être un peu exagéré. La directrice allait se demander pourquoi un flic se tenait ainsi à la disposition de la jeune femme. Tant pis, c'était fait.

— C'est d'accord. J'espère que vous avez raison et que c'est juste un problème médical. Comme vous dites qu'elle n'a pas son portable, elle n'a peut-être pas pu avoir accès à un téléphone si elle n'est pas bien.

— S'il y a quoi que ce soit, vous n'hésitez pas à m'appeler, insista Louis avant de couper la communication.

Une fois son portable rangé dans sa poche, préoccupé, le lieutenant leva les yeux vers le ciel chargé de nuages de plus en plus noirs. Une rangée de pigeons se tenaient serrés les uns contre les autres sur le rebord d'une fenêtre condamnée dans le bâtiment d'en face. En dessous, le trottoir était maculé de leurs déjections. Louis n'aimait pas ces volatiles. C'étaient des oiseaux des villes, sales et envahissants. Quand il avait la chance d'apercevoir un rouge-gorge dans cette capitale polluée, son cœur s'allégeait comme à la vue d'un visage ami au milieu d'une foule hostile.

L'absence non justifiée d'Agathe Delcourt assombrit sa journée déjà morose à cause du temps pluvieux. Le visage fermé, il remonta dans les bureaux et prévint les autres qu'il partait à Argenteuil, au domicile des Prudhom, pour voir les lieux en personne.

Ismaël se fit rabrouer lorsqu'il proposa de l'accompagner. Louis ne se montra pas agressif, mais il déclara qu'il avait besoin d'être seul. C'était la deuxième fois en peu de temps que Salvant-Perret manifestait ce désir. Cela n'avait pas échappé à Maud, qui ne fit cependant aucun commentaire à ce sujet.

Au lieu de prendre le véhicule de service, il s'installa dans sa propre voiture, même si cela n'était pas du tout réglementaire parce qu'il n'aurait pas accès à la radio de la police. Mais c'était justement le but de la manœuvre dans l'esprit du lieutenant.

Avant de se rendre à Argenteuil, il fit un détour par une petite cave de sa connaissance, où il acheta une bouteille de Médoc qu'il comptait apporter à Daniel Mespouille, comme il le lui avait promis.

L'expert se montra beaucoup moins désagréable dès qu'il eut le Graal entre les mains, mais il reconnut toutefois qu'il ne méritait aucune récompense étant donné qu'il avait fait chou blanc.

— En tout cas, fit quand même remarquer Mespouille avant que Louis ne reparte avec le portable d'Agathe, je peux te dire que ta petite psychologue n'a pas du tout envie qu'on accède à ses données personnelles. C'est un véritable *bunker,* son mobile !

— Vraiment ? C'est-à-dire ?

— Eh bien, à part ses SMS et le journal d'appels, tout le reste est méga-protégé par des pare-feu et des mots de passe bien chiadés. J'ai pas tenté de les craquer parce que c'est pas ce que tu m'avais demandé, mais cette fille, soit c'est une déesse de l'informatique, soit c'est une dingue paranoïaque. Voire les deux.

Louis passa les deux mains dans ses cheveux, très affecté par ces dernières paroles. Est-ce que Mespouille était bien en train de parler de la magnifique jeune femme qui le remuait tant ?

— T'exagères pas un petit peu ? lui reprocha-t-il sur un ton badin.

— Oh ! Moi, je dis ça...

Les bras levés en un geste de défense, il n'acheva pas sa phrase et retourna à ses affaires, laissant Louis tout à fait incrédule. Pour lui, Agathe n'avait rien d'une folle et le fait de protéger ses données personnelles relevait à son avis davantage de la prudence que de la paranoïa.

Le mobile de la jeune femme en poche, il suivit son idée d'aller tourner autour de la maison de la famille Prudhom en attendant d'avoir des nouvelles de madame Bosquet ou mieux, d'Agathe elle-même.

Chapitre 18

La circulation jusqu'à Argenteuil fut un enfer. Il passa un temps infini bloqué derrière une Kangoo aux vitres recouvertes d'un papier blanc opaque qui empêchait de voir ce qui se passait devant. Ce genre d'ajouts devrait être interdit, pestait Louis, tout comme les vitres teintées l'étaient depuis peu.

Pour couronner le tout, les feux stop du véhicule ne fonctionnaient pas. S'il n'avait pas été de bonne constitution, il serait descendu pour verbaliser le conducteur. Mais il prit son mal en patience, branché sur une radio musicale de grande écoute qui passait dix fois par jour les mêmes standards à la mode.

À une dizaine de kilomètres de sa destination, il reçut un appel sur son portable, directement transmis sur l'écran de bord de son SUV, qui afficha le nom de son ex.

Il ne manquait plus qu'elle avec la pluie qui s'intensifiait !

Il hésita un instant, mais répondit quand même. Contre toute attente, le ton qu'elle employa était étonnamment doux et affectueux, comme aux premières heures de leur idylle.

Méfie-toi, Louis ! disait sa voix intérieure.

Anne était souffrante et, comme elle était seule,

elle ne pouvait soi-disant pas se déplacer jusqu'à la pharmacie pour aller chercher les médicaments que le docteur lui avait prescrits.

— Tu ne pouvais pas y aller en sortant de chez le médecin ?

— C'était une consultation à domicile, j'ai le dos bloqué.

— Je n'ai pas le temps dans l'immédiat, Anne. Tu n'as pas une amie qui pourrait y aller pour toi ? Si mes souvenirs sont bons, ta bonne copine Chantal ne travaille pas.

— Elle est à Ibiza jusqu'à la semaine prochaine et toutes mes autres copines travaillent, on est jeudi.

— Je le sais, qu'on est jeudi, c'est bien pour ça que je ne peux pas me libérer. En plus, je ne suis pas du tout dans les environs et j'en ai pour un moment.

— Mais après, quand tu auras terminé ? S'il te plaît, je n'ai que toi...

Après tout ce qu'elle lui avait fait endurer à la suite de leur séparation, Louis trouva qu'elle ne manquait pas d'air de se comporter de la sorte ; comme s'il ne s'était rien passé. Il aurait dû l'enregistrer à l'époque, et le lui faire écouter en lui demandant si elle ne se fichait pas un peu de lui.

Cependant, désireux d'en finir au plus vite, il préféra éviter le conflit :

— Écoute, je ne te promets rien, mais j'essaierai de passer si j'ai un moment de libre.

— Avant l'heure de fermeture des pharmacies, précisa-t-elle encore. Sinon, tu seras obligé de courir à une pharmacie de garde.

Louis leva les yeux au ciel, retenant un soupir d'exaspération. En coupant la communication, il se dit qu'il était vraiment trop con. Il ne lui devait plus rien. Déjà, il avait fait preuve d'une extrême générosité en la laissant s'installer dans l'appartement de Boulogne et elle en profitait.

À tout prendre, il aurait préféré que ce soit Agathe Delcourt qui le sollicite pour aller chercher des médicaments. Il y serait allé avec plaisir. Repenser à elle lui fit regarder l'heure. Il n'était pas loin de onze heures, la directrice de l'institut attendait certainement midi ou treize heures avant de se rendre au domicile de la psychologue manquant à l'appel. Il espérait vraiment que madame Bosquet le tiendrait au courant et surtout qu'Agathe était effectivement souffrante et que c'était pour cette raison qu'elle n'avait pas pu prévenir de son absence.

Mais il avait l'intuition que ça ne serait pas le cas. S'il s'était écouté, il aurait foncé lui-même à l'appartement de la jeune femme pour en avoir le cœur net. Il savait où elle habitait, il avait fait des recherches. Le problème était de justifier une autre visite dans le Calvados auprès d'Amary. Déjà qu'il lui avait fait une réflexion au sujet de son comportement, se rendre tous les quatre matins sur le lieu de travail de la thérapeute serait très mal vu, ou du moins suspect.

Elle avait pourtant quelque chose de spécial qui l'attirait malgré lui. Il sentait chez elle une sorte de fragilité, un côté insaisissable qui ajoutait à son charme naturel.

Comme le quartier où il se rendait était plutôt ouvrier et que pratiquement tous les habitants étaient au travail, Louis put passer au ralenti devant le 37 de la rue des Vignes aux Moines sans gêner la circulation. Des hommes coiffés de casques de chantier étaient sur le toit en réfection tandis que des maçons s'affairaient à l'intérieur de la maisonnette, dont la porte d'entrée était ouverte.

Il alla se garer à quelques mètres de là, puis décida d'entrer jeter un œil dans la maison. Au pire, si quelqu'un lui barrait le passage, il sortirait sa carte de police et l'affaire serait réglée.

Lorsqu'il franchit le seuil, personne ne l'en empêcha. C'est à peine si on le remarqua. Un homme était agenouillé devant une auge de plâtre qu'il venait de préparer, un autre prenait des mesures. Aucun d'entre eux ne fit attention à lui. Quand il passa devant eux, il les salua sans que cela déclenche la moindre curiosité de leur part.

L'intérieur était complètement vide. Les murs ainsi que toutes les surfaces avaient été mis à nu, le plafond détruit puis refait. On entendait les ouvriers parler entre eux au-dessus, grimpés sur la charpente. Ils riaient fort, donnaient des coups de marteau, faisaient vrombir les visseuses et les perceuses.

Le tour de la maison fut vite fait et n'apporta pas grand-chose au lieutenant, qui repartit comme il était venu, dans l'indifférence générale. Peut-être les ouvriers l'avaient-ils pris pour un promoteur ou le propriétaire des lieux, qui sait ? En tout cas, Louis s'était fait une bonne idée de l'agencement des pièces et, dans sa tête, il avait imaginé le placement des corps retrouvés morts dans cet espace en devenir. Cela lui permettait une meilleure compréhension des événements.

En sortant, il regarda autour de lui. La rue était assez longue et la maisonnette se trouvait côté nord. À droite, un alignement de bâtisses construites sur le même modèle architectural. À gauche, à une centaine de mètres de là, il avisa un petit immeuble vers lequel il dirigea ses pas, sans vraiment savoir ce qu'il comptait trouver. Juste après le bâtiment, il y avait un terrain vague sommairement clôturé par une palissade faite de planches de bois dont plusieurs étaient manquantes, les autres à moitié pourries.

Il glissa la tête dans un des interstices. Devant lui, un espace rectangulaire pouvant accueillir au moins trois maisons. La terre semblait stérile, étouffée par des mauvaises herbes et des gravats. Toutes sortes de détritus encombraient la surface. Des cannettes de bière et de soda en quantité, des emballages de nourriture provenant de restaurants rapides, du verre cassé, une poupée dépourvue d'yeux, nue, avec des cheveux qui semblaient avoir pris feu.

Qui semblaient avoir pris feu ?

Un déclic se fit dans sa tête. Il passa un pied à travers la palissade, puis la jambe, prudemment pour ne pas accrocher ses vêtements, enfin tout le corps.

Camouflé à l'angle droit de la palissade et du petit immeuble, il découvrit le repaire d'un SDF qui le regardait s'avancer dans sa direction avec un sourire édenté des plus répugnants. Il était secoué de spasmes comme s'il riait de plus en plus fort et oui, en se rapprochant, Louis se rendit compte que c'était bien le cas.

Le pauvre hère était assis sur un monticule d'effets en tous genres. Il s'était construit un abri sommaire avec des cartons, du papier journal, des vieilles couvertures et d'autres choses encore dont on ignorait la nature. À intervalles réguliers, il portait un mouchoir de tissu immonde à sa bouche, qu'il respirait à grandes bouffées, et il éclatait de rire dès qu'il éloignait le tissu de son visage.

Louis soupçonnait l'individu de se défoncer à la

colle à rustines ou un autre produit bon marché à l'effet hilarant. Ça allait être difficile de tirer quelque chose du bonhomme.

Il le salua néanmoins et l'autre leva un bras en signe de bonjour, incapable d'aligner trois mots cohérents pour le moment. Avec douceur, Louis prit le mouchoir du bout des doigts pour l'éloigner un peu de son propriétaire, qui se laissa déposséder sans réagir.

— J'ai besoin de vous parler, lui dit le lieutenant gentiment. Vous voulez bien qu'on discute, vous et moi ?

— Rends-moi mon mouchoir.

— Oui, dans un moment.

— Tu me rends mon putain de mouchoir, sale con !

— Oui, d'accord, je vais vous le rendre dans deux petites minutes, calmez-vous. J'ai juste deux ou trois questions à vous poser, ensuite je vous laisse tranquille.

— T'es qui, toi ? Un flic ?

— Ça n'a pas d'importance, qui je suis. Je veux juste savoir si ça fait longtemps que vous êtes dans le coin.

— Je te réponds si tu me rends mon mouchoir.

— Si je vous le rends, vous allez le respirer et vous ne serez plus en état de répondre.

— File-moi du blé, alors !

L'homme commençait à s'énerver. Fini le rire béat, sa respiration se faisait plus rapide et plus bruyante, ses lèvres se retroussaient en une grimace haineuse. Il fallait que Louis aligne quelques billets, sinon il n'obtiendrait rien.

— OK, voilà vingt euros, proposa Louis en sortant

le billet bleu de son portefeuille. L'incendie au numéro 37 en novembre dernier, vous l'avez vu ?

— Un peu que je l'ai vu ! Un beau feu de joie qui m'a réchauffé toute une nuit. Ces connards de pompiers voulaient me faire dégager, mais je connais le coin, je me suis planqué et j'en ai profité un max. D'autant que ça pelait, cette nuit-là.

Après avoir donné sa réponse, l'homme arracha le billet des doigts de Louis à une vitesse surprenante étant donné son état.

— Vous êtes entré dans la maison après l'incendie ?

Le SDF lui lança un regard mauvais, s'attendant bien sûr à ce qu'on l'accuse de tout et n'importe quoi sous prétexte qu'il vivait dans la rue.

— Nan !

Louis s'était rapproché. Trois matelas les uns sur les autres étaient empilés, dont l'un portait des traces de brûlures marron.

— Et ce matelas, là, il ne vient pas de la maison qui a brûlé ?

— Tu me fais pas chier, d'accord ? hurla l'homme, un doigt accusateur pointé sur le visage de Louis, qui se recula d'un pas, non pas à cause de la menace, mais en raison de l'odeur insoutenable qui se dégagea lorsque l'homme se leva.

— Je ne suis pas en train de vous accuser de quoi que ce soit, n'ayez pas peur, il ne vous arrivera rien. C'est très important. Me laisseriez-vous jeter un coup d'œil, s'il vous plaît ?

— C'est à moi !

— Je ne vais pas vous le prendre. Enfin, en principe. Tenez, reprenez votre mouchoir.

Comme l'individu avait tendance à devenir

agressif lorsque les effets de sa drogue disparaissaient, mieux valait qu'il se remette à rire. Il ne se fit pas prier et replongea le nez dans le mouchoir crasseux. D'un léger mouvement, Louis le prit par le bras pour l'aider à se déplacer. Se laissant enfin convaincre, le pauvre bougre se blottit dans un coin pendant que le lieutenant dégageait l'amas de tissus sans nom qui recouvraient les trois matelas, évitant autant que possible de respirer tant la puanteur lui soulevait l'estomac.

À première vue, les grabats étaient empilés selon leur ordre d'acquisition. Celui du dessous était positivement lamentable, dépourvu de tout rembourrage. Il était usé jusqu'à la trame, dévoré par les souris et couvert de taches dont Louis préférait ignorer l'origine.

Il se focalisa sur celui du dessus, qui avait attiré son attention. Une fois dégagé de toutes les frusques, de larges surfaces marron apparurent, ne laissant aucun doute quant à ce qui était arrivé à ce matelas : il avait cramé à plusieurs endroits.

D'un ample mouvement, Louis le retourna et, comme il s'y attendait, il vit une lettre tracée au marqueur noir, là, sous ses yeux.

Un « C ».

De la même écriture, semblait-il, que les deux autres.

On y était. Il n'avait plus qu'à faire avouer au SDF que la paillasse provenait bien du 37 rue des Vignes aux Moines et il aurait la preuve que la famille Prudhom avait, elle aussi, été victime du même tueur que les Aubry et les Lemonnier.

Il prit son téléphone, composa le numéro des renseignements, obtint celui des Emmaüs de La

Garenne-Colombes, à qui il demanda s'ils avaient des matelas disponibles. La réponse étant positive, il appela Ismaël dans la foulée pour qu'il le rejoigne avec une des fourgonnettes de service.

– Tu passes chez les Emmaüs de La Garenne-Colombes, tu embarques un matelas deux places le moins abîmé possible et tu me rejoins rue des Vignes aux Moines, à Argenteuil. Je ne bouge pas, je t'attends dans la rue, tu me verras. Je t'expliquerai quand tu seras là.

Louis réalisa qu'il était plus de midi et qu'il n'avait rien avalé depuis le deuxième petit déjeuner d'Isabelle, au commissariat. Il ajouta *in extremis* avant de couper la communication :

– Tu me rapportes un jambon-beurre en même temps, s'il te plaît ?

Rien que de prononcer le nom du *sandwich* lui provoqua une crampe d'estomac tellement il avait faim.

À quelques pas de lui, le SDF était allé s'affaler contre la palissade avec son mouchoir plaqué sous le nez, mais il semblait s'être endormi, car il ne bougeait plus. Un instant, Louis eut même peur qu'il ait passé l'arme à gauche. Il s'approcha et fut rassuré : sa poitrine se soulevait à intervalles réguliers. Ce n'était pas encore son heure.

Quelques minutes plus tard, alors qu'il continuait de déblayer la tanière en prévision de l'enlèvement du matelas qui l'intéressait, il reçut le coup de fil qu'il attendait de la directrice de l'institut Saint-Jean.

Elle s'était rendue chez Agathe Delcourt, avait sonné tant et plus, mais personne n'avait répondu. Elle se trouvait encore devant son appartement, un de ses voisins lui avait permis d'entrée dans l'immeuble, elle avait pu monter jusqu'à son étage. Elle avait collé l'oreille contre le bois de la porte, mais aucun bruit ne lui était parvenu. Poussée par l'anxiété, elle avait même osé regarder par le trou de la serrure, en vain.

— N'a-t-elle pas un parent chez qui elle a pu se réfugier si elle est souffrante ?

— Je ne crois pas, non. Je me suis posé la même question que vous et j'ai vérifié dans son dossier, il n'y a personne à prévenir en cas d'urgence. Elle ne parle jamais de sa vie privée, vous savez. Nous ne discutons que des enfants dont nous avons la responsabilité. Elle est si professionnelle !

— Elle est orpheline ? questionna Louis, de plus en plus intrigué.

— Je ne saurais vous dire. Vraiment, vous me voyez tout à fait désemparée et confuse d'en savoir si peu au sujet d'une de mes meilleures thérapeutes.

— Eh bien, fort heureusement, elles n'ont pas tendance à disparaître sans laisser de trace, d'habitude, essaya-t-il de plaisanter.

Mais son trait d'humour tomba à l'eau. Il réfléchit un instant, puis :

— N'y a-t-il personne au sein de l'institut dont elle soit proche ? Souvent, les personnes avec qui on travaille deviennent des amis.

Il y eut un court silence durant lequel madame Bosquet fouilla dans sa mémoire.

— Il y a bien cette jeune religieuse qui fait partie de la congrégation des sœurs de Saint-Jean. Constance, je crois. Je les ai vues quelquefois discuter ensemble dans le parc. Mais je ne vois pas comment cette fille pourrait nous renseigner sur l'endroit où mademoiselle Delcourt se trouve.

— On ne sait jamais. Essayez de la voir dans la journée et attendons peut-être jusqu'à ce soir. Si vous n'avez toujours aucunes nouvelles à ce moment-là, nous aviserons. Et si elle vous contacte, vous m'en informez ?

— Bien entendu, oui, assura madame Bosquet.

Louis avait vraiment espéré que la directrice trouverait Agathe chez elle, alitée et dans l'incapacité de prévenir de son absence puisqu'elle lui avait confié son téléphone et qu'elle n'avait *a priori* pas de ligne fixe.

Son téléphone !

En faisant les cent pas sur le trottoir le temps qu'Ismaël le rejoigne, Louis entreprit de passer en revue les contacts dans le répertoire du mobile de la psychologue.

Aucune entrée au nom de *papa*, *maman* ou *parents*. Des noms et des prénoms sans aucune connotation affective. Déjà, lorsqu'il avait jeté un œil sur les SMS, il avait pu constater que ceux-ci ne concernaient que son travail. Des messages de collègues thérapeutes, de laboratoires médicaux ou d'hôpitaux. Rien de personnel.

Décidément, cette femme demeurait insaisissable. Louis ignorait s'il devait s'en inquiéter ou au contraire s'en émerveiller. Soit elle cachait un lourd secret, soit le sort s'acharnait contre elle et elle pouvait passer pour une personne froide et sans cœur. Ce qu'elle n'était pas. Louis l'avait vue en présence des enfants et en règle générale, il se trompait rarement sur les gens.

Elle était attentionnée, douce et patiente avec ses petits malades. De plus, avec lui, quand il avait tenté de la séduire de façon si maladroite, elle s'était montrée compréhensive alors qu'elle aurait été en droit de l'envoyer proprement balader. D'ailleurs, il avait appris de la bouche de Maud que le commissaire avait pris un malin plaisir à lui faire croire qu'Agathe s'était plainte de son comportement quelques semaines plus tôt alors qu'en réalité, il n'en était rien. Amary avait inventé tout cela parce que ça l'amusait de voir Louis s'empêtrer auprès d'une femme qui, de toute évidence, ne le laissait pas indifférent.

En attendant, où pouvait-elle bien être ? Lui était-il arrivé malheur ? Entre ces coups de fil anonymes qu'elle recevait et la mauvaise blague du cadavre de chat sur son paillasson, on pouvait s'attendre à ce qu'un détraqué l'ait dans sa ligne de mire et soit passé à la vitesse supérieure.

Malheureusement, Louis ne savait absolument rien de la jeune femme et même la personne qui travaillait avec elle tous les jours ne semblait pas davantage au courant de sa vie en dehors de l'institut Saint-Jean.

La fourgonnette de la police apparut au bout de la rue alors que Louis venait de s'assurer que le SDF dormait toujours, avachi à même le sol. Il avait pris la précaution de retirer le mouchoir de devant le nez du pauvre bougre, déjà suffisamment défoncé ; ce n'était pas la peine de lui faire respirer ces relents de mort jusque dans son sommeil.

— Qu'est-ce que t'as trouvé ? fit Ismaël en ouvrant les deux portes arrière.

— Un SDF et un matelas.

— Formidable !

Ismaël attendit la suite, un sourcil curieux levé.

Tout en déchargeant le matelas provenant des Emmaüs, Louis résuma la situation.

— Il faut qu'on amène ce type au poste pour prendre sa déposition. C'est pas gagné, il est défoncé à la colle ou à je ne sais quoi.

— T'inquiète, je sais m'y prendre avec ce genre de population, je vais le gérer. Tu as dit qu'on avait un « C », cette fois-ci ? L, A, C... Un lac ?

— Il doit y avoir un ordre, Ismaël.

— Mais comment tu expliques qu'il n'y ait pas eu une lettre aussi dans l'affaire qui date de novembre 2000 ?

— Je ne l'explique pas. Je me pose des questions, comme toi.

Le chargement était léger et en bien meilleur état que celui qu'ils s'apprêtaient à enfourner dans la fourgonnette. Ismaël se chargea de convaincre le SDF de les accompagner après qu'ils eurent installé le matelas marqué de la lettre « C ». Louis ne sut pas comment il s'y était pris ou ce qu'il lui avait dit, mais l'homme les suivit et monta à l'arrière.

Ils durent ouvrir toutes les vitres et même là, l'odeur était infecte. Et dire qu'il faudrait le raccompagner ensuite ! songea Louis. Ils seraient bons pour une désinfection totale du véhicule après cette journée.

Dieu merci, Louis récupéra son véhicule, devant lequel Ismaël le déposa avant qu'ils se dirigent vers leur destination suivante. Le calvaire fut d'autant plus long pour Ismaël à cause de ce détour par les locaux du laboratoire afin d'y déposer la paillasse. Louis ne parvint à manger son *sandwich* qu'après être descendu de la fourgonnette, pendant que deux policiers déchargeaient. Ils portaient des masques blancs, chanceux qu'ils étaient ! Ismaël les avait prévenus de la nature de ce qu'ils allaient réceptionner.

Même après le dépôt de l'objet, sa puanteur demeurait, doublée de celle du sans-abri, qui s'était rendormi durant le trajet qui les amenait au commissariat.

Comme il l'avait prévu, Ismaël obtint la déposition attendue. Courageusement, il s'enferma avec le SDF malodorant dans le seul bureau libre disposant d'une fenêtre, qu'il ouvrit en grand afin d'échapper à l'asphyxie. Un gardien de la paix fut désigné pour raccompagner le pauvre bougre avec vingt euros de plus en poche grâce à Ismaël, et un matelas presque neuf pour remplacer celui qu'ils avaient saisi pour les besoins de l'enquête.

Dans la salle de travail, les deux lieutenants et Maud Cortès relurent ensemble la déposition du sans-abri, dénommé Pascal Maher. Ce dernier avait passé toute la nuit de l'incendie à se *chauffer la couenne*, comme il disait, puis, lorsque la voie avait été libre, il était entré dans les maisons mitoyennes, moins touchées par l'incendie mais évacuées, afin de récupérer ce qui pouvait l'être. Il confirma ainsi que le grabat saisi provenait bien du domicile des Prudhom.

– On a donc trois lettres, raisonna Maud. Si on part du principe qu'il y a une certaine logique dans la démarche du tueur, on peut supposer que l'ordre de ces lettres correspond à celui dans lequel les meurtres ont été commis.

– C, L, A, prononça Louis lentement.

– Ça peut être n'importe quoi, on tourne en rond avec ces foutues lettres ! s'exclama Ismaël.

— Si comme je le crois, toutes les affaires ont un lien entre elles, je dirais qu'il faut chercher du côté de chaque membre de chaque famille.

Louis ouvrit ses dossiers et se mit à faire la liste de tous les noms et prénoms des quatre familles.

— Il n'y a qu'avec la famille Albert que je trouve une correspondance. Deux même : Claude, le père, et Claire, la fille aînée.

— La fille aînée, répéta Maud. Y'a un truc qui nous échappe avec les aînés.

— Oui, approuva Louis. Et la famille Albert est la seule chez qui l'on n'a pas retrouvé de lettre.

— Par conséquent, tout porte à croire que le tueur nous désigne Claire Albert, termina Ismaël. Mais pourquoi ?

— On sait qu'un des membres de cette famille a survécu, fit Louis. Son identité a été soigneusement camouflée. Et c'est justement la fille aînée qui a eu le visage écrasé par un individu inconnu, sans doute le tueur qu'on n'a jamais retrouvé.

— Le petit ami de cette fille qui se vengerait des années après ? proposa Maud.

— Mais pourquoi attendre quinze ans pour se venger ? Et pourquoi s'en prendre à des familles entières qui n'ont aucun rapport entre elles ni avec la famille Albert ?

— Il y a forcément un élément déclencheur.

Le silence retomba entre les trois lieutenants.

— Il faut chercher du côté de cette famille Albert, dit Louis. Je suis quasiment sûr que tout est parti de là.

Chacun de leur côté, ils replongèrent dans le dossier qui les intéressait, échangeant leurs idées ou leurs découvertes au fil de leur analyse. Les heures défilèrent sans qu'ils parviennent à une hypothèse cohérente. Cependant, il devenait évident pour Louis que celui qui avait assassiné la famille Albert en novembre 2000 ne pouvait pas être le même que celui qui avait tué les autres familles entre novembre 2014 et avril 2015.

Toute l'équipe tomba d'accord avec lui. La position dans laquelle avaient été retrouvés les corps des Albert était différente des victimes suivantes. Les premiers avaient été attachés les uns aux autres en rond au milieu du salon, par les poignets, se tournant le dos. Ensuite, pour une raison inconnue, le cercle avait été rompu. Puis, ils avaient été exécutés. Sauf, justement, la fille aînée, Claire, qui avait été tuée en premier et n'était pas dans le cercle. D'ailleurs, elle ne présentait aucune marque de liens autour des poignets comme les autres.

Selon le rapport du médecin légiste, après Claire, ce fut au tour de Marie-Christine, sa mère. Ensuite, Mélissa avait eu la gorge tranchée et le benjamin, Victor, avait succombé juste avant que son père ne meure par pendaison. Les enfants avaient été éliminés du plus âgé au plus jeune.

Dans les autres affaires, il n'y avait pas cet agencement en cercle ni un ordre particulier dans les meurtres des enfants. Restait à découvrir le mobile de ces assassinats.

La lumière déclinait lorsque Maud regarda sa montre.

— Zut ! Vingt heures trente déjà, il faut que j'y aille !

— Quoi, déjà ? lui fit écho Ismaël en décollant de son siège pour atteindre le portemanteau. Les chéris, c'est pas que je m'ennuie, mais on verra tout ça demain. Au fait, repas samedi soir à la maison, vous deux, OK ?

— C'est si gentiment demandé, ironisa Maud en le talonnant.

— Et toi, petit prince ?

Louis marmonna dans sa barbe quelque chose qui ressemblait à un assentiment tandis que les deux autres le saluaient.

Il était absorbé. Ce n'est que quelques minutes après que tout le monde fut parti qu'il se rappela qu'Anne attendait qu'il aille à la pharmacie pour elle. Son portable étant sur silencieux, quand il l'attrapa, il vit qu'il avait pas moins de dix appels en absence, autant de messages sur son répondeur et cinq SMS.

Merde ! pensa-t-il.

Il prit sur lui, rappela son ex, qui hurla dès qu'elle l'eut en ligne. On était loin du ton charmeur adopté quelques heures plus tôt. Il la laissa vociférer trois bonnes minutes puis, une fois qu'elle fut hors d'haleine, prise d'une violente toux, il en profita pour la prier de se débrouiller toute seule car il n'avait pas le temps de s'occuper de ses médicaments. Ce n'était pas la peine d'essayer de le rappeler.

Et il raccrocha, un peu surpris lui-même de son audace toute nouvelle.

Aussitôt après, madame Bosquet l'appelait pour le prévenir qu'il n'y avait toujours aucun signe de vie d'Agathe Delcourt.

— D'accord, on va attendre le délai de quarante-huit heures pour la déclarer disparue. Mais je vais quand même venir faire ma petite enquête dans son quartier. Si vous pouviez juste me confirmer que j'ai bien la bonne adresse, s'il vous plaît ?

Louis lut à haute voix les coordonnées qu'il avait

récoltées. Il s'agissait bien de l'adresse de la thérapeute. La directrice de l'institut le remercia en priant pour qu'il récolte des informations susceptibles de les renseigner sur l'endroit où Agathe se trouvait.

Chapitre 19

Il était onze heures passées quand Louis Salvant-Perret se gara sur la place centrale de la petite ville du Calvados où Agathe Delcourt vivait, à une vingtaine de kilomètres de l'institut Saint-Jean, et à seulement une heure de route de chez les parents du lieutenant.

Le centre-ville n'étant pas très étendu, il décida de marcher jusqu'au petit bâtiment de construction récente dans lequel la jeune femme occupait un appartement.

Debout sur le trottoir d'en face, il aperçut des lumières à tous les étages sauf au deuxième, là où il aurait espéré en voir. De toute évidence, il n'y avait personne, et comme l'entrée de l'immeuble possédait un digicode, il ne put pénétrer à l'intérieur. Il était trop tard pour sonner chez un voisin, c'était un coup à provoquer la peur et il y avait peu de chances pour que quelqu'un entre ou sorte un soir de semaine. Il attendit tout de même une dizaine de minutes, faisant les cent pas au pied du bâtiment, sans succès.

D'après ses renseignements, Agathe habitait ici depuis deux ans. Elle avait certainement ses habitudes dans le quartier. Toutes les boutiques étant fermées, il fallait faire une croix sur les petits commerces. Mais son GPS lui avait indiqué deux restaurants et un bar qu'il pouvait toujours visiter.

Il doutait fort que la psychologue fût du genre à traîner dans les bars, néanmoins, Louis alla y faire un tour, par acquit de conscience. Dès le premier coup d'œil, il s'aperçut qu'il n'y avait aucune femme dans l'assistance. L'endroit était plutôt glauque, les rares consommateurs lui lancèrent des regards hostiles lorsqu'il commanda un demi, qu'il se dépêcha de boire pour partir au plus vite.

Il prit ensuite la direction de l'un des deux restaurants : un chinois. Comme dans la plupart de ces établissements, la devanture vitrée était surmontée d'une énorme enseigne lumineuse rouge où l'indication *buffet à volonté* clignotait afin d'attirer la clientèle. Deux gigantesques statues de dragons encadraient la double porte et, alors qu'il se rapprochait, il ajusta son regard, croyant reconnaître la silhouette de France-Alix derrière l'un des animaux factices dans les bras d'une autre jeune fille à l'allure gothique qu'elle embrassait à pleine bouche.

Ce n'était pas possible, il avait mal vu ! Ça ne pouvait pas être sa fille ! Il crut que son cœur allait sortir de sa poitrine quand le visage de France-Alix se dégagea nettement, ne laissant plus aucun doute. Le choc fut terrible.

Son premier réflexe fut de faire demi-tour pour ne pas être vu. Tête baissée, Louis alla se réfugier à l'abri d'une porte qui présentait un renfoncement.

Voilà une chose à laquelle il ne s'attendait pas. Sa fille, homosexuelle ? Depuis quand ? Comment n'avait-il rien vu ? Anne était-elle au courant ? Elle le lui aurait dit, quand même ! raisonna-t-il.

Les questions se bousculaient dans sa tête. Sa confusion était sans commune mesure. Une envie viscérale de téléphoner à sa mère le tenailla. Il était tard, elle dormait peut-être. Tant pis, c'était une urgence ! L'affaire était d'importance.

Sans plus attendre, il s'éloigna davantage du restaurant et appela Hélène sur son portable. La réponse ne tarda pas. La voix de sa mère n'était nullement ensommeillée. En fait, elle était devant le troisième épisode d'une série policière américaine qu'elle suivait assidûment.

La voix de Louis, ainsi que l'heure indue pour un coup de fil, l'inquiétèrent tout de suite :

— Qu'est-ce qui se passe, mon chéri, ça ne va pas ?

— Où est France-Alix ?

— Comment ça, où est France-Alix ? Qu'est-ce qui te prend ? N'as-tu donc aucune confiance en tes propres parents ? Elle est de sortie avec son amie Léa. Elles sont allées au nouveau restaurant vietnamien, ton père doit passer les récupérer d'ici une petite demi-heure. Pourquoi cette question à bientôt minuit ?

— Je l'ai vue, maman. France-Alix. Avec cette fille, en train de s'embrasser en pleine rue, devant tout le monde.

Il y eut un silence. Louis se sentait fiévreux, une sorte de boule s'était formée dans son ventre qui lui bloquait la respiration et l'empêchait d'avoir les idées claires.

— Elles s'embrassaient, la belle affaire, finit par dire Hélène le plus calmement qu'elle put. Quel est le problème ?

— Mais, maman, elle embrassait *une fille* !

— Louis Joseph Ambroise Salvant-Perret ! s'emporta-t-elle alors. T'ai-je élevé dans un esprit obtus et discriminatoire ?

Elle avait utilisé tous ses patronymes, ce n'était pas bon signe ! Le ton était monté, elle continua :

— Ta fille se drogue-t-elle ? Couche-t-elle à droite à gauche avec le premier venu ?

— En l'occurrence, ce serait plutôt avec *la* première venue, releva Louis en regrettant aussitôt cette remarque malheureuse.

— Épargne-moi ton humour déplacé, rétorqua Hélène. Et puis d'abord, comment as-tu pu la voir ? Tu es dans le coin ?

— Je suis sur une affaire. Peut-être une disparition. Mais là n'est pas la question, n'essaie pas de détourner la conversation. Depuis quand es-tu au courant de ses... tendances ?

Il ne savait même pas comment exprimer cela tant il était confus. Il avait vaguement conscience que sa réaction était détestable et excessive, rétrograde même, mais il n'avait pas été préparé. Il se sentait trahi.

— Pourquoi crois-tu qu'elle ait voulu se réfugier ici ? Elle a un père et une mère, mais personne à qui se confier. Tu n'es pas vraiment présent dans sa vie et Anne est davantage occupée à se trouver un nouvel amant qu'à écouter sa fille. Mais ce n'est pas le moment de discuter de tout ça, il est tard et tu n'es pas objectif. Nous en reparlerons à tête reposée, quand tu seras calme.

— Je suis parfaitement calme ! cria Louis, qui tremblait, les nerfs à fleur de peau.

Bien entendu, il réalisa le ridicule de la situation. Sa mère coupa la communication en lui souhaitant une bonne nuit, et il n'eut pas l'occasion de prononcer un mot de plus.

Il se retrouva seul et complètement assommé sur le trottoir de cette ville endormie, à ne plus savoir très bien ce qu'il faisait là. Bouleversé, il se mit à marcher droit devant, sans but, essayant de retrouver son calme. Tant pis pour le restaurant vietnamien, il y retournerait une autre fois. Ce n'était pas tant le fait d'avoir surpris France-Alix dans les bras d'une autre fille qui le gênait, mais plutôt de le découvrir brutalement. Il avait l'air de tomber comme un cheveu sur la soupe, de débarquer vingt-quatre heures après la bataille puisque sa mère semblait au fait de la chose depuis un moment déjà.

Et c'est lui qui se faisait enguirlander, en prime ? C'était un comble ! Par ailleurs, qu'est-ce que ça voulait dire de laisser sortir une gamine de quinze ans en plein milieu de la semaine jusqu'à pas d'heure quand elle avait classe le lendemain ? Hélène ne lui aurait jamais permis ce genre de liberté quand il avait le même âge. Soit elle se radoucissait en vieillissant, soit France-Alix avait usé de moyens de persuasion que seule une jeune fille maligne est capable de développer. Toujours est-il que Louis maudissait sa mère intérieurement, sans relâche, ressassant sa colère, parce qu'il avait besoin de s'en prendre à quelqu'un.

Petit à petit, il finit par se calmer. La raison pour laquelle il était venu dans cette ville lui revint et la pensée d'Agathe dont on était sans nouvelles mit sa fille au second plan. Mais c'était comme une musique lancinante dans son crâne, l'image de France-Alix et de cette fille était gravée au fer rouge dans sa mémoire.

L'application GPS piéton de son portable le mena jusqu'au second restaurant ; une *pizzeria* qui ne payait pas de mine, mais d'où il vit sortir une bonne dizaine de personnes qui riaient et chahutaient après un repas sans doute bien arrosé.

L'entrée était banale, on aurait dit la porte d'une simple maison d'habitation, avec une plaque métallique indiquant qu'il s'agissait d'un restaurant. Dès qu'il entra, une jeune employée leva la tête de la table qu'elle était en train de débarrasser, alertée par le carillon qui s'était déclenché à l'ouverture de la porte.

— Le service est terminé, monsieur, annonça-t-elle bien fort pour couvrir le son d'une musique italienne monté au maximum. Sergio ! Baissez la musique, par pitié, on ne s'entend pas !

Aussitôt, ce fut plus vivable quand le son fut au minimum. La serveuse soupira en levant les yeux au ciel, visiblement soulagée.

— Je ne viens pas pour manger, expliqua Louis en sortant sa carte de police et en se présentant. Je suis à la recherche d'une jeune femme qui habite pas très loin d'ici et je me demandais si vous la connaissiez.

— On voit beaucoup de monde, vous savez. Mais si vous avez une photo...

— Désolé, je n'ai aucune photo à vous présenter, juste son identité et une description si besoin. Elle s'appelle Agathe Delcourt, cheveux longs châtains, bouclés. Assez grande, dans les un mètre soixante-dix, mince, yeux noisette.

Louis vit tout de suite que sa description éveillait quelque chose dans l'esprit de la serveuse car son visage s'illumina et un sourire se dessina sur ses lèvres couleur framboise.

— C'est drôle, ça ! J'ai justement sympathisé hier soir avec une femme prénommée Agathe qui correspond parfaitement à ce que vous me dites. Mais je ne connais pas son nom de famille. Par contre, je sais où elle habite parce que comme il était tard et qu'elle était seule, je lui ai proposé de la déposer devant chez elle. Est-ce qu'il lui est arrivé quelque chose ?

Son visage avait changé du tout au tout à l'idée qu'un malheur ait pu frapper une personne avec qui elle venait à peine de faire connaissance. Louis voulut d'abord savoir à quelle adresse elle avait déposé la jeune femme en question et, comme cela correspondait avec celle de la psychologue, il n'y avait aucun doute possible, ils parlaient bien de la même Agathe.

— Si un inspecteur de police demande après elle, c'est que c'est grave, insista la serveuse. Soit elle a fait quelque chose de mal, soit c'est quelqu'un qui lui a fait du mal. Vous ne voulez pas me dire ce qui se passe ?

— Je suis lieutenant, pas inspecteur, commença par rectifier Louis, habitué à cette erreur. On ne sait pas encore s'il est arrivé quelque chose à cette personne, nul besoin de paniquer. Son employeur m'a contacté parce qu'elle n'est pas venue travailler aujourd'hui et il n'y a personne à son domicile. Ça ne veut pas dire qu'il faille s'inquiéter pour autant, elle est peut-être simplement chez un ami ou autre part. Si elle ne reparaît pas d'ici deux jours, là, il faudra se poser des questions. Vous avez dit qu'elle était seule hier soir. Est-ce qu'elle vient souvent dans ce restaurant ?

— Oui, assez. Au moins une fois par mois et

toujours toute seule. Pourtant, elle est très jolie, ça fait bizarre de voir quelqu'un d'aussi bien sans personne pour l'accompagner. Mais bon... À ce propos, elle avait dit qu'elle viendrait dîner au restaurant ce soir, mais elle n'est pas venue.

— Est-ce qu'elle vous a paru en bonne santé la dernière fois que vous l'avez vue ? Elle n'avait pas l'air différente de d'habitude, préoccupée ?

— Non, elle allait très bien, j'en suis sûre. Ça ne date que d'hier soir, vous savez. On a discuté un bon moment et on a même plaisanté. Elle est vraiment très gentille. Un peu réservée peut-être, mais on ne se connaît pas, elle n'allait pas me raconter sa vie non plus !

— Très bien. Et vous n'avez pas remarqué une personne qui aurait pu vous paraître étrange ou au comportement suspect à une autre table, par exemple ?

— Non, répondit-elle après un court instant de réflexion. Il n'y a pas eu grand monde, c'est toujours comme ça le mercredi. On a eu la fameuse Agathe à sa table habituelle, un couple d'amoureux là-bas au fond, et puis une mère avec son jeune fils qui viennent régulièrement. Sans compter les gens qui viennent chercher les *pizzas* à emporter, bien sûr. Mais ceux-là, c'est Sergio qui s'en occupe, le patron. Je ne fais pas trop attention à qui attend sa commande au comptoir. Je n'ai pas que ça à faire, vous comprenez.

Louis n'en demandait pas tant. Il avait l'impression qu'elle n'allait jamais s'arrêter de parler. Mais il fallait reconnaître qu'elle faisait preuve de précision et il fut fixé quant à la santé de la psychologue la veille au soir. À moins qu'elle ne se soit trouvée mal pendant la nuit, rien n'expliquait pour l'instant son absence.

— D'accord, je vous remercie, votre aide est précieuse. Si jamais vous la voyez d'ici demain ou après-demain, vous pourrez me prévenir ?

Il lui laissa sa carte, qu'elle mit aussitôt dans la poche arrière de son jean *slim* sans la regarder.

— Je n'y manquerai pas. J'espère que vous allez la retrouver, inspecteur.

— C'est toujours lieutenant, sourit Louis malgré son humeur maussade.

La serveuse se frappa le front en riant tandis qu'il quittait les lieux.

En temps normal, il se serait fait une joie d'aller passer la nuit au domaine de ses parents. Ce soir-là pourtant, il opta pour la villa à Deauville, dont il gardait toujours un double de clefs dans sa voiture. Il faisait encore frais à cause du temps humide, mais les chauffages tournaient au minimum jusqu'à fin mai, au cas où quelqu'un déciderait d'y séjourner durant la morte-saison.

Faire face à sa mère, ou même à sa fille le lendemain matin était au-dessus de ses forces. Il était trop choqué, trop en colère. Le pire, c'est qu'il était plus en colère contre lui-même que contre qui que ce soit d'autre. Il s'en voulait de n'avoir rien soupçonné d'une part, et de ne pas être un assez bon père pour que France-Alix se soit confiée à lui d'autre part.

En même temps, étant donné sa réaction, il était peut-être préférable que sa fille ne se soit pas épanchée sur son épaule. Mais il était trop englué dans sa propre colère pour s'en rendre compte.

La pluie s'était mise à tomber à verse. Il était

trempé lorsqu'il atteignit sa voiture et cela ne s'arrêta pas jusqu'à ce qu'il arrive à la villa, une trentaine de minutes plus tard.

Il était presque une heure du matin quand il se glissa enfin dans les draps froids de sa chambre attitrée, dont le matelas était un peu trop mou à son goût. Il s'y enfonça comme dans du chamallow, mais ses yeux restèrent désespérément ouverts malgré la fatigue qui le tenaillait. Il était en guerre contre lui-même, il ressassait tous les événements de la journée en finissant par tout mélanger. Il se rappelait sa fille devant le restaurant. Le visage d'Agathe venait se superposer à celui de la jeune gothique et, dans le demi-sommeil qui l'avait gagné, il les voyait s'embrasser toutes les deux tandis que le carillon de la porte de la *pizzeria* tintinnabulait encore et encore avec un son cristallin agaçant.

Louis se redressa dans le lit. La sonnerie était bien réelle bien qu'il ne parvînt pas à l'identifier. Cela provenait de la chaise où il avait laissé ses vêtements pêle-mêle. Il se leva, fouilla dans la poche de son blouson, d'où il extirpa le mobile d'Agathe.

Trop tard.

Quelques secondes après, alors qu'il vérifiait le journal d'appels, un message se chargeait, émettant un piaillement d'oiseau. Le numéro qui venait d'appeler était masqué, ainsi que celui du SMS que Louis ouvrit et lut :

JE TE CROYAIS PLUS PERSPICACE, PETIT PRINCE.

C'EST DOMMAGE POUR LA PSY.

Louis relut le message vingt fois, en caleçon au milieu de la chambre, où l'obscurité devint totale dès que l'écran du portable s'éteignit. Il était décidément écrit qu'il vivrait la pire soirée de sa vie !

L'auteur du SMS s'adressait personnellement à lui, et pas de n'importe quelle manière : il employait le surnom que seuls ses collègues au sein de la police lui donnaient. Sa première pensée fut qu'il s'agissait peut-être d'un flic comme lui. Cela impliquait tellement d'ennuis que sa tête se mit à tourner. Et comment savait-il qu'il était en possession du portable de la thérapeute ?

Une chose en tout cas était maintenant certaine : Agathe avait été enlevée. Ces deux phrases laissaient planer une menace doublée d'une volonté de faire culpabiliser Louis. La première phrase l'accusait clairement de ne pas avoir su anticiper ce qui allait arriver à la jeune femme. Mais pour quelle raison aurait-il soupçonné qu'un tel danger la menaçait ?

Comme un zombie, il alla préparer du café dans la cuisine. Maintenant que la puissance des chauffages avait été augmentée, il faisait bien meilleur dans la maison.

Une fois assis à la table ronde au centre de la pièce, il but une première tasse d'un trait, se brûla le palais et la langue, puis s'en servit une seconde rasade qu'il sirota en repensant à ce qu'il savait.

Il paraissait évident que l'auteur du message était la même personne qui avait passé les appels anonymes à Agathe et, s'il savait que Louis avait ce portable, c'est que la jeune femme le lui avait dit ou qu'il l'avait surveillée de très près. On pouvait donc espérer qu'elle fût toujours en vie. En revanche, il paraissait hautement improbable qu'Agathe eût été en mesure de révéler à son ravisseur qu'il était surnommé le *petit prince,* car d'après lui, elle n'en savait absolument rien.

Alors comment pouvait-il avoir connaissance de ce détail ? Qui en dehors des membres du commissariat et de sa propre famille connaissait ce sobriquet ?

Beaucoup plus de monde qu'il ne l'aurait imaginé, en fait, car si l'on y réfléchissait, entre les proches et les amis des uns et des autres au sein du commissariat, ça faisait du monde. Ce détail avait très bien pu filtrer. Ce n'était pas un secret d'État, après tout !

Mais pourquoi chercher à communiquer avec lui en particulier ? S'agissait-il de quelqu'un ayant un contentieux avec lui ? En tout cas, c'était tout sauf une plaisanterie.

Dans l'immédiat, il ne pouvait rien faire. Il était presque quatre heures du matin et il fallait qu'il dorme s'il voulait être opérationnel le lendemain. Avec tout ce qui venait de lui tomber dessus, cela promettait des journées bien remplies et une fin de nuit compromise.

Automne 2000

L'homme ôta son masque de chat, qu'il roula pour le glisser à l'intérieur de son pantalon, contre son ventre. Il transpirait à grosses gouttes. D'un revers de sa main gantée, il s'épongea le front, puis resta un moment à contempler son œuvre.

Sa force physique avait toujours impressionné son entourage quand il était jeune. À présent, anonyme derrière la vitre de son guichet, personne ne lui prêtait attention. Il n'avait eu aucun mal à transporter le corps de Claude Albert sur une épaule, comme il aurait porté un sac de pierres. Le suspendre par le cou avec sa propre ceinture n'avait pas posé le moindre problème non plus.

Il se balançait encore tout doucement au-dessus, surplombant le massacre de sa femme et de ses enfants, qu'il n'avait pas su protéger.

Cela avait été facile, finalement. Il s'en était fait toute une montagne, mais maintenant qu'il était passé à l'acte, il saurait exactement comment procéder la prochaine fois. Et ils verraient à qui ils avaient affaire ! Ce n'était que le début. Des familles comme celle-là, il en voyait défiler des centaines par jour au bureau. Qui venaient quémander leur allocation comme si avoir des enfants leur donnait tous les droits.

Il allait faire du ménage, lui ! Et si les gens n'arrivaient pas à décider qui devait vivre et qui devait mourir, il se chargerait de choisir pour eux. Et tant mieux s'ils y passaient tous. Bon débarras ! La planète ne s'en porterait que mieux.

Devant le spectacle de ce qu'il venait d'accomplir, il se sentait grand, grisé par la toute-puissance de sa main armée du couteau à cran d'arrêt. Désormais, il ne se poserait plus tant de questions. Il était dans son droit, c'est lui qui avait raison, il agissait pour le bien de l'humanité. Pour les générations à venir. Celles qui seraient choisies. Ce serait un travail fastidieux, il devrait agir souvent, sans faillir. Mais il se sentait plus sûr de lui maintenant qu'il avait entamé sa croisade. Et rien ne l'arrêterait.

Il manquait juste la touche finale. Ce qui deviendrait sa signature. Calmement, il se dirigea vers la cuisine, évitant avec soin de marcher dans les flaques de sang qui s'étalaient sur le sol. Comme il s'y attendait, personne n'avait songé à sortir le sac poubelle qui vomissait ses détritus. Papiers et films plastique d'emballages, pots de yaourt, bouteilles en verre, morceaux d'aliments mélangés à du marc de café et bien d'autres choses encore que cette famille ne prenait pas la peine de trier. Le couvercle ne fermait plus tellement le sac était rempli.

Il se saisit de la poubelle sans se préoccuper de tout ce qui tombait, puis entreprit de vider tout son contenu à travers le salon. L'odeur fut épouvantable, mais l'odorat n'était pas son sens le plus développé. Aussi n'était-il pas incommodé par les relents de sang, d'excréments, d'urine et de déchets mélangés qui auraient agressé n'importe quel individu normalement constitué.

Ces gens salissaient la planète, c'est dans leurs immondices qu'ils méritaient de pourrir.

Une grande sérénité l'habitait lorsqu'il rejoignit le petit hall d'entrée. Et là, alors que son regard se posait sur son visage dans le miroir en partie caché par l'entassement de vêtements pendus autour, il remarqua une photographie coincée dans l'encadrement, tout en bas.

Il la prit entre ses doigts gantés, l'observa avec de plus en plus d'attention et ce qu'il vit le fit bondir intérieurement. Le cliché en main, il retourna sur ses pas, se pencha sur la première de ses victimes, dont il dégagea le visage caché par sa chevelure afin de comparer cette figure à celle qui posait sur la photo.

Aucun doute possible : ce n'était pas la fille aînée, Claire Albert, qui gisait là. Les cheveux de sa victime étaient d'un blond très clair alors que la véritable Claire avait les cheveux châtain foncé et ondulés. Il n'y avait pas d'erreur, au dos de la photo, il était écrit :

Famille Albert, 1999

Le cliché était donc récent. Il n'avait pas tué la bonne personne.

Comment avait-il pu commettre une telle faute ? Tout lui avait semblé si parfait, les choses s'étaient si bien déroulées ! Toute la cohérence de son travail s'en trouvait gâchée.

La colère monta en lui comme une vague déferlante. Son visage s'empourpra, sa respiration se fit anarchique, ses oreilles se mirent à bourdonner, il se mordit la lèvre inférieure jusqu'au sang et il se mit à répéter : « Salope ! Salope ! » tout en s'acharnant à grands coups de pied sur le visage de la jeune fille.

Sa rage dura plusieurs minutes avant de se dissiper lentement. Il était hors d'haleine, tremblait de tous ses membres. À cause de cette fille, il avait raté sa première œuvre. Qui était-elle ? Qu'est-ce qu'elle foutait là et où était la fille aînée ?

Après tout, peu importait. Tant pis pour elle, elle s'était trouvée au mauvais endroit, au mauvais moment. Ce qui était fait était fait, il ne pouvait plus revenir en arrière.

À peu près maître de ses moyens, il quitta finalement la maison silencieuse, monta dans sa voiture, où la buée avait envahi le pare-brise. Sans attendre que le système de soufflerie la fasse disparaître, il démarra, encore sous le coup de sa rage et de sa déception.

Il n'avait pas fait plus de deux kilomètres en dehors de la ville qu'un chien traversa sous ses roues. Il braqua pour éviter l'animal au moment où un camion semi-remorque arrivait en face.

La voiture, volée la veille au soir sur un parking de bâtiments HLM, s'encastra dans le camion. Le conducteur, mort sur le coup, méconnaissable et sans aucun papier sur lui, ne fut jamais identifié, son œuvre à peine commencée inachevée.

Chapitre 20

Quand Agathe revint à elle, la tête près d'exploser, elle eut d'abord l'impression qu'un rouleau compresseur lui était passé sur le corps. Tous ses membres étaient douloureux, sans parler de ses cervicales, qui semblaient rouillées tant son cou était raide.

Reprenant peu à peu ses esprits, elle comprit pourquoi elle avait si mal. On l'avait assise par terre, sur un sol de terre battue glacé, les mains attachées dans le dos et, comme elle avait été inconsciente un certain temps, son corps s'était affaissé sur lui-même, entraînant des courbatures sévères.

Il faisait très sombre, mais l'odeur qu'elle sentait lui fit tout de suite comprendre qu'elle devait se trouver dans une cave. Face à elle, elle distingua ce qui devait être un soupirail d'où filtrait une faible lueur extérieure ; la lune peut-être.

Des larmes ne tardèrent pas à embuer ses yeux au fur et à mesure qu'elle réalisait dans quelle situation elle se trouvait. Elle avait envie de crier, mais la peur la tétanisait, elle ne parvenait qu'à gémir misérablement à travers ses larmes et sa respiration qui s'affolait.

Brusquement, comme prise de frénésie, elle se

mit à secouer ses bras pour essayer de faire céder les liens. Elle se démena furieusement, totalement paniquée, désespérée, haletante. Tout ce qu'elle réussit à faire, c'est se blesser douloureusement aux poignets tandis que sa tête heurtait ce qui semblait être une autre tête. Elle hurla pour de bon, cette fois-ci.

Elle se tourna vers ce qu'elle prit pour une autre personne, attachée comme elle et assise sur le sol.

— Aidez-moi ! cria-t-elle.

Mais comment pouvait-elle imaginer que ce malheureux, aussi prisonnier qu'elle, puisse l'aider ?

— Vous m'entendez ? insista Agathe, ne comprenant pas pourquoi son voisin d'infortune ne lui répondait pas.

Puis, tournant la tête de l'autre côté, maintenant que sa vision s'était ajustée à la pénombre, elle distingua une autre forme humaine aux poignets ficelés dans le dos. Se contorsionnant malgré les crampes, elle vit qu'ils étaient quatre attachés dos à dos, en cercle au milieu de cette cave lugubre, froide et humide.

— Pourquoi vous ne me répondez pas ?

Et puis soudain, elle comprit. Quand elle donna un léger coup de coude à son voisin de gauche, c'était rigide. Il ne s'agissait pas d'un être humain. Non, c'était un mannequin comme on en voit dans les grands magasins, fixé par des liens rivés au sol.

— Qu'est-ce que c'est ? bégaya-t-elle, encore plus affolée par sa découverte.

Car les trois formes qui se trouvaient là étaient des êtres factices. En regardant plus attentivement, elle se rendit compte qu'il y avait un adulte et deux enfants : un petit garçon et une fille un peu plus âgée.

Abattue, elle se mit à pleurer sans pouvoir s'arrêter.

Chapitre 21

Finalement, Louis parvint quand même à dormir quelques heures avant de se réveiller en sursaut vers huit heures. Le jour était levé depuis un bon moment, il aurait déjà dû se trouver au commissariat à cette heure-là.

Sans perdre un instant, il appela sur la ligne directe du commissaire Amary. S'il voulait faire les choses en règle, il n'avait pas le choix : il devait expliquer à son supérieur tout ce qui venait de se passer, des appels anonymes à répétition reçus par la psychologue jusqu'à son enlèvement présumé, en passant par le SMS qui lui avait été adressé la veille sur le portable de la jeune femme.

Amary le laissa parler sans l'interrompre, comme il le faisait toujours quand il sentait que c'était important. Puis il posa pas mal de questions pour avoir des détails sur le pourquoi du comment.

Louis voulait en priorité pouvoir entrer dans l'appartement de la thérapeute. Le texto reçu par le lieutenant tendait à faire soupçonner une disparition inquiétante, l'enlèvement était probable, le commissaire fut on ne peut plus coopératif :

— Je contacte le procureur pour obtenir la réquisition d'un serrurier au plus vite, Salvant-

Perret. Rendez-vous au poste le plus proche, je vous confirme tout ça d'ici une heure. Faites-vous accompagner par les gars du coin et tenez-moi informé. Je vous envoie vos équipiers et je leur dis pour le message.

Il avala un petit déjeuner rapide. De toute façon, il n'y avait qu'une malheureuse boîte de céréales dans le placard de la cuisine, et du lait en poudre. La maison était inhabitée la plupart du temps, c'était un de leurs voisins, dont ils étaient devenus proches au fil des années, qui venait une fois par mois vérifier que tout allait bien. Il possédait un double des clefs et s'arrangeait pour qu'il y ait toujours le minimum vital au cas où des invités arriveraient à l'improviste.

Après une douche salutaire, Louis passa chez Romain Chatel pour le prévenir qu'il avait passé la nuit à la villa, qu'il ne fallait pas qu'il s'inquiète si des choses n'étaient plus au même endroit dans la maison. Il ne put échapper à une tasse de café chez le brave homme, dont le veuvage pesait sur ses épaules. Dès qu'il avait l'occasion de discuter, il alpaguait les gens pour alléger sa solitude.

Louis avait toujours bien aimé le bonhomme. Il le connaissait depuis qu'il était enfant. Le voisin l'avait vu grandir et feu sa femme l'avait même gardé quelquefois, lorsque Vincent et Hélène Salvant-Perret avaient un événement imprévu où ils ne pouvaient pas emmener leur jeune fils.

Romain voulut savoir comment Louis se débrouillait dans sa nouvelle vie de divorcé ; ce que devenait sa ravissante fille et si le boulot au commissariat n'était pas trop dur. Révéler à l'homme que France-Alix vivait désormais avec Vincent et Hélène provoqua une mélancolie chez Louis. Il ne put s'empêcher de se remémorer l'épisode de la veille et ses paroles dures et probablement injustes envers sa mère.

Il regrettait.

Dès qu'il fut sorti de chez Romain Chatel, il monta dans sa voiture et appela Hélène.

– Es-tu dans de meilleures dispositions ? attaqua-t-elle d'entrée, avant même qu'il n'eût prononcé un mot.

Quelle femme clairvoyante ! Elle savait déjà que son fils avait dû cogiter et réaliser à quel point sa réaction avait été démesurée et arbitraire.

– Je regrette, maman, j'étais énervé et ça m'a surpris. Je ne m'attendais pas à une chose pareille et j'ai pété les plombs. Je suis désolé.

– Je sais, mon chéri. Tu as l'air sur les nerfs, en ce moment, tu devrais te ménager. Tu sais, France-Alix n'a que quinze ans, elle est un peu déstabilisée et elle se cherche. Ce n'est sans doute que temporaire, il ne faut pas te mettre dans des états pareils. Et puis, si finalement elle persiste dans cette voie, eh bien ! Nous ferons avec. Parce que nous l'aimons quoi qu'il arrive et que nous ne souhaitons que son bonheur, n'est-ce pas ?

– Bien sûr, oui. Mais je t'en supplie, surveille-la bien. Et dis-le-moi quand quelque chose d'aussi important lui arrive. Ça m'a fait un choc, quand même !

– Je ne savais pas trop comment te l'annoncer et, comme je te l'ai dit, ce n'est peut-être qu'une passade. Mais tu ne dois pas t'en faire, je suis là et ton père et moi veillons sur elle.

– Papa est au courant ?

Il y eut un léger temps de flottement.

— Non, finit-elle par reconnaître. Je n'ai pas jugé bon de lui en parler et France-Alix ne tenait pas à ce que je le fasse.

— Et à moi, elle comptait m'en parler ?

— Elle l'aurait fait. Mais elle n'a pas trouvé l'occasion, ou le courage, va savoir. Où as-tu dormi, cette nuit ? À la villa ? ajouta-t-elle pour changer de sujet.

— Oui, avoua Louis. C'était plus près que de venir au domaine.

— Tu as dû avoir froid, c'est ridicule. Tu aurais pu pousser jusqu'ici.

Hélène Salvant-Perret n'était pas née de la dernière pluie et elle connaissait son fils par cœur. Elle savait très bien que s'il n'était pas venu, ce n'était pas une question de kilomètres mais de fierté.

Néanmoins, cette conversation matinale avec sa mère soulagea la conscience vite saturée de Louis. Il n'avait jamais supporté d'en vouloir à quelqu'un plus de vingt-quatre heures, et encore. Savoir qu'il était en mauvais termes avec une personne aimée le rongeait jusqu'à l'épuisement moral. Quand il était enfant, s'il s'était disputé avec l'un de ses parents ou un camarade d'école, il ne fermait pas l'œil de la nuit. Il pouvait même tomber malade tellement les conflits lui étaient intolérables. En prenant de l'âge, cette faiblesse n'avait jamais complètement disparu, mais il prenait sur lui. De toute façon, il faisait preuve de suffisamment de force de caractère par ailleurs pour ne pas avoir une réputation de chochotte ; ce qu'il n'était certainement pas.

Le poste de police le plus proche était situé à dix minutes à peine en voiture. Il connaissait bien l'un des officiers, qui vint à sa rencontre dès qu'il se fut annoncé à la réception.

— Alors, Salvant-Perret, toujours pas décidé à demander ta mutation dans notre belle région ? fit joyeusement le lieutenant Lorenzatto en lui tapant sur l'épaule avec une virilité sismique.

Salvatore Lorenzatto, dont les origines italiennes ne pouvaient être reniées, passait tout son temps libre dans les salles de musculation. Son corps était taillé dans le roc, aussi son coup de patte amical secoua Louis jusque dans ses entrailles.

À la tête que faisait le lieutenant Salvant-Perret, Lorenzatto éclata de rire, l'entraînant avec lui dans son bureau. Ce commissariat était bien mieux agencé et en meilleur état que celui d'où venait Louis. Salvatore possédait un bureau qu'il ne partageait qu'avec un seul coéquipier, absent ce jour-là, quand Louis devait se contenter d'un espace commun minuscule avec ses deux autres collègues.

— On a réquisitionné ton serrurier, fit-il en tendant une enveloppe. J'ai cru comprendre qu'Ismaël devait te rejoindre. Comment se fait-il que vous ne soyez pas venus ensemble ? Tu étais chez tes parents ? Comment se portent-ils, au fait ?

Ça faisait beaucoup de questions d'un seul coup, mais Louis s'efforça de répondre à chacune d'entre elles, sans toutefois s'étendre sur les raisons de sa présence dans le Calvados seul. Il gardait à l'esprit qu'il pouvait y avoir une taupe à l'intérieur des services de police, dans son entourage, qui renseignait le ravisseur d'Agathe sur ses agissements. Mieux valait rester discret, en dire le moins possible.

— On t'a accordé deux gars pour vous accompagner. On attend ton équipe ici ou tu préfères sortir boire un café au PMU ?

— PMU, choisit Louis. J'envoie juste un SMS à Cortès pour la prévenir de nous y rejoindre. J'ai besoin d'une double dose de caféine, ce matin.

Une fois installés à une table un peu en retrait, les deux hommes commencèrent à discuter du cas qui occupait Louis et son équipe depuis plus d'un mois à présent. L'affaire ayant été à la une de tous les quotidiens, il eût été difficile de passer à côté.

— Tu sais que je connais bien Stan et Fred. Ils ont été les premiers sur la scène des homicides à Savigny. J'ai entendu parler des lettres que vous avez retrouvées sous les lits des gamins. Tu sais à quoi elles correspondent ?

— On commence à y voir plus clair, mais on n'est encore sûrs de rien. La presse n'est pas au courant de ces détails-là, je ne saurais trop te conseiller de garder ça pour toi.

— La confiance règne ! lança Lorenzatto sur un ton faussement offusqué.

— Tu sais bien comment ça marche, temporisa Louis. En plus, cette affaire prend des proportions hors du commun. Neuf enfants tués, tu avoueras que c'est une enquête particulièrement difficile, même pour un flic qui a vingt ans de maison.

— Vous avez des suspects ?

— Des pistes, rien de concret.

— Pourtant, vous avez l'ex de la fille Aubry en garde à vue, non ?

— Il a été incarcéré, mais pas pour les meurtres, juste pour détention et revente de stupéfiants. On ne s'en occupe plus. Et de ton côté, vous êtes sur quoi en ce moment ?

Louis voulait détourner la conversation, peu désireux d'en dire trop à quelqu'un d'étranger à son équipe, même si Lorenzatto jouissait d'une excellente réputation au sein des forces de l'ordre. Le SMS qu'il avait reçu la veille revenait sans cesse, avec cette façon de l'appeler *petit prince*. Il éprouvait une sensation étrange au souvenir de la syntaxe choisie par l'auteur du message ; quelque chose de malsain qui le mettait mal à l'aise.

Quand enfin, Maud et Ismaël se présentèrent devant les deux lieutenants, ces derniers en étaient à leur quatrième expresso. Les nouveaux venus refusèrent le café que Lorenzatto leur proposa. La matinée tirait déjà à sa fin, il fallait s'activer.

Au bas du petit bâtiment, il y avait donc un rassemblement assez conséquent pour éveiller la curiosité des passants et du voisinage. Deux voitures de police stationnaient en double file, gyrophare tournoyant, ce qui attirait forcément les bavards. On se demandait ce qui se passait dans cet immeuble tranquille. On parlait même de la présence d'un terroriste extrémiste vivant là. Les commentaires les plus farfelus circulaient.

Une femme envoyée par le syndicat de copropriété s'engagea la première dans la cage d'escalier, suivie du serrurier, d'un des gardiens de la paix, puis des lieutenants Al Bakir, Cortès, Lorenzatto et Salvant-Perret. Le deuxième gardien de la paix fermait la marche tandis qu'un autre s'était posté à la porte d'entrée de l'immeuble.

Sur le palier du deuxième étage, un homme d'une cinquantaine d'années, en tricot de peau d'une propreté douteuse, se tenait devant son logement, regardant ce défilé d'un œil morne.

– Rentrez chez vous, monsieur, ordonna Ismaël d'un ton sans appel. Nous viendrons vous voir si nous avons besoin de vous interroger.

L'homme parut fort mécontent, bougonna des propos incompréhensibles, mais finit par obtempérer.

— À croire que personne ne bosse, dans ce quartier ! fit remarquer Ismaël à Maud, qui l'avait doublé.

— Les joies des RTT, répondit-elle.

Puis, désignant Louis d'un signe de tête :

— Il a l'air inquiet. Tu crois qu'on va encore retrouver un cadavre ?

— J'espère pas ! Il risquerait de ne pas s'en remettre. Pour une fois qu'il a l'air d'avoir des sentiments pour une nana...

Après la découverte de tous ces corps durant les semaines passées, Maud Cortès redoutait les déplacements comme celui-ci. Heureusement, elle n'était pas en tête de file. La femme qui avait ouvert la marche fut priée de rester à l'extérieur, sur le palier, en compagnie d'un des agents et du serrurier, pendant que Louis, Ismaël et Salvatore se déployaient dans toutes les pièces, arme au poing étant donné la menace palpable.

Les uns après les autres, ils annoncèrent qu'il n'y avait rien à signaler dans les pièces qu'ils venaient d'inspecter. Aucune trace de la présence de la psychologue nulle part. En revanche, l'on n'entendit pas la voix de Louis. Après avoir échangé un regard, Ismaël et Maud le rejoignirent à l'entrée de ce qui semblait être la chambre à coucher d'Agathe Delcourt. Il se tenait immobile face au lit et avait le regard fixé au-dessus. Sur le mur blanc, écrite au marqueur noir, ils découvrirent l'inscription :

— Tu penses ce que je pense ? demanda Ismaël, les yeux rivés sur le mur.

— Quoi ? fit Maud, affolée.

Louis sortit son portable, rechercha quelques instants dans ses fichiers, puis fit défiler les photos de chacune des lettres retrouvées sous les matelas des enfants dans leurs trois dernières affaires.

— Pour moi, c'est la même écriture.

— Qu'est-ce que tu en penses, Maud ?

Les trois lieutenants restèrent penchés sur l'écran quelques secondes, comparant la couleur de l'encre utilisée, la forme des lettres et la force donnée dans les traits.

— Y'a pas à dire, on dirait que c'est la même écriture.

— Je préviens Hébrard, annonça Ismaël.

Avant de contacter leur capitaine, le lieutenant prit une photo de l'inscription, qu'il envoya en pièce jointe à son message. Quelques minutes plus tard, alors que Louis faisait le tour de l'appartement en demandant que l'on ne touche à rien, la réponse d'Hébrard arriva : une équipe allait venir expertiser la chambre. Ils détermineraient si l'auteur de cette phrase était le même que celui des trois lettres de l'alphabet.

— Il faut que tu appelles Amary, dit Ismaël à Louis, il veut te parler et c'est urgent.

Une sorte de désespoir s'était emparée de ce dernier. La psychologue visée par l'homme qui assassinait des familles entières, comment était-ce possible ? Il avait pressenti que la jeune femme cachait quelque chose, mais il n'aurait su dire quoi.

Il avait la conviction qu'il n'allait pas tarder à le découvrir.

Il partit s'isoler dans la cage d'escalier, où il s'assit sur une marche, la tête un peu vide. Le commissaire décrocha aussitôt que Louis eut composé le numéro ; il attendait son appel.

— Vous êtes assis, Salvant-Perret ? annonça-t-il sans préambule. Claire Albert, l'aînée des enfants Albert, n'est autre qu'Agathe Delcourt.

Louis éprouva quelques difficultés à déglutir quoiqu'au fond de lui, il s'y fût attendu plus ou moins.

— La nuit où sa famille a été attaquée, elle était partie dormir chez une camarade de classe qui fêtait son anniversaire. Elle avait dix-sept ans au moment des faits. Comme on a vite supposé qu'il s'agissait d'homicides, elle a été évincée de la partie, je ne sais pas encore comment, jusqu'à ce qu'on retrouve le coupable.

— Mais il n'a jamais été retrouvé, termina Louis sombrement.

— C'est tout à fait exact.

— Mais il y avait cinq cadavres, objecta alors le lieutenant, dont le cerveau recommençait à fonctionner. Qui était la cinquième victime si ce n'était pas Agathe ? Enfin, Claire, je veux dire.

— C'était une amie de Mélissa, la fille cadette. Elle s'appelait Éva Portal. Bref, comme l'aînée n'était pas là et que les sœurs partageaient la même chambre, la gamine est restée dormir dans son lit. Elle était plutôt développée physiquement pour son âge, on pouvait facilement lui donner l'âge de Claire. On peut supposer que le tueur a fini par se rendre compte qu'il n'avait pas eu toute la famille et qu'il s'est mis en tête de terminer le travail. Reste à déterminer depuis quand il sait qu'il n'a pas tué Claire et comment il s'est débrouillé pour découvrir sous quelle identité elle vivait.

— Oui, dit Louis d'une voix éteinte, incapable pour l'instant de penser de façon cohérente.

— Je suis désolé pour la petite psy, je sais que vous l'aimez bien. J'espère qu'on va la retrouver. À vous de jouer, Louis. Je mets Hébrard sur le coup pour les recherches ici.

Après ces révélations plus que troublantes, Louis tâcha de mettre de l'ordre dans ses idées avant de rejoindre les autres. Claire Albert et Agathe Delcourt étaient donc une seule et même personne. L'unique survivante d'un massacre qui remontait à quinze ans. Celle qui avait été tuée à sa place avait aussi été la seule des victimes dont le visage ait été mutilé à coups de pied. Au cours des trois dernières tueries, aucune violence de ce genre n'avait été constatée. Seule Emma avait subi un viol particulièrement sauvage, mais son visage était intact. Le tueur de cette famille, il y avait quinze ans, savait-il qu'il ne s'agissait pas de la fille aînée ? Avait-il fini par s'en apercevoir d'une façon ou d'une autre ? Était-ce pour cette raison qu'elle avait eu droit à un tel traitement ? Et dans ce cas, pourquoi attendre tant d'années pour retrouver la véritable fille aînée des Albert ? Et pourquoi continuer à tuer des familles en semant des cailloux menant à Claire ?

Quelque chose n'allait pas dans ce scénario.

Depuis le début, il lui semblait qu'il y avait deux tueurs distincts et cette idée se confirmait. Encore s'agissait-il de le prouver.

Lorsqu'il exposa à Maud et à Ismaël la tournure

que prenaient les événements, il y eut un flottement dans l'atmosphère. Ses coéquipiers ne savaient pas trop comment Louis appréhendait la nouvelle de la double identité de la psychologue à laquelle il semblait s'être attaché. Le regard de Maud était chargé de compassion alors qu'Ismaël tâchait de conserver une attitude professionnelle tout en ménageant son collègue et ami.

— Il devient évident qu'Agathe est le lien entre toutes ces tueries, fit-il remarquer après un silence qui s'éternisa pendant une partie du trajet qui les ramenait au poste de Lorenzatto.

— C'est elle qui est désignée à chaque fois, approuva Maud. Mais pourquoi ? Qu'est-ce qu'elle a bien pu faire qui justifie que l'on ait tué toute sa famille et trois autres, quinze ans plus tard ?

— Si ça se trouve, il y a eu d'autres meurtres et on ne le sait pas, observa Ismaël.

— Non, Yvan Duval a bien cherché dans les données du SALVAC, il n'y a pas d'autres concordances nulle part ailleurs et ça m'étonnerait que notre gars soit allé à l'étranger pour commettre d'autres meurtres. Il a un but, une logique dans sa démence. Depuis le début, il fait tout pour qu'on lui coure après, qu'on le retrouve. Comme s'il voulait qu'on découvre pourquoi il agit comme ça. Il a quelque chose à reprocher à Aga... Claire Albert. Il faut savoir quoi. Je propose que nous restions ici jusqu'à demain, j'ai de la place pour dormir à Deauville. C'est d'accord pour vous ?

— Ça me va, approuva Maud, mais je dois prévenir à la maison et j'ai besoin de quelques affaires de rechange.

— Moi aussi, suivit Ismaël. Un tour au

supermarché ne sera pas superflu.

— Ne vous préoccupez pas d'affaires de toilette, il y a tout ce qu'il faut. On passera faire quelques courses en fin d'après-midi. Je tiens à être présent quand le graphologue va venir.

— Je sens que ma soirée de demain va tomber à l'eau, maugréa Ismaël.

— Ne t'inquiète pas, on sera rentrés demain.

— Quand même, il y a quelque chose qui m'intrigue, dit alors Maud. Comment le tueur a-t-il fait pour connaître la nouvelle identité de Claire Albert ? Même nous, on n'a pas accès à ce genre d'informations.

— C'est justement là que je bute, fit Louis sombrement. Depuis le SMS que j'ai reçu où l'expéditeur s'adresse à moi en utilisant mon surnom au poste, je soupçonne fortement une fuite dans nos troupes.

— Une taupe ? s'écria Maud, scandalisée.

— On garde ça pour nous, pour l'instant.

— On n'en parle même pas au commissaire ? insista la jeune femme.

— Pas tant qu'on n'est sûrs de rien. D'après moi, le tueur a un contact qui suit de près notre enquête. Agathe a été enlevée pile au moment où on allait découvrir qui elle était en réalité. D'après moi, ce n'est pas un hasard.

— Ça veut dire qu'on ne peut faire confiance à personne, conclut Ismaël. Ça risque de nous compliquer la tâche.

— En tout cas, on a de nouveaux éléments. S'il s'avère que c'est le même type qui a tué les familles et enlevé la psychologue, il a fait une erreur. Sa première. J'espère que l'équipe qu'ils envoient sur place va trouver des traces exploitables. Déjà, si on a la confirmation que l'écriture est identique, on aura avancé.

Même si la situation paraissait sombre pour le devenir de la thérapeute, Louis voyait un espoir. S'ils n'avaient pas retrouvé la jeune femme assassinée chez elle, si le ravisseur avait pris la peine de l'enlever, c'est qu'il voulait obtenir quelque chose d'elle. Et pour cela, il avait besoin qu'elle soit en vie ; ce qui était plutôt positif.

— Comment on va s'y prendre pour démasquer la taupe ? questionna Maud, que cette situation rendait nerveuse.

— D'abord, on va se montrer discrets, répondit Louis. Trouvons-nous un bureau où travailler. À partir de maintenant, c'est entre nous trois.

— Mais le capitaine Hébrard est aussi sur le coup, observa Maud. Est-ce qu'on doit aussi se méfier de lui ?

— Je ne pense pas que Stéphane représente une quelconque menace, jugea Louis. Mais soyons prudents et parcimonieux dans les infos qu'on transmet là-haut. Personne ne dit rien à personne sans en avoir informé les autres, d'accord ?

— C'est d'accord, approuvèrent Ismaël et Maud en chœur.

Comme ils accédaient à la réception du commissariat, Lorenzatto les guida jusqu'à une salle qui ressemblait à une petite cafétéria, avec une machine à café expresso, un distributeur d'eau minérale et un autre de *snacks* bourrés de graisses végétales.

— Je suis désolé, c'est le seul endroit de libre.

— Question intimité, ça va pas être terrible, fit

remarquer Ismaël.

— Vous inquiétez pas, tout le monde sait que vous êtes là, on ne viendra pas vous emmerder pour venir chercher à boire ou à manger. On a une autre machine à café là-haut. Ici, c'est l'ancienne salle de repos. Les chips du distributeur doivent être périmées depuis deux ans au moins. Par contre, la machine à expresso fonctionne très bien, il suffit de la brancher et de mettre de l'eau. Les dosettes sont dans le meuble en dessous.

— Périmées aussi ? plaisanta Ismaël.

— Nan ! Je vous fais installer un PC dans cinq minutes, faites comme chez vous.

Lorenzatto disparut tandis que Maud s'affairait à ouvrir les placards à la recherche du nécessaire pour préparer un café à chacun d'entre eux. Le lieutenant revint rapidement avec une tour sous un bras et un écran plat sous l'autre, des fils de branchement pendus autour de son cou.

— C'est bon, je vais gérer, dit Ismaël en débarrassant l'officier de tout son attirail. Montrez-moi juste où sont les prises.

De son côté, Louis avait une mine à faire peur. Il s'était approché d'une des fenêtres et regardait à l'extérieur sans rien voir. Son esprit était ailleurs. Tourné vers la jolie Agathe qui n'avait pas eu suffisamment confiance en lui pour avouer qu'elle vivait sous une autre identité. Qui n'avait pas été totalement honnête envers lui lorsqu'elle lui avait parlé des coups de fil anonymes. Car elle devait bien se douter alors qu'ils étaient peut-être liés à son passé tragique. Tout comme elle devait avoir été alertée par les nouvelles familles décimées de la même façon que l'avait été la sienne. Lui se sentait tout à fait ridicule de ne pas avoir su décrypter cette réserve un peu formelle dont elle faisait preuve depuis le début. Il aurait dû deviner que derrière cette retenue, il y avait une immense souffrance.

Il n'était pas étonnant qu'elle fût si évasive au sujet de sa famille. Elle n'avait plus de famille. On la lui avait arrachée d'un seul coup et qui sait quels tourments avaient été les siens durant les années qui avaient suivi cette nuit d'horreur.

Il comprenait à présent pourquoi aucun nom ne figurait dans son dossier à l'institut Saint-Jean à la rubrique « personne à prévenir en cas d'urgence ».

Elle était seule.

Chapitre 22

Elle avait froid. Si froid !

Ses dents claquaient, impossible de contrôler ses mâchoires. Tous ses muscles étaient tendus, à tel point qu'elle souffrait de partout à la fois, à l'intérieur et à l'extérieur.

Depuis combien de temps était-elle là ? Trois heures, quatre ? Davantage ?

Pas moyen de consulter sa montre, ses poignets étaient attachés dans le dos. Sa seule certitude, c'est qu'il faisait nuit dehors. La petite fenêtre face à elle donnait sur l'extérieur, et le jour n'était pas encore levé.

Il n'y avait aucun bruit, hormis celui de ses pleurs par intermittences et celui de son souffle lorsqu'elle essayait de recouvrer son calme. Aucun moteur, elle devait donc se trouver dans un endroit isolé, à la campagne.

Entre deux crises de larmes, elle tâchait d'écouter, penchait la tête en cessant de respirer pour savoir s'il y avait quelqu'un au-dessus. Mais elle n'entendait absolument rien. Pas un mouvement, pas un grincement. Le silence était sa seule compagnie.

Avec les quatre mannequins.

Son ravisseur était arrivé par-derrière lorsqu'elle

se trouvait dans sa chambre, face au mur où cette phrase glaçante avait été écrite en énormes lettres noires. Agathe avait eu l'impression qu'on venait de la violer quand elle avait compris que quelqu'un était entré chez elle, dans sa chambre à coucher.

Et puis elle avait ressenti un choc terrible derrière la tête. Ensuite, plus rien jusqu'à ce qu'elle se réveille dans cette cave lugubre qui puait la moisissure et l'humidité. Elle n'avait pas vu son agresseur. Elle ne l'avait même pas entendu s'approcher d'elle alors qu'il devait être dissimulé quelque part dans l'appartement.

Bêtement, ses pensées se tournèrent vers Sherlock. Avait-il pu ressortir après qu'elle avait été emmenée ? Elle se souvenait d'avoir laissé la fenêtre de la cuisine entrouverte quand le chat était entré. L'animal s'était sûrement sauvé en voyant qu'on emportait sa maîtresse occasionnelle. Du moins l'espérait-elle. Elle ne supporterait pas que l'on ait fait du mal à cet animal.

Penser à Sherlock lui fit un peu de bien. Tout au moins, cela lui permit-il d'oublier sa condition durant quelques minutes, même si elle tremblait de tous ses membres. Elle essayait de se persuader que de toute façon, pleurer ne l'aiderait pas. Tout comme elle comprit très vite qu'il ne servait à rien de hurler, personne ne l'entendait.

Sans arrêt, elle se répétait que si elle avait échappé à la mort, cette fois, elle ne serait pas épargnée. Toute sa vie, elle avait vécu dans cette hantise et ça se réalisait. C'était son tour. Les âmes tourmentées de ses parents, de ses frère et sœur la rappelaient auprès d'elles.

Qu'est-ce qu'elle croyait ? Qu'elle pourrait s'en

tirer si facilement et passer toute sa vie dans une insouciance bienheureuse ?

Inconsciemment, elle s'était mise à gémir à chaque expiration en se balançant légèrement d'avant en arrière, les yeux fermés, ses cheveux pendouillant misérablement devant son visage. De toute façon, elle était incapable de repousser cette masse, ses mains étaient liées et elle n'avait plus aucune force.

Le désespoir avait atteint chaque parcelle de son être lorsque les premières lueurs de l'aurore éclairèrent faiblement le sous-sol. Le temps s'écoulait comme dans le pire des cauchemars. Au ralenti. Avec une lenteur qui permettait à la peur de s'insinuer dans chaque fibre.

À travers le rideau épais de sa chevelure, Agathe commença à distinguer des murs de pierre brute qui s'effritaient. Le sol était recouvert d'une espèce de poussière blanchâtre où l'on devinait la présence de champignons microscopiques en abondance. Il n'y avait absolument rien dans cette cave. Elle était totalement vide, à l'exception du cercle formé par les mannequins et elle-même. Des tuyaux couraient le long du plafond vétuste. Il devait y avoir une maison d'habitation au-dessus. Elle crut même reconnaître un compteur électrique lorsqu'elle tourna la tête pour regarder ce qui se trouvait derrière elle. Il y avait également un escalier de bois dont les marches lui parurent démesurément grandes, et une ampoule nue qui pendait au milieu du plafond.

Mais alors que la lumière devenait de plus en plus forte, ce qui retint l'attention d'Agathe, ce furent les vêtements dont les mannequins étaient affublés. Elle crut que son cœur allait sortir de sa poitrine en reconnaissant les pyjamas que portaient sa mère, sa sœur et son petit frère à l'époque où ils avaient disparu.

Un des mannequins représentait sa mère avec sa chemise de nuit couleur fuchsia décorée de strass autour du col et des poignets. Celui de Mélissa portait son pyjama blanc avec une tête d'ourson sur le devant et une inscription au dos où il était écrit *Teddy*. Victor, son tendre petit frère, avait une grenouillère verte. Agathe l'avait surnommé « crapaud » à cause de cette tenue.

La mise en scène macabre ne laissait aucun doute. Son ravisseur voulait la punir d'avoir survécu au reste de sa famille. Bien sûr, ça ne devait pas être les véritables vêtements de nuit ayant appartenu aux défunts, mais tout y était, jusqu'aux cheveux de chacun des personnages que l'on aurait pu prendre pour les originaux. Comment son ravisseur pouvait-il savoir avec une telle précision quelles tenues les membres de sa famille portaient ce soir-là ?

Le tout était terrifiant. Agathe sentit que son sang se glaçait. Les larmes recommencèrent à rouler le long de ses joues.

L'homme qui avait exterminé tous ses proches l'avait retrouvée. Comment ? Elle vivait sous une autre identité depuis quinze ans, avait fait un énorme travail sur elle-même afin de se fabriquer une nouvelle personnalité, une nouvelle vie, aux antipodes de celle qu'elle avait menée jusque-là avec des parents sans arrêt dans le besoin.

L'État l'avait très bien accompagnée et elle voulait s'en sortir. Déjà, avant la tragédie, elle était ambitieuse. Elle n'avait jamais aimé la vie précaire que ses parents leur offraient. Surtout sa mère, dont les diverses addictions étaient connues de tous, sauf de son petit frère, à qui Agathe racontait que leur mère était malade pour justifier son état perpétuellement comateux et sa consommation hallucinante de médicaments.

Elle avait tellement pleuré Victor ! Elle s'en était voulu de ne pas avoir été à ses côtés, de ne pas être morte en même temps que lui. Par quel concours de circonstances avait-elle été absente ce soir-là ? Pourquoi le destin l'avait-il choisie pour survivre si elle devait mourir maintenant, aux mains du même monstre ? Car elle n'en doutait pas, il devait l'avoir cherchée durant toutes ces années en s'apercevant, elle ne savait comment, qu'elle lui avait échappé.

Depuis cette nuit funeste où la police était venue la chercher chez sa copine Céline pour l'arracher à tout ce qui lui avait été familier, Agathe avait vécu dans la peur d'un malheur de ce genre. Parce qu'il lui semblait impossible qu'elle s'en sorte. Parce que n'ayant pas assisté à ce qui était arrivé, elle avait imaginé des choses terribles. Bien plus terrifiantes sans doute que ce qui s'était réellement produit.

Cent fois, elle avait vu en songe le visage du meurtrier. Toujours plus repoussant, toujours plus horrible. Ses nuits étaient peuplées de son épouvantable présence, ses jours voilés d'un épais rideau de crainte et de noirceur. Toutes ces années, son ombre l'avait talonnée. Quoi qu'elle fasse pour lui échapper, il était là, tapi dans les recoins de son esprit, l'empêchant d'envisager des relations saines, un équilibre moral, une vie normale. Des années de thérapie n'avaient fait qu'atténuer son sentiment de culpabilité. Mais elle parvenait quand même à vivre du mieux qu'elle le pouvait.

Le temps passait sans qu'elle sache si elle devait compter en minutes ou en heures. Ses pensées se bousculaient, sa raison allait et venait. Elle était entre la folie et l'hyperconscience.

À travers la fenêtre crasseuse du sous-sol, l'on ne distinguait qu'une lumière du jour terne, comme si le ciel était chargé de lourds nuages gris. Elle avait l'impression d'être arrivée au bout de quelque chose en ayant échoué dans toutes ses entreprises.

Elle allait crever ici, seule, et personne ne pleurerait sa perte. Elle ne manquerait à personne puisqu'elle avait toujours pris soin de fuir toute attache.

Combien de temps mettait-on à mourir sans eau ni nourriture ?

Les heures passant, elle retenait une furieuse envie d'uriner qui lui donnait un mal de tête terrible tellement elle était contractée. Son estomac commençait aussi à la tirailler sérieusement. Sa gorge était sèche, ses yeux la brûlaient d'avoir tant pleuré. Des crampes l'assaillaient de toutes parts à force d'être assise dans la même position. Seules ses jambes pouvaient bouger, mais c'était une bien maigre consolation.

L'attente était insoutenable. Et d'ailleurs, qu'est-ce qu'elle devait attendre ? Pourquoi ne l'avait-il pas déjà tuée ? Peut-être voulait-il la garder prisonnière pendant quinze ans, pour la punir de lui avoir couru après si longtemps ?

Tout à coup, sa vessie lâcha. Elle n'en pouvait plus. Et tandis que le liquide chaud s'écoulait sous ses fesses, elle éclata en sanglots, à bout, humiliée. Soulagée d'un côté, son agonie redoubla lorsque après quelques minutes, l'urine ayant refroidi, elle se mit à trembler de plus belle. C'était un calvaire sans nom. Son corps tout entier était une plaie béante. Elle voulait mourir, en finir là, tout de suite.

Un cri de bête blessée s'échappa de sa gorge, long, déchirant, mais parfaitement inutile. Les quatre mannequins gardaient le regard fixe dans le vide, caricatures grotesques des membres d'une famille disparue depuis si longtemps qu'Agathe ne se rappelait même plus les traits de leurs visages.

Alors qu'elle sombrait dans une semi-conscience, il lui sembla percevoir un bruit lointain de moteur qui se rapprochait. Elle tendit l'oreille, entre espoir et terreur. Ça venait plus près. D'un coup de reins, elle se redressa, aux aguets.

Une voiture.

Il y avait des graviers au-dehors. Peut-être une allée. Elle reconnaissait le son que faisaient les roues sur les petits cailloux. Le véhicule s'arrêta. Le moteur tourna une ou deux minutes pendant que la voiture était immobilisée, puis il s'éteignit et l'on entendit une portière claquer.

Une seule.

Ensuite, des pas qui crissaient et se rapprochaient.

On ne pouvait rien voir à travers cette maudite fenêtre.

Au-dessus d'elle, une porte s'ouvrit, puis se referma. Quelqu'un marchait avec des talons, semblait-il.

Une femme ?

Agathe suivait les moindres déplacements, oubliant pour un temps ses douleurs et la faim qui la torturaient. On ouvrit un robinet dont le tuyau, donnant dans le sous-sol, se mit à émettre le bruit caractéristique du flux de l'eau circulant à l'intérieur.

Était-ce son ravisseur ? Allait-on la tuer ? Ou bien venir lui dire pourquoi elle était retenue prisonnière depuis des heures ? La personne là-haut savait-elle qu'Agathe était là ? Fallait-il qu'elle crie pour manifester sa présence ?

Quelque chose la frappa comme un coup de poignard : si on avait voulu l'empêcher de crier, on l'aurait bâillonnée. Or, elle ne l'était pas. Ce qui signifiait que celui ou celle qui venait d'arriver était parfaitement au courant qu'elle était attachée dans cette cave immonde. Cela signifiait aussi que l'on ne craignait pas que ses cris fussent entendus. Un abattement sans nom s'empara d'elle, un désespoir au-delà du supportable.

À chaque fois qu'elle faisait un mouvement avec ses jambes, l'odeur désagréable de sa propre urine remontait à ses narines. Maintenant qu'elle savait ne plus être seule, une sueur froide courait le long de son dos, les relents de sa transpiration, acre à cause de la peur, se mêlaient aux autres odeurs.

Il y eut du remue-ménage en haut. On aurait dit des casseroles qui s'entrechoquaient. Les pas ne se déplaçaient plus que sur de très courtes distances. Les talons faisaient du sur-place dans une même pièce ; la cuisine très probablement.

Allait-on lui apporter à manger ?

Rien qu'à cette pensée, son ventre se mit à gargouiller bruyamment. Mais l'énorme tache d'urine qui devait maculer l'arrière de son pantalon la faisait mourir de honte. Même si elle n'était pas responsable de cet accident, elle n'en ressentait pas moins une humiliation sans bornes. La personne qui allait descendre devait bien s'attendre à la voir dans cet état. Car c'était à cause d'elle si elle en était rendue là. On voulait la salir, la soumettre, lui faire vivre l'enfer que sa famille avait vécu avant elle.

Elle entendit un meuble léger que l'on déplaçait tandis que les bruits de pas cessaient. L'inconnu était-il en train de manger ? Plus aucun son pendant un moment qui sembla durer l'éternité. Cette attente lui mettait les nerfs à vif. L'incertitude dans laquelle elle se trouvait lui torturait l'esprit, son corps la faisait souffrir de partout à la fois, elle allait devenir folle.

Après un temps infini, un autre raclement se fit entendre. Une chaise que l'on bougeait. Puis des pas, et de l'eau qui coula pendant plus longtemps que la première fois. Les talons claquèrent.

De plus en plus près.

Ils se rapprochaient.

Le cœur d'Agathe accéléra sa cadence, une bouffée de chaleur lui monta au visage alors que dans son dos, la porte de la cave s'ouvrait. D'un coup, la lumière crue de l'ampoule l'aveugla quelques secondes. Elle ajusta sa vision avec difficulté, car elle avait fixé la lumière, surprise par la soudaineté de cet éclairage. Il faisait en fait beaucoup plus sombre qu'elle ne se l'était imaginé.

L'inconnu descendit la première marche, s'arrêta. Agathe n'osait pas se retourner pour lui faire face, elle avait trop peur de ce qu'elle allait découvrir.

Une autre marche, puis une troisième, lentement, sans prononcer la moindre parole. Agathe avait l'impression qu'un souffle froid courait dans son cou au fur et à mesure que son ravisseur continuait de descendre l'escalier.

De ce qu'elle avait pu voir, les marches étaient si

dangereuses qu'il était nécessaire de faire preuve d'une grande prudence afin d'éviter une chute, surtout avec des chaussures à talons.

Il avait atteint le sol.

Agathe baissa la tête, terrorisée, refusant de porter son regard sur ce monstre qui semblait l'avoir traquée depuis toutes ces années.

Elle entendit qu'il faisait lentement le tour du cercle de mannequins et soudain, il fut devant elle.

Des chaussures de femme. Grises, avec des talons assez larges, hauts d'environ cinq centimètres. Des jambes fines portant des collants noirs opaques. Surprise que ce ne soit pas un homme, Agathe leva peureusement les yeux, détaillant l'inconnue qui la dominait de toute sa hauteur.

Elle portait un ensemble jupe tailleur gris perle sur un chemisier de soie rouge et un élégant *trench* noir la protégeait de la fraîcheur ambiante. L'écartement de ses jambes était un peu trop marqué, comme si elle n'avait pas l'habitude de se trouver dans cette posture. Une chevelure blonde soyeuse, un visage aux traits durs mais pas disgracieux, et des yeux qui hésitaient entre le marron et le vert.

Leurs regards se croisèrent. L'inconnue eut un petit rictus qui souleva légèrement sa lèvre supérieure alors qu'Agathe baissait bien vite les yeux, affolée par la cruauté qu'elle venait de déceler dans l'expression de celle qui lui faisait face.

En une fraction de seconde, elle comprit qu'elle allait mourir ici, sous le joug de cette femme dont elle ne savait rien, à qui elle n'avait rien fait.

— Tu te plais ici ? questionna soudain l'inconnue.

Sa voix était un peu étrange, comme si elle se

forçait à employer un ton plus doux que son timbre naturel.

— J'ai pris soin de t'entourer de ta famille disparue. Quoique j'aie cru comprendre que tu ne t'étais pas gênée pour les oublier bien vite. N'est-ce pas, Claire ?

Ce nom avait été prononcé de façon très distincte, pour bien insister sur le fait que la véritable identité d'Agathe était parfaitement connue de sa geôlière.

C'était donc cette femme qui avait organisé toute cette mise en scène. Pourquoi ? Qui était-elle ? Malgré son état déplorable, le cerveau d'Agathe fonctionnait à plein régime. Cette inconnue semblait jeune, plus jeune qu'elle peut-être. Vingt-cinq ans, certainement pas plus de trente. Ce qui signifiait qu'il était impossible qu'elle ait quelque chose à voir avec les meurtres des membres de sa famille quinze ans plus tôt. À l'époque, elle devait avoir entre dix et quinze ans, c'était tout bonnement inenvisageable. Ou alors, elle avait été envoyée par le véritable auteur des massacres. Tant de questions sans réponse !

Alors, pourquoi ? Que lui voulait-elle ?

— As-tu pensé à moi pendant toutes ces années ?

La question était directe, l'inconnue attendait une réponse. Ce fut d'une voix qu'elle ne reconnut pas qu'Agathe répondit après quelques secondes :

— Je ne sais pas qui vous êtes.

— Tu ne sais pas qui je suis ?

La femme avait crié ces mots d'une voix suraiguë, comme si sa réponse constituait une aberration.

— N'as-tu jamais eu une pensée pour celle qui est morte à ta place ce soir-là ? N'as-tu jamais cherché à savoir qui elle était, qui elle aimait, et qui l'aimait en retour ? Es-tu à ce point imbue de ta petite personne que tu ne ressentes aucune pitié, aucun remords envers celle qui aurait dû vivre ? Moi, j'ai beaucoup pensé à toi. J'ai attendu pendant longtemps que tu te manifestes, que tu fasses un geste pour t'excuser. Ne serait-ce qu'une lettre. Ça t'aurait fait mal d'envoyer rien qu'un mot pour dire que tu regrettais ?

Elle s'arrêta tout à coup de parler alors que les pleurs d'Agathe résonnaient dans cet espace vide. Au milieu de ses sanglots, la jeune psychologue bredouillait :

— Je n'ai rien fait. C'est pas ma faute...

Telle une chape de plomb, le silence pesa.

— Je suis Éva, articula la femme d'une voix forte et volontaire, cette fois.

Puis elle tourna les talons et disparut.

La lumière s'éteignit.

Les pas s'éloignèrent.

Elle était de nouveau seule.

Chapitre 23

Contre toute attente, le capitaine Hébrard les rejoignit lors de l'expertise de l'appartement d'Agathe Delcourt.

— Stéphane ? s'étonna Louis en le voyant apparaître sur le pas de la porte. Qu'est-ce que tu fais là ? Je pensais que tu devais faire des recherches au poste.

— Je les ai faites, répondit-il d'un air bonhomme. J'avais besoin de prendre l'air du large. Fontaine est sans arrêt sur mon dos, je ne sais pas ce qu'il a, en ce moment. Et puis j'avais envie de voir ce qu'il y a à se mettre sous la dent dans le Calvados, ajouta-t-il, grivois comme à son habitude.

— Ta petite secrétaire t'a lâché ? le taquina Ismaël.

— Je crois que nous n'irons pas plus loin, elle et moi. La différence d'âge, précisa-t-il alors que tout le monde savait qu'il essuyait échec sur échec avec les femmes ; l'âge n'avait rien à voir là-dedans.

— On fait le point ce soir à la maison, reprit plus sérieusement le lieutenant Salvant-Perret. Le graphologue vient d'arriver avec les photos des trois premières lettres pour comparer. On y va.

Dans la chambre de la jeune psychologue, il n'y

avait que des hommes, à part Maud Cortès qui, au milieu de toute cette testostérone, détonait bigrement avec ses manières pleines de délicatesse et sa voix douce.

— Faites attention à ça, c'est du Chanel N° 5, ça coûte très cher ! Il s'agirait de ne pas faire tomber le flacon.

— Cortès, laissez les gars faire leur travail, la reprit le capitaine, une main furtivement glissée dans le cou de la jeune femme.

— Si vous n'enlevez pas votre main de là, le prévint-elle, je vous attaque pour harcèlement. En plus, elle est glacée !

Bien sûr, elle plaisantait. Hébrard et Cortès s'entendaient à merveille, mais ils adoraient se chambrer dès que l'occasion se présentait.

— Petite nature, maugréa Hébrard en enserrant le cou de Maud un peu plus fort avant de retirer sa main, ce qui la fit frissonner.

Puis, s'adressant à l'un des techniciens qui répandait de la poudre sur chaque poignée de porte ou de meuble :

— Des empreintes ?

— Des tas. Mais je suppose que la plupart appartiennent à l'occupante de l'appartement. Vous êtes pressé ?

— Moi, non. Le procureur, oui. On a des cadavres en veux-tu en voilà depuis le mois dernier et maintenant un enlèvement. M'est avis que ça va être la goutte d'eau.

Louis, placé aux côtés du graphologue, ne perdait rien de ses déplacements ni de ses réflexions à voix haute. Ils avaient obtenu les résultats de l'analyse de l'encre utilisée sur les matelas et, effectuées en priorité, celles de l'encre sur le mur. Peu après, le graphologue concluait qu'il s'agissait très probablement du même auteur, car il y avait de nombreuses similitudes dans le tracé.

Le capitaine Hébrard, qui reçut le coup de fil concernant les résultats, annonça qu'il y avait correspondance. Il s'agissait du même marqueur qui avait été utilisé à la fois sous les matelas et sur le mur de la chambre. Agathe Delcourt avait bel et bien été enlevée par le coupable des multiples meurtres de ces dernières semaines. Il était à espérer que les techniciens trouveraient des traces du ravisseur quelque part dans l'appartement. Et il y en aurait pour de longs jours avant d'obtenir les résultats.

Alors que Louis semblait errer à travers l'appartement, passant d'une pièce à l'autre comme une âme en peine, Maud le rejoignit. Elle lui glissa à l'oreille :

— On va la retrouver, ne vous inquiétez pas.

— Je l'espère. Mais vu le sort qu'il réserve à ceux qui tombent entre ses griffes, je crains le pire. Les heures passent et plus on mettra de temps à la retrouver, plus il y aura de risques qu'il la tue.

— Selon toute vraisemblance, il a un compte à régler avec elle. S'il avait vraiment voulu la tuer, c'est un cadavre qu'on aurait eu ici à la place d'un graffiti. Je ne sais pas ce qu'il a en tête, mais je sens qu'il ne veut pas la tuer. Du moins, pas tout de suite. Il n'aurait pas perdu son temps à semer tous ces indices pour se débarrasser si rapidement de sa proie. Il va jouer avec elle comme il joue avec nous. Avec vous en particulier puisque c'est vous qui avez reçu le SMS. C'est le jeu du chat et de la souris. Et j'ai l'impression qu'il cherche à être attrapé.

— Oui, vous avez certainement raison. Mais dans ce cas, ça veut dire qu'il va la torturer. C'est une vengeance.

Il avait prononcé cette dernière phrase comme s'il venait à l'instant de réaliser la portée de ce que cela impliquait. En partant du principe qu'il y avait deux tueurs distincts — un ayant opéré en novembre 2000 et un autre entre novembre 2014 et mai 2015 —, Louis se demanda qui pouvait en vouloir à ce point à Claire Albert. Or, une jeune fille avait trouvé la mort à la place de l'aînée des Albert. Tout à coup, c'était comme si les nuages noirs qui obscurcissaient son ciel s'effilochaient pour laisser la place au soleil. C'était de ce côté-là qu'il fallait chercher.

— On s'en va, dit Louis de but en blanc, quittant l'appartement sans vérifier si les autres le suivaient.

Maud rameuta les troupes. Chacun dans son véhicule, ils se suivirent jusqu'à Deauville, dans la villa des Salvant-Perret, où Louis leur attribua une chambre.

Ismaël et Stéphane Hébrard connaissaient déjà les lieux. L'un pour y avoir été invité avec sa femme, l'autre pour y avoir séjourné en galante compagnie à plusieurs reprises. Maud découvrit la maison avec enchantement.

— Il y a un supermarché au sud-est de la ville, allez-y, je reste ici installer ce qu'il faut. Prenez de quoi dîner ce soir et déjeuner demain matin, il n'y a rien dans le réfrigérateur.

— Et un petit pinard ? suggéra le capitaine Hébrard.

— Je préfère la bière, objecta Ismaël.

— Faites au mieux, trancha Louis, trop préoccupé pour esquisser le moindre sourire aux tentatives de ses collègues pour détendre l'atmosphère.

À leur retour, Louis avait déposé des draps, des housses de couette propres ainsi que des serviettes de toilette sur chaque lit. La maison disposant de deux salles de bains, ils ne se bousculeraient pas trop le lendemain matin.

Après avoir pris leurs marques dans leurs chambres respectives, ils se retrouvèrent tous dans la cuisine pour la préparation du repas et le dressage de la table dans la salle à manger attenante. La discussion s'orienta tout de suite sur leur enquête. Au moins ici, pas d'oreilles indiscrètes, ils pouvaient parler librement. C'est ce que fit remarquer Maud, que la suspicion d'une taupe rendait très nerveuse.

– Je suis soulagée que vous abordiez le sujet, dit aussitôt le capitaine Hébrard lorsqu'il fut question d'une fuite. Dès qu'on a établi qu'il y avait eu un survivant en 2000, j'ai commencé à faire des recherches de mon côté, à réfléchir. Tu nous as exposé quatre affaires dont l'une est la raison d'être des trois autres. En l'occurrence, la première. Les lettres désignaient Claire Albert, c'est donc de ce côté qu'il fallait concentrer les recherches. Et quand j'ai commencé à fouiner et à faire marcher mes contacts ici et là, j'ai appris que je n'étais pas le seul à avoir posé des questions sur cette personne. Un autre flic s'était renseigné, et ce bien avant qu'on fasse le rapprochement entre les quatre familles.

Tout le monde était suspendu aux lèvres du capitaine Hébrard.

– Tu sais qui c'est ? demanda Louis d'une voix fébrile.

– Je n'ai pas de nom. Mais j'y travaille.

– Vous croyez que c'est forcément quelqu'un de

chez nous ? demanda Maud, la voix plaintive.

— Pas forcément, la rassura Ismaël. Rappelez-vous qu'il y a eu une équipe sur l'affaire en novembre 2000. Et les supérieurs de Stan et Fred sont forcément au courant de notre enquête puisqu'ils étaient les premiers sur les lieux pour la famille Aubry. La seule chose dont on soit sûr, c'est que le tueur a eu besoin d'une taupe pour découvrir l'identité actuelle de Claire Albert et qui sait quels renseignements encore.

— Agathe a commencé à recevoir des coups de fil anonymes il y a un moment déjà, dit Louis, dont le cerveau fonctionnait à plein régime. Mespouille m'avait donné le relevé de tous les appels masqués sur son portable et ça a commencé juste après les homicides de novembre de l'an dernier.

— Ce mec est un taré pour tuer des familles et des enfants juste pour se venger. Stéphane, tu as découvert qui est mort à la place de Claire Albert ?

Tout en discutant, le repas étant fini d'être cuisiné, ils s'assirent autour de la table et commencèrent à se servir. Les garçons avaient bien entendu choisi des charcuteries en guise d'entrées, tandis que Maud avait diététiquement opté pour une salade au saumon toute prête. Des pâtes à la sauce bolognaise suivaient ; plat simple à préparer qui tenait au ventre et que tout le monde appréciait.

— La fille s'appelait Éva Portal. Treize ans au moment des faits. J'ai mené mon enquête dès que j'ai eu connaissance de son identité. Ses parents sont décédés depuis quelques années. La mère est tombée en dépression à la suite de l'assassinat de sa fille et son père s'est mis à boire. Suicide de la mère en 2003, cancer généralisé du père deux ans plus tard.

Il a été emporté en quelques mois. Le seul qui reste, c'est un frère. Et tenez-vous bien : un frère jumeau !

— Et on a quoi sur lui ? questionna Louis, qui avait à peine touché à son jambon de pays.

Le capitaine Hébrard avala quelques rondelles de chorizo accompagnées d'une bonne tranche de pain beurré avant de répondre, l'air satisfait de quelqu'un qui est sûr de son fait.

— J'attendais que vous me le demandiez. Entre une sœur assassinée, une mère suicidée et un père alcoolique, autant vous dire que c'était pas gagné ! Le gamin a passé une bonne partie de son adolescence en hôpital psychiatrique.

— Comment s'appelle-t-il ? questionna Maud.

— William.

— Il souffrait de quel genre de trouble ? voulut savoir Ismaël.

— Il n'y a rien eu à faire, ils n'ont pas voulu me le dire : secret médical.

— On sait ce qu'il est devenu ?

— Il a quand même réussi à faire des études de droit tout en gagnant sa vie à la caisse d'un cinéma le soir et les *week-ends*. Après, chômage. Il touche le RSA.

— C'est lui ! s'écria Maud avec une sorte d'excitation apeurée. Ça ne peut être que lui ! Des jumeaux, ça a des liens qu'on ne peut pas comprendre. Si l'un des deux meurt, l'autre meurt un peu aussi. J'ai lu pas mal d'études sur le sujet, c'est absolument fascinant et assez flippant, il faut l'avouer.

— C'est vrai qu'il fait un coupable tout à fait plausible, dit Louis. On a son adresse ?

— C'est là que ça coince. Tout son courrier arrive

dans une boîte postale et il retire son argent mensuel directement au guichet. Il est interdit bancaire et ne possède pas de véhicule. S'il paie des factures d'électricité ou autres, il doit s'arranger pour le faire en liquide, parce que je n'ai rien trouvé et de nos jours, c'est quand même pas banal.

— Aucune trace de lui dans les foyers sociaux ?

— J'ai vérifié. Personne à ce nom. Mais ça ne veut rien dire. Il peut très bien utiliser un autre nom ou être inscrit dans un autre département, je n'ai fait que l'Île-de-France.

— Aucun bien du côté des parents ?

— Leur maison a été vendue quand le père est décédé.

— Les nouveaux propriétaires ?

— Un couple du nom de Babinet. Ils n'y viennent que durant l'été, c'est une maison secondaire pour eux. Faut dire qu'elle est située en pleine *pampa*, y'a rien à moins de dix kilomètres à la ronde.

— Il pourrait très bien y retourner sans que personne le sache, suggéra Louis.

— Et y retenir Agathe prisonnière, ajouta Maud.

— Tu as l'adresse exacte ?

Le capitaine fournit le renseignement à contrecœur. Il savait comment ça allait finir et la perspective d'une nuit blanche ne l'enchantait guère. Mais inexorablement, ce qu'il redoutait se produisit la seconde suivante :

— On y va ! lança Louis d'un ton décidé.

— Il nous faut des renforts, objecta Maud.

Les cours théoriques fraîchement en tête, elle avait toujours tendance à se montrer très à cheval sur les procédures. Sauf que dans certaines circonstances, on ne pouvait pas respecter les règles à la lettre.

— Si on appelle la cavalerie, la taupe risque fort d'être au courant de ce qui se passe et de prévenir le suspect, intervint le capitaine en soupirant.

— Je sais que ça ne plaît à personne, dit Louis, mais on va devoir agir seuls. Maud et Stéphane, vous n'êtes pas obligés de nous suivre. Vous pouvez rester là et si besoin, vous appelez les renforts.

— Cortès reste ici, rectifia Hébrard, moi, je viens avec vous. Ce gars m'a l'air bien dérangé, on ne sera pas trop de trois s'il est armé.

— Il ne s'est jamais servi d'une arme à feu, fit remarquer Ismaël. Son arme de prédilection, c'est le couteau. Soit pour reproduire fidèlement les premiers assassinats de 2000, soit par choix personnel. Mais on n'est pas à l'abri d'un fusil ou d'une arme de poing obtenue de façon illégale. Tu as regardé dans le fichier d'autorisation de détention d'armes ?

— Absolument rien à son nom, affirma le capitaine.

— Mouais, ça veut rien dire.

Puis, après une hésitation, Ismaël fit signe à Louis, qu'il entraîna un peu à l'écart des autres, discrètement. Il s'était levé, son assiette vide à la main pour l'apporter dans le lave-vaisselle. Louis le suivit :

— Il faut en parler à Amary, quoi que tu en penses, raisonna Ismaël. Non seulement on ne sera pas couverts s'il arrive une tuile, mais en plus, il pourra sûrement chercher de son côté d'où vient la fuite. Il a toujours été réglo, je ne vois pas pourquoi tout d'un coup, il trahirait son équipe. La fuite ne peut pas venir de lui, tu es bien d'accord ?

— La question n'est pas là. Si Amary est informé, il sera obligé de mettre en route le processus d'intervention.

— Laisse-moi lui parler, proposa Ismaël.

Louis parlementa encore quelques minutes, mais finit par accéder à la requête de son coéquipier, plutôt doué en diplomatie, il fallait le reconnaître. Si quelqu'un pouvait convaincre le commissaire Amary de les couvrir sur ce coup, c'était bien lui.

Pendant qu'Ismaël s'isolait dans une autre pièce afin de s'expliquer avec le commissaire, Louis rejoignit le capitaine Hébrard, déjà en train de vérifier le bon fonctionnement de son arme de service sur la table que Maud était en train de nettoyer d'un coup d'éponge, la mine soucieuse.

— Vérifiez bien que vos téléphones soient chargés, conseilla-t-elle. Il faut que je puisse vous joindre à tout moment, et inversement. En espérant que vous aurez du réseau. Si c'est aussi isolé que vous le dites...

— Arrête de t'en faire, la bleue, lui dit Hébrard avec sa bonhomie rassurante. C'est pas la première fois qu'on part coincer un méchant, ça va aller.

— Mais ce n'est pas pour vous que je m'inquiète, c'est pour cette malheureuse Agathe Delcourt !

— Oh ! se renfrogna l'officier. Moi qui pensais que j'aurais une chance si jamais tu devenais veuve. Tous mes espoirs s'évanouissent.

Maud lâcha un soupir exaspéré pendant qu'en silence, Louis s'asseyait à un coin de la table, s'assurant que la batterie de son portable était bien chargée, comme l'avait préconisé sa collègue. À contrecœur, il se saisit de son pistolet, dont il vérifia que la sécurité était bien enclenchée avant de le glisser de nouveau dans son *holster*. Il détestait avoir à se servir de son arme de service, même à l'entraînement. Malheureusement, lors de ce genre d'intervention, c'était un mal nécessaire.

– J'aimerais que vous fassiez quelque chose en mon absence, Cortès, dit Louis avec douceur.

– Tout ce que vous voudrez.

Il lui tendit un morceau de papier qu'il avait déchiré de son carnet :

– Téléphonez à ce numéro et demandez à parler à monsieur Dupontet. C'est le commissaire qui était sur l'affaire Albert en 2000. Il est à la retraite, mais peut-être pourra-t-il vous donner des renseignements supplémentaires sur le dénouement de cette enquête. Expliquez-lui ce qui se passe et voyez ce que vous pouvez tirer de lui. Ils devaient bien avoir des suspects à l'époque, de ceux que l'on n'interpelle pas, faute d'éléments probants.

– Je le ferai, assura Maud. Bonne chance.

Sans trop savoir pourquoi, en se levant, Louis l'embrassa sur la joue avant de disparaître avec les autres.

Chapitre 24

La voiture était repartie tout de suite après la visite de cette étrange femme. Des heures et des heures défilèrent encore, sans rien à boire ni à manger.

Son pantalon était à présent innommable, souillé à plusieurs reprises. Si on la retrouvait vivante, elle espérait ne pas être consciente tant elle mourrait de honte qu'on la découvre dans un tel état de déchéance. Sa propre odeur lui donnait envie de vomir. Au moins, ses compagnons de misère ne pouvaient pas être importunés par ces effluves, c'était déjà ça. Immobiles, muets, froids, ils étaient les témoins passifs de sa souffrance.

Elle n'avait rien dans le ventre depuis la veille au soir et la matinée devait être déjà bien entamée. Le souvenir de la *pizzeria* et de Lou, la serveuse qui l'avait si gentiment raccompagnée chez elle, lui revint en mémoire.

Comme cela lui paraissait loin ! Elle avait l'impression d'être enfermée dans cette cave depuis des mois. C'était comme si elle n'avait jamais rien connu d'autre et qu'il n'y aurait rien après.

Le visage de l'inconnue et ses paroles, n'arrêtaient pas de tourner dans sa tête, encore et encore.

Éva.

Ce prénom ne lui disait absolument rien.

Après l'assassinat de sa famille, on l'avait éloignée de tout ce qui lui avait été ordinaire jusqu'alors. Elle n'avait jamais su qui était mort à sa place. Certainement une amie de sa sœur, mais Mélissa et elle n'avaient jamais été proches. Elles étaient même comme chien et chat. Agathe – ou plutôt Claire – ne se préoccupait pas des fréquentations de Mélissa, et il en allait de même pour cette dernière. À l'époque, plus que sœurs, elles étaient surtout rivales. Combien elle avait regretté toutes ces petites chamailleries après la tragédie !

En toute logique, cette fameuse Éva devait être une des nombreuses copines de sa sœur. Malgré leur condition sociale, celle-ci était très populaire, contrairement à elle, qui était plutôt d'un caractère introverti. À l'époque, à part Céline, cette amie chez qui elle avait passé la nuit en novembre 2000 et qu'elle n'avait jamais revue par la suite, elle ne fréquentait pas grand monde en dehors du lycée. Et elle aurait eu honte d'inviter qui que ce soit dans le taudis qu'était leur maison.

Elle s'était bien promis de ne jamais ressembler à sa mère, d'avoir un intérieur irréprochable et surtout, si un jour elle avait des enfants, d'avoir les moyens de leur offrir une vie meilleure que celle à laquelle elle avait eu droit.

Mais comment était-il possible que cette fameuse Éva fût sa geôlière puisqu'elle était morte quinze ans plus tôt ? Tout comme sa famille, dont les pantins macabres lui tenaient compagnie. Agathe ne croyait pas aux fantômes et la femme qui lui avait rendu visite tout à l'heure était bien réelle, aucun doute là-dessus. Son parfum sucré flottait encore dans l'air, mêlé à toute la puanteur ambiante.

Quelque chose l'avait gênée dans l'apparence de cette inconnue, mais elle n'arrivait pas à définir ce que c'était exactement. La sensation d'un manque de naturel, si tant est que la situation fût propice à une attitude normale. Éva avait l'air d'en faire trop, comme un acteur qui surjoue. Trop de maquillage, trop de poses, trop de mélodrame dans sa voix. On aurait dit un travesti.

Oui... c'était bien ça.

Il y eut comme un déclic dans la tête d'Agathe, qui comprit qu'elle avait eu affaire à un homme travesti. Même si l'ensemble paraissait convaincant au premier abord, la position des jambes manquait de féminité, le timbre de la voix avait une sonorité grave malgré les efforts évidents pour l'adoucir. Mais avec l'émotion, il était difficile de tenir longtemps et Agathe aurait dû se rendre compte du subterfuge. Elle ne se rappelait pas avoir distingué la pomme d'Adam, mais cela pouvait s'expliquer car elle avait délibérément évité de trop poser son regard sur l'individu en face d'elle.

Elle en était certaine à présent : celui qui se faisait appeler Éva était un homme.

Restait à savoir qui il était et pourquoi il se faisait passer pour cette fille, morte des années auparavant. Quelqu'un qui avait été très proche d'elle, évidemment. Qui souffrait encore de sa disparition brutale. Mais surtout, quelqu'un de dérangé, de profondément malade et dangereux. Quelqu'un ayant développé une psychose dont elle était l'objet.

Le cas de ce forcené relevait de la psychiatrie. Ce n'était pas simplement un phénomène lié à une homosexualité frustrée. C'était plutôt un dédoublement de personnalité, ce qu'il était convenu d'appeler un trouble dissociatif de l'identité, sans doute provoqué par la mort d'Éva, dont il s'était approprié la personnalité et le sexe. Mais quel lien existait-il entre eux ?

Étant donné l'âge qu'elle lui donnait, Agathe repoussa l'idée qu'il puisse s'agir d'un petit ami. Elle pencha plutôt pour un frère. Et celui-ci l'avait jugée responsable de la mort de la jeune fille, alors qu'elle aussi avait perdu tous les siens cette nuit-là. Elle aussi avait perdu un frère auquel elle était très attachée. Mais elle ne s'était pas mise à assassiner des gens par vengeance ! Elle ne comprenait même pas comment on pouvait en venir à de telles extrémités après avoir vécu la perte d'un proche d'une manière aussi atroce. Cela la dépassait.

Il fallait qu'elle trouve un moyen de raisonner cet homme maintenant qu'elle l'avait cerné. Après tout, elle avait des années d'études en psychologie derrière elle, et quelques autres de pratique dans différents services.

Malgré tout, ce qu'elle savait des troubles de la personnalité multiple ne collait pas avec la simple perte d'un proche. Généralement, ces cas découlaient de traumatismes, souvent d'ordre sexuel, subis durant la petite enfance de façon récurrente. L'apparition d'une personne *autre* sert à protéger l'individu victime de sévices, à le mettre en retrait par rapport à la gravité des violences endurées.

Son persécuteur avait-il vécu ce genre de cauchemar ? Ou son désordre mental était-il lié au traumatisme causé par la perte de sa sœur ? Dans ce cas, leur attachement devait être exceptionnel.

L'homme éprouvait-il alors des sentiments répréhensibles par la morale envers sa sœur ? Dans ce cas, il ne ressentirait pas le besoin de devenir *elle.*

Des jumeaux !

C'était la seule explication tangible pouvant justifier le développement d'une dissociation de l'identité chez cet individu. De cette façon, il ne la perdait pas vraiment. Sa sœur continuait de vivre à travers lui. Et qui sait ce que l'esprit de la défunte lui susurrait à l'oreille ? Elle devait réclamer vengeance et il était sans doute plus facile de retrouver Agathe que le monstre réellement responsable des assassinats d'Éva et de sa famille à elle. Il était aussi bien plus commode de s'en prendre à une femme seule qu'à un homme probablement dans la force de l'âge quand on était bâti comme cet inconnu au physique androgyne.

Il fallait qu'elle se sorte de là. Elle n'était en aucune façon responsable de ce qui était arrivé cette nuit-là. Les journaux avaient parlé de toute une famille égorgée ; ce n'était pas elle qui tenait le couteau. C'est Mélissa qui avait invité cette fille à dormir chez eux, c'était à elle qu'il fallait s'en prendre. Mais évidemment, elle n'était plus de ce monde depuis longtemps et elle s'en voulut de déplacer la faute sur sa pauvre sœur défunte.

Son esprit divaguait. Elle cherchait des responsables afin de se disculper elle-même, mais au fond, elle s'était toujours sentie coupable. Peut-être qu'elle méritait ce qui lui arrivait.

Tandis que tout son être était au supplice, la lumière se mit à décliner. Elle allait donc passer une autre nuit ici, seule, misérable, condamnée à mourir dans ce trou à rat, enchaînée à des mannequins.

Chapitre 25

Le coup de téléphone d'Ismaël laissa le commissaire Amary dubitatif pendant quelques minutes. Mais cela ne dura pas. Une taupe dans les rangs ? Cela n'allait pas se passer comme ça !

Selon le raisonnement du lieutenant Al Bakir, seul un officier pouvait avoir renseigné le tueur des trois dernières séries d'homicides au sujet de la nouvelle identité de Claire Albert.

Il regarda l'heure sur l'écran de son ordinateur : vingt heures trente. Dans le deuxième tiroir de son bureau, il avait rangé le dossier rassemblant les affaires de meurtres des quatre familles. Profitant du calme relatif lié à l'heure tardive, il se replongea dans celui des Albert, en novembre 2000, chercha tout ce qui concernait Claire Albert, absente au moment des faits.

À l'époque, on ne s'était pas rendu compte tout de suite que le corps gisant en dehors du cercle formé par le reste des membres de la famille n'était pas celui de l'aînée. Pourtant, le fait que le cadavre était à distance des autres était significatif en soi. Mais qui pouvait dire ce qui se passait dans l'esprit d'un assassin ? Était-ce un acte délibéré de l'écarter des autres ou un pur fruit du hasard ? Étant donné l'état du visage de cette pauvre fille, le commissaire Dupontet et son groupe n'avaient pas été en mesure d'affirmer qu'il s'agissait de la même personne que celle posant sur une photographie retrouvée par terre, froissée, près du corps mutilé.

Ce n'est que le lendemain que l'identité de la jeune fille avait été révélée, lorsque la mère d'Éva Portal était venue la chercher au domicile des Albert et que la police l'avait accueillie. La pauvre femme, ivre de douleur, avait été prise en charge immédiatement par les services d'urgence médicale appelés sur place après qu'elle eut fait un malaise.

Il avait été un peu plus compliqué de savoir où était Claire Albert mais, dans la chambre commune à Mélissa et à sa sœur aînée, ils avaient trouvé son journal intime, où un seul nom figurait à plusieurs reprises en dehors de ceux de ses proches : Céline Desclos, chez qui elle allait dormir assez souvent. On avait envoyé une voiture de police ainsi qu'un éducateur des services sociaux pour la prendre en charge. Il était juste spécifié qu'elle avait été envoyée au centre psychiatrique spécialisé de Cadillac, en Gironde, très loin du lieu de la tragédie. Et ce afin de la protéger puisqu'il s'était avéré rapidement qu'il s'agissait d'un multiple homicide dont le coupable était dans la nature. La presse n'avait jamais eu accès à ces dernières informations. Pour le grand public, Claire Albert était décédée avec les autres membres de sa famille et les Portal, qui venaient de perdre leur fille, avaient été tenus au secret. De toute façon, ils avaient été tellement anéantis par cette perte qu'ils avaient sombré dans une hébétude morbide, refusant d'être pris en main par les services d'aide aux victimes.

On perdait ensuite la trace administrative de Claire Albert puisqu'elle avait été officiellement déclarée morte. Alors comment avait-on procédé pour lui obtenir une nouvelle identité ?

Elle était mineure au moment des faits, et comme il ne lui restait plus aucun parent, il fallait bien qu'un adulte se fût chargé des démarches auprès des services du garde des Sceaux. Mais il lui paraissait très peu probable que la voie légale eût été suivie étant donné la dangerosité de la situation.

Après un long moment le nez plongé dans ce dossier épineux, Antoine Amary décida de contacter le lieutenant Cortès. Il savait de la bouche d'Ismaël qu'elle était restée à Deauville sous les recommandations de Salvant-Perret, toujours prompt à épargner les interventions sur le terrain au lieutenant stagiaire, on ne savait pas trop pourquoi.

Il se doutait bien que le prince du central lui aurait donné des directives pendant leur absence et il ne fut pas déçu : elle avait réussi à joindre le commissaire Dupontet, à la retraite depuis quelques années, et avait glané pas mal d'informations qui ne figuraient nulle part dans le dossier.

— Le cas de Claire Albert était très particulier, expliqua Maud Cortès. Le tueur qui s'en était pris à sa famille pouvait parfaitement se mettre à la traquer jusqu'à ce qu'il ait fini le travail. À cause des coups de pied au visage qu'Éva avait reçus, ils en ont déduit que l'assassin devait être furieux quand il s'est rendu compte de sa méprise et qu'il ferait tout pour retrouver celle qui manquait à son tableau de chasse. Par conséquent, il fallait qu'elle disparaisse de la circulation. En suivant les démarches légales, il fallait passer par un officier de l'état civil et toutes les informations la concernant — ancien patronyme, nouveau, adresse, date de naissance, etc. — auraient été visibles dans le Journal officiel. Le procureur a jugé que c'était trop dangereux. N'importe qui, armé de patience, peut retrouver le J.O. où figure le changement.

— Qu'ont-ils décidé de faire, alors ? la pressa Amary.

— Ils lui ont obtenu des vrais-faux papiers avec l'aide d'un ami du commissaire Dupontet, membre de la DST à l'époque. Tout s'est fait dans la clandestinité. Rien d'officiel, pas de trace. Claire Albert a été déclarée morte la même nuit que le reste de sa famille et on a inventé une enfance d'orpheline à Agathe Delcourt.

— Avec l'aval du procureur ? s'étonna Amary.

— D'après Dupontet, tout aurait été beaucoup plus facile si en France, on avait un système de protection judiciaire comme aux États-Unis.

— Il faut reconnaître que la gamine était dans une situation assez inédite et délicate, approuva le commissaire.

— Oui, et à situation exceptionnelle, mesures exceptionnelles, renchérit Maud Cortès. C'est donc quelqu'un de la DST qui s'est chargé des formalités, si j'ose m'exprimer ainsi.

— Autrement dit, on entre dans le monde merveilleux du secret-défense, traduisit Amary à sa façon. Si la fuite vient de chez eux, ça va être difficile de remonter jusqu'à la taupe. À moins que ce soit notre commissaire à la retraite qui ait lâché le morceau moyennant finance, histoire d'égayer ses vieux jours.

— William Portal est au RSA, je ne vois pas

comment il pourrait se permettre de payer ce genre de renseignement auprès d'un ancien officier de police judiciaire ! J'opterais plutôt pour une opération de chantage de sa part. Mais de la façon dont Dupontet s'est confié, je suis quasiment certaine qu'il n'a parlé à personne d'autre de cette affaire et qu'il n'est victime d'aucun chantage. Il a même continué à mener sa propre enquête après son départ à la retraite et il pense avoir retrouvé l'assassin de la famille Albert.

– Vraiment ? Expliquez-moi ça, Cortès.

– Eh bien, c'est tout à fait officieux, mais il y a quelques années de ça, Dupontet est tombé sur un fait divers dans un journal local qui faisait mention d'un accident de la route entre un semi-remorque et une voiture que le propriétaire s'était fait voler la veille du drame. Le conducteur était un homme inconnu qui n'a jamais été identifié. Ça s'est produit à deux ou trois kilomètres du domicile des Albert, la nuit de leur assassinat, et personne n'a fait le rapprochement parce que l'enquête a changé de main quand Dupontet est parti à la retraite. Et le dossier avait été classé comme affaire non élucidée, faute de suspect.

Le commissaire avait quitté son fauteuil de bureau pour aller se préparer un café tout en écoutant le récit passionnant du lieutenant Cortès, qui continua :

– Bref, l'ex-commissaire a fait des pieds et des mains pour retrouver qui s'était occupé du corps de l'accidenté et d'après lui, les chaussures qu'il portait correspondaient avec celles qui avaient défoncé le visage de la présumée Claire Albert.

– Comment a-t-il fait pour comparer les

chaussures ? Il n'a tout de même pas exhumé le corps !

— Vous savez comme moi qu'il faut des autorisations à n'en plus finir pour ça, commissaire. Non, il a fait appel à l'entreprise de pompes funèbres. Après un accident pareil, les vêtements des victimes sont en lambeaux, on les lui avait retirés. Mais avant ça, il y avait eu des photos de l'accident et du corps auxquelles Dupontet a pu avoir accès. C'est ainsi qu'il a été capable de comparer les empreintes de semelle incrustées sur le visage de la malheureuse Éva Portal avec celles des chaussures de l'accidenté. Afin d'en avoir le cœur net, il s'est adressé à un expert de sa connaissance encore en fonction, et son analyse a démontré qu'il s'agissait bien des mêmes chaussures. Mais ça ne l'avançait pas à grand-chose puisque non seulement il était à la retraite, mais en plus, le dossier était classé depuis longtemps. Même s'il n'y a pas prescription pour les homicides.

— Il n'a donc jamais réussi à découvrir l'identité du tueur.

Ce n'était pas une question, plutôt un constat.

— Malheureusement, non. Mais en tout cas, ça veut dire que l'assassin de la famille d'Agathe est mort depuis longtemps. Quant à ses motivations, elles demeureront toujours un mystère. Mais il y a un détail qui m'a frappée.

— Allez-y, Cortès. Je suis tout ouïe.

— Sur la scène de crime, il y avait des détritus partout, comme si on avait volontairement vidé la poubelle sur les corps.

Amary feuilleta son dossier, son téléphone coincé entre son épaule et sa joue, à la recherche des photos de la scène de crime en question. En effet, sur les clichés, il vit que le sol était jonché de matières plus ou moins identifiables. Il parcourut les lignes des rapports qui forcément devaient faire état de la présence des déchets. Il n'y avait pas prêté attention, mais Amary finit par trouver le passage où l'un des lieutenants présents décrivait la pièce en précisant que la poubelle avait été renversée, son contenu disposé sur et autour des cadavres.

– Je n'avais pas relevé ce détail, reconnut le commissaire. S'il s'agit bien de l'assassin des Albert qui est mort dans cet accident, on ne saura jamais quelle psychose l'a poussé à commettre tous ces meurtres. Et cela ne nous renseigne pas davantage sur la personne qui a pu informer le tueur des trois autres familles au sujet de la nouvelle identité de Claire Albert.

– Ben, on sait déjà que ça peut pas venir de quelqu'un de chez nous. Je veux dire, puisque c'est la DST qui a été impliquée, ça vient peut-être de chez eux.

Rien n'était moins sûr, mais c'était éventuellement une piste à suivre. Même si cela n'arrangeait pas les affaires d'Amary. Autant mettre le nez dans un nid de frelons ! se disait-il. Le bon côté de la chose, c'est que la plupart des hommes de la DST étaient des anciens membres des forces de l'ordre – tout comme c'est le cas pour la DGSI à l'heure actuelle – et le commissaire avait quelques connaissances parmi eux.

Il avait le choix entre deux contacts : Jean-Louis Vallès ou Bernard Lamothe. Finalement, il opta pour ce dernier, avec qui il avait travaillé pendant une bonne dizaine d'années au début de sa carrière.

Il remercia un peu vertement le lieutenant Cortès,

l'esprit déjà tourné vers son prochain coup de fil, puis rouvrit le dossier Albert. Le procureur chargé à l'époque de cette affaire était un dénommé François Montagnier, ce qui ne l'avançait guère, car il n'avait jamais eu affaire à lui. De plus, après quelques recherches, il apprit que le magistrat n'était plus en fonction depuis trois ans et qu'il vivait dans le sud de l'Espagne où il coulait une retraite paisible avec sa femme. Décidément, tous les acteurs de cette enquête avaient pris le large.

Cela faisait pas mal de temps que Bernard Lamothe et Antoine Amary ne s'étaient pas revus, mais lorsqu'ils eurent échangé les premiers mots au téléphone, ce fut comme s'ils s'étaient quittés la veille. Leur complicité de l'époque revint comme par magie, les souvenirs qu'ils évoquèrent ne manquèrent pas de les faire rire comme au bon vieux temps. Il y a des gens avec qui ni la distance ni les années n'ont d'emprise sur les sentiments qui vous lient à eux. Il en allait ainsi entre les deux hommes.

— Tu as besoin de quoi ? finit par demander Bernard Lamothe.

— Un nom. Ça concerne une affaire qui date de novembre 2000.

Le commissaire Amary résuma la tragédie en quelques phrases, puis expliqua qu'un gars de la DST s'était chargé de mettre Claire Albert en sécurité en lui fournissant de faux papiers. Il voulait savoir, très officieusement, de qui il s'agissait.

Évidemment, son ancien collègue demanda pour quelle raison il lui fallait l'identité de cet agent. Amary lui fit alors part de ses soupçons à propos d'une fuite qui aurait mené un autre tueur sur la piste de Claire Albert.

— Ben dis donc, vous vous ennuyez pas, chez vous ! plaisanta Bernard Lamothe. Tu sais que même si je te trouve le gars qui était sur l'affaire, ça va pas être simple d'enquêter sur lui comme ça ?

— Je ne t'en demande pas tant, le rassura Amary. Trouve-moi déjà le type en question, ce sera un grand pas de fait.

— Et je gagne quoi en échange ?

— Tu veux pas une bouffe au Fouquet's, quand même !

— Le Ritz suffira, plaisanta Lamothe. Je te recontacte le plus vite possible.

Le commissaire Amary était sûr de pouvoir compter sur son ancien collègue, il dénicherait rapidement l'oiseau qu'il cherchait. Quant à savoir si ce dernier avait pu révéler l'identité d'Agathe Delcourt, c'était une autre paire de manches. Il devrait enquêter sur un enquêteur…

Pour cela, il devrait faire appel à un autre homme, Benoît Pallas, spécialiste en informatique, afin qu'il jette un œil sur les *emails* et les relevés téléphoniques de la personne dont Lamothe lui donnerait le nom. En attendant, il jugea que le commissaire Dupontet, malgré la bonne impression qu'il avait laissée à Cortès, pouvait très bien être l'informateur qu'ils recherchaient. Il donna des directives au technicien à ce sujet :

— Tu me passes la vie de ce type au peigne fin et tiens-toi prêt à faire la même chose pour un autre gars de la maison dans pas longtemps.

Ce qui plaisait avant tout au commissaire Amary chez Benoît Pallas, c'est qu'il ne posait jamais de questions. Et, cerise sur le gâteau, lorsqu'il était sur une piste, il était pire qu'un limier sur les traces d'un gibier. Il ne lâchait rien, retournait la vie des pauvres gens qu'on lui demandait de mettre à jour jusqu'aux zones les plus obscures de leur passé. Et pour ne rien gâcher, il ne comptait pas ses heures. Une qualité très appréciée par l'officier de police.

Dans le cas présent, Amary donna pour consignes de voir si l'ancien commissaire avait reçu des coups de fil suspects, des appels masqués à répétition, des mouvements de fonds anormaux sur ses comptes en banque, ou s'il avait un quelconque lien avec un certain William Portal.

— D'ailleurs, tant que tu y es, fais des recherches sur celui-ci aussi. Mes gars n'ont pas trouvé grand-chose à part l'adresse de ses défunts parents. J'aimerais tellement savoir où il se terre ! Regarde dans les foyers pour SDF et dans les listes des Restos du Cœur. Le type est au RSA, je suppose qu'il ne doit pas avoir de quoi aller au supermarché une fois par semaine et on n'a aucun antécédent, il est *clean*. Par contre, comme il a fait un long séjour en hôpital psychiatrique, regarde du côté des thérapeutes, il est peut-être suivi. Vois s'il n'est pas sous traitement, on pourrait éventuellement le coincer à sa pharmacie habituelle.

Benoît Pallas émettait quelques sons gutturaux en guise d'assentiment aux directives d'Amary. Cela signifiait qu'il était déjà en train d'ouvrir une multitude de fenêtres de recherche sur ses différents écrans.

Lorsqu'il fut clair que le commissaire en avait terminé avec lui, le technicien se contenta d'articuler un « je suis dessus » avant de couper la communication.

Antoine Amary soupira longuement, se calant

dans son fauteuil, la tête renversée contre le dossier moelleux. Les chiens étaient lâchés : son équipe s'était lancée dans le sauvetage d'Agathe Delcourt, Bernard Lamothe était sur la piste de l'agent de l'ex-DST, et Benoît Pallas sur celles de Dupontet et de William Portal.

Malheureusement, en matière de taupe, le policier avait beau retourner ça dans tous les sens, les possibilités étaient nombreuses, les suspects potentiels pullulaient. Car même si le changement d'identité de Claire Albert s'était effectué dans la clandestinité, il restait néanmoins bon nombre de gens ayant eu vent de la chose. À commencer par la personne qui avait fourni les faux papiers en question ; sans compter les intermédiaires que cela présupposait, les officiers de police judiciaire impliqués dans cette affaire au même titre que le commissaire Dupontet ; et l'amie de Claire Albert, chez qui celle-ci avait passé la nuit du drame, ainsi que les parents de cette camarade.

Ils n'avaient pas cherché de ce côté-là. Or, en y réfléchissant, la famille qui avait en quelque sorte sauvé la vie de Claire Albert savait qu'elle n'avait pas péri avec le reste des siens. Quel était le nom de cette gamine, déjà ?

Amary feuilleta le dossier encore une fois, finit par tomber sur ce qu'il cherchait : Céline Desclos. Les deux jeunes filles étaient-elles restées en contact après les assassinats ? Ça valait peut-être le coup d'approfondir la question. Tant qu'à se servir des talents de Benoît Pallas, autant y aller à fond ! Il lui envoya un *mail* lui demandant de prendre des renseignements sur Céline Desclos en plus des deux autres. Le message retour fut un « OK » laconique.

Étant donné l'ampleur de la tâche, Amary ne comptait pas obtenir des résultats avant le lendemain, car même si Pallas était performant, il n'allait pas passer une nuit blanche derrière ses écrans simplement pour lui faire plaisir.

Chapitre 26

L'ancienne maison de la famille Portal ne pouvait pas être plus isolée. Perdue au beau milieu d'une forêt, on y accédait par un chemin de terre que même le GPS ne connaissait pas. Ils étaient passés devant trois fois sans le voir avant de le repérer enfin, sur un grand cri du capitaine, qui aperçut des traces de pneus conséquentes à un endroit précis de la petite route qu'ils sillonnaient à la lisière de ce fameux bois. Comme il faisait nuit, Hébrard était dangereusement penché à la portière, sa lampe de poche balayant le sol. C'est ainsi qu'il les dirigea vers la bonne voie.

La bâtisse paraissait assez grande, de plain-pied, avec des tuiles d'ardoise et une parabole fixée sur l'aile droite de la maison. Pas de garage, aucune voiture en vue ni à l'avant ni à l'arrière. Aucune lumière ne filtrait à travers les persiennes. Ils firent le tour au ralenti avec leur véhicule, inspectant les alentours à la recherche du moindre signe de vie, mais apparemment, il n'y avait personne.

Louis se gara sous les arbres. Silencieusement, les trois hommes se préparèrent à sortir, après que Salvant-Perret eut envoyé un SMS à Maud pour la prévenir qu'ils étaient sur les lieux. La jeune femme se garda bien de répondre, attendant à la villa la suite des opérations.

Chacun prit soin de ne pas faire de bruit en refermant sa portière, les armes furent dégainées. D'un coup d'œil entendu, ils se séparèrent. Le capitaine Hébrard emprunta le côté gauche, Ismaël celui de droite, tandis que Louis inspectait le devant de la maison. Tous les volets étaient clos et l'accumulation de feuilles mortes sur les marches suggérait qu'il n'y avait pas beaucoup d'allées et venues sur les lieux.

En revanche, le pas de la porte semblait plus dégagé que le reste. Quelqu'un était entré récemment. Par ailleurs, des traces de pneus étaient visibles sur le chemin de terre qu'ils avaient emprunté, fraîches, et menaient aux abords de la maison. Avec la pluie de ces derniers jours, difficile de passer à côté.

S'éloignant de l'entrée, Louis repéra des fenêtres au ras du sol, équipées de barreaux de fer. Il avait beau faire attention, ses pas crissaient sur le gravier qui tapissait tout le pourtour de la bâtisse. Il se rapprocha de l'une des fenêtres, s'agenouilla, plaqua ses deux mains autour de son visage contre la vitre pour tenter d'apercevoir quelque chose. Mais le verre était couvert de poussière à l'intérieur comme à l'extérieur, et la nuit n'arrangeait rien.

Si par chance, Agathe se trouvait là, il lui était impossible de la voir. En revanche, il pouvait peut-être se faire entendre d'elle, en espérant que son ravisseur ne se trouve pas dans les parages. Cela dit, il en doutait, car c'était inenvisageable de se rendre en ce lieu éloigné de tout sans véhicule. Il se mit donc à frapper contre cette vitre à l'aide de son majeur replié. Doucement d'abord, regardant de nouveau à l'intérieur pour voir s'il y avait du mouvement, puis plus fort, renouvelant la même opération, l'oreille tendue. À défaut de distinguer quoi que ce soit avec ses yeux, il espérait entendre une plainte, un raclement de meuble, quelque chose.

Elle était peut-être inconsciente, ou pire. Ou bien ils s'étaient trompés et elle n'était pas là.

Il sentit du mouvement sur son côté droit en même temps qu'un son différent des autres se faisait entendre faiblement. Louis fit signe au capitaine Hébrard, qui l'avait rejoint, de stopper afin de mieux écouter. L'homme s'arrêta net. Le bruit se renouvela, plus distinct cette fois. Et c'est bien une voix de femme qu'il entendit.

Elle était là, dans cette cave ! Ismaël apparut à son tour et tous les trois entendirent nettement une voix qui criait :

— Ici ! Je suis là !

Ensemble, ils foncèrent en direction de la porte d'entrée.

— Je fais le tour, j'ai vu une issue qui donne derrière, annonça Ismaël en courant. On ne sait jamais.

Le lieutenant Salvant-Perret et son chef de groupe se retrouvèrent devant la porte verrouillée, qu'il fallait ouvrir.

— Bouge pas, mon bon prince, je reviens.

Malgré son surpoids, Hébrard disparut quelques secondes et revint en un temps record, armé d'un bélier à frapper qu'il balança avec force, laissant la voie libre à Louis, qui s'engouffra à l'intérieur, arme au poing, faisceau de sa lampe dirigé droit devant lui.

C'est alors que l'on entendit une déflagration qui assourdit le capitaine en même temps qu'elle l'aveugla. Il fut projeté en arrière, se retrouvant sur les fesses dans le gravier, complètement sonné, mais vivant.

— Putain de merde ! jura-t-il en se relevant péniblement.

Il voyait des papillons, ses oreilles bourdonnaient. Rapidement, il vérifia qu'il avait encore tous ses membres. Du sang maculait son visage, il avait reçu un morceau d'explosif à la tempe, mais ça n'avait pas l'air bien grave, il ne sentait même pas la blessure tant la poussée d'adrénaline était forte. Tout ce qu'il avait à l'esprit, c'était Salvant-Perret, dont on ne distinguait plus la silhouette à travers la fumée et la poussière.

Il appela les secours et une unité de déminage dès qu'il eut repris ses sens. C'est alors qu'Ismaël apparut sur le pas de la porte, Louis sur ses épaules. Le lieutenant était inconscient, son blouson était déchiqueté du côté de son bras droit, qui dégoulinait de sang.

— J'ai appelé du renfort et les secours, annonça le capitaine. Occupez-vous de Salvant-Perret, je file au bout du chemin les attendre pour ne pas qu'ils le loupent. On aura les démineurs. Si ça se trouve, cette foutue baraque est bourrée d'explosifs.

Alors que le capitaine Hébrard galopait en direction de la route, Louis, allongé en position latérale de sécurité, sembla revenir à lui. Ismaël lui conseilla de ne pas faire de mouvements inconsidérés, il lui avait fait un point de compression à l'endroit où Louis était touché et s'était servi de sa ceinture pour empêcher le sang de s'écouler. Mais ils ignoraient s'il avait d'autres blessures moins visibles, mieux valait ne pas bouger jusqu'à l'arrivée des secours.

— Agathe, fit-il faiblement, comme s'il peinait à respirer.

— Elle ne risque rien, je pense. On l'a entendue, on va la sortir de là, t'inquiète pas.

— Fais-lui savoir qu'on est là, reprit Louis.

— OK.

Ismaël couvrit le haut du corps de son collègue avec son propre blouson, puis se dirigea vers le soupirail, dont il brisa la vitre à l'aide de la crosse de son arme.

— Mademoiselle Delcourt ? appela-t-il.

— Oui, oui ! lui répondit une voix remplie de désespoir. Qu'est-ce que c'était ? Pourquoi ça a explosé ?

— Tout va bien, on va venir vous sortir de là, n'ayez pas peur, la rassura Ismaël. Pouvez-vous me dire si une arme quelconque est pointée sur vous ? Voyez-vous une minuterie ou entendez-vous un cliquettement régulier ?

— Non... Non, rien de tout ça.

— Êtes-vous assise sur une chaise ? Y a-t-il des fils électriques autour de vous ?

— Non. Je suis assise par terre.

L'affolement avait gagné la captive à l'aube de sa délivrance.

— C'était une bombe ? demanda-t-elle encore.

Tout en essayant d'enrayer la panique qui montait chez Agathe Delcourt, Ismaël éclaira la cave à l'aide de sa lampe torche, qu'il promena partout. Il vit la jeune femme effectivement assise par terre, ses jambes recroquevillées sous elle. Ses cheveux cachaient son visage, mais elle n'avait pas l'air d'être blessée. Elle était attachée les mains dans le dos et le lieutenant distingua des mannequins de différentes tailles, vêtus de ce qui semblait être des pyjamas, en cercle au milieu de la pièce, tous reliés par des liens que l'on avait fixés au sol.

Ismaël lui demanda si elle allait bien, si aucun mal ne lui avait été fait. Comme elle répondait par la négative, il lui expliqua ce qui venait de se passer et ce qui allait suivre avec l'arrivée d'une équipe de déminage, des renforts policiers et des secours d'urgence médicale. Puis, alors que le faisceau de la lampe s'éteignait, Agathe poussa un petit cri d'angoisse :

— Ne me laissez pas toute seule, je vous en prie...

Elle se mit à pleurer, mais Ismaël ne pouvait pas rester auprès d'elle indéfiniment. Il lui parla doucement, lui expliqua que son collègue avait besoin de lui le temps que les secours arrivent, qu'elle allait être délivrée le plus vite possible.

Il l'abandonna donc à son triste sort et découvrit Louis en train d'essayer de se mettre debout. Il l'en empêcha avec autorité :

— Hep ! Reste tranquille, petit prince. De toute façon, on ne fera rien de plus tant que les renforts ne sont pas arrivés.

— Comment va-t-elle ? s'enquit le lieutenant Salvant-Perret.

— Elle flippe, mais elle n'est pas blessée, apparemment.

Ismaël décrivit ce qu'il avait vu dans cette cave. Louis fit tout de suite le rapprochement avec la scène de crime de novembre 2000, dont il avait étudié chaque photo en détail.

— J'espère qu'il ne l'a pas assise sur une bombe, fit-il sans aucune trace d'humour dans la voix.

— Non, elle est par terre et à première vue, il n'y a rien qui présente un danger. J'ai pas pu voir le mur du côté du soupirail évidemment, mais le reste est complètement vide à part les mannequins et Agathe.

— Je m'y attendais pas, à celle-là, fulminait Louis, en colère contre lui-même d'être entré dans cette maison sans se méfier.

— Rien ne laissait supposer ce genre de mauvaise surprise, relativisa Ismaël. Tu devrais te calmer, t'es blanc comme un linge. Tu fais chier !

— Quoi, je fais chier ? le reprit Louis sans comprendre.

— Tu vas être bon pour un séjour à l'hôpital. Du coup, ça fout en l'air ma soirée.

— Ça fout en l'air rien du tout ! Il est hors de question que je traîne mes guêtres dans un hôpital, la nourriture y est exécrable !

— Tu vas avoir besoin de points, si tu veux mon avis.

— C'est rien, assura Louis en essayant de bouger son bras.

Mais la grimace qui déforma les traits de son visage démentait ses allégations et il dut s'avouer vaincu lorsque deux ambulances arrivèrent, l'embarquant dans l'une d'entre elles afin que les urgentistes effectuent les premiers soins.

Le capitaine Hébrard vint lui rendre une courte visite dans le véhicule pour s'assurer qu'il allait bien. Puis il repartit assister de loin à l'intervention de l'équipe de déminage. Il sembla à Louis que cela prit des heures avant qu'il n'aperçoive enfin le brancard où Agathe avait été allongée, saine et sauve. Pendant les longues minutes qui avaient précédé sa délivrance, il s'était attendu à tout moment à entendre une nouvelle déflagration. Mais rien ne se produisit ; seule la porte d'entrée avait été piégée.

Il fut surpris de se réveiller dans une chambre d'hôpital. Il avait dû perdre connaissance dans l'ambulance parce qu'il ne se souvenait de rien en dehors des portes du véhicule de secours qui se refermaient alors qu'Agathe lui faisait un petit signe de la main depuis la civière où on l'avait installée. Après, le trou noir.

Son bras droit était soigneusement bandé au niveau du biceps, il avait la tête comme dans du coton.

Quelle heure pouvait-il bien être ?

On était sans doute au milieu de la nuit parce que les volets roulants étaient fermés aux trois quarts et il n'y avait pas de lumière à l'extérieur. Quelques bruits feutrés de portes que l'on referme doucement se faisaient entendre, mais rien d'autre. Pas de voix, pas de son de télévision ni de conversations d'infirmières dans le couloir.

Une petite veilleuse diffusait une lumière orangée au-dessus de la porte. Il se rendormit en la regardant trembloter.

— Papa ?

France-Alix ?

Comme dans un rêve, Louis écoutait cette voix qui l'appelait sans être sûr qu'il l'entendait vraiment. Ça résonnait comme s'il se trouvait dans une grande pièce vide. Et ça bourdonnait dans ses oreilles. Il avait l'impression d'avoir assisté à un concert de *hard rock* juste à côté des enceintes.

— Ce sont les antidouleurs qu'ils lui injectent, ma chérie, ça le fait dormir...

À qui appartenait cette voix-là ? Il essaya de réfléchir, mais penser lui était difficile. Tout s'embrouillait, tout lui échappait, tout glissait sur lui. Finalement, cette sensation était agréable. Rien n'avait d'importance. Il n'avait qu'à se laisser aller, et advienne que pourra.

À plusieurs reprises, il ouvrit les yeux, mais ne parvint pas à distinguer ce qui l'entourait. Il voyait du blanc, des silhouettes qui se penchaient au-dessus de lui. Un brouhaha inintelligible inondait ses tympans à chaque reprise de conscience, si bien que ce bruit insupportable le faisait retomber dans un sommeil artificiel sans repos.

— Est-ce qu'il va mourir ?

— Bien sûr que non, qu'est-ce que tu racontes ? Ça fait juste un peu trop longtemps qu'il n'a pas pris de vraies vacances, alors il fait sa Belle au bois dormant.

Ismaël.

Cette fois, les brumes de son esprit se dissipèrent. Louis se réveilla pour de bon peu à peu, reconnaissant son ami et collègue ainsi que France-Alix, qui pianotait nerveusement sur l'écran de son téléphone.

— Tiens, regarde ! Il a entendu la voix du prince charmant, il revient parmi les vivants.

Sa fille se jeta sur son torse un peu trop vivement, ce qui lui arracha un cri en même temps qu'il réalisa que sa poitrine était également bandée. Comme il grimaçait et poussait un gémissement de douleur, France-Alix se recula, mortifiée, et se confondit en excuses.

— Oh ! pardon, mon petit papa, je suis désolée. Je ne voulais pas te faire mal. Je suis tellement contente que tu te réveilles enfin !

— Ça fait combien de temps que je suis là ? parvint-il à articuler, la langue pâteuse.

— Trois jours, répondit la jeune fille en lui prenant la main. Tu nous as fait peur, tu sais.

— J'ai pas fait exprès, crois-moi.

Il essaya de se redresser, mais la douleur du côté droit l'en empêcha. Il éprouvait même des difficultés à parler et à respirer.

— C'est quoi, ce que j'ai autour du torse ? s'irrita Louis.

— Tu as une côte fêlée et une lésion à un poumon. On ne s'est pas aperçus de tout ça aussitôt parce qu'il n'y avait que ton bras qui saignait, mais c'est sérieux, mon pote, j'ai bien peur que tu rates le bouquet final.

Louis considéra Ismaël en fronçant les sourcils.

— Vous l'avez coincé ?

— Pas encore. Mais on sait où il va chercher son courrier chaque fin de mois. Il y a des hommes en planque pendant que je te parle et je m'y colle dès que je repars.

Ismaël voyait bien que Louis crevait d'envie de savoir ce qui s'était passé pendant son séjour à l'hôpital. Mais il hésitait à s'exprimer devant la toute jeune France-Alix, qui voulait certainement profiter de son père maintenant qu'il avait repris conscience.

— Écoute, on en discutera plus tard, je repasserai en fin de journée. En attendant, essaie de récupérer au mieux et ne pense plus à tout ça.

— Dis-moi au moins si la psy va bien, insista Louis.

— Elle était déshydratée et très secouée, mais elle va très bien. On a eu sa déposition et d'ailleurs, elle est venue te rendre visite. Mais France-Alix va t'expliquer tout ça mieux que moi. À plus tard, petit prince !

Quand il fut parti, la jeune fille aida son père à se redresser en ajoutant un oreiller derrière son dos. La douleur dans sa poitrine était vraiment aiguë. Il profita de la visite d'une infirmière pour lui demander s'il était possible de lui administrer un antidouleur. La femme acquiesça.

Pendant qu'elle partait chercher ce qu'il fallait, il fit signe à sa fille de se rapprocher. Dans un élan de tendresse, il passa une main derrière sa nuque et déposa un baiser sur son front.

— Je suis heureux que tu sois avec moi, lui dit-il, de l'émotion plein la voix.

Elle eut un petit sourire gêné et essuya une larme qui dévalait le long de sa joue d'un revers de main, visiblement émue elle aussi.

— Je voulais te dire, commença Louis sans trop savoir où cela allait l'emmener. Je suis désolé pour tout ce qui s'est passé. Je voudrais tellement qu'on recolle les morceaux, tu comprends...

— Je sais, coupa France-Alix. Je me suis mal comportée, moi aussi. Mais je t'en voulais, tu sais.

Elle n'acheva pas sa phrase et éclata en sanglots. Ce qui fit chavirer le cœur de Louis, qui sentit les larmes envahir ses yeux à son tour.

— Oh, merde ! Ne pleure pas, Alix, s'il te plaît.

Quand elle se rendit compte qu'ils étaient en pleurs tous les deux, elle se mit à rire, entraînant son père avec elle. Toute la nervosité, la rancœur accumulées ces dernières années semblèrent s'évacuer pendant ces quelques instants de pur bonheur où ils se sentirent de nouveau une famille. Malgré les douleurs, il prit sa fille dans ses bras et ils restèrent ainsi un bon moment, heureux de se retrouver après tant d'épreuves et de tensions.

— Je sais que je t'ai déçue, chuchota Louis à l'oreille de France-Alix. Le problème, vois-tu, c'est qu'il n'y a pas vraiment de mode d'emploi à l'usage des parents. On fonctionne en *free-style*. Je ne me cherche pas d'excuses, je n'en ai aucune. J'aurais dû essayer plus fort de rester proche de toi et j'ai lamentablement perdu ta confiance.

— Mais non, répondit la jeune fille, c'est pas ta faute. J'ai trop écouté maman alors que c'étaient vos histoires, pas les miennes.

Comme dans la plupart des cas de couples qui s'affrontent lors d'une séparation ou d'un divorce, France-Alix s'était sentie obligée de choisir son camp, en quelque sorte. Vivant avec sa mère jusqu'à ces dernières semaines, il était naturel qu'elle prenne son parti. Louis se doutait bien que cela avait été délicat pour sa fille, il ne lui en voulait pas.

Sentant que leur étreinte devenait douloureuse, France-Alix reprit sa place sur le fauteuil réservé aux visiteurs, sécha ses larmes, le sourire aux lèvres maintenant qu'ils étaient réconciliés.

— Alors, tu as fait connaissance avec Agathe Delcourt ? voulut savoir Louis afin de changer de sujet après toutes ces émotions.

— Elle est géniale ! s'exclama aussitôt sa fille avec l'exubérance liée à son jeune âge. Elle était là hier, on a papoté tout l'après-midi, jusqu'à ce que grand-mère vienne me chercher. Elle a dit que c'est en voulant la sauver que tu avais failli mourir.

— Je n'ai pas failli mourir, relativisa Louis.

— Mais bien sûr que si ! le contredit aussitôt la voix de l'infirmière qui entrait dans la chambre juste à ce moment-là, munie d'une seringue dont elle injecta le contenu dans le cathéter. Le chirurgien est intervenu sur votre poumon. Votre pronostic vital était engagé quand vous êtes arrivé ici.

– Je ne le savais pas, on ne m'a rien dit.

– Vos proches ont voulu vous ménager, sans doute.

– En même temps, il vient juste de reprendre ses esprits, fit remarquer France-Alix.

– C'est vrai, approuva l'infirmière. Alors autant que vous le sachiez, vous allez pouvoir rentrer chez vous d'ici deux jours, mais ce sera repos pendant au moins trois semaines, voire davantage. Le médecin va venir vous voir cet après-midi.

Elle avait réinstallé les coussins derrière la nuque de Louis et ce dernier ressentait les effets bénéfiques de l'antidouleur qui se diffusait dans ses veines.

– Ça va mieux ? s'enquit la femme, bien qu'elle vît parfaitement au visage de son patient qui se détendait que c'était le cas.

– Merci, souffla Louis, soulagé.

France-Alix et lui reprirent leur conversation dès qu'elle fut repartie.

– De quoi avez-vous parlé avec Agathe ?

– De toi, bien sûr ! plaisanta France-Alix. Elle dit que les hommes ne sont pas mûrs avant quarante ans, mais que dans ton cas, elle a bon espoir.

– Quoi ! s'exclama-t-il dans un éclat de rire qui lui arracha un cri de douleur. C'est quoi, ces bêtises ? Dis-moi plutôt si elle s'est remise de son enlèvement. Elle t'en a parlé ?

– Pas beaucoup, en fait. Elle a juste dit qu'elle était partie habiter pour un temps avec les sœurs de l'institut Saint-Jean parce qu'elle ne se voyait pas rester dans son appartement après ce qui s'était passé. Et puis elle a parlé des gamins dont elle s'occupe et qui lui manquent. Tu sais, elle m'a fait des confidences sur son passé, de sa famille qui a été tuée et qu'Agathe, eh ben, c'est pas son vrai nom. Mais elle ne s'est pas étendue sur le sujet.

— Elle a vécu des choses terribles, oui. Ça ne doit pas être évident pour elle d'en parler, surtout après les derniers événements. Elle est venue seule à l'hôpital ? s'inquiéta-t-il soudain.

— Non, il y avait un flic qui a attendu dans le couloir tout le temps où elle était là. Est-ce qu'Ismaël va retrouver celui qui l'avait enlevée ?

— On va le retrouver, oui, ça, c'est moi qui te le dis !

— Comment ça *: on* ? Tu ne comptes pas courir après ce déglingos dans ton état, quand même ? fit France-Alix, alarmée. Tu as entendu l'infirmière.

— J'aime quand tu joues les petites mamans avec moi ! Mais il y a déjà ta grand-mère dans ce rôle, et pour faire de la surveillance assis dans une voiture, pas besoin d'un entraînement intensif.

France-Alix secoua la tête, mécontente de ce que ces paroles présageaient. Son père n'avait visiblement aucune intention de rester au repos comme le préconisait son état.

— Ça veut dire que tu ne vas pas écouter les conseils des médecins ?

— Ça veut dire que le vrai malade, il est dans la nature et que je ne vais pas risquer la vie d'Agathe encore une fois. Sans compter les familles à qui il peut s'en prendre.

— Tu promets au moins qu'on se fera une soirée rien que tous les deux, disons... une fois par mois ? proposa-t-elle.

— Bien sûr, tout ce que tu voudras, ma grande.

Au fur et à mesure qu'ils parlaient, les paupières de Louis devenaient de plus en plus lourdes à cause du médicament. France-Alix avait allumé la télévision, qu'elle ne regardait pas, accaparée par son portable. Il finit par s'endormir au son d'un reportage animalier.

Quand il revint à la réalité, la première chose qu'il entendit fut le bruit de la pluie qui s'abattait avec force à l'extérieur. Le capitaine Hébrard avait pris la place que France-Alix devait avoir quittée quelques heures plus tôt, il était profondément endormi dans le fauteuil. Ses ronflements vinrent s'ajouter au tambourinement des gouttes sur les bâtiments et la tôle des véhicules garés en contrebas. C'était sans doute ce vacarme qui l'avait réveillé, d'ailleurs.

Automatiquement, Louis tendit le bras gauche en direction de la table de nuit où quelqu'un avait eu la délicatesse de déposer son portable. Le moindre mouvement était pénible, mais Dieu merci, l'appareil était à sa portée.

Il supposa que sa mère ou France-Alix avaient eu la présence d'esprit de mettre le téléphone à charger, car il avait toutes les barres sur son écran et l'icône en forme d'enveloppe lui signala qu'il avait un message.

Il provenait d'Agathe, qui le remerciait d'être venu à son secours et le prévenait qu'elle s'était permis de récupérer son téléphone portable, que sa fille avait déniché dans une des poches de son blouson. Elle lui souhaitait de se remettre rapidement, promettait de lui rendre visite dans les prochains jours s'il était toujours hospitalisé.

Tout en fermant le SMS, Louis se remémora la

conversation qu'il avait eue avec la pédopsychologue à propos des tensions entre sa fille et lui. Il se demanda si elle n'avait pas profité de leur rencontre pendant son sommeil pour arrondir les angles entre eux. Le revirement de France-Alix avait quelque chose de tellement inespéré ! Mais peut-être était-ce simplement lié au fait qu'elle avait cru le perdre. Quoi qu'il en soit, si son corps ressemblait à une épave, son moral était bon.

— Quoi de neuf, Stéphane ? cria-t-il sciemment afin de réveiller le capitaine de sa sieste improvisée.

Celui-ci eut un soubresaut digne d'un acteur de comédie avant d'émettre des bruits de bouche non encore répertoriés.

— Mon bon prince s'est enfin réveillé ? bafouilla Hébrard en se redressant sur son siège.

— C'est toi qui ronflais comme un sonneur de cloches, lui retourna Louis.

— Pas du tout ! Je veillais mon subalterne.

— Et de mauvaise foi, en plus ! Comment ça se fait que je n'aie pas encore vu Maud ?

— Sa petite dernière est malade, tu ne la verras pas avant demain. Mais elle est venue hier, pendant que tu dormais.

— Qu'est-ce qui s'est passé pendant ces trois jours ? On en est où ? Ismaël m'a dit que vous étiez en planque devant le bureau de Poste où Portal a sa boîte. On est quel jour, d'ailleurs ? Je suis à la ramasse.

— On est mardi. Le 19 mai, lui précisa le capitaine Hébrard. Et ne t'en fais pas pour Portal, on va le coincer, c'est une question de jours. La petite psy est bien surveillée et Fontaine a bossé de son côté. Amary et lui ont remué ciel et terre pour débusquer la taupe. Le commandant, on l'a pas vu pendant les trois jours où t'as été dans le coaltar, mais il nous a trouvé le lascar ; brigadier-chef de son état.

Hébrard raconta que le commandant Fontaine, aidé de Benoît Pallas — le technicien informatique mis sur le coup par Amary —, avait fait des recherches sur chacune des personnes ayant eu un lien, de près ou de loin, avec les assassinats de la famille Albert. Tout le groupe d'enquête de l'époque avait été passé au crible : leur niveau de vie d'alors comparé à celui de maintenant, leurs relevés bancaires ainsi que ceux de leurs enfants s'ils en avaient, une plainte déposée pour harcèlement ou disparition inquiétante, une arrestation pour détention de drogue ; tout ce que l'informatique pouvait révéler avait été analysé. Un travail fastidieux et qui, contre toute attente, avait fini par payer.

Celui qui avait retenu leur attention s'appelait Mathieu Gilbert et ce nom n'était pas étranger à Louis.

— Je me rappelle très bien ce gars, dit-il. Quand j'étais lieutenant stagiaire, il était simple gardien de la paix et on a eu un accrochage, lui et moi.

— Rapport à ton statut social, oui, absolument. L'incident est de notoriété publique dans le XIIe.

— C'était ma première affectation.

— Notre brigadier-chef y est toujours et il stagne à ce grade parce que passer officier ne l'intéresse pas. Avant d'être au central du XIIe, figure-toi qu'il était à Argenteuil. De service la nuit des assassinats de la famille d'Agathe. C'est lui qui a conduit le commissaire Dupontet chez Céline Desclos et qui, ensuite, a accompagné Claire Albert, avec un autre de ses collègues, en région bordelaise pour assurer sa sécurité. Il était là quand le gars de la DST est venu pour expliquer à la gamine qu'ils allaient lui procurer des faux papiers et qu'elle disparaîtrait de la circulation au cas où le tueur voudrait lui courir après.

— On a retrouvé le gars de la DST ?

— Oui, mais peu importe. Mathieu Gilbert est en garde à vue au moment où je te parle.

— Mais on sait s'il est entré en contact avec William Portal ? demanda Louis.

— Pas encore. Mais on va bien le cuisiner.

— Et le mec de la DST, vous avez vérifié de son côté ?

— Aucun contact avec Portal. Rien de suspect dans ses *emails* ni dans ses appels téléphoniques, professionnels ou privés.

— Je n'aime pas être cloué au lit pendant que les choses avancent, se plaignit Louis en soupirant de frustration. Et Agathe, qu'est-ce qu'elle a dit de son ravisseur dans sa déposition ? Elle l'a vu ?

— Ah ! Là, c'est intéressant. Figure-toi que ce taré s'est présenté à elle déguisé en femme, sous le nom d'Éva.

— Sa sœur ?

— Précisément. La pédopsy connaît assez mal ce genre de maladie mentale, mais d'après elle, Portal a subi un grave traumatisme dû à la mort tragique de sa sœur jumelle, ce qui aurait entraîné un trouble dissociatif de l'identité. Elle pense qu'il a l'habitude de se travestir comme ça. Sa façon de s'habiller et de se maquiller révèle une pratique régulière.

— Il est homosexuel ? Il traîne peut-être dans les boîtes *gays*. Vous avez pensé à y faire un tour ?

— Ismaël a fait deux *night-clubs* différents hier soir, sans succès. En même temps, on ne possède aucune photo de Portal en femme, on ne sait pas à quoi il ressemble une fois travesti, alors c'est difficile de voir avec les habitués s'ils le connaissent. Comme apparemment, il se fait passer pour Éva, on cible juste une personne évoluant sous ce nom. Agathe nous a donné la description de Portal dans sa version féminine : longs cheveux blonds et vêtements classiques mais élégants. Ce soir, j'y retourne avec lui, on va inspecter deux autres boîtes.

— Tu aurais une photo de ce William Portal ?

— Ah ! Oui, tu fais bien d'en parler, Ismaël l'a reconnu. Attends...

Hébrard extirpa son portable au moment où Ismaël entrait à son tour dans la chambre du malade. Puis, il tendit la photo du suspect qui apparaissait sur l'écran :

— C'est cet abruti de journaliste qui nous a interpellés après l'intervention à Aulnay-sous-Bois, devant chez les Lemonnier !

— Absolument, confirma Ismaël en s'asseyant au bord du lit entre les deux hommes. Il n'est pas plus journaliste que toi et moi, d'ailleurs. Le canard pour lequel il nous a dit qu'il travaillait n'existe même pas.

— Il avait pris contact avec Agathe, réalisa soudain Louis, dont les souvenirs remontaient peu à peu à la surface. Rappelle-toi quand on est retournés chez les Lemonnier pour voir où le gosse avait pu se planquer, il était en train de l'emmerder dans la rue.

— Je me souviens. Et le lendemain, on retrouvait les cadavres de la famille Aubry avec ce déchaînement de violence sur la fille aînée.

— On s'est demandé d'où venait cette colère.

C'était à cause de mon intervention. Et c'est pour ça qu'il s'est adressé directement à moi dans le SMS. Je l'avais empêché de régler ses comptes avec Agathe.

— Ça se tient, approuva le capitaine Hébrard.

— Ça veut dire qu'il jouait avec sa proie et qu'on l'avait sous le nez depuis le début, ragea Louis. Qui interroge le brigadier-chef ?

— Le commandant Fontaine, répondit Ismaël. Je voulais le faire, mais il a insisté. Et il voulait le faire seul.

Bizarre, pensa Louis. En général, le commandant laissait ses lieutenants s'occuper des interrogatoires. Il croisa le regard du capitaine, qui semblait, quant à lui, désabusé.

— Je me demande quelle mouche l'a piqué, à celui-là, finit-il par dire, à personne en particulier. Amary est au poste aujourd'hui ?

— Non, il est parti pour la journée.

— On devrait l'informer que Fontaine mène l'interrogatoire, proposa Louis.

Il y eut un silence un peu gêné entre les trois hommes.

— Pourquoi ? questionna enfin Ismaël. C'est son droit d'interroger un suspect s'il en a envie. C'est quoi, le malaise ? ajouta-t-il en fronçant les sourcils.

Ismaël sentait qu'il y avait des non-dits qui polluaient l'atmosphère, mais il n'arrivait pas à définir ce qui travaillait les deux autres.

— Fontaine s'est vraiment montré taciturne ces derniers temps, commença Hébrard. Quand les premiers meurtres nous sont tombés dessus, c'est à peine s'il s'y intéressait. Il a dit qu'il avait d'autres affaires en cours et je sais que c'était le cas. Mais quand même ! C'est pas tous les jours qu'une enquête de cette ampleur vous est confiée. Son manque d'intérêt me paraissait pas net.

Nouveau silence. Il reprit malgré lui, voulant aller jusqu'au bout de son raisonnement.

— Et à partir du moment où on a su que Claire Albert était en réalité Agathe Delcourt, alors là, changement radical d'attitude : je l'ai eu sur le dos du matin au soir. Il s'est mis à fouiner de tous les côtés sans rien dire à personne, mais j'ai l'œil, je l'ai vu faire. Même Amary le regardait bizarrement s'agiter comme ça.

— Qu'est-ce que tu es en train de sous-entendre ? fit Ismaël d'une voix blanche.

— On ne le connaît pas des masses, mais c'est vrai qu'il n'est pas comme d'habitude depuis quelque temps, reconnut Louis. Cela dit, il a peut-être des problèmes personnels que nous ignorons. Tout le monde est à cran avec tous ces meurtres. Ça crée des tensions au sein du groupe.

— Ben justement, il a bossé en solo sur ce coup, sans l'équipe. Même Amary m'a demandé plusieurs fois ce qu'il fabriquait à disparaître tout le temps.

— Attends, attends, attends ! s'écria Ismaël, agitant les mains devant lui. Tu te contredis, Stéphane. D'abord tu dis qu'il est sans arrêt derrière toi, et après tu dis qu'il disparaît : faudrait savoir !

— Les gars, vous me connaissez. Je n'ai pas pour habitude de critiquer qui que ce soit dans le dos et d'ailleurs, c'est pas le genre de la maison. Si je vous parle de l'attitude de Fontaine, c'est qu'elle me paraît vraiment pas nette. Vous, vous êtes le plus souvent sur le terrain, vous ne le voyez pas aussi souvent que moi.

Il est vrai que Stéphane Hébrard était plutôt un

homme de bureau, tout comme le commandant Fontaine ou Amary de par leurs fonctions. Il fallait également reconnaître que le commandant n'était dans le groupe que depuis un an et qu'il ne faisait pas beaucoup d'efforts pour s'intégrer réellement.

– OK, trancha Louis. Tu penses qu'il pourrait cacher des informations à propos de notre enquête ? Mais pourquoi il ferait ça ?

– Je dis que j'attends de voir ce qu'il va tirer du brigadier-chef. Parce que malgré tous les éléments contre ce type, il n'y a aucun lien entre Portal et lui. Et en plus, j'ai parlé en personne au gars qui bossait à la DST et il est formel : Mathieu Gilbert n'a eu aucun moyen de savoir quelle était la nouvelle identité de Claire Albert. Tout s'est finalisé après que la gamine a été emmenée au centre psychiatrique, en privé. Le bleu était reparti depuis belle lurette à Paris.

– Tu veux dire que Fontaine a menti ? fit Ismaël, de plus en plus incrédule.

– On verra bien sur l'enregistrement vidéo ce que l'interrogatoire aura donné, déclara Louis.

– Tu ne verras rien du tout, le contredit aussitôt Ismaël. Tu es en arrêt pour un bon moment, je te rappelle.

– C'est ce qu'on verra, maugréa Louis.

Chapitre 27

Pendant trois semaines, le lieutenant Salvant-Perret fut confiné chez ses parents, où il fut choyé comme un enfant convalescent. Même sa fille fut aux petits soins. Contre toute attente, ces deux-là se redécouvraient, et c'était un plaisir de les voir ensemble, père et fille.

Par un bel après-midi de printemps, France-Alix vint chercher son père en le prenant par la main, le sortant des dossiers dans lesquels il était plongé sur son ordinateur, jamais vraiment au repos.

Elle avait installé deux chaises longues à l'ombre des chênes. Deux grands verres de citronnade attendaient sur la petite table de jardin qu'elle avait déplacée toute seule, sans l'aide de personne, jusque-là. Sur chacun des transats était déposé un livre de poche qu'elle avait soigneusement choisi dans la bibliothèque de sa grand-mère, espérant que le titre qu'elle avait pris pour Louis serait à son goût : un roman policier de Pierre Lemaitre dont elle avait entendu parler, mais qu'elle-même n'avait jamais lu. Quant à elle, un Fred Vargas lui avait fait de l'œil.

Louis se laissa entraîner sans discuter, le sourire aux lèvres, se tenant néanmoins le côté droit en marchant à cause de la douleur toujours bien vivace lorsqu'il se déplaçait.

Elle l'aida du mieux qu'elle put à s'installer dans la chaise longue qui lui était destinée et prit place dans l'autre, ne cessant de lui lancer des coups d'œil à la fois amusés et protecteurs.

— Excellent choix, ce Lemaitre, apprécia Louis en regardant la couverture du livre. Et toi, tu as pris quoi ?

— Le dernier Vargas. Grand-mère l'a trouvé génial. Moi, je ne connais pas, mais Léa est totalement accro de cette romancière.

Une sonnette d'alarme s'activa dans la tête de Louis au nom de Léa. Cela faisait des semaines qu'il mourait d'envie d'éclaircir cette histoire de baiser qui l'avait tant choqué.

— Pourquoi tu ne me l'as jamais présentée, ton amie Léa ? tenta-t-il avec la sensation de marcher sur des œufs.

Il y eut une légère hésitation, perceptible, puis France-Alix répondit :

— J'ai entendu dire que tu n'appréciais pas vraiment mes nouvelles fréquentations. En même temps, maman et toi n'appréciiez pas non plus les anciennes.

— Je suppose que les rumeurs proviennent de ta grand-mère ?

Un silence s'installa de nouveau. Louis avait les yeux braqués sur sa fille, dont le regard s'était fait fuyant. Elle feuilletait les pages de son livre pour se donner une contenance, mais on voyait bien qu'elle réfléchissait à ce qu'elle allait dire.

— Tu sais, j'avoue que ça m'a fait un drôle de coup quand je vous ai vues toutes les deux en train de vous embrasser. Ne prends pas cet air surpris, je sais bien que grand-mère t'a tout dit à ce propos. Je ne m'y attendais pas. Mais j'ai eu le temps d'y réfléchir et, tout bien considéré, je pense que j'aurais eu la même réaction s'il s'était agi d'un mec.

France-Alix se tourna d'un coup vers lui et éclata de rire, incrédule en voyant le petit sourire provocateur qu'il arborait.

— T'es sérieux ?

— Oui. Je crois que ce qui m'a le plus vexé, ce n'est pas le fait que tu embrasses une fille, mais plutôt que tu ne m'aies jamais parlé de ta vie sentimentale.

— C'est-à-dire que t'es mon père, fit-elle en grimaçant. Déjà, avec maman, j'ai du mal, alors avec toi... Et puis de toute façon, on ne fait plus ça, avec Léa. Je veux dire, on s'embrasse plus, quoi. C'est fini. On est juste amies. C'était pas trop mon truc, en fait. Et elle non plus.

Inconsciemment, Louis respira plus librement. Les ados...

— Tu veux dire que tu n'es plus lesbienne ?

— Non, je ne le suis pas, papa, répondit-elle en riant franchement, cette fois, de lire le soulagement sur le visage de son père. Mais tu ne m'aurais plus aimée si je l'avais été ?

— Bien sûr que si ! Il m'aurait juste fallu un temps d'adaptation, c'est tout. Mais je t'aimerai toujours, Alix, quoi que tu fasses.

C'était la première fois depuis une éternité qu'il lui disait des mots aussi forts. France-Alix en avait le cœur qui s'affolait tellement elle était heureuse de les entendre de la bouche de ce père qu'elle avait fui et tenté de détester pendant si longtemps. Parce qu'au fond, à chaque fois qu'elle faisait mine de l'ignorer, c'était son amour qu'elle réclamait en silence.

— Je t'aime aussi, papa, finit-elle par lâcher, comme pour se débarrasser d'un poids énorme.

— Oh, merde ! On va pas se remettre à chialer ! s'exclama Louis qui, évidemment, ne pouvait pas retenir ses larmes.

Et leur rire résonna dans le jardin jusqu'à l'intérieur de la maison, où Hélène les observait derrière la verrière de son jardin d'hiver. Elle était si heureuse à cet instant !

Depuis que Louis l'avait laissée en plan pour l'histoire de la pharmacie, Anne ne lui adressait plus la parole. Ce qui en soi n'avait rien de désagréable. Elle était tout de même bien contente d'occuper l'appartement de Louis où, d'après France-Alix, qui lui rendait des visites régulières, elle avait déjà reçu deux amants différents.

Louis déplorait l'impact que la légèreté sentimentale de sa mère pouvait avoir sur France-Alix, qui avait déjà du mal à se trouver elle-même. En tout cas, il évitait d'aborder le sujet. D'abord parce que ça le rendait mal à l'aise, ensuite parce qu'il ne voulait pas monter France-Alix contre sa mère et inverser la vapeur par rapport à la situation précédente.

Quelques jours après les émouvantes mises au point entre sa fille et lui, Louis reçut la visite d'Agathe Delcourt. Toujours aussi belle et attirante, la jeune femme semblait cependant avoir changé. Louis la sentit à la fois plus sereine et plus triste.

Hélène insista pour la garder au déjeuner. La visiteuse n'eut pas d'autre alternative que de céder, d'autant que France-Alix appuya sa grand-mère avec effusion.

Après le repas, elles passèrent d'ailleurs un long moment ensemble, lors d'une promenade dans le parc où Louis ne put les accompagner. Agathe le rejoignit alors qu'il s'était réfugié dans la bibliothèque.

— Puis-je entrer dans la tanière de l'ours brun ? fit-elle en guise d'introduction.

Absorbé par le livre dans lequel il s'était plongé, Louis leva la tête vers la jeune femme resplendissante en lui souriant :

— Alors, c'est ainsi que vous me voyez ? Vous dites ça parce que j'ai pris du poids à force de rester inactif ?

— Je ne me le permettrais pas ! Et puis votre ligne est irréprochable, je vous assure.

— La vôtre aussi.

Qu'est-ce qui lui avait pris de répondre un truc pareil ! Évidemment que la délicieuse Agathe avait une silhouette parfaite. Mortifié par sa propre bêtise, refoulant une forte envie de disparaître sous le canapé dans lequel il était à demi allongé, il l'invita néanmoins à entrer, désignant un des fauteuils en face de lui.

Mais la jeune femme lui fit un petit signe de refus de la main et se dirigea à la place vers les rayonnages.

— Quelle impressionnante bibliothèque ! Et comme vous avez de la chance d'être aussi bien entouré.

Le regret était perceptible dans sa voix. Comment ne pas comprendre l'admiration d'Agathe ? Elle qui n'avait connu que la précarité, suivie de la vie en foyer jusqu'à ce qu'elle termine ses études et obtienne son premier emploi.

— J'espérais que vous viendriez me voir à

l'hôpital, risqua Louis sans la quitter des yeux alors qu'elle avançait lentement le long des étagères, effleurant le dos des livres d'une touche légère à son passage.

Comme il aurait aimé être l'un de ces livres qu'elle caressait amoureusement !

— Je n'étais pas prête, déclara-t-elle soudain, évitant son regard. Et puis j'ai eu mille choses à faire après cette effroyable histoire.

— J'imagine, oui, compatit Louis. J'ai appris que vous aviez trouvé refuge chez les sœurs. N'est-ce pas un peu... austère ?

Il la vit qui souriait sans cesser de déambuler dans la pièce avant de prendre place dans le fauteuil qu'il lui avait proposé précédemment.

— Vous savez, je ne suis pas quelqu'un d'exigeant. Je me contente de peu pour vivre. Rester dans cet appartement, après ce qui s'était passé, était au-dessus de mes forces. Même avec une présence policière. Je l'ai entièrement fait repeindre, j'ai déposé mon mobilier au garde-meuble et j'ai proposé à une amie intéressée d'en être locataire dès que les travaux seraient finis. C'est la serveuse de la *pizzeria* que vous avez interrogée, vous vous souvenez ?

Louis se la rappelait parfaitement.

— Vous avez repris le travail ? Comment va le petit Nathan ?

— C'est très difficile pour lui. Grâce à vous, il passe beaucoup de temps au piano. Il faudrait que vous reveniez, il fait ses gammes à la perfection, maintenant.

— Je viendrai avec grand plaisir, promit Louis, dès que je pourrai de nouveau conduire.

Un silence s'installa. Et avec lui, une certaine gêne

due au fait qu'ils étaient parfaitement conscients de l'attirance qu'ils éprouvaient l'un pour l'autre. Ce fut Louis qui brisa la glace le premier :

— Agathe ? l'appela-t-il doucement.

Elle le regarda, et leurs yeux restèrent comme aimantés. Le temps de trois respirations, une sorte de complicité s'installa, sans qu'aucun mot fût nécessaire.

Elle attendait qu'il continue, mais il n'osait pas.

— Vous vouliez m'inviter à dîner encore une fois ? l'encouragea-t-elle, à sa grande surprise.

Il ne put réprimer un sourire qui se transforma en rire, puis en gémissement lorsque ses côtes le rappelèrent à l'ordre. Tout son visage exprimait la douleur. Agathe fut à ses côtés en un instant, agenouillée au pied du canapé, l'air soucieux :

— Oh, pardon ! C'est ma faute, je vous ai fait rire.

Il prit doucement la main qu'elle avait posée sur le coussin du canapé devant elle et la porta à ses lèvres pour y déposer un baiser. Elle la retira en fronçant légèrement les sourcils, baissa les yeux, mais resta dans la même position :

— Pardonnez-moi, Louis, mais il va me falloir un peu de temps, souffla-t-elle avec peine.

— Je ne suis pas pressé, répondit celui-ci avec une grande douceur.

Du revers de sa main, il lui caressa la joue où une larme se frayait un chemin.

— On va commencer par un restaurant, ça vous va ?

Soudain, elle fut debout, reniflant discrètement, le visage trahissant une vive émotion. D'un mouvement gracieux qui lui rappela sa fille, elle rabattit ses cheveux derrière ses épaules et essaya de prendre une voix assurée, sans vraiment y parvenir.

— Appelez-moi dès que vous vous sentez mieux. Je dois y aller. J'ai été contente de vous voir. Remerciez votre mère pour le repas, c'était très agréable. Au revoir.

Que de précipitation ! Louis n'eut pas le temps de la retenir ni de dire quoi que ce soit qu'elle avait déjà mis son sac à l'épaule et disparaissait.

Il aurait tellement aimé pouvoir l'embrasser ! Il était un peu déçu, mais désormais, tous les espoirs étaient permis.

Chapitre 28

Le brigadier-chef Mathieu Gilbert fut relâché au bout de quarante-huit heures. L'on n'avait pu établir aucun lien entre William Portal et lui, il niait ne serait-ce que connaître ce nom. Il s'était défendu bec et ongles, clamant sa bonne foi et sa conscience professionnelle, remises en doute par ces soupçons infondés. Tout ça parce qu'il avait eu le malheur de s'accrocher avec le prince du central des années auparavant ! Ses états de service étant irréprochables, on dut admettre qu'il n'était pas à l'origine de la fuite.

La surveillance du bureau de Poste où Portal possédait une boîte ne donna absolument rien. Certainement au courant de la présence policière consécutive à l'explosion qui avait blessé un lieutenant sur le lieu où Agathe Delcourt était retenue prisonnière, l'homme ne s'était pas montré. L'événement avait fait la une des journaux, il ne pouvait pas l'ignorer et se doutait bien qu'on allait le traquer. Il était aux abois. Il ne s'était pas manifesté non plus auprès d'Agathe, qui avait fait changer son numéro de ligne. D'ailleurs, on l'avait mise sur écoutes sur ordre du substitut du procureur Sack.

Grâce au Ciel, aucune autre famille n'avait été

attaquée. Portal finirait bien par avoir besoin d'argent. Alors, comme il ne montrait pas le bout de son nez au bureau de Poste, il fut décidé de surveiller la CAF.

Le versement du RSA s'effectuait toujours en début de mois, entre le 4 et le 7. Dès le 3 juin, Louis avait repris son poste et, avec Ismaël, Maud et Stéphane Hébrard, ils se postèrent en surveillance dans le bâtiment de la CAF où ils savaient que William Portal venait retirer son paiement en liquide, directement au guichet. Le commandant Fontaine, contrairement à ses habitudes, participa à l'opération sur le terrain. Ce tueur n'ayant rien d'ordinaire, le commissaire Amary ne trouva rien à redire à ce que tout le groupe soit sur le pont pour coincer ce malade.

Comme chaque matin depuis deux jours, ils arrivèrent une demi-heure avant l'ouverture des bureaux au public. Une bonne trentaine de personnes patientaient déjà devant les portes closes. Maud et Ismaël se firent passer pour un couple *lambda* tandis que Louis jouait le chômeur solitaire un peu paumé, assis sur le rebord d'une énorme jardinière en pierre à l'intérieur de laquelle on ne voyait même plus la terre tellement elle regorgeait de mégots de cigarettes.

Le capitaine Hébrard était resté dans la Mégane banalisée. Quant au commandant Fontaine, il jouait son propre rôle, un peu à l'écart du groupe de sans-emploi, une cigarette roulée éteinte au coin de la bouche, mains dans les poches, le regard insondable, la mine peu engageante. Il ressemblait à un inspecteur du Trésor public en mal d'impayés.

Son comportement énigmatique de ces dernières

semaines avait éveillé la curiosité et la méfiance du groupe, y compris de la part du commissaire, à qui les lieutenants et le capitaine s'étaient confiés de façon officieuse.

Amary avait également remarqué un changement chez son subalterne et, toujours officieusement, il n'avait pas perdu son temps ces derniers jours, profitant de la présence de Fontaine sur le terrain.

Se remettant sur la piste des boîtes de nuit *gays* de la capitale déjà suivie par Ismaël sans succès, le commissaire repassa dans ces mêmes lieux, mais avec la photo de Fontaine, cette fois-ci. Il espérait sincèrement se tromper, et lorsqu'il essuya les deux premiers échecs, il se prit à croire qu'il avait fait fausse route. Malheureusement, dans le troisième *night-club*, un des serveurs interrogés reconnut le commandant comme l'un des habitués.

Il n'y avait plus grand-chose susceptible d'étonner Antoine Amary. Cette découverte le contraria vivement néanmoins. Le commandant aurait pu avoir l'excuse de se trouver sur une affaire concernant le milieu homosexuel, ce qui aurait expliqué qu'il fréquentât ce lieu. Mais Amary était au courant de toutes les enquêtes courantes et aucune n'avait de lien avec cette population.

Il pensa que peut-être, Jules Fontaine épiait quelqu'un de sa famille, par exemple. Mais il n'avait qu'une fille et celle-ci vivait en Guyane depuis des années ; ils ne s'adressaient plus la parole. Quant au reste de sa famille, s'il en avait, il n'en parlait jamais. Il essaya vraiment de trouver des explications, mais il dut se rendre à l'évidence : l'homme avait réellement des penchants homosexuels qu'il avait réussi à dissimuler jusque-là.

À partir de ce constat, Amary refit appel à Benoît Pallas. Cette fois, le technicien dénicha des *emails* dans la boîte personnelle du commandant provenant d'une certaine Éva Portal. Autrement dit, de William. Les courriers étaient tout à fait explicites. Pallas avait réussi à récupérer leur correspondance jusqu'à un an avant les premiers meurtres. Les deux hommes avaient entretenu une relation amoureuse des plus sulfureuses que Fontaine avait tenté d'effacer en supprimant les *emails,* mais en bon *hacker*, Pallas avait récupéré toutes les lettres qu'ils avaient échangées. Et la passion avait cédé la place aux menaces, puis au chantage, car William Portal ne voyait en Jules Fontaine qu'un moyen de parvenir à sa cible : Claire Albert.

Portal n'avait pas eu à menacer longtemps. Comme il l'avait annoncé dans un de ses *mails* afin que Fontaine lui révèle l'identité actuelle de Claire Albert, il avait assassiné la première famille, les Prudhom, en novembre 2014. Le commandant avait cependant refusé de lui donner l'information qu'il réclamait, engendrant la fureur de l'autre homme. Celui-ci avait donc massacré une deuxième famille : les Lemonnier.

Fontaine avait lâché le nom d'Agathe Delcourt, mais la folie meurtrière de William Portal s'était déchaînée, il ne pouvait plus s'arrêter. D'où la sauvagerie des derniers homicides, où il s'en était pris sexuellement à la fille aînée des Aubry, substitut d'Agathe/Claire.

Amary obtint toutes ces informations alors que son groupe était en opération pour appréhender William Portal, ce vendredi 5 juin 2015. Enfermé dans son bureau depuis six heures trente du matin, il avait demandé à n'être dérangé sous aucun prétexte et s'était plongé dans la lecture de la correspondance de Fontaine et de Portal.

Ce travail terminé, la lumière faite sur les agissements du commandant, il contacta Hébrard, lui demandant de l'appeler impérativement dès qu'ils auraient repéré William Portal. Puis, il informa l'IGPN de la situation.

Les trois lieutenants et le commandant Fontaine s'étaient éparpillés dans le hall du bâtiment de façon à couvrir toutes les issues. Tous avaient bien en tête le visage de William Portal. On était vendredi, c'était le dernier jour ouvrable pour venir chercher les allocations ou les indemnités, il viendrait forcément.

Il ne se passa rien le matin. Ils battirent en retraite dans un café qui proposait des plats du jour à un prix abordable. Le commandant prétendit qu'il préférait rentrer chez lui, il les rejoindrait à l'ouverture, en début d'après-midi.

— Et s'il se pointait habillé en femme ? suggéra fort justement Maud, que cette idée obsédait depuis le matin.

— Les versements se font à la personne qui y a droit, ils demandent une pièce d'identité, répliqua Ismaël.

— Il peut très bien avoir rédigé une procuration, objecta Louis.

— Ça n'empêche pas qu'il lui faut quand même une pièce d'identité.

— Les faux papiers constituent un marché parallèle fort lucratif, comme chacun sait, ironisa Hébrard, la bouche pleine, les joues rouges, les yeux fixés sur le contenu déclinant de son assiette.

— C’est la merde ! On ne sait absolument pas à quoi il ressemble quand il se travestit, déplora Ismaël. Même avec la description qu’Agathe nous a donnée, il peut avoir dix perruques différentes, ça ne nous avance à rien.

— En tant que femme, je saurai reconnaître une personne qui n’est pas de mon sexe, je vous assure.

— Si ça se trouve, il est déjà passé sous notre nez et on n’a rien vu, fit Louis.

— Ça m’étonnerait, reprit Maud, cette idée me turlupine depuis qu’on a commencé la surveillance, et j’ai bien fait attention aux hommes autant qu’aux femmes.

— Vous trouvez pas ça bizarre que Fontaine n’ait pas déjeuné avec nous ? demanda alors Ismaël. Le temps de rentrer chez lui et de revenir pour l’ouverture, il a quoi ? Dix minutes à tout casser pour se préparer un truc et le manger !

Un bref silence s’installa, comme à chaque fois qu’ils évoquaient le comportement asocial du commandant. Chacun pensait la même chose : ils le soupçonnaient tous d’être l’indic qu’ils avaient cherché en vain parce qu’il était sous leurs yeux.

Ce fut Hébrard qui mit les pieds dans le plat, après avoir consciencieusement essuyé sa bouche et poussé un soupir rassasié.

— Amary m’a demandé de le prévenir dès qu’on aurait Portal en visuel. Il ne l’a pas demandé à Fontaine, il me l’a demandé à moi. Je crois qu’on commence tous à se rendre à l’évidence : Fontaine, pour des raisons que j’ignore, est celui qui a renseigné Portal et d’après moi, il sent le vent tourner. Il se doute que les soupçons se portent sur lui.

— Mais pourquoi il aurait fait une chose pareille ? s'indigna Maud. Il est de la maison ! Et comment peut-on mettre en danger une personne qui a déjà subi de telles horreurs par le passé ? Surtout, je ne comprends pas qu'on puisse se ranger du côté d'un homme qui tue ainsi des enfants. Putain ! Merde à la fin ! Quel salaud !

Maud Cortès était rouge de colère, au comble de l'exaspération. On n'avait jamais entendu de tels propos sortir de sa bouche. Les trois autres la regardèrent avec de grands yeux tant ils furent ébahis par ce langage fleuri. Deux larmes coulèrent le long de ses joues, sa voix chevrota lorsqu'elle termina :

— Je me suis attachée à chaque membre du groupe, moi. Vous êtes ma famille...

— On est avec toi, Cortès, ne put s'empêcher de la réconforter Louis. Tu sais bien que dans toutes les familles, il y a une brebis galeuse, un mouton noir.

— Oh, putain ! s'exclama alors Ismaël en riant. Il va neiger !

Tous le regardèrent sans comprendre le motif de son hilarité à un moment aussi chargé en émotion.

— Qu'est-ce qui te prend ? On est au mois de juin, qu'est-ce que tu nous chantes avec ta neige ? lança Hébrard.

— Louis vient de tutoyer Maud !

Le commandant Fontaine ne reparut pas cet après-midi-là. Les portes automatiques s'ouvrirent, la masse compacte des allocataires s'engouffra à l'intérieur et, au bout d'une demi-heure, ne voyant pas reparaître leur supérieur, Hébrard décida d'en informer le commissaire.

— C'est lui ? demanda simplement le capitaine au téléphone.

Il n'avait pas besoin de préciser, Amary comprit immédiatement le sens de sa question.

— Oui, fit-il gravement. On en reparle avec tout le monde dès que vous en avez fini de votre côté.

— On pense que Portal pourrait se présenter sous les traits de sa sœur.

— Ce n'est pas impossible, ouvrez l'œil. Et on procède comme j'ai dit, je tiens des renforts à disposition au cas où ça tournerait mal. Vous appelez dès que vous avez un visuel et vous l'appréhendez en douceur. N'oubliez pas que vous êtes dans un lieu public, il ne s'agirait pas qu'une balle se perde. Avec l'histoire de Fontaine, Sack ne nous loupera pas si on merde sur cette arrestation.

Le capitaine Hébrard assura le taulier qu'ils agiraient selon ses directives et fit passer le mot par SMS tandis qu'il attendait dans la voiture et faisait une première analyse des physionomies qui entraient et sortaient.

Beaucoup de femmes étaient coiffées de foulards, ou alors trop jeunes ou pas assez pour correspondre aux critères recherchés. Aucun des hommes ne ressemblait au suspect non plus.

La journée s'étira jusque peu avant l'heure de fermeture. Entre-temps, le capitaine avait informé ses collègues que le commandant Fontaine était bien la taupe, ainsi qu'ils l'avaient soupçonné.

Un quart d'heure avant la fermeture, une inconnue attira enfin l'attention d'Hébrard, qui la prit en photo. Plus grande que la moyenne, trop bien habillée pour cet endroit, trop maquillée aussi ; et des cheveux d'une longueur remarquable. Il prévint les autres et Amary dans la foulée.

À l'intérieur, les trois lieutenants se cherchèrent du regard, repérèrent tout de suite la femme en question qui passait les portes d'un air faussement dégagé.

Elle donnait vraiment le change si c'était réellement un homme ! pensa Ismaël en se rapprochant sensiblement de la cible. Les deux autres lieutenants se tenaient au guichet voisin de celui où la suspecte s'arrêta, faisant mine d'attendre leur tour dans la file, le visage tourné à l'opposé pour ne pas être reconnus.

— C'est pas une femme, j'en suis sûre, souffla Maud à l'oreille de Louis. Il faut le coincer maintenant.

Sur un infime mouvement de la tête en direction d'Ismaël, celui-ci se jeta sur le travesti, le plaqua au sol et, avec une dextérité toute professionnelle, lui passa les menottes dans le dos. La foule était en état de choc, un cercle de curieux se forma aussitôt pendant qu'Ismaël, retournant le suspect comme une crêpe, lui collait brutalement sa main entre les jambes :

— C'est bien un mec, annonça-t-il en grimaçant, mais content de lui.

À l'entrée, ils aperçurent le capitaine Hébrard, le téléphone à l'oreille, le pouce levé et un grand sourire aux lèvres. L'intervention s'était bien déroulée, le suspect avait perdu une chaussure pendant son arrestation et n'avait pas prononcé un seul mot. Ce n'est que lorsque Louis fut près de lui qu'il lui adressa ces mots pleins de fiel :

— J'avais espéré que ma petite surprise te péterait à la gueule, histoire d'effacer ce petit air princier à la con.

Louis ne répondit pas. En revanche, Ismaël lui asséna un coup derrière le genou qui le fit vaciller, mais il se rattrapa et évita la chute.

— J'en ai une, de surprise pour toi, lui chuchota-t-il à l'oreille. C'est pas la gueule qu'ils vont te péter, en taule, c'est ton petit cul d'assassin. En plus, les tueurs d'enfants, à l'ombre, ils leur font regretter d'être nés.

On entendit des sirènes qui se rapprochaient. Le groupe d'Hébrard attendait sur le parvis avec leur prise, dont la perruque avait pris un tour comique. Les commentaires au sujet du travesti allaient bon train, les lieutenants avaient hâte de quitter cet endroit.

William Portal monta dans un véhicule de police où deux agents en uniforme s'engouffrèrent à sa suite. Le groupe rejoignit la voiture banalisée qu'Hébrard conduisait.

Ils se retrouvèrent en salle de réunion, assis autour de la grande table que le commissaire Amary présidait, pour le *débriefing*.

— Messieurs, madame, c'est du bon travail, commença-t-il quand tout le monde fut installé.

Pour une fois, il n'avait pas oublié qu'une femme faisait partie du groupe, ça s'annonçait bien.

— Ça manque de croissants, se plaignit le capitaine.

— Désolé, Isabelle a fini plus tôt aujourd'hui, on est vendredi. Mais puisez donc dans vos réserves, capitaine, vous n'en manquez pas.

Les rires fusèrent puis, après ces quelques instants de détente, une sorte de malaise s'installa. Il fallait crever l'abcès. Ce fut Louis qui lança la première question :

— Et Fontaine ? dit-il simplement.

— Disparu de la circulation, répondit Amary sombrement. Mais ce n'est plus de notre ressort, l'IGPN fera son boulot. À partir de maintenant, capitaine Hébrard, vous passez commandant. Et Salvant-Perret, vous êtes nommé capitaine.

Spontanément, Maud Cortès se mit à battre des mains comme une enfant au spectacle. Ismaël donna une tape amicale sur l'épaule de Louis, puis sur celle d'Hébrard pour faire bonne mesure.

— Tout ça ne nous dit pas pourquoi Fontaine a risqué sa carrière en trahissant son groupe, dit alors Louis après l'euphorie des promotions.

Le commissaire leur raconta alors ce qu'il avait découvert concernant la vie cachée du commandant, son lien et sa correspondance avec William Portal, dont il avait été l'amant, puis la victime.

— Pourquoi ne nous avoir rien dit ? fit Maud avec innocence.

— Il n'était pas avec nous depuis suffisamment longtemps pour confier de tels secrets. Et puis sans doute avait-il honte de ses penchants, je n'en sais rien, répliqua Amary. Toujours est-il qu'il s'est retrouvé piégé à partir du moment où il a donné une information confidentielle à un assassin qui, en plus, a continué à tuer même après avoir obtenu ce qu'il voulait. Fontaine s'est rendu complice de meurtre, il était coincé. Je pense que jusqu'au dernier moment, il espérait régler ses comptes avec Portal avant que vous l'arrêtiez. Mais c'était perdu d'avance, il a vu qu'il ne s'en sortirait pas. S'il est intelligent, il est déjà loin à l'heure qu'il est et on ne le reverra pas.

Ce fut un coup dur pour tout le groupe, mais ils étaient suffisamment soudés pour rebondir. À présent, ils avaient un nouveau commandant et celui-là, ils étaient certains qu'il aimait les femmes. De toute façon, Hébrard était tellement bonne patte que même s'il avait préféré les hommes, personne n'aurait trouvé à y redire. Sauf peut-être les secrétaires qu'il couvrait de cadeaux dans l'espoir toujours avorté de les séduire.

Épilogue

Ce ne fut qu'après un long mois que Louis Salvant-Perret se décida à appeler Agathe Delcourt. Si cela n'avait tenu qu'à lui, il aurait craqué bien avant, mais la douleur persistante au niveau de ses côtes, son bras en écharpe et sa peur imbécile l'en avaient empêché.

Ce qui lui laissa amplement le temps de cogiter. Un peu trop. Plus les jours passaient, plus il hésitait, plus il se demandait à quoi le mènerait une relation avec la pédopsy, et moins il se sentait de courage.

Ses collègues le chambraient gentiment, prêchaient le faux pour savoir le vrai. L'avait-il revue ? Comptait-il la revoir ? C'est que des paris étaient ouverts !

Enfin, par un torride après-midi d'août, alors que tout le monde semblait fonctionner au ralenti à cause de la chaleur qui s'abattait sur la capitale, Ismaël surprit Louis au téléphone. Il allait pénétrer dans le bureau de l'ex-commandant Fontaine où Louis s'était isolé, mais se ravisa quand il entendit la voix inhabituellement suave de son collègue murmurer des mots doux.

Il se plaqua dos au mur, tendit l'oreille vers l'espace laissé par la porte entrouverte et intercepta

Maud par le bras avant qu'elle n'entre là-dedans. Celle-ci sursauta, mais garda le silence en voyant Ismaël lui faire signe de ne pas faire de bruit et d'écouter.

Au bout d'un moment, ce fut la moitié du service qui fut à l'écoute derrière la porte, le commissaire Amary compris.

Lorsqu'ils entendirent Louis prononcer la phrase « Je t'embrasse aussi, Agathe. On se voit ce soir », un chahut effroyable se déclencha, chacun réclamant à l'autre la somme qu'il avait pariée sur le couple Louis/Agathe.

Quand il raccrocha, Louis se demanda ce qui se passait. Il fut accueilli à la porte par une armée de policiers surexcités, transpirants et hilares qui lui tapèrent sur l'épaule comme s'il venait de remporter une victoire olympique.

Il obtint le fin mot de l'histoire grâce à Maud, la seule à ne pas avoir parié, la seule aussi à ressentir un immense bonheur à l'idée que Louis avait trouvé l'âme sœur.

Remerciements

Que serait un auteur de romans policiers sans un ami des forces de l'ordre ? Je tiens à dire un grand merci à Charles Cauquil, commandant de police honoraire pour sa patience, sa disponibilité, son esprit pédagogue, son sens de l'humour et sa gentillesse.

Pour ce roman, bien différent de la série qui m'a occupée quelques années, j'ai eu un grand besoin de lecteurs(-trices) qui, patiemment, lisaient les aventures de Louis, Ismaël, Maud etc. Par épisodes, souvent frustrés que ça s'arrête au beau milieu d'une action mais toujours enthousiastes. De cet enthousiasme qui vous pousse et vous encourage à avancer. Merci à Caroline Hayot, Llewellyn, Muriel Leroy, Louise Canal, Céline Tanguy et Dominique Este : vous avez été mon moteur pendant ces mois en apnée.

Merci enfin aux éditions Eaux Troubles de me faire confiance.

Impression : mars 2024
ISBN : 978-2-940606-77-1
Dépôt légal : mai 2024
Imprimé en UE